Praise for *Law School Confiden...*

"Miller covers every aspect of the law school experience—from surviving the first semester to seeking summer internships—which makes this book unique. He presents experiences of other law students to help readers understand what is expected of them and how these expectations will affect their social and personal lives. The author emphasizes that discipline and conviction are the keys to successfully completing law school. Chapters are of course included on how to study for entrance tests and select an appropriate school. Recommended for all college and larger public libraries."

—*Library Journal*

"*Law School Confidential* walks the reader through the law school experience, from the decision to go to law school through that real-world graduation from law school, the bar exam. Nine recent law school graduates—'mentors'—assist. . . . A useful and worthwhile book."

—*New York Law Journal*

"Know someone who wants to apply to law school or is getting ready to start law school this fall? A new book being published this month might be a worthwhile addition to their summer reading lists. Written by a recent graduate of the University of Pennsylvania Law School, it offers step-by-step advice on the entire process: deciding where—and whether—to go; taking the LSAT; getting the most out of law school; identifying and applying for appropriate jobs and judicial clerkships; and passing the bar exam."

—*Chicago Daily Law Bulletin*

"[Miller] has decorously armed his readers. . . . Investment in this book for the first 75 pages alone is profitable for anyone wrestling with the decision of 'to be or not to be' (a lawyer, that is). . . . Excellent advice concerning 1L and 2L summer internships, law school journals, the bar exam, and choosing a firm is accompanied by informative sections summarizing required law school courses and demystifying judicial clerkships. This abundance of information is just the remedy for the nerves of a student anxious to enter law school."

—*The Docket* (Denver Bar Association)

"Today, with the help of one book, law students and those considering the field of law can prepare themselves for what awaits. *Law School Confidential*, by Robert H. Miller, is that book. The book is a step-by-step manual that explains it all. Topics include the mystery of the LSAT, the first set of law school exams, the bar exam, and everything in between. Although the book is lengthy, it is effortless reading: well written and to the point. As a law student entering my second year, I wish I had read *Law School Confidential* before starting my first year. The book's detailed and honest explanation of what to expect from the first year of law school is invaluable . . . the book is a must for anyone attending or thinking about law school."

—*The Houston Lawyer*

"*Law School Confidential* (Revised Edition) delivers again! The much-anticipated revised Second Edition of the bestselling law school preparatory book adds three new mentors, two new chapters, updated financial aid, recruiting and judicial clerkship advice, and much, much more. You'll find no fluff in the revised edition's hefty [432] pages. Just a whole lot of solid, tested advice, eloquently delivered with humor and style. Author Robert H. Miller, a former federal judicial clerk, law review editor, and graduate of UPenn Law School, covers every aspect of the law school experience in thoughtful detail. Whether you are a college student just starting to think about law school, a student in the midst of law school applications, someone who has already been admitted, or someone already in law school, *Law School Confidential* is a book you should not be without." —*The Princeton Review*

"Whether you're just starting to think about applying to law school, or you're a 3L getting ready to sit for the Bar, *Law School Confidential* is a great book. The author and his team of 'mentors' from law schools across the country pull no punches in providing revealing and honest chronological advice for all three years of the law school experience, from picking the law school that's right for you and funding your legal education, to how to study and properly assess job opportunities. This is a must-read for anyone entering law school." —*Law Preview*

"One of the better books that gives advice on how to handle law school . . . Written by a graduate of the University of Pennsylvania Law School along with a dozen law students, this book takes an informal approach in discussing how to succeed in law school and how to obtain clerkships and other legal jobs after graduation." —Duke University School of Law/Student Affairs

"[A] landmark book." —UVA Law Blog

"*Law School Confidential* has built up a formidable reputation since its publication as a must-read book for every aspiring or current law student. If you ask an actual law student, you will find that most, if not all, have a copy of this book sitting in their book library. The book is more than just a guide to law schools in the United States; it is a veritable tome of inside information on choosing, getting in, and excelling. . . . The greatest strength of *Law School Confidential* has to be its conversational style. Rather than talking at you, it talks to you—an asset rarely found in a law book, which have a tendency to become loaded with legal jargon. This book isn't filled with fluffy nonsense; every chapter, word, and letter is included on its own merit. . . . If you are seriously planning to study law, then this book is a definite buy. Period." —EzineArticles.com

"*Law School Confidential* is considered the 'little black book' of law schools around the United States. *Law School Confidential* aims to be a complete guide to the entire law school experience. It walks the reader through what it feels like to be inside a law school. The author frequently uses the experiences of former law students to make its points clear, and at that it is quite effective. The strongest point of the book, and one that has made it so popular among most law students, is its no-nonsense, conversational tone. Most law books tend to throw legal mumbo jumbo at their readers—a tradition among lawyers themselves—but *Law School Confidential* keeps the verbose to a minimum, and focuses on delivering frank information that can be actually useful to those thinking of, or attending, law school." —JDJungle.com

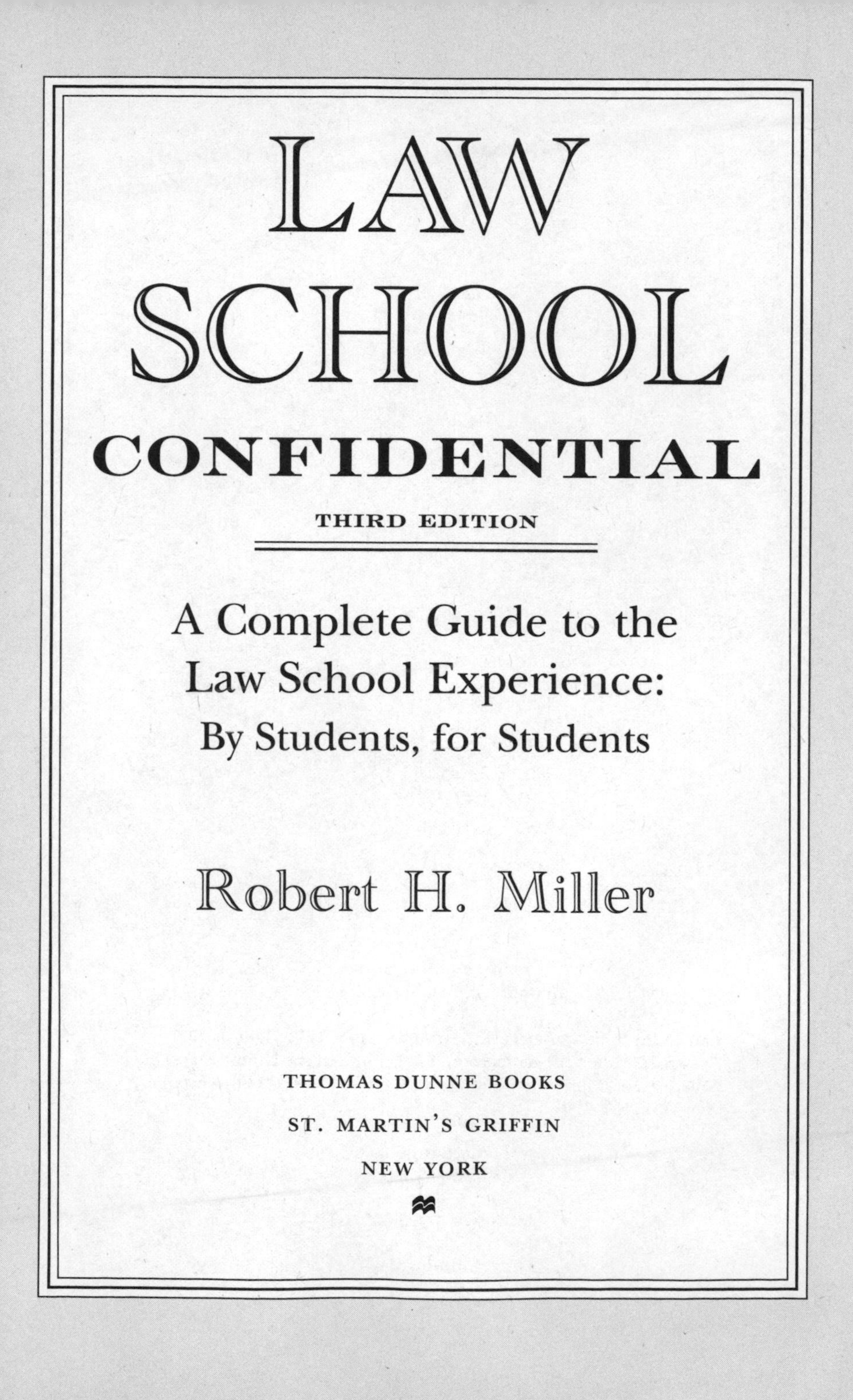

LAW SCHOOL CONFIDENTIAL

THIRD EDITION

A Complete Guide to the Law School Experience: By Students, for Students

Robert H. Miller

THOMAS DUNNE BOOKS
ST. MARTIN'S GRIFFIN
NEW YORK

THOMAS DUNNE BOOKS.
An imprint of St. Martin's Press.

www.thomasdunnebooks.com
www.stmartins.com

ISBN 978-0-312-60511-7

Third Edition: May 2011

For Mom and Dad,
who made it possible for me to live the life
of a country lawyer. And for Carolyn,
who kept the faith that someday
we'd walk in the sun.

Contents

PART THREE

THE SECOND YEAR, THEY WORK YOU TO DEATH

AUTHOR'S NOTE

A LOT HAS HAPPENED since the first edition of *Law School Confidential* was published in the summer of 2000. First, the dot-com bubble burst, sending scores of disappointed entrepreneurs scurrying for the safe harbor of graduate schools. Law schools scooped up a not insignificant percentage of these folks, and a higher than normal percentage of college graduates in the ensuing years set their sights on law school. This led to a significant increase in the number of applicants that top law schools saw each year—at some places, 60–80 percent more in the middle of the past decade than just three years earlier—and that, in turn, led to higher yields and lower admission rates at these schools.

In the middle of the last decade, when the second edition of this book came out, it was harder than it had ever been to get into law school.

Then, in 2008 and 2009, the economy completely collapsed, and with it, much of the work that kept the machinery of many of our nation's largest law firms running. That, in turn, made the end of the first decade of this new century the worst climate in memory to be an associate in a firm or a law student trying to find a job. Everywhere, firms were downsizing, jettisoning associates, dumping paralegals, assistants, and staff, and closing or shrinking offices in an effort to avoid the ultimate failure—being forced to close up shop completely, or exploding under the pressure of it all, resulting in a spectacular interstellar storm of lawyers streaming across the country into new firms to begin the cycle anew. Meanwhile, summer associates wined and dined on shrimp and caviar only months earlier were offered paid leave to travel or to work in the public interest until things got figured out (if they were lucky) or simply told that their offers had been rescinded and wished good luck (if they were unlucky). Remarkably, many of the lucky ones refused these yearlong paid holidays or once-in-a-lifetime chances to work at a meaningful public interest job while actually getting paid enough to reduce their debt burden—fearful that such too-good-to-be-true furloughs would later be held against anyone who took one.

It was a cluster$%# the likes of which our profession hadn't seen in many, many years.

The result? Thousands of first-year associates crammed into lifeboats lolling in the slack tide along the docks, doing nothing and waiting to be allowed ashore to the positions they had once been promised, and everyone looking at each other wondering what was going to happen next.

As of this writing (October 2010), this "lost generation" of law students is slowly being reabsorbed back into their firms, if their firms survived the recession, or back into the hiring pool if not. Firms have, however, at least for now, learned their lesson and responded by slashing the size of their incoming associate classes by up to 50 percent, instituting hiring freezes, and cutting starting salaries and bonuses.

That, of course, makes this a terrible time to be coming out of law school.

That's the bad news.

The good news is that history proves that the legal economy is cyclical. I'm writing this at what we all hope is the absolute bottom of the down cycle, and we're starting to see some telltale signs of recovery. Hopefully, by the time you're reading this, the larger economy will be on its way back to full recovery, and law firms will once again be hiring like crazy. When that happens, people will once again want a piece of the action and will again flood into the law schools like an incoming tide—and the cycle will begin again. It may well be that when we do the next edition of this book in a few years' time, we'll once again be talking about how hard it is to get into law school.

The better news is that no matter what stage of the economic cycle you find yourself in when you're reading this, the book you are now holding has helped many people beat the odds, get into the law school of their choice, get the job of their choice, and make that job work for them—and it can help you do the same.

As I have traveled the country speaking to prospective and current law students, and in responding to your countless e-mails and phone calls, I have eagerly solicited and collected advice and suggestions about how to make this book better and more responsive to the needs of today's students. To that end, this new, completely revised and updated third edition of *Law School Confidential* has been brought totally up-to-date in all its content and advice for today's law students. This new edition features a long and significant new chapter on cutting-edge trends in legal education, and advice, throughout the book, from three brand-new mentors. It also contains the most recent financial aid information and the most recent guidance available about how to navigate the new federal judicial clerkship rules.

I hope you'll find the additions to this book helpful and useful, and as always, that as you travel this road, if you have ideas or suggestions about how to make this guide better, you'll continue to get in touch with me to share your ideas! I'm always happy to hear from you.

Of course, no edition of *Law School Confidential* would have come together without the help of many people who need to be called forward into the spotlight. First, another rousing boomalacka to my literary agent, Jake Elwell, of Harold Ober and Associates, for giving me my start and providing me with such sound professional guidance over the past ten years. Every young writer needs a champion, good counsel, and a steady hand, but few have the great fortune that I've had to have an agent who has provided all three.

To my original editor, Melissa Jacobs, for believing in this book and having the courage to reach out to a new writer; to Carolyn Chu, who edited the second edition, for taking over this project with the enthusiasm that has fueled its progress before eventually heeding its advice and heading off to law school herself (!); and finally, to my newest editor, Peter Joseph, for embracing this project in its newest iteration as if it were his own. Special thanks, as well, to Steve Boldt for his excellent work copyediting this manuscript.

To Dean Gary Clinton, who, to the great fortune of Penn Law students, remains the heart and soul of Penn Law's "atmosphere of cooperation," for all the things he does to make Penn a different and better place than most law schools, and for again honoring me with his foreword to this book.

To Dean Richard Geiger of the Cornell Law School for giving so freely of his time and wisdom to take us all on a voyage into the often seemingly inexplicable world of law school admissions policy, and, more important, for his willingness to help future generations of law school applicants better understand what animates the process.

To Heather Flanner, a newly minted lawyer out of the University of New Hampshire Law School, for taking the time to read every word of this manuscript and suggest the necessary updates and changes to bring it into the age of social media.

And finally, to my outstanding team of mentors: Carolyn, Keith, Joel, Steve, Alison, Allan, Pat, Bess, Elizabeth, John-Mark, Yvette, Patrick, Megan, Lindsay, and Shruti for finding both the time in your busy schedules and the emotional fortitude to go back and relive your law school experiences in order to offer your good counsel to others. It is an honor for me to be associated with all of you for posterity in the pages of this book.

—Robert H. Miller
Hopkinton, New Hampshire
October 2010

Foreword

Several years ago, at a law school orientation party, one of the new students came up to me and, without introduction, threw his arms wide-open, taking in the full sweep of Penn Law's summer-green courtyard, and proclaimed to me, "I own this place!"

I laughed. In fifteen years of law school administration, no one—no dean, no trustee, no faculty member, no administrator, and certainly no student—had ever before said that. Quickly thinking it over, however, I realized that he was absolutely right.

Since then, that message has become the core theme of advice I give to people contemplating a legal education, students starting out their first year, or those already deep into law school. Own the place, own the process, own your own time, and own the direction of your future.

Viewed from the outside, law schools are intimidating. Viewed from the inside, legal education is often a confusing and sometimes a seemingly pointless process. Neither is necessarily true—and neither is deliberately true. Both views alienate the layperson from the attorney, and the law student from the educational process. After seeing this education up close for more than twenty years now, I can, however, assure you that neither of these factors is deliberately crafted.

These views come about in part because legal education is neither sentimental nor romantic. Law school is a hard-edged training ground, meant to take the worldview of each law student (those things I describe as what we each inherently hold to be "good and true and right and just and beautiful") and shake this worldview to its foundation. The goal is to allow the gut "feelings" we each carry with us to be challenged right to their intellectual, rather than their emotional, roots. When this process is over, the process may have altered the student's values, bringing these values to a "higher" (some might say a more cynical) plane, or the student's values may precipitate out into exactly the same system held before. In either case, however, the student should now know the reasoning behind that value system. The core goal of legal education is to teach the student to ask the critical questions "Why?" and "How?" of any situation. The student must learn to accept nothing at face value, but to learn the relationship of facts, learn to know why this is not that, and how any number of seemingly disparate situations, facts, ideas, or problems are related.

This brings me back to the notion of ownership, because as your world is turned around, your ideas are challenged, and you come to feel that not only do you not know, but you do not know how to know, it is natural to feel that the process is alienating and cruel, and that you are not nearly as smart as you thought you were. Ownership, however, means coming to understand and accept that you are now part of a larger process, and at the same time, that you are becoming a product of that process. This recognition allows you to use the process to better advantage. The goal is to walk through the door each day feeling that you understand, if not each night's reading for each class, at least that you are fully involved in the process of your education.

The other significant aspect of taking ownership of your education lies in the contact you make with your classmates, professors, and administrators outside the classroom.

Most law schools attract a remarkably well-rounded group of individuals. Life and work experiences, political and social points of view, interests, career goals, hobbies, and educational values will cover a broad spectrum. Use that to your advantage. Stretch yourself, and allow your ideas and viewpoints to be challenged.

The student I quoted at the outset was, in some ways, the last person I would have expected to instantly know how to maximize his experience at law school. This student, in his midthirties, was a former street gang member from South Central LA who had finished college late and had held a series of jobs. Yet, his sense of joy in the opportunity, and his sense of ownership of that opportunity, never faded. He threw himself into it during his three years, eventually becoming president of a large student group, president of the student government, and vice president of his class.

When this student graduated, one of our professors—a man who had recently won both the law school's and the university's awards for distinguished teaching—said to me, "I always liked having Michael in my classes because he could be depended to wade on in when everybody else was looking down pretending to search their texts. He wasn't always right, but he was always willing, and he always advanced the class. He took the chance of being wrong. And that's what I call a fine student."

Rob Miller was another such student. He came to Penn and jumped right in on every level. His eyes and ears were open, not just to the cases, but to the multilayered processes of attending a law school. He too "owned" his experience and made it work for him. The result is this fine book that will teach you how to do the same.

—Gary Clinton
Dean of Student Affairs
The University of Pennsylvania Law School

PART ONE

So You Wanna Be a Lawyer . . .

How to Use This Book

Is there anyone so wise as to learn
by the experience of others?
—Voltaire

Congratulations! By picking up and opening this book, you have just taken the first significant step toward building a productive, successful, and perhaps an even pleasant law school experience. Though you may not know it yet, law school can be an incredibly intimidating, foreign, and isolating place. Sure—at many law schools, you'll be assigned a 2L or 3L to serve as your "mentor," and if he or she isn't too busy, you might glean a few nuggets of wisdom from that relationship. Your school may offer a dean of student affairs, a team of orientation counselors, or a lecture to help you "transition" from undergraduate life or the working world into the new experience of law school. At the end of the day, though, it's still going to come down to you. In those desperate hours (and trust us, there will be many) after your mentors and counselors have given you all they can, it's going to come down to you alone, beneath the glow of your reading lamp, hiding behind closed doors wondering, panicking, and crying out for answers.

And that's where I, and the rest of your *Law School Confidential* mentors come in.

We can relate because we've just been there. We've given the "wrong" answer to a Socratic professor and sounded stupid in front of an amphitheater full of fellow students. Collectively, we've been caught unprepared, fallen behind in our reading loads, botched exams, and received some horrible grades. We've papered our walls with rejection letters from employers and judges, thought about dropping out, considered alternative careers, and anguished about choosing between coasts, cities, firms, and practice areas. We've feuded with members of our study groups and broken up with girlfriends and boyfriends who couldn't understand why we didn't have time to call or visit. We've worked on law reviews and journals, and we've been rejected by law reviews and journals. We've had articles published and articles rejected.

We've thrived and stumbled in moot court competitions and legal clinics. We've pulled the all-nighters, blanked out during exams, cried behind our own closed doors, and felt the isolation firsthand.

Despite all of that, we also graduated, passed bar examinations in six different jurisdictions, got the jobs we wanted, and have moved on into the world of legal practice.

We're not professors twenty-five years removed from the law school experience, clueless about the demands and requirements of law firm life, and waxing nostalgic about how wonderful law school is. We were students, just like you, and three short years ago, we were where you are. We know that law school often isn't wonderful, and that it can be a cold, cruel experience for the unprepared.

We're here to give you the confidential "scoop" about law school—all the stuff the books written by professors will never tell you about. If you want the truth about law school—what it's going to take to get in, get what you want out of it, and get out with your self-esteem and personality intact—this is the book you want. We expose all the traps, dispel all the myths, cut through the rhetoric, and raise the veil that has for so long shrouded the law school experience in mystery and dread.

Possessing this book and applying its teachings will give you a distinct advantage over your classmates in almost every aspect of the law school experience. Most of all, however, it will give you some peace of mind and help you to avoid making the same mistakes we made during the many weeks and months of hard work and isolation that lie ahead.

In a moment, I'll be introducing you to your mentoring team—the group of recently graduated students from law schools around the country who will guide you through the next three years with their wisdom, advice, and experiences. First, though, a bit of advice about how to get the most out of this book. Whether you are a college student thinking about law school, a working person contemplating a career change, a student already in law school, or the parent, friend, or significant other of someone in law school just trying to understand what your loved one is going through, this book has something to offer you. Determine which of the following sections is most applicable to you, and read accordingly.

I am a college student thinking about applying to law school, or I'm thinking about changing careers and applying to law school

Great! If your law school experience has not yet begun, you've just stumbled upon a wealth of information and resources that will make your entire experience easier, less stressful, and, we hope, more successful. We suggest that you read this book from cover to cover before you begin the application process to confirm that you really do want to go to law school, and to get a good overview of the entire experience to help inform your interviews and application essays. Once you've read the material, familiarized yourself with law school terminology, and have a basic grasp of how the law school experience will proceed, you should then go back and read each of the individual chapters again as they become applicable to your experience.

I've already been admitted to law school, and I'm nervous . . .

Yeah, well, join the crowd! Almost everyone entering law school is nervous about it because of the mystique associated with the experience. You, however, have come to the right place at the right time. Unlike your classmates, who will nervously fumble through the first few weeks if not the entire first semester not knowing exactly how to proceed, you will be escorted around the pitfalls and provided with a step-by-step, proven plan drawn from the experiences of the mentors you're about to meet.

Take the time between now and the first day of classes to read this book cover to cover. Don't worry if you don't understand everything right away. Just familiarize yourself with its content and with some of the basic ideas and concepts it presents. Then, when law school begins, keep *Law School Confidential* within arm's reach and let it be your escort through each week of each semester, guiding you safely through the jungle that so many of your classmates will get lost in. Use it to measure your progress and to keep track of where you are.

This is a book of collective wisdom. Put it to work for you.

But I'm already in law school . . . I wish I'd found this sooner

Yeah, us too. The difference between us, though, is that at least you can still benefit from this book. We had to learn most of this stuff the hard way! The fact is, it's never too late to start.

If you are already in the throes of law school, we recommend reading the entire book anyway—as there may be some earlier hints and suggestions that you can still capitalize on and apply. Then simply go to the table of contents, find where you are in your law school career, and begin in earnest. Read forward to the end of the book to get a feel for what's to come, then concentrate on specific chapters as they become applicable to you.

I'm the parent, friend, sibling, or significant other of someone going to law school

Want to give your friend or loved one the best gift you could ever give her at the time she needs it most? You have it in your hands. Before you wrap it up, though, you may want to skim it over yourself. In it, you'll soon discover why your law student isn't returning your phone calls, letters, or e-mails, doesn't have time to come home to visit, and is frequently tired and cranky when you call. If you're close to a law student, the experience will touch you too—and the better understanding you have of law school's incessant demands on time and energy, the easier it will be to accept the virtual loss of your loved one for the next three years. Your job is to be as understanding and forgiving as possible, and to place as few demands as you can on your law student. Reading *Law School Confidential* will help you to understand why by giving you some familiarity with the experience.

That said, it's now time to meet the mentors who will guide you through the next three years. As you progress through this book, you'll be able to follow their progress, recognize and learn from their mistakes, and watch their careers develop before your eyes. You can and should model some of their actions, choices, strategies, and experiences.

At the end of our law school careers, we all walked away from law school shaking our heads and muttering to ourselves, "I wish I knew then what I know now." You are in the fortunate position to have that wish granted before you start.

It's time to get busy!

The *Law School Confidential* Mentors

Pat Closson
Exeter, New Hampshire

B.A. University of New Hampshire
J.D. Boston College Law School

Boston College International and Comparative Law Journal

1L summer: New Hampshire Attorney General's Office
2L summer: summer associate, McLane, Graf, Raulerson & Middleton, Manchester, NH

After graduation: associate, McLane, Graf, Raulerson & Middleton, Manchester, NH

I majored in history in college and decided in my senior year that I was not interested in pursuing a career as a historian. Having made that decision, the remainder of my senior year I struggled to figure out what I wanted to do with the rest of my life. In the midst of this uncertainty, I adopted law school as a contingency plan. I figured if I got into law school, I could put off answering "The Question" for a few more years. On the day I graduated from college, I had a stack of rejection letters and had been wait-listed twice. I then started looking for a job and ended up as a customer service representative for an HMO, answering questions from New Yorkers who were angry with the service they were getting. After about two weeks on that job, I had learned all I could about angry New Yorkers and HMOs, and I realized that whatever career I chose, it would have to be something that challenged me every day. Shortly after that, I received an acceptance letter from Boston College, and I knew law school was my next step.

A career as a lawyer includes many of the things I was looking for in a career—including the ability to solve problems, help people, and be intellectually challenged. Knowing what I know now, I would do it again. A solid foundation in the law is useful in any pursuit, and the skills learned in law school are transferable to most careers.

ELIZABETH DECONTI
Albany, New York

B.A. Yale University
J.D. University of Miami Law School

University of Miami Yearbook of
International Law
Vice President, Moot Court Board

1L summer: studied evidence and European community law at University College, London
2L summer: summer associate, Pyszka, Kessler, Douberly & Massey, Miami, FL

After graduation: associate, Holland & Knight LLP, Tampa, FL

When I entered my senior year of college, I was torn between going to graduate school and going to law school. My prospective field of study in graduate school was very narrow, and there was not much room to grow. Teaching positions were at a premium, and the "greats" under whom I had studied did not look to be ready to vacate their posts for a long time. I was determined that whatever I did should be worthwhile both to me and to society, and I began to get the idea that I would not have the opportunity to leave much of a mark on the world as an academic.

I decided that more opportunities would be available to a lawyer. The field was wide open, jobs were plentiful (that year), and the law seemed to be a door opener to a variety of other careers including business and politics. Even within the law, I saw many opportunities, including working for a law firm, public interest group, or even in the judiciary. It did not occur to me then that the world is overflowing with lawyers, that jobs are not easy to come by, and that, most of all, it takes something special to distinguish oneself from the crowd.

Would I do it all again? I honestly don't know. At times I miss spending my day studying the perspective of a Renaissance painting. . . . Now, though, my days are filled with different kinds of excitement—finding a client a way out of a difficult business trap, arguing hearings, and developing well-reasoned legal arguments in briefs to courts. I suppose if I had not had the "legal experience," I would not know what I was missing. Surely I would have been a very happy academic. As a lawyer, though, I can keep my love of art history and Shakespeare as a hobby and have the law as a career. It would have been difficult to do the reverse.

Bess Franzosa
Durham, New Hampshire

B.A. University of New Hampshire
M.S. Boston University College of Communication
J.D. Boston College Law School

Boston College Law Review

Law clerk, Hon. Paul Barbadoro, Chief Judge, United States District Court, NH

1L summer: legal department, City of Waltham, MA
2L summer: summer associate, Goodwin, Procter & Hoar, Boston, MA

After graduation: associate, Goodwin, Procter & Hoar, Boston, MA

I went to law school because I wanted to be a prosecutor. I had worked for four years as a reporter and editor, and I had covered and/or followed coverage of many heinous crimes. I found myself frustrated—because I was a journalist, I was forced to be a constant bystander. I wanted to do something rather than simply watch and criticize or comment.

If I could go back, however, I would not do it again. The cost of law school, financially and personally, has outweighed the benefits for me.

The loans I had to take out to pay for law school will preclude me from becoming a prosecutor for a long time, so my original motivation for going to law school now seems foolish, or at least naïve. By the time I have paid off the debt, I don't know that I will even want to continue to practice law. I think it is particularly poignant that at a graduation party for one of my classmates from law school, one of the guests asked all five of us graduating law students there about our plans. All five of us said, on the day after graduation, that we weren't sure we wanted to be lawyers.

I wanted to be a prosecutor, but joined the labor and employment group at a large firm because I have to pay back $1,100 per month in loans. I enjoy labor and employment law, so it may turn out to be a good change that I'll stick with. I do wish I had inquired more about law school and the legal profession before I went into it, though.

ALISON GABEL
Brooklyn, New York

B.A. SUNY Binghamton
J.D. University of Pennsylvania Law School

Journal of International Economic Law

1L summer: Public Interest Healthcare Outreach Project—Senior Citizen Judicare
2L summer: summer associate, Simpson Thacher & Bartlett, NYC

After graduation: associate, Simpson Thacher & Bartlett, NYC

I decided to go to law school because I thought the law would be a good way to satisfy a bunch of different interests I had (public service, public speaking, and being challenged intellectually daily) all in one. I also decided to go to law school because it's what I thought smart people did if they didn't go to med school. Getting into a good law school seemed to be a good way to prove to those around me that I was smart. I didn't have the foggiest idea what I was going to do with my law degree.

Through my participation in this book, I hope to give some advice about getting through the many hard, negative parts of law school. It's important to focus just as much on enjoyment as achievement, since much of law school is so competitive, and you can't win everything. I want to help people understand how to achieve, get better grades, and be successful on the job search, but most important, I want to help explain how to keep your perspective in order to come out of the law school experience a happier, better person for it.

I now practice trusts and estates at a big law firm in Manhattan. I like both my job and my firm. From first to third year, I learned a great deal about balance—I worked hard in school, but I made time for part-time jobs and tried to keep active socially. I still try to do that today. I have to say that if I could go back, I wouldn't change much. I learned a great deal, both academically and personally, and I found law school enjoyable, rewarding, and valuable.

MEGAN HERTLER
Winslow, Maine

B.A. Wheaton College, 2008
J.D. University of New Hampshire School of Law (formerly Franklin Pierce Law Center), 2011

Webster Scholar

1L summer: summer associate, Sheehan, Phinney, Bass & Green, Manchester, NH
2L summer: summer associate, Sheehan, Phinney, Bass & Green, Manchester, NH
After graduation: associate, Sheehan, Phinney, Bass & Green, Manchester, NH

I went to a liberal arts school and took a wide range of classes. While I got good grades, I was never a "natural" at anything; I had to put in excruciating amounts of work to get the grades that I got. It always seemed that other students could spend less time studying and still perform better than I could. During the second semester of my freshman year, I took a mini law course. It met once a week, and 100 percent of the grade was determined by a law-school-style, issue-spotter exam. Taking that class, I learned that legal propositions come naturally to me; it took much less work for me to understand the information, organize it, memorize it, and excel. I took two other such classes while in college, and after confirming that I both enjoyed the material and that it came easily to me, I applied to law school. My choice to go to law school was not about money or prestige; I wanted the degree because law was something that I enjoyed.

I would strongly encourage any undergrad who is considering law school to take any law classes, or classes on the legal process, that his or her school offers. That is a good way to determine whether legal concepts interest the student. Additionally, I think it is beneficial to have conversations with lawyers. What do they do day to day? What are their hours like? How do they maintain their work-life balance? Having this sort of conversation with several lawyers, preferably lawyers from a broad range of practice areas, can help to illuminate the life and work of a lawyer, which will help a person determine whether that is a life and a job that he or she is interested in pursuing.

ALLAN KASSENOFF
West Orange, New Jersey

B.S. Columbia University
J.D. University of Pennsylvania Law School

Journal of International Economic Law

1L summer: New Jersey Attorney General's Office
2L summer: summer associate, Kaye, Scholer, Fierman, Hays & Handler, NYC

After graduation: associate, Kaye, Scholer, Fierman, Hays & Handler, NYC

I decided to go to law school because the work involved seemed both interesting and stimulating to me, and because it pays well. I enjoyed law school. Once you get the hang of it, it is a rewarding experience. I am now practicing litigation at Kaye, Scholer in New York City. From day one of law school, I always planned to work at a large New York City firm, and it has worked out well. I love what I do 90 percent of the time.

LINDSAY ROSE KENNEY
Washington Township, New Jersey

B.A. Pennsylvania State University
J.D. Rutgers School of Law

Winner: Senior Class Day Award for Outstanding First-Year Legal Research & Writing

1L summer: Philadelphia District Attorney's Office, Family Violence & Sexual Assault Unit
2L summer: Philadelphia District Attorney's Office, certified to try municipal court cases

I realized I wanted to go to law school in fourth grade when my reading teacher asked the class what a sewer was, and I eagerly raised my hand and responded, "A sewer is someone who sues people in court—a lawyer." Wrong answer, but something clicked, and I realized then that I wanted to be a lawyer. No one in my family was a lawyer; I never even met a lawyer until I started law school. Nevertheless, something inside of me just felt that this was what I was meant to do. Ever since that day, I made it my mission to get into law school.

My family and I grew up with the mantra that school comes first, but we always made time for volunteering, especially for causes that were close to our hearts. Accordingly, I worked hard to get to a place where I could help others for a living. I was always fascinated with criminal law and specifically interested in the physical and sexual abuse of women and children. Therefore, a career in criminal prosecution seemed like the perfect marriage of my interest in helping those who are not in a position to help themselves and criminal law. I feel lucky that my hard work enabled me to get the education I needed to allow me to be the voice for others and do what I love every day.

Determining whether law school is right for you is an entirely personal decision, so it's important to take the time to gather as much information as you can to make an informed decision. I recommend reading up on, in books such as this one, what is expected of you in law school, careers in the legal profession, and the lifestyles of lawyers, as well as talking to law students and lawyers and even sitting in on actual law school classes. It is important to be realistic about your interests and abilities—you know yourself the best, so carefully evaluate your study habits and time-management skills, your ultimate career interests, and the type of lifestyle you want to have. If you do not like competitive environments, hard deadlines, long hours, and doing lots and lots of reading, law school is probably not for you.

KEITH KOEGLER
Bronxville, New York

B.A. Amherst College
J.D. Vanderbilt University Law School

Vanderbilt Journal of Transnational Law

1L summer: internship with criminal law judge
2L summer: summer split doing part-time work for two Nashville, TN, law firms

After graduation: in-house counsel for start-up technology company

Like many people, I backed into law school. At Amherst, I received the classic liberal arts education, which meant that I didn't really start thinking about a career until my senior year, when I began scrambling to find a way to support myself after graduation. I chose to paralegal for a large national law firm for a year because I couldn't think of anything better to do. The experience was miserable, and after a year I applied to law school because what else was I going to do with my B.A. in history?

I now work doing corporate securities work for a start-up technology company, and I couldn't be happier. My hours are reasonable, the work is interesting, and the people are fantastic. But I think I'm unusual—most of my friends are at large national law firms and are miserable.

Carolyn Koegler Miller
Bronxville, New York

B.A. Tufts University
J.D. University of Pennsylvania Law School

H. Clayton Louderback legal writing instructor

1L summer: summer associate, Dow, Lohnes & Albertson, D.C.
2L summer: summer associate, Bingham Dana, Boston, MA

After graduation: associate, Sulloway & Hollis, Concord, NH

I went to law school because (1) I was told by a number of people that law school teaches you how to "think" in a way that even the best undergraduate education does not; (2) because I felt that no matter what career I ultimately chose, even if I decided not to practice law, people would take a woman with a law degree more seriously than they would take a woman without one; (3) because I thought that a law degree would open up more opportunities for me; and (4) because I majored in history in college and I wasn't sure what else to do with that degree!

I don't regret my decision to go to law school at all, but I think this is because my father was generous enough to pay for it. As a result, I don't have to worry about paying off student loans, and I was able to take the kind of position I really wanted. I got a terrific education and a degree that has opened up opportunities to me that I would never have had without it. I also feel that people take me more seriously when they find out that I have a law degree.

Having said all this, I would not necessarily have made the decision to go to law school had I been required to pay for it myself. I have a number of friends who are very unhappy practicing law, but cannot leave their jobs because they have to pay off enormous student loans. After struggling through a tough three years in law school, they are now stuck in jobs they despise for the better part of the next decade. I enjoy my present job, working in a smaller law firm, in a smaller community, where I am getting a lot of hands-on experience, and where the work I do actually impacts clients I know and talk to. Knowing that if I ever stop enjoying it, I could just decide to do something else without worrying about having to make loan payments makes a big difference.

Shruti Krishnan
Dallas, Texas

B.S. Rensselaer Polytechnic Institute
M.S. University of Texas Southwestern Medical Center Graduate School of Biomedical Sciences (biochemistry)
J.D. Southern Methodist University Dedman School of Law

1L summer: studied abroad at University College in Oxford, England
2L summer: Finnegan, Henderson, Farabow, Garrett & Dunner, D.C.

Five years after I graduated from college, I matriculated in law school. I went to graduate school and earned a master's degree in biochemis-t... orked as a sales and marketing liaison for a biochemical com-... nd finally interned at a large law firm as a scientific adviser before deciding to go to law school. I have a science background and wanted to be able to use that, so I became interested in patent law. Instead of just taking the patent bar and becoming a patent agent, I wanted to pursue the J.D. so that I could also litigate if I wanted to.

I would advise anyone thinking of applying to law school to try to get an internship at a law firm where they can shadow an associate, work with a paralegal, or work as a file clerk to get an idea of what life is like at a law firm. You owe it to yourself to see it on the inside to determine if you think you yourself could do it in the future.

YVETTE Y. ROBINSON
Boston, Massachusetts

B.A. Boston University
J.D. Suffolk University Law School

1L summer: Hale and Dorr/
Harvard Law School
Community Enterprise Project
2L summer: summer associate,
Foley, Hoag & Eliot, Boston, MA

After graduation: law clerk, Hon. James
Duggan, Associate Justice, New Hampshire Supreme Court

I've wanted to be an attorney at least since I was in the fifth grade. I was always the kid on the playground standing up to the bully, trying to talk people out of fighting, or standing up for the kid who was getting teased. I think I was just a natural advocate. In high school, I wrote for the school paper and enjoyed being argumentative, writing controversial pieces, and stirring things up. I won the Law Day Award, and at the ceremony I met a lot of attorneys who encouraged me to pursue a career in law, and it seemed that being an attorney would be a productive career given my natural spirit of advocacy. Throughout college, I interned with attorneys and worked in law offices every chance I got in an effort to learn as much about the profession as possible before I applied to law school.

For me, law school felt natural given my love of advocacy, reading, writing, and expressing my ideas in words. I would advise anyone thinking of law school to spend some time working for an attorney to get a real sense of it. When I did this, I relished the challenge of thinking on my feet and developed a thick skin for criticism. You have to be willing to put your work on the table and take the heat. You also need to appreciate not only the subject matter, but the environment, the personalities, and that not every day is going to be like what you see on *Law & Order.*

PATRICK SINCLAIR
Shirley, New York

B.A. George Washington University
J.D. Boston University School of Law

1L summer: United States Attorney's Office, Boston, MA
2L summer: summer associate, McDermott, Will & Emery, NYC

After graduation: associate, McDermott, Will & Emery, NYC

I've wanted to be an attorney since I was in elementary school and was on the moot court team in fifth grade where I prosecuted Goldilocks for burgling the home of the three bears. From there, I participated in youth and government programs and moot court in high school, and I had congressional and White House internships in college. Thinking about and wrestling with legal issues is what I like to do.

There are so many reasons to go to law school. My corporate-minded colleagues hated classes on administrative and constitutional law, but got excited about the contents of proxy statements and issues around shareholders' rights. There truly is something for everyone. All lawyers, though, must be fastidious, hardworking, detail-oriented, and comfortable interacting with people.

John-Mark Turner
Chapin, South Carolina

B.S. University of South Carolina
J.D. Boalt Hall School of Law, University of California at Berkeley

California Law Review

1L summer: U.S. Department of Justice (Environmental Enforcement Section), D.C.
2L summer: summer associate, Davis Wright Tremaine LLP, Seattle, WA

After graduation: law clerk, Hon. Michael Murphy, United States Court of Appeals (Tenth Circuit), Salt Lake City
Associate, Sheehan, Phinney, Bass & Green, P.A., Manchester, NH

Like a lot of people, I fell into law. I had gotten my undergraduate degree in math, which I didn't find to be particularly marketable. Teaching jobs were plentiful, but after a year of teaching, I found that I didn't enjoy it. I considered graduate school, but my older brother was just finishing up his doctoral dissertation in math and hadn't enjoyed it, so I decided I'd take a different path. My girlfriend at the time (now my wife) was taking the LSAT, so I did too. As I waited for my scores, I started to really get into the idea. I attended a few conferences and talks at Tulane Law School that were open to the public and became intrigued by the perspective that professors, lawyers, and law students brought to bear on issues that mattered to me. It was a pragmatic, "let's get things done" attitude. For me, college was spent developing a firm idea of all the things that I wanted to change about the world, but it didn't give me the tools I needed to bring about those changes. A legal education offered the ability to develop an attack plan and to advocate forcefully for the things I believe in.

Before you apply to law school, you need to answer that kindergarten question *What do I want to be when I grow up?* More specifically, do you understand what it means to practice law for a living, and is that what you want to do? Sometimes, it is difficult to get a good sense for what the practice of law is like unless you are able to observe it firsthand. You may want to consider spending some time as a paralegal or interning in a law office to get a better sense of it. You might also want to get to know law students and get their reactions to their summer jobs.

As in any career, practicing law has pros and cons. The hours are long, but they are usually happily spent in absorbing material. Much of your time is spent fighting or haggling with other lawyers, but it can be an exciting game of cat and mouse. You might represent people and causes you find morally repugnant, but you might also change the world. Before deciding on law, you need to determine if the trade-offs are worth it to you.

JOEL WATTENBARGER
Red Bank, New Jersey

B.A. Yale University
J.D. Harvard Law School

Harvard Law Review

1L summer: summer associate,
Kirkpatrick & Lockhart, D.C.
2L summer: summer associate,
Ropes & Gray, Boston, MA

After graduation: associate, Ropes & Gray, Boston, MA

The biggest factor in my decision to go to law school was the three years I spent as a paralegal in Washington, D.C., after graduating from college. I found that I enjoyed the atmosphere in that firm—I had never experienced such a concentration of bright, motivated, and responsive people. I also enjoyed the work I was doing, helping companies understand and respond to complex legal and business problems. I was also attracted, unsurprisingly, by the money that can be made by lawyers. A word of warning, though: because I had to take out significant loans, it will take close to a decade for my "investment" in law school to start "paying off."

Knowing what I know now, I would probably do it again. However, I would consider business school more seriously than I did four years ago—anyone who is considering a career in corporate law should consider life as a client, rather than as a lawyer!

Know what you're getting yourself into. I almost applied to law school as a senior in college, primarily because I didn't have any idea what I wanted to do, and law school seemed like a respectable way to put off the decision for a few years. In retrospect, applying at that time would have been a huge mistake. I wasn't then emotionally prepared for three more years of any school (much less law school), and I wouldn't have had any clear idea of where I might be headed at the end of the three years, but I would have been deep in debt nevertheless. If you don't know why you're going to law school, don't go.

STEVEN WEITZMAN

B.A. University of Maryland at College Park
J.D. University of Pennsylvania Law School

University of Pennsylvania Journal of Labor Law

1L summer: summer associate, Thomas Foley, Wilmington, DE
2L summer: summer associate, Seward & Kissel LLP, NYC

After graduation: associate, Seward & Kissel LLP, NYC

I didn't decide to go to law school—it was just something I was always going to do. When I was a little kid, my cousin came to visit my family. He was a lawyer in New York, and he had a nice car and told interesting stories and seemed to have a glamorous life. From that, while I was just a little boy, I decided that I would be a lawyer too. It seemed to fit me personally, since I was always argumentative, logical, and quick-thinking. Nothing better ever came along to replace that aspiration, so here I am.

Knowing what I know now, I would definitely still go to law school. It was a great experience for me, and it has led me to a great career.

CHAPTER 1

Thinking About Law School? Think Again . . .

Know thyself.
—SOCRATES

THE MOST IMPORTANT PIECE of advice that can possibly be given to you, the prospective law student, is simple. Surprisingly, perhaps, it has nothing to do with how to study or how to write a good exam. It is not about how to glean wisdom from the dusty pages of the U.S. Supreme Court opinions that shaped our country, or how to make the law review, or how to impress an employer in a job interview. Those things are important, but they're all secondary.

The most important advice that you can get as a prospective law student isn't even about law school. It's about you—and it can be summed up succinctly but completely with a single word.

Commit.

That's it. "To carry into action deliberately." Commit.

Show up for your first day of law school with only a vague notion of why you're there—without a clear set of reasons for putting yourself through the punishment you're about to endure—and you'll be setting yourself up for a miserable and unfulfilling three years. Show up committed, with a well thought-out set of goals supported by reasons for attaining them, and the experience can be exhilarating.

The choice is yours. You picked up this book looking for answers, or maybe a "quick fix" that will put you ahead of your competitors in the rough-and-tumble world of law school. You have it in one word: commit. That's it. Don't "decide" to go to law school. Don't "try" law school. Commit to law school. That is the pure axiom of law school success. Commit, or forget it—for in law school, to quote the ancient Jedi master Yoda, "there is no try."

Still with me?

Now . . . about the cocky guy next to you who just put this book back on the shelf with a "Hrumph" after reading these first few paragraphs—don't worry about him. That's the overconfident guy who will spend the first weeks of law school casually reading cases, partying in the bars, and teasing you about studying too much. Learn to love that guy because he's someone you're going to flog on your first-semester finals. Trust me on that because I used to know that guy.

He was me.

Step number one on the road to your commitment to law school is to ask yourself one critical question. Why do you want to go to law school?

No really. Think about it. What's driving you? Force yourself to come up with an answer. Now be honest. Does your answer, or something like it, appear on this list?

- because my mom/dad/sibling/relative/friend is a lawyer
- because I took the LSAT and got a good score
- because I'm not good at science and wouldn't be able to get into med school
- because lawyers make good salaries and have financial and/or job security
- because most of the people at my school are applying to law/med school
- because I watch *Law & Order* reruns and think they're interesting
- because I've read all of John Grisham's novels and find them fascinating
- because I don't know what else to do and law is a respectable profession
- because my parents/relatives/teachers/friends think I'm a "born lawyer"

Okay. So if your rationale for going to law school appears above, all is not lost. It just means that you need to rethink your motivations because these just aren't going to cut it for you. Let's dispel some illusions.

My relative the lawyer made me do it

First of all, what is it about your parent/sibling/friend the lawyer that makes you want to follow him into his profession? Is it the money? The prestige? Do you even know whether this person is happy practicing law? Have you asked him lately? More important, have you ever followed this person through a typical day—or even better, a typical week? Ever ask this person what he likes least about the law, or about how much time he spends in court compared to how much time he spends with his nose buried in the books? Ever ask how long it took him to make partner, or how many hours a week he had to work to become partner? Ever ask him how much time he gets to spend with his kids, on his hobbies, or exercising? How her relationships are with her family and friends? These are revealing questions that may help you explore a career in law more realistically. Ask them before you romanticize your relative the lawyer.

I can't ignore this amazing LSAT score, can I?

Why not? The LSAT is allegedly an aptitude test that predicts how well you'll do in law school, but the accuracy of this correlation is controversial and much debated. A good LSAT score is a tremendous asset when applying to law schools. A whole chapter in this book is devoted to teaching you how to get the best possible score. However, the test bears almost no resemblance to what you'll be doing in law school, and even less to the actual practice of law. Both law school and law practice require well-developed research and writing skills, and to a lesser extent, oral advocacy proficiency, none of which is tested on the LSAT. No legal concepts are tested on the LSAT, which is basically a souped-up, trickier SAT. Yet some would use a good LSAT score to justify law as a career choice. A good LSAT score may bring you to the dance, but it's no guarantee that you'll be happy to be there.

I don't have a mind for science, so . . .

Otherwise known as the old "I can't be a doctor because I couldn't hack orgo, so I might as well be a lawyer" rationale. Trust me, I get it . . . I took orgo twice myself, but seriously, where's the logic in that argument? We're not playing the game of Life here—this is the real thing. Contrary to the beliefs of many, there are other career choices besides law, medicine, and investment banking. Maybe you should explore some of them. Take a year off to travel, learn a language, teach, write, or work for a nonprofit or volunteer organization. Start your own business. Think a little and figure out what it is that you like to do. Don't just fall into this ridiculous mind trap and go straight for the law school applications because all your friends are doing it. To quote your mom, "If all your friends jumped off the Brooklyn Bridge . . ."

It's the economy, stupid

This is one of the biggest misconceptions of all. If you're going into law because you think it's your road to riches, stop and go directly to business school or ignore the advice in the last section and become an I-banker. That's where the real money is. While associates in big-city law firms *do* make six-figure salaries right out of law school, in a good year I-bankers at comparably large investment firms commonly make that much in their holiday bonus. Similarly, a successful business idea can bring you a partner-level salary two or three years after start-up, not to mention stock options, a flexible work schedule, and the pleasure of being your own boss.

Remember this—the average lawyer's salary in the United States is still only about $40,000 per year. Sure, partners at big-city firms may pull down over a million a year . . . but those big salaries generally belong only to the real rainmakers, and it may have taken even them fifteen to twenty years of eighty-hour weeks, two failed marriages, and a heart attack to get there. Clients don't just grow on trees or fall out of the sky. You have to earn the right to represent clients, and that takes serious time and effort. Meanwhile, the prosecutors you've romanticized from television or the novels you've read may make as little as $25,000 a year while working the same hours. So don't kid yourself. A career in law does provide some job security and a good assurance that you and your family won't starve on the streets, but if money is your primary motivator, there are much easier ways to make your millions.

This ain't Hollywood, son

That brings us to the unspoken reason why many people go to law school—the secret longing to be Tom Cruise in *The Firm*, Gregory Peck in *To Kill a Mockingbird*, Sam Waterston in *Law & Order*. Unfortunately, this too is a romanticized notion of the law. Most lawyers never make guest appearances on CNN or get to parade secret, star witnesses into court to the gasps of the gallery. The vast majority of cases settle before trial, and the work between intake and settlement is a long, private grind of discovery battles, document review, motion practice, and many hours spent reading, writing, and thinking far from the limelight. If your aspirations about law school center on supercharged days before a jury and invitations to appear on national television after your latest victory, it's time to wake up to the reality of what the practice of law is really like.

Most lawyers, even the really good ones, typically toil in the state and lower federal courts, often on mundane legal issues. Most lawyers will never argue before the U.S. Supreme Court, and an appearance before a circuit court of appeals or a chance to break new legal ground may only occur once or twice in a career. That's not to say that your days as a lawyer won't be interesting or intellectually challenging. Many of them will be. But they won't be like what you see in the movies.

Finally, remember that even what you see on *Law & Order* is the culmination of hundreds of hours of hard work in the library reading cases, developing theories, drafting court briefs and memoranda, and taking depositions from unwilling witnesses in law firm conference rooms—things the producers will never show you on television. For every hour of court time you log, you may spend hundreds of hours reading, researching, and writing. If you become a civil or criminal litigator or a prosecutor, you'll have your days in court before a judge and jury—but if you go to work for a big-city firm, it may take you five to ten years to even see the inside of a courtroom, and even longer to try your own cases. In the meantime, you'll be a researcher—analyzing issues, finding applicable cases, and writing memoranda to the more senior associates and partners in the firm. You'll typically be asked to work sixty-to-eighty-hour weeks, late nights, and at least some weekends.

Your fate is typically better in a smaller firm, or working for a state or federal prosecutor. Doing so can bring these opportunities much more rapidly—often within the first year or two, but these positions typically pay much less.

On the corporate side, it is much the same story. If you want to become a dealmaker in a large city, you'll need to get in line. For the first few years, you'll be paid handsomely to draft boilerplate agreements and spend late nights at the printer arguing over the placement of commas in merger agreements and initial public offerings. Remember that at a big firm, there may be sixty to eighty starry-eyed associates in your "class," all of whom want the same plum assignments that you do. Someone has to do the scut work, though, and for the first few years, that will be you. While smaller firms again offer more rapid opportunity, the deals are also smaller. Further, someone still has to proofread these agreements—and that someone is still going to be you. Oh—and if you're thinking of going the in-house route, remember that most corporations won't even consider hiring someone right out of law school. You'll need some years of firm experience first, unless you hook up with your friend's start-up company, and if you do, remember that 95 percent of these "start-up" companies never actually get anywhere.

Of course, there are exceptions to all these scenarios. Partners in big firms will occasionally take promising young associates under their wings, channel them interesting and important work, or provide them with uncommon opportunities to sit "third chair" in a trial, or to help "put the deal together." Be clear, though: These are the exceptions, not the rule. The road to partnership is paved with disillusioned associates who became bored and disenchanted with the work they were given and left voluntarily, or who, after seven years spent toiling in the mines, were told that they were not on the partner track and should look elsewhere for employment. In a typical large firm, of an entering class of forty to eighty associates, only a small handful, maybe three to five, will survive to make partner eight or ten years later.

Hey, you! Yeah, you—the one with the distressed look on your face about to reach for that copy of *Med School Confidential* instead. Relax. It's not all bad. It's just that there are so many people out there with misconceptions about law practice that we need to clear away the delusions up front to approach this experience with more realistic expectations. Now that we've done this, it's time for more introspection. Let's explore whether you have an accurate picture of what your law school experience will entail. As you read the questions that follow, carefully consider the answers that come from within. Pay particular attention if a "Yeah, but . . ." comes up. Trust me—it's better to deal with this crisis now than to experience it a month into your first semester.

A Realistic Evaluation of Your Fitness for Law School

Go somewhere where you can be undisturbed for the next thirty minutes or so and force yourself to answer the following questions honestly. What follows is a realistic picture of the day-to-day grind of law school. In many ways, it's also an accurate picture of the day-to-day life of a young lawyer. So forget the glamorous pictures of law practice you've seen on television and in the movies and be honest with yourself. While few people will find themselves completely in love with the thought of spending their next three years holed up in a library, if what you see below is too far out of sync with what drives you, your misery may last much longer than the three years you'll be in school.

- How comfortable are you with the idea of spending the majority of each day in silence, reading difficult material?
- Do you or could you have the stamina to read dry, complicated material for four to six hours a day, every day?
- Are you self-reliant, or do you depend on others for constant encouragement, evaluation, and/or affirmation?
- Can you seize the main points of an assignment and move on, or do you typically get hopelessly bogged down in detail?
- Are you disciplined enough to get up and attend classes every day?
- Are you comfortable speaking out in class and arguing in front of others?
- Have you been able to "will" yourself through difficult periods in your life?
- When you don't understand something, are you capable of teaching yourself?
- Do you enjoy doing research, searching through books in a library or online databases, for pieces to a puzzle or "the answer" to a problem?
- Do you like to write critically and analytically?
- Is your personality more proactive than reactive?
- When you've given your best effort, will you be able to sleep at night knowing that you've done the best you could, or are you more likely to beat yourself up wondering if there was more you could have done?
- Are you ready to make the law your life for the next three years by subverting most of your hobbies, other interests, and your social life to serious academic dedication?

It's probably obvious from the way these questions were worded, but you're looking for mostly yes responses—or at least the probability that you'll be able to work up to yes responses on each of these questions. If you've had too many "oh-ohs" during this evaluation, you should take that as a warning. For example, if you don't like to read, you're making a big mistake applying to law school.

"If you are reading this while you are still an undergrad, I would strongly encourage you to take any law classes or classes on the legal process that your school may have to offer," Shruti suggested. "That is a very good way to determine whether legal concepts really interest you. I also think it is very beneficial to have some conversations with actual, practicing lawyers. Find out what they do on a day-to-day basis. What are their hours like? How do they maintain their work-life balance—or do they? Having this sort of conversation with several lawyers, preferably from a broad range of practice areas, can help to illuminate the life and work of a lawyer, which in turn will help you determine whether that is a life you want."

To help you examine your readiness for law school, let's develop these areas more completely.

The reading load

The typical law student will read in excess of three thousand pages of case law, hornbooks, and outlines during a fifteen-week semester. In the typical semester of 105 days, that means roughly thirty pages of reading every day if you read seven days a week without ever taking a day off. At an average analytical reading rate of ten pages per hour, that means three hours of reading per day, every day, with no weekends, holidays, or excuses. Naturally, that's an unrealistic expectation—but when you start taking days off, the missed reading starts backlogging and piling up on other days. In my own experience, in the first year of law school, I generally read for about four hours a day, six days a week. That, of course, is in addition to class time, and time spent outlining what you've read. But we're not talking about the time commitment yet, just the reading. Recognize what you're signing up for. If you can't fathom yourself reading law for about four hours a day, six days a week, you might want to start reevaluating your career choice.

The discipline

In law school, there is really no substitute for discipline. The problem is, unless you are coming to the law from the military, most of us have never had to exhibit the kind of discipline that law school requires, and many prospective law students underestimate just how much discipline that is. Whatever your practices were in college—

skipping classes because they were too early in the morning, too boring, or because you were too tired from staying up too late playing poker online or too hungover from your bender—they must become a thing of the past when you get to law school. Missed classes mean missed notes, and even if you get the notes from someone else, chances are you won't understand them. Since classes often build on the material introduced in prior classes, if you miss a critical class, you might fall off the wagon. Trust me when I say there is no greater discomfort than realizing that because you missed an important lecture, you are the only person in your section who still doesn't understand a concept.

There is simply no substitute for putting in the time. You must go to class every day, struggle through the difficult material, take notes on the professor's hypothetical scenarios (called hypos), and pay special attention to what parts of the material the professor stresses in class. The benefits will soon be obvious, as it is often these very things that show up on exams.

In your upper years, after you have a few semesters of law school under your belt, these rules will change somewhat, and we'll get into these modifications in later chapters—but you, the prospective 1L, are looking at the need to string together two to three semesters of near-perfect attendance. Are you disciplined enough to force yourself through those tough days when pulling the covers over your head sounds a lot better than a 9:00 a.m. lecture on collateral estoppel?

Of course, just being there isn't enough. You need to be there with the reading done and outlined, taking supplemental notes, and ready to respond when that fateful day arrives when you are called upon to be the Socratic crash-test dummy for the class. Given that we've established that you can't afford to miss classes, "I didn't do the reading, so I'll just blow off the class" doesn't work in law school. Knowing the importance of discipline and preparedness, the professors can be unforgiving if they catch you unprepared.

During my first year at Penn Law, the unthinkable happened in only one class, during the second-to-last week of the first semester. The unfortunate individual, a friend of mine, had already started studying for exams and had not read the case being discussed that hour. The class, Civil Procedure, was being taught by the acting dean of the law school—a younger but equally intimidating incarnation of Professor Kingsfield from *The Paper Chase*. The exchange went something like this:

"Mr. Brown [not his real name]—what happened in *Hanna v. Plumer*?"

A long silence, in which heads began to turn and stare at Mr. Brown.

"Mr. Brown?"

Mr. Brown furiously scrambled to locate the proper page in his commercial outline. Members of the class, starting to realize what was about to happen, began to whisper to each other and giggle nervously.

"Is something wrong, Mr. Brown?"

More silence, then . . . "Uhh . . . I'm going to have to pass."

"I don't think so, Mr. Brown!"

More silence as the professor and the student stared each other down.

"Mr. Brown, are you trying to tell me that you are unprepared to discuss this case?"

Poor Mr. Brown didn't manage to find anything sensible to say about *Hanna v. Plumer* and was badly humiliated before the entire section of almost eighty students. He was the first and last student caught unprepared by the professor that semester. He was also called on for two consecutive days after that day—and I'm happy to report, he gave good answers both times. However, even if your law school has blind grading, you really don't want this to happen to you.

A couple of more practical thoughts to close this section on the requirements of discipline. The average yearly tuition in a private law school now tops $50,000. Assuming eight subjects per year, or four per semester, that breaks down to $6,250 per subject, and assuming three classes per week in each subject during a fifteen-week semester, nearly $150 per class. For every class you miss, you're throwing away $150. Think about that.

If that doesn't work for you, this—the ultimate example of why you need discipline in law school—probably will. As we've previously discussed, to accomplish your reading load for the semester, you need to read about thirty pages a day, every day. If you blow off Friday's reading for whatever reason, that means you'll need to read forty-five pages on Saturday and on Sunday to be ready for Monday. If you really goof off and don't read on Saturday, you've left yourself ninety pages to read on Sunday, which is more than can realistically be handled in a day. Once you get that far behind, the stress and the worry start to build, hang over your head, and make your entire experience miserable. This is why there are no weekends off in law school, and this example clearly illustrates just how easy it is to get hopelessly behind in your reading load.

You must be disciplined!

The atmosphere

The study of law is lonely. Yeah, there are study groups, but you don't get to a study group until you've read the material for the week, and you won't stay in one for long if you don't keep up with the work. Can you sit alone in a library carrel and read for a few hours after class every day, then go home and outline the day's reading alone under the midnight oil? Isolation is a reality of law school that many people have difficulty with. My group of friends made it a point to get together on Sunday nights for a few hours to play poker; but aside from that, during the first year, I often went the entire week without seeing them outside of class. You need to be ready for that. While some schools may tout softball leagues, intramural sports, and other activities, for your first two years of law school, those things will be much more the exception than the rule. For most people, the cappuccino after class, the hour at the gym, or the thirty-minute "library break" dinner you grab with a friend will be the extent of your social life. That takes some getting used to. Is it something you can handle?

Other people have substantial difficulty getting used to the competitiveness and contentiousness of everyday life in law school. If you dislike competitiveness, you have some options—such as applying to schools known for a more cooperative atmosphere—but this won't completely eliminate your problem. Most schools still operate, at least during the first year, via the Socratic method. In other words, you'll go to class, and a professor will ask a question related to the reading for that lecture and then call on someone to respond—perhaps even requiring the student to stand while responding. The interrogation rarely ends with one question, often stretching for fifteen minutes or more, while you're up there, intellect exposed to the entire class, sweating out answers. In many cases, when you're stumped, other students will eagerly volunteer the correct answers (though in chapter 10, we'll suggest that you not do this), which can leave you feeling humiliated and incompetent, and questioning your fitness for the experience. Even the most intellectually confident people are not immune from these feelings of doubt.

Finally, at some of the most competitive law schools, the competition can get truly ugly. People hide books needed for common assignments or hoard the best outlines passed down by upperclassmen to give themselves an advantage in exams. Sometimes, people even intentionally play mind games with you to try to throw you off. Some schools are notorious for harboring atmospheres like this, and I encourage you to surf the various law school message boards and blogs, identify these places, and then avoid them like the plague. But the truth is, at any school where students are graded on an absolute curve, there is bound to be some nastiness as exams draw near. If you are easily rattled or respond badly to the stress of academic competition, you may want to reconsider how well your personality fits with the realities of the law school experience.

The writing

Words are the lawyer's tools, and writing is the lawyer's craft. If you don't like to write, and if you're not fully committed to becoming a master legal wordsmith, you're in for a miserable three years and an even worse career. At a minimum, all lawyers draft letters to each other and to their clients. Corporate lawyers spend a lot of their time drafting or amending contracts and other agreements. Litigators can spend weeks crafting motions and memoranda of law to various courts.

Given the importance of writing in legal practice, you'll have a first-year class that will teach you the finer points of legal research (where to find cases, statutes, legislative history, and the like in books and online) and writing (everything from how lawyers write, to proper legal citation form). You'll do a lot of writing in this class, encompassing everything from an opinion letter to a client to a full-blown appellate brief to the U.S. Supreme Court. Your instructor will dismantle your current writing style and, hopefully, turn you into an economic, laser-sharp legal tactician. The conversion will likely be rough on you because legal writing emphasizes precision. Every word must be chosen carefully to convey the desired meaning—nothing more, and nothing less. There is no room for flowery prose. Many students find this Spartan style arduous and frustrating. Don't make a critical mistake by taking this class lightly, because after graduation, your legal research and writing skills will define your aptitude as a lawyer more than anything else. How much real estate law you remember, however, may never matter to you again.

You'll utilize your legal writing skills at almost every turn in law school—in writing essay exams, in the law review writing competition, in moot court competitions, in writing a law journal "Note" or "Comment," and in any externship you may pursue. Every employer will require a writing sample as a prerequisite for a callback interview, and no judge will grant you a clerkship without first evaluating your ability to write.

I trust that you get the message here. If you don't like to write precisely, and don't think you can warm up to it, you might want to consider a different line of work.

The commitment

At least for the first two years, law school is an all-encompassing task. Nights, weekends, and holidays will all be sacrificed to the cause. You'll be eating, sleeping, and dreaming law. Most of your conversations will center on law, to the point where you may discover that you have difficulty talking about much else. There will be stretches during the first two years when you won't have enough time to return phone calls. Letters will go unanswered, and bills will go unpaid. You'll be forced to abandon most if not all of your most cherished hobbies. There simply won't be enough time left in the day for most things. Not if you're going to stay on schedule.

Sure—you can cut corners and turn in a lackluster performance now and then. It's your future. But every grade you get, particularly the ones you get during your first year, counts.

A lot.

Every stumble closes a door. In a great legal market when the economy is booming, you might survive a stumble or two. If the market tightens, however, or if you're after one of the really plum jobs or a high-level federal clerkship, you can't afford putting forth anything less than your best effort every day. In the rough-and-tumble world of law school, sometimes even your best effort won't be good enough.

The law is a jealous mistress. Be forewarned.

Taking time off before you apply

Many people wonder about the merits of taking a year or two off after college prior to applying to law school. As Dean Geiger explains in his lengthy interview in chapter 3, law school admissions committees generally do not care whether an applicant has taken time off between college and law school. What is critical, though, both in Dean Geiger's eyes, and in the opinion of your mentors, is that you not apply to law school until you feel certain that you actually want to go to law school—and further, that you have worked out your wanderlust and your urges to ski-bum, write a novel, teach, work in the Peace Corps, or live a bohemian lifestyle as a musician.

If you feel these competing urges as you approach graduation from college, indulge them.

Embrace them.

Chase your dreams and make them happen. Just do it now—before you wake up when you're forty years old and wish you had.

Law school is no place to try to find yourself. Law school is the kind of place that will force you to repress just about every other competing interest in your life as you struggle to stay afloat. There are no free summers and no vacations. Once you matriculate in law school and the train starts rolling, it is hard to get off. Inertia kicks in; before you know it, you're ten years into a law career with a spouse and children, wondering how you never got to hike the Appalachian Trail, backpack through Europe, or write that novel.

For some, law school is the terminal dream—the thing they've been working toward since childhood. If this is you, fantastic. Get on with it.

If it isn't, though . . . or if you're not sure . . . or if you are haunted at night by a nagging wonder about whether you'd rather be a chef, for God's sake stop and figure it out. If you don't, you're setting yourself up for a lot of miserable years until finally, at some point, you either give up your life's dream and settle for something else or have a midlife meltdown to the detriment of your family.

> The biggest mistake I made was not taking time off between college and law school. Once you start law school, you begin down the path to becoming an attorney, and once this process has begun, there is no looking back. The first year is very stressful, and after that, you become focused on getting a job.
>
> —Pat

"It was a mistake for me to attend law school directly out of college. I experienced a lot of personal growth in the years immediately after college," Patrick noted. "While my friends were out learning how to work and support themselves in major cities around the country, I was still living in the utopia of a university campus as a first-year law student. As I was dealing with the pressures of being a first-year law student, I was also dealing with the emotional turmoil associated with 'coming out of the closet.' The latter experience would have been easier to handle if I didn't have to read cases, prepare briefs, and make a new group of friends all at the same time."

"I think some time away from studies is a great opportunity to explore the world and gain some insight into oneself," John-Mark advised. "Keep in mind, though, that it is not necessarily an either/or proposition. You can usually apply, get in, and then defer admission for a year. That year out can be spent exploring other career possibilities, paying off undergraduate loans, traveling, or just plain relaxing."

"I wasn't ready for law school right after college," Yvette admitted. "My grades were pretty average, so I had to raise my senior-year grades to better demonstrate my academic ability. Throughout college, I was more interested in partying than studying. By the time I got to law school, I had worked all of these things out, and all I wanted to do was study, and I was quite content."

"I also noticed that at my law school, many of the top students took time off before returning to school, so I think there is something to say about the maturity, perspective, and time-management skills of returning students," Lindsay added.

Don't rush the decision to go to law school. Take as much time as you need to be certain that the decision is right for you. The legal profession is littered with unhappy people who failed to properly consider the choice to go to law school—and who are now trapped in a career they don't want. Don't add yourself to their number.

Plan Your Application Process

Well, you're still with us, which is a good sign. Although chapter 3 will take you step-by-step through the law school application process, we need to address some significant scheduling issues now, while you're still thinking about law school. Most schools use "rolling" admissions, meaning that they admit, wait-list, or reject students as their applications arrive instead of commencing evaluation on a stated date. Some schools using rolling admissions will make offers to attractive candidates (or reject unqualified candidates) within a week to ten days of the completion of your application. This means you must have your applications complete, filed, and ready for evaluation as early as possible to give yourself the maximum opportunity for success.

If one of your top-choice schools admits you early on, your application stress will be greatly reduced, and you'll be in a much better position to haggle over money and/or to secure loans at favorable rates. If you wait until the last minute, most of the slots at your top-choice schools may already be filled, leaving you to compete for whatever slots and whatever financial aid has not already been committed to other candidates.

Recommendations

Most law school applications require two or three recommendations. Unless you're coming to the law from another career, two of these recommendations must be from college professors, and the third from the source of your choice. Obtaining recommendations takes time, particularly if the professors have to write them for many people, or if you need many versions personalized to each different school. Accordingly, a good benchmark is to disseminate your recommendation forms sixty days in advance of the date you hope to complete your applications. In chapter 3, we'll address how to select and solicit your recommenders and provide several hints about how to keep the process running smoothly. For now, just remember to plan sixty days ahead for the receipt of your recommendations.

Essays

Most law school applications require two to five essays. Many or all may have word limits or space restrictions. You heard it when you applied to college and you'll hear it again here—essays can make or break your application. Near-perfect grades and LSAT scores are commonplace in admissions offices at the best law schools, so in making the tough calls between numerically identical candidates, nothing is more impressive to an admissions committee than concise, well-crafted prose. Good writing takes time and considerable effort. Don't expect to have the luxury of essay overlap that you enjoyed in college, where you could simply adapt the same essay to every school you applied to. For law school, you may have to craft at least one different essay for every application you file.

Request your law school applications in July so you'll receive them as soon as they are published, typically in mid-August. Make a list of the different essay topics, determine how much overlap there is, and get started as early as possible.

Your criminal history

Huh?

That's right. Your criminal history. You are applying to law school, and most schools will be asking you to document any arrests and any court appearances you've made for anything other than routine traffic tickets—and they may even want to know about those if you've had too many of them. If you have any skeletons in your closet, assemble the documentation now so your applications won't get held up.

If you've ever been arrested or been a defendant in a court proceeding, admissions committees will want to know the name of the court, its address and phone number, the date and docket number of your case, the disposition, and any fines or other punishment you received. For those of you considering a cover-up at this stage—don't. You might get away with it, but most law schools won't automatically disqualify individuals with checkered pasts. Three years down the road, however, an extensive character and fitness background check awaits you before you can sit for the bar exam. Investigators will find anything you've tried to cover up—and they won't be as forgiving as the admissions office might be.

If you have a criminal history, contact your state bar association and inquire about the effect your past might have on your ability to pass the character and fitness investigation. Better to find out now than to spend the tuition and three years of your life only to find out that no state considers you fit to practice law.

The LSAT

Finally, you must determine when you will face the LSAT—the great law school gatekeeper. The LSAT is offered four times a year, in February, June, October, and December. Scores can take up to six weeks to be processed and sent to the schools, and your application will not even be looked at until your scores are in. Accordingly, most applicants will take the LSAT in June or October in order to complete their applications by November. Taking the exam in June is the wisest choice because it leaves room in case you are sick, have a family emergency, or experience one of the few circumstances that warrant canceling your scores. We'll address the LSAT more fully in the next chapter.

The big picture

You should have penciled in (1) a June or October LSAT date, (2) compiled a final list of schools and written application-request letters to be sent out no later than August 1, and (3) made your recommendation requests no later than September 15.

Your applications should begin arriving at the beginning of September, and you should immediately dissect them. Make a list of all the essay requirements, figure out how how many separate essays you'll need, and get busy writing.

Remember, your deadline is to have everything in the mail by November 1.

CHAPTER 2

Your Five Most Critical Hours: How to Beat the LSAT

Labor conquers all things.
—HOMER

THE LAW SCHOOL ADMISSIONS TEST, OR LSAT, is the "great equalizer," theoretically designed to measure aptitude and fitness for law school. Its goal is to take the entire pool of law school applicants and "level the playing field" by evaluating everyone on a single objective scale. Such a measurement is needed, the argument goes, because the inherently subjective nature of essays and recommendations and relative degrees of grade inflation make it otherwise difficult to separate applicants based on merit.

The LSAT, the gatekeeper to the doors of law school, comes with a healthy dose of both good and bad news.

First the bad news.

The LSAT is required for admission to any of the over two hundred law schools that are members of the Law School Admissions Council (LSAC). Not surprisingly, all of the top law schools, and the overwhelming majority of second- and third-tier schools, are members of the LSAC.

Most law schools take LSAT scores extremely seriously. Although exact admissions "equations" are among law schools' most closely guarded secrets (see the interview in the next chapter for more on this), most law schools use some kind of formula that combines a student's undergraduate grade-point average and strength of undergraduate institution with that student's LSAT score to compute a raw score for that student called an admissions index. This index is then used to rank the applicants. At many schools, an applicant whose admissions index falls well outside the school average may not ever get a second look. And the news gets worse. Although exact figures are not known, at the majority of schools, LSAT scores account for at least half, and in many cases more than half, of the admissions index. Bombing the LSAT will, in many cases, be fatal to your admissions hopes.

> When I decided to try to get into law school, I realized that my score on the LSAT was going to decide where I went to law school, and prepared with that in mind.
>
> —Pat

So what, you ask, is the good news?

The LSAT is nothing more than a big game, and it is a game that you can get good at. The structure of the exam is virtually identical from year to year, and the content of the test rarely surprises anyone. The exam employs a finite number of "tricks," simply rehashing the same tricks over and over in subtly different ways. Although the LSAT is challenging and poses severe time constraints, the challenge can be overcome if you are willing to put in the preparation. The LSAT's formidable reputation as the "great equalizer" and the "breaker of dreams" has primarily been earned from the experiences of the unprepared and the uninformed. This is not a test that you'd be advised to take cold, but it is certainly a test you can master.

So What Is This "LSAT" Anyway?

The LSAT allots 175 minutes for a hundred multiple-choice questions (including one unidentified experimental section used to test future exam questions) and 35 minutes for an essay question. The exam is divided into five thirty-five-minute timed sections, each testing one of three different categories of questions. These categories include reading comprehension, logical reasoning, and logic games. The LSAT will always have two logical reasoning sections, one reading comprehension section, and one logic games section. The wild card is the experimental section, which can be another section of any of the above types. During any given exam session, more than one experimental section will be tested, so one student's exam may contain an experimental section of logic games, while another student's exam may have an experimental reading comprehension section. There is no way to tell which section of an exam is the experimental section, so you have to treat each of the five sections the same way.

Your "raw score" on the exam is the number of questions you answered correctly. No subtraction is made for incorrect answers, so you should fill in an answer choice for every question even if you have to guess blindly at some. Your raw score will be converted to a "scaled score" between 120 to 180 based on a formula that will normalize the LSAT you took with LSATs given in the past five years to account for differences in difficulty between exams. Your scaled score will then be assigned a percentile ranking, which will compare your score to the scores of all other students who took the identical exam.

The reading comprehension section

Don't be lulled into complacency—this is not the same reading comprehension section you aced on the SAT. This is major-league reading comprehension. The dense passages of up to 450 words each will be chosen from one of four general fields: law, humanities, social sciences, or natural sciences. Each passage will be followed by five to eight questions. You are allotted thirty-five minutes to complete the entire section, usually comprising four passages and twenty-seven total questions. Although reading comprehension is usually perceived to be the least threatening of the LSAT categories, it often poses the most serious time constraints. Accordingly, building speed will probably be the focus of your practice in this section.

Logical reasoning

With two multiple-choice sections of twenty-four to twenty-six questions each (forty-eight to fifty-two total questions), logical reasoning questions constitute half of the LSAT. Generally, these questions pose a short argument and then one or two questions requiring you to analyze or evaluate that argument or draw logical inferences from it. These questions generally follow one of several basic patterns that you should memorize and learn to recognize as part of your preparation.

Logic games

The logic games section is almost always the most dreaded of the LSAT sections, in large part because it is the least familiar. Invariably, four different scenarios, or "games," are each followed by four to seven questions based on it. A typical game poses a hypothetical example, such as having eight seats around a table, and eight dinner guests. Several statements follow about who will and won't sit next to whom, who must be seated together, etc., and you will then be asked several questions about possible seating arrangements.

Although these games can be fascinating and fun to work out casually on an airplane or sitting in front of the fire on a rainy day, they can bring students to tears under the strict time constraints of the LSAT. Accordingly, on this section more than any other, studying the different "types" of games and their hidden tricks and the strategies for dealing with them can pay huge dividends on exam day. Allan notes, "The only way to master the games section is to take multiple practice-exam sections and learn the tricks."

Usually the logic games section of the LSAT is what causes students to panic and waste time fretting—leading to exam disasters. Knowing this ahead of time, and preparing accordingly, will give you a big advantage over your competitors.

The minutiae and related suggestions

As noted, the LSAT is offered four times a year, in June, October, December, and February. You should take the exam no later than October of your application year to ensure that admissions offices have your completed application as early as possible.

In 2010–11, the registration fee for the exam was $136 (which can be waived upon proof of financial hardship and the filing of the proper forms) and had to be received one month prior to the administration date. With an additional late fee of $68, you can register up to three weeks before the exam.

You'll have a wide choice of test administration centers, and you should not overlook the advantages of a wise selection. At the time I registered, I was living in New Haven, but despite the familiar exam center and setting, I had no desire to take the exam in a room filled with several hundred frenetic Yale students and a bunch of way-too-serious graduate-student proctors. Instead, I opted to travel home to New Hampshire for the weekend to take the LSAT at the exam center at the tiny liberal arts college in my hometown—where I felt that I would have a psychological advantage and might benefit from more relaxed proctors. Instead of taking the exam in a room with 250 others, I took it in a room with 10. My friends in New Haven tell me that their graduate-student proctors were confiscating food and beverages at the door. My proctor allowed us to have whatever we wanted and actually baked cookies for us to eat at the break. Although food is technically "prohibited" during the LSAT, you should try to bring in at least a couple of rolls of Life Savers or some raisins for a little sugar boost when you need it, an energy bar to eat at the break, and a bottle of water. If they get confiscated, they get confiscated. You might, however, get lucky.

Maybe you don't care about any of these little "advantages," and that's fine. I, however, find stress to be contagious, and I wanted to assure myself of every possible edge I could get. The LSAT was hard enough by itself, and I found that my choice of test centers made a big difference to me.

Wherever you decide to take the exam, you should visit the exam center at least a day before the exam to get a sense for where it is located, what the room is like, and how warm or cold it is, so you can dress properly. No matter where you take the exam, I'd also bring a pair of earplugs and plan to use them. If the guy next to you has a cold and sniffles incessantly, it will disturb your concentration and throw you off your game. I've known people who would have gladly paid $100 for a pair of earplugs to counter a clanking radiator, a jackhammer out in the street, or construction noises in the exam building. The day you take the LSAT will be one of the most critical days of your academic life. Plan for every contingency.

"And don't talk to other test takers about the exam during the exam breaks," Lindsay counseled. "It will only stress you out and make you second-guess yourself. Stay relaxed."

So what about the test prep courses?

Kaplan and the Princeton Review both offer excellent LSAT preparation courses that you can take either on tape or live and in person. I've had many friends who have taken one or the other and been extremely satisfied with them. The courses are relatively expensive, generally around $1,500, but by most accounts are well worth the investment.

"I took the LSAT twice. The first time, I prepared minimally on my own and ended up scoring in the ninetieth percentile. This wouldn't have gotten me into the schools I wanted to go to, so I took the Princeton Review prep course, took the test again, and scored in the ninety-fifth percentile. I would definitely recommend taking one of these courses," Keith noted.

I had a personal tutor from Kaplan. While this person was very helpful, I do not believe that I was any more successful than I would have been had I chosen to take a prep class instead. Asking for clarification and interacting with the teacher is still an option in the classes, and I am fairly certain that the extra expense for a personal tutor was unnecessary, at least for me. Beyond the tutor, I did a significant amount of studying on my own. I blocked off thirty minutes on weekdays and practiced doing one practice section at a time. On the last three or four Saturdays prior to the exam, I spent the morning doing full, timed sample exams. These methods were very helpful. I think that one of the most important parts of preparing for the LSAT is *practice.* The more that I practiced, the more accustomed I became to the types of questions that typically appear on the test. The more accustomed I became to the questions, the faster I could answer them, and my score steadily increased with each test. I advise students thinking about taking the LSAT to first pick up an LSAT study book from the bookstore. For some people, the types of questions and the logic games come naturally, and a class is not necessary. If the student is unsatisfied with his or her performance after working with that book under real-time conditions, I suggest taking a prep course. It is my understanding that Kaplan and the Princeton Review are comparable, and both very good. Beyond that, the student should block off a good amount of time for studying—make studying part of his or her daily and weekly routine. I blocked off periods of time for studying in advance, and then I treated it like a class that I had to attend. I also think that it is important to do two or three full, timed practice exams. Two of the hardest parts of the LSAT are (1) the mental endurance necessary to complete a full exam, and (2) the time pressure associated with completing each section within the allotted period. If a student has never taken a full, timed practice exam, he may find that he is so mentally exhausted after the first few sections that he performs poorly throughout the remainder of the exam, so you'll need to be ready for that.

—Megan

"I took the Princeton Review prep class, which forced me to focus and study. The class helped because it taught me what to expect so that I was not surprised. I was able to feel comfortable and confident throughout the exam. To me, peace of mind alone is worth the cost," Yvette said.

"I took a few weeks before the exam and studied on my parents' porch on Long Island. I bought a few books and did sample questions. I did okay on the LSAT, but my score did not allow me to realistically apply to the top fifteen law schools. My friends who took prep classes generally did better than I did," Patrick added.

"I am a runner and have trained for marathons, and training for a race is similar to training for the LSATs—you have to work every single day to exercise your muscles and perfect your form. I scheduled LSAT prep into my daily schedule as if it were a regular college class," Lindsay noted. "I quarantined myself in a cubicle in our student center and left my computer and phone at home so I would not be distracted and purposely did not tell anyone where I was to avoid people stopping by to say 'Hi!' and distract me."

"One other helpful thing I did was set an alarm for the week before the exam and wake up every day and do practice questions so I could get used to thinking like that early in the morning," Alison noted.

In light of the increased significance that even small differences in LSAT scores now carry in law school admissions (see the interview with Dean Geiger of Cornell in the next chapter for details), I cannot recommend strongly enough taking one of the test prep courses prior to taking the LSAT. Scores are just too important, and even small gains of three to five questions can make a huge difference. A preparation regimen that forces you to apply yourself to learning the "tricks," practicing the questions over and over, and learning from your mistakes is well worth the investment. In today's admissions environment, you must do everything in your power to get the highest score possible. With so many applicants now taking these classes, can you afford not to?

You probably know someone who took the LSAT without any advance study and pulled a 175. I know someone like that too, but it wasn't me, and you shouldn't expect it to be you either. It took me six weeks of intense training to get in range of the score I needed. Whether you do a course with one of the reputable test preparation centers or prepare on your own, plan for about the same time frame and take test preparation seriously.

I bombed it—I know it—so should I cancel my score?

Many, many students walk out after the LSAT thinking that they did significantly worse than they actually did. Unless you were physically ill during the exam or you know that you drastically underperformed on more than one section (say, by wild guessing on many more questions than you intended in more than one section), you should consider allowing your test to stand and see where you are after your score comes out. Do not simply cancel your score because you are nervous about your performance. Everyone is.

> Don't cancel your score just because you feel bad when the exam is over. I came out of the exam feeling terrible about it and thought seriously about canceling my score. I don't know if it was that I did badly on the experimental section and lucked out, or whether it was a tough exam for everybody, but I ended up scoring in the ninety-third percentile, which was enough to get me into the school I wanted. Unless you know you misbubbled or seriously mistimed the exam and therefore had to guess on huge numbers of questions, you are better off letting it ride.
>
> —A mentor

You'll have five days after the administration of an exam to decide whether to cancel your score. The Law School Data Assembly Service, or LSDAS, reports aborted exam attempts to the law schools you selected to receive score reports, and law schools are suspicious of canceled exam attempts. Further, you cannot take the LSAT more than three times during any two-year period—and canceled exams count.

If you take the LSAT more than once, LSDAS will report each separate score and then average the two scores together. Many schools will look at the average as the more accurate indicator, although as Dean Geiger explains in his interview, if the scores are significantly different, many will chalk up your low score as the product of a bad day and look at the higher score as the better measure of your ability.

Chapter 3

Applying to Law School: Bait the Hooks Carefully and Cast the Nets Wide

'Tis fate that flings the dice,
And as she flings
Of kings makes peasants,
And of peasants, kings.
—John Dryden

Most of us who applied to college filed applications with a relatively small number of schools. Your guidance counselor probably advised you to pick two or three schools in each of three tiers. The highest tier contained your "reach" schools, where your chances of admission were unlikely or uncertain, but most desired. The middle tier contained the schools that were a good numerical match for you based on their mean GPA and SAT numbers, where your chances of admission were good. Finally, the third tier contained your "safety" schools, one or two places, typically including your state university system, where your admission was virtually assured. For others, a single application to their state university may, for financial or other reasons, have been the only choice.

The law school admissions process, however, is entirely different. The admissions criteria are different, the required documentation is different, there isn't always a state school available to you, and admission is virtually never certain. Accordingly Joel notes, "For applicants with borderline numbers, I recommend applying to as many as fifteen or even more schools. There is less variance between law school applications than between college applications, so it's not that hard to crank out a bunch of apps without diluting the overall quality of each one."

Steve agrees: "Apply to four or five schools that you think you can get into and that you would not mind going to, and then apply to as many other schools as you can in the range above those schools. While it may seem like a waste of money and a waste of time to send out so many applications, you never know where you're going to get in, and so the time and money spent applying must be viewed more like a long-term investment. If the result is that you get into a school that is higher on the list than you expected you would get accepted to, the time and money will be well worth it."

Megan, who knew where she wanted to live and practice after law school, had a slightly different take. "I applied to five schools, all of which were located in Maine, New Hampshire, or Massachusetts. I did this because I wanted to stay on the East Coast near my family and had no intent of establishing roots elsewhere. I was told that employers, particularly when recruiting summer associates, are more likely to hire someone if they are convinced that the person is likely to come back if given an offer. With respect to the particular schools that I applied to, I spoke with the law professor at my college and, based on my GPA and my LSAT score, he helped me to figure out my odds of getting into various schools that I was interested in. Of the schools to which I ultimately applied, I was fairly certain that I would get into three of them, and two of them were 'reach' schools. I only applied to schools that I knew I would be satisfied attending; it was not worth the application fees to apply to schools that I knew I would never attend. If I had not gotten into any of my choices, I planned to retake the LSAT and try again."

Another mentor expressed his frustration at the seemingly random way the process is conducted, and the even more random array of results he got from applications. "It made no sense at all. I got into the number three school in the country and rejected by one of my safety schools. I just have no idea what the admissions people are looking for."

With this is mind, *Law School Confidential* is proud to present the advice and insights of Dean of Admissions Richard Geiger of the Cornell Law School. Dean Geiger brings fifteen years of law school admissions experience to your side at this critical time, and he speaks with unsurpassed candor and alacrity. We trust you will find his advice useful.

Interview with Richard Geiger, Cornell Law School

Dean Geiger, first of all, I'd like to thank you for taking the time out of your busy schedule to speak directly to the future generations of law students who will read this book. As you know, the purpose of this book is to provide prospective and current law students with as much information as possible to help demystify the experience; and I have to say, speaking from my own experiences, there was nothing more baffling or unpredictable than the law school admissions process—so I'm really thrilled that you agreed to participate in this project!

You're welcome. I have read your book, and it provides information in a very responsible way, so it's great to be a part of it.

Let's start with a little bit about your background and how you came to be the dean of admissions at the Cornell Law School.

I graduated from the Boston University School of Law in 1980 and then clerked for then–chief judge Raymond Pettine of the United States District Court for the District of Rhode Island, a wonderful experience with a truly inspirational jurist. From there, I did regulatory appellate work in the Washington, D.C., office of Sidley & Austin while my wife was doing a clerkship on the D.C. Circuit Court of Appeals. After that, we moved back to Boston, where I practiced at a medium-sized Boston law firm, that is now gone, for three years. It was at that point my wife got the academic bug, which was not a surprise—we sort of knew that was probably going to happen. But what we didn't know was that she'd get enticed by Cornell, and to make a long story short, we packed up and came to Ithaca. When we came, I became international counsel at Corning, which is about an hour down the road from here. And then when the dean of admissions job opened up in 1987, I followed up on that; and the rest is history.

So you've been the dean of admissions at Cornell for quite a while. . . .

You know, I found a professional niche that I enjoy. My wife and I fell in love with this kind of world—with this nonurban lifestyle. And now, I can't imagine anything different. I've certainly seen a lot during my tenure here. . . .

This is certainly an interesting time in law school admissions. What has been happening with the admissions numbers over the past couple of years, both at Cornell and nationally? What trends are you seeing?

Last year at Cornell, we got about 4,100 applications. That was something like a 13 or 14 percent increase from the year before. This year we're up another 15 or 16 percent, and we'll probably end up with something like 4,700–4,800 applications. I think the national trend has been pretty close to that. The underlying theme is that over the last two years or so it has been increasingly difficult to get into law school.

Do you attribute that to the slow economy?

I think so. The last time admission to law school was this competitive was during the economic downturn of the early nineties. That all changed in the midnineties when we had the dot-com boom, which took a huge number of very worthy candidates out of the law school applicant pool to go off and try to make millions designing Web sites or whatever [laughing]. Then that bubble burst, and suddenly, everyone who wasn't lucky enough to cash out at the height of the market came flooding back into the law school admissions pool! So the return of all of those people, added to a higher than normal tide of college grads coming out and applying to law school because of the poor employment climate, accounts for the record numbers of applicants we're seeing today.

And naturally, that has made it harder to get in?

Yes. As getting admitted to law school has gotten more and more competitive over the past several years, our yields have been creeping up steadily. Last year we made fewer offers than the year before, and this year we'll probably make still fewer offers. I think last year we made offers to about 17 percent of our applicants, to seat a class of 185. We had an unexpectedly high yield, though, and we ended up with a first-year class of 210. And applications are way, way up this year. Given what happened last year, I'm pretty sure we're going to end up making even fewer offers, so that the admission rate is going to go down even more.

On that happy note, let's start at the beginning. Who is generally on an admissions committee at a law school?

There's no legislation that requires that a committee look any particular way, so in a strict sense, it is up to the dean to decide what the committee looks like. But in my experience over the sixteen years I've been here, our Admissions Committee consists of faculty and senior administrators, usually our dean of students, and me. The faculty members on the committee represent the entire range of the law school faculty—junior members, clinical faculty, and tenured professors. The size of the committee has ranged, from year to year, from as small as five to as large as eight or nine people, depending on interest and who is available to serve.

Does the composition of the committee change dramatically from year to year or is it pretty consistent?

It varies quite a bit, although there are some of what I would call "admissions junkies"—people who have a lot of experience with the process or have particular interests in certain segments of the pool, people with particular knowledge or expertise about undergraduate education, and that sort of thing. So there is some continuity among those people, but there is also always an effort to try to bring in new blood to spice things up.

How does an admissions committee formulate admissions policy? Who decides what the policies are?

We're not the kind of place that has a lot of formal policies that are written in stone. One of the beauties of being an administrator or faculty member at a relatively small, but resource-rich, school like Cornell is that we are able to do most things on a case-by-case basis. So that's really how we approach our admissions process. Every year, there is a general consensus among the members of the committee that builds out of having meetings or talking about files—about what it is that we're looking for, and what makes a "good" student. That general consensus tends to build every year—but it's not around any particular ideology or anything that you can really point to and say, "These are our criteria for admission." I think it's fair to make some generalizations that every year we tend to look for people who can thrive in and contribute to a very academically driven, intellectual environment . . . but by the same token, we don't want people who will spend all their time in the library. There has to be some evidence in a candidate's file that they're the type who is going to get out there and participate in the life of the school and the community, engage in all of the things that are going on here, and be, you know, significant contributors—agenda setters we like to say. If someone has not shown any propensity to do that in their past, we don't assume that they're going to come to Cornell Law School and suddenly turn this on. That's important, because it makes a difference once a law student graduates into the professional world. We're looking for people who we feel exhibit the kind of traits that are going to make them both successful lawyers and successful leaders in their communities. So we look at academic success, personal achievement, leadership skills—all of those things are taken into account. We're fortunate enough to have an applicant pool where a lot of the time we can get all those things in the same candidate. In an ideal world, that's what we would get in every case. That policy isn't written down anywhere, and there isn't a final, numbers-based calculus for measuring those criteria, but that's what we try to do on a case-by-case basis. It's a really subjective evaluation—informed by as much data as we can reasonably acquire.

You said a lot there. Let's try and break the criteria for admissions down one by one . . . and since applicants tend to be most worried about the impact of their LSAT score on their chances of admission, let's start there. Is the LSAT score the be-all and end-all of a candidate's chance of admission? Is there a cutoff below which an application gets tossed without any further consideration?

I know that the LSAT is the source of major concern out there, and I also know that people out there are thinking, "You have this entire academic record, four years of college, maybe some work experience, maybe some graduate work, letters of recommendation, a great array of performance-related information, and what you're going to do is make me take this four-hour test that refines itself down into a single number, which suddenly is going to take on all this weight. . . ." And when you put it that way, it sounds awful. And if that's what actually happened, it would be awful. What we try to do at Cornell is use the LSAT as one component in the overall review. There are a lot of countervailing forces at work, though, that interfere with the way a lot of law schools use the LSAT.

Can you explain what you mean by that?

The LSAT is only intended to be one piece of a much larger equation. It gets used in law school admissions because it is a relatively good predictor of actual performance in the first year of law school. We know that because law schools actually test it every year—they do correlation and validity studies. And it turns out that the LSAT really is a much better predictor of performance in the first year of law school than undergraduate GPA or any other factor we can measure. That's not to say that it is perfect, but as a test—as an admissions tool, it does have some validity. So the challenge for any admissions committee is to figure out how to incorporate that, and how much weight to accord to small differences in scores. For example, is the difference between a 160 and a 164 significant from a prediction standpoint? Should that matter in the admissions process? The answer is probably not—but does it matter in the admissions process? Yes. But that's partly for reasons that have nothing to do with what the LSAT should be doing in an admissions process.

I suspect you're alluding to the impact of a school's median LSAT score on its ultimate ranking?

Right, rankings have something to do with it, but it's not all about rankings. The test is such a seductive thing to admissions committees mostly because it's a pretty good predictor of future performance in law school, so some committees end up using it to the hilt, and in those cases it ends up magnifying small differences in test scores and making those differences much more important than they really are. Then that tendency gets exaggerated by the law school rankings that take median LSAT scores into account as a factor in ranking the schools. So on top of the natural tendency to overrely on the test because it is empirically, at least, the best predictor of performance, you also have law schools worried about the incoming median LSAT score of their classes—because it's significant to them in terms of their ranking in *U.S. News & World Report*. So you have the compounded problem of a test that on its merits is very seductive, and a ranking scheme that takes schools' median LSAT scores into account, and the net result is that schools make distinctions between applicants based on one-point differences in their LSAT scores.

That's crazy! That one-point difference could be based on nothing more than a guess!

There's certainly no predictive difference at all based on one point. But that's the reality of the regime that has been created, where outside factors start to influence the process and put too much weight on distinctions that are not real. It's a real problem.

In your opinion, what should the LSAT be doing in the admissions process?

What it should be doing is, like I said, giving you some ability to get a feeling for whether the applicant has some of the raw tools to thrive academically in law school. And those raw tools are measured in the various sections of the LSAT—reading comprehension at a very high level, deductive reasoning, inductive reasoning, abstract thought. Those are the things that the LSAT tries to test. And they all have relevance in the law school setting. It's a package of tools that almost everyone would agree is very important when it comes to someone's ability to succeed in law school. So what that test should do is allow an admissions committee to come to a conclusion about whether a candidate has the package of tools necessary for success at their school when that evaluation is combined with the other relevant elements of the candidate's application. Used that way, the LSAT is a very important and effective piece of the whole equation.

Is that how you use the LSAT at Cornell?

Well, to be frank, we're subject to the same human frailties as every other school. We constantly have to remind ourselves that small differences don't have predictive significance, that not all people do well on standardized tests, and that the test isn't an accurate predictor for everyone. But unfortunately, we're also influenced by the fact that this score plays a role in our rankings, and that exerts pressure the other way when we look at applications. So there's now this tension that exists—a person applies who has a good record and is otherwise a great candidate, but his LSAT isn't quite up to where you might want it to be. Because I've been here for fifteen years, I can remember the days in admissions when that didn't matter. Now, I think there would be a lot of admissions people around the country who, when faced with that situation, would take a look and try to make a judgment about how much effect admitting that candidate might have on their median LSAT score.

You'd think that these tiny point distinctions just wouldn't matter that much. If Cornell's ranking dropped, say, from number seven to number thirteen as a result of taking a stand on this issue and refusing to play the rankings game, would that really change the quality of the yield or the type of students who ultimately matriculate at Cornell? I guess I'm trying to figure out why the deans of admissions at a number of similarly ranked schools don't just band together and stop* U.S. News *from driving the admissions process like that?

I think the simple answer to that is that, as a group, we're just ridiculously competitive. Everyone assumes that at law schools like ours, you can get anybody you want. But incremental differences in the rankings do matter—applicants clearly pay attention—and everyone is always angling for the next higher group of applicants. As an institution, we're always comparing ourselves and measuring ourselves against our peer schools and trying to outachieve them. It may be that this simply is the nature of an institution that's basically run by a bunch of lawyers. So no matter where you are in the pecking order, you compete intensely with your peer group for the best students, for the best faculties, for the most pages of law review articles published—basically anything that can be measured.

Before we leave the subject of the LSAT—a couple of strategy questions that people always want to know. First of all, do you think it is possible to study for the LSAT?

Oh, absolutely. I don't think you necessarily need to take expensive classes to do well on the LSAT, but at a minimum, several months before you intend to take the exam, you ought to be sitting down with a book of actual old exams, training under real-time test conditions, and developing strategies. It is definitely possible to improve your score this way; and let's face it, the score you get is an important factor, so it's worth taking the time to prepare.

What advice do you have for the student who bombs the LSAT? Would you advise that student to take the test a second time?

I think you really need to take a look at what happened in that particular circumstance. Was the score you got wildly anomalous, and by that I'm talking about at least half a standard deviation away—not just a couple of points—from the scores you were getting on your practice tests? Were you sick on the day of the test, or was there a serious distraction in the test center, like a jackhammer outside the window? If so, then you should definitely take the test again. If your score represented something close to what you were getting on your practice tests, though, and there wasn't anything you can point to that distracted you from an optimal performance, you should probably stand pat, because chances are, your score is not going to meaningfully improve.

How does an admissions committee handle multiple scores?

We usually look at the scores, and if the scores are meaningfully different, we typically use the higher score. In situations like this, knowing that multiple administrations of the test under normal conditions should not result in dramatically different scores, if there is a meaningful difference, we assume that there was a distraction or that the student had a bad day, and that the better score is the better indicator of that student's "real" ability.

Let's move on to a candidate's GPA. How important is the GPA, and how does an admissions committee account for the difference between a GPA from a top-tier college and a GPA from a lower-ranked school?

Well, interestingly, the undergraduate GPA by itself is better than random in terms of its predictive ability as to how well someone will perform in law school. So the challenge for any admissions committee is to figure out what the GPA is supposed to tell you, and to try to get behind it to give it more meaning than simply what you get from the number. There are lots of ways of doing that. One way we do it is to scrutinize transcripts very closely. LSDAS [the Law School Data Assembly Service] gives us a tool that helps us get started understanding what a GPA might mean. For example, it gives us the distributions of all GPAs from an undergraduate school for every law school applicant over a three-year period. Armed with that chart, you can take someone's GPA, plug it into that distribution, and figure out where it fits. This is a way of dealing with differences in grading factors for schools that have a lot of grade inflation. You can use that distribution to figure out what a school's mean and median GPAs are for law school applicants, compare that data to other schools, and then make appropriate adjustments from there.

So let's take the undergraduate program at Cornell University as an example. What you are saying is that LSDAS will give you a distribution chart with the GPAs of all Cornell undergraduates who have applied to law school in the past three years?

Right.

So you can look at a Cornell undergraduate's 3.65 GPA and immediately know where that places that person in comparison to his peers over the past three years.

Exactly. So you're getting apples to apples on the grade point average, which is a big help because it helps you get a feeling for the grading factors in a particular situation.

But that still doesn't tell you objectively how that 3.65 in the Cornell undergraduate curriculum stacks up against a 3.81 in Stanford's or Georgetown's undergraduate curriculum, for example.

That's true, but LSDAS gives us a rudimentary tool for that, too. In the case you raise, you're trying to judge the respective qualities of the student bodies. To start the process, LSDAS gives you the mean LSAT score of all students who graduated from a particular institution during the past three years. You'll have schools that have high mean LSAT scores, and you'll have schools that have not so high mean LSAT scores. So that gives you a very rough measure of the quality of the student body of a particular school, and how those student bodies compare to each other—at least as measured by the LSAT, which, as I mentioned before, isn't perfect but is the best indicator we have.

So does the committee read every file completely, or is there a way that you cut some files off? For example, if somebody comes in with a 135 LSAT or a 2.2 GPA, does it go immediately to the reject pile without getting reviewed? How does the committee deal with files that really fall outside the mean?

Even the files that look like they're going to be outliers always get a complete review by at least one person. And most of the files in our pool get a complete reading by at least two. Some files get a complete reading by as many as seven or eight people. But even the outliers get at least one very thorough reading. The reason for that is that I still remember the days when we routinely took some of those outliers, and they turned out to be some of the most special students we have ever had. That's the miracle of the admissions process. You can always find somebody who may not have your typical numbers, but when you look at the file, you can just tell that the person is going to be a great law student, and a great citizen, or contribute in other ways to the benefit of the class. If we didn't have a way of piercing through all of the superficial indicators like grade and test scores, we'd miss those folks. Don't get me wrong, I'm not saying that we're ever going to admit a lot of low outlier applicants, but you've got to at least give them the chance. We've seen enough cases where those people turned out to be great that we don't take the risk of losing them by simply doing things by the numbers. Again, that is one of the great things about a flexible process that isn't a slave to formulas.

So for someone who really loves Cornell and really wants to come here but has numbers that fall below Cornell's target numbers, it is still worth applying if they feel they have a compelling story to tell?

Definitely. Especially if they've looked hard at us, and they've decided that there's something about us—whether it's our size, whether it's a particular academic focus, where we are, or whatever—if there's something about us that makes them think this could be the place for them, it's definitely worth taking a shot. You know, median means median. The twenty-fifth percentile is just that—the twenty-fifth percentile—so every year there are people above that and people below that. There's a whole matrix of factors that goes into the admissions decision. If you just look at the numbers and disqualify yourself, you're basically taking the rest of that matrix out of the equation.

Having said all of that, does Cornell calculate an admissions index to help you organize files?

We don't calculate one to help us organize files. We calculate one as an aspect to our correlation studies. We use a combination of the student's LSAT and GPA as most schools do and do a regression analysis. Every year, we test the index against performance, and there's a pretty strong correlation there. But that's the sole reason for doing it; we don't use it as a ranking factor.

So how is the admissions index calculated, and how is it used?

LSDAS does that for us. Validity studies have shown that a combination of LSAT score and undergraduate GPA is the very best predictor of law school performance; so every year, we send each student's first-year grades to LSDAS, and they take that data, along with each student's undergraduate GPA and LSAT score, and perform an analysis to determine by what relative weight our students' undergraduate GPA and LSAT scores predict their first-year grades. Each year, we get that report back, showing what our formula should be—what our optimal coefficients are to weigh the LSAT and GPA to best predict first-year grades.

So does a student's admissions index matter more than other factors?

You would think it would, right? But it doesn't, and I'll tell you why. The validity studies are nice, and there is a pretty strong correlation between the index and first-year performance. But again, it's just one factor we look at. We think we can do even better by looking at transcripts, analyzing the rigor of the courses and curriculum a student has taken, looking at the letters of recommendation, looking at trends in grades, looking at the institution attended—all of those things. We think we can improve on the predictive value of the admissions index by doing our own legwork. Numbers can only tell you so much about someone.

So if you don't use the admissions index to rank files, with 4,700 applications coming in, is there a way that you prioritize files, rank files, or decide which files you're going to read first in order to get offers out to your most desirable applicants early in the rolling admissions process?

In general terms, our theory is, first in, first out. It doesn't really work that way because it's much more complex than that. We don't have a sort of straight-line way of evaluating every single application. It's also complicated by the requirements of our Early Action program, which requires us to get a bunch of decisions out by mid-December.

Would you describe how the Early Action program works?

We have a nonbinding Early Action program, which means that for those files that are complete by November first, we guarantee an admissions decision by mid-December. The theory is that it allows applicants to stick their toe in the water early at the schools that they most care about and see how they do, and to try to determine whether they need to make any kind of midcourse correction in their application strategy. It's great for people who can get organized early. You can apply to as many programs as you want. If you get into the school you most want to go to, you don't have to send out fifteen more applications; you can start planning, rent an apartment, and get everything all taken care of well in advance. If you don't get into the schools that you apply to Early Action, you still have a chance to send out a few more applications to a wider array of schools.

Can you explain the difference between Early Action programs and Early Decision programs?

Early Action programs are nonbinding, so you can indicate your interest to one or more schools, get a decision by mid-December, and then either accept an offer or continue the process. An Early Decision program contractually binds you to accept an offer of admission from a school if one is made and to withdraw all other applications you may have filed. A binding Early Decision program is good for people who know that there is one particular law school they absolutely will go to if they get accepted and are willing to shut the doors to all other places and go to that one school if they're accepted.

What percentage of your applications come by way of the Early Action program?

About 25 percent.

And how many offers of admission generally flow from that process?

We received over 1,100 applications and made approximately 250 offers to that group.

Two hundred and fifty offers out of the seven hundred–plus that you know you're going to make? So in other words, at least this year, more than a third of the allotment of seats in the class was filled by the time the Early Action process was complete.

Well, that's not quite right because I'm guessing that our yield may be lower for that group, and remember, they don't have to make a commitment until the spring.

And the admit rate was about 23 percent, compared to something around 17 percent overall.

Right.

How many law school applications would you generally advise people to send out?

Well, the average number of applications that law school applicants file is between five and six. If you're smart about the application process, you ought to be able to fairly easily narrow the field to seven or eight schools or perhaps even fewer if you're limiting yourself geographically. The other thing I tell people is to never apply to a school that you would not go to. I'm always amazed talking to people in the application process who ask me about reapplying to Cornell because it was their first choice who tell me, "I got into blank, blank, blank, and blank, but I don't want to go to any of those schools because I really want to go to Cornell." What kind of rational process is that? Why would you bother to spend money to apply to a law school that you would not go to if they admitted you? I think a lot of people could save themselves a lot of time and expense if they'd just approach it that way. Only apply to law schools that you'd be happy to attend if admitted. Why waste your energy applying anywhere else?

If someone already knows the city or at least the region of the country where they want to end up, do you think they should factor that into their choice of a law school?

I think an applicant owes it to herself to do her due diligence before beginning the application process. If the person already knows where she wants to end up, she should go to a law school that can show her a placement record that establishes that it puts people in that city or region on a consistent basis. Every law school collects placement data. Most of it is now on law school Web sites. Don't accept the label that the school applies to itself—go look at the data or call the placement office and say, "I want to be in Los Angeles. What are my chances of doing that coming out of your school?" Whoever you talk to should be able to whip out the data and say, "Seven percent of our graduates every year end up in Los Angeles," or whatever the figure is, and then compare that number to the ones you get from the other schools you are applying to.

Okay, now that we've dealt with the nuts and bolts regarding a candidate's LSAT and GPA, can you take us through an evaluation of a particular candidate's file from the moment it arrives in the office to the time a decision is made on it?

Once a file comes in and is completed, the selection process begins here in my office. I, or one of the other two admissions officers, read all the files first. One of us will read every file and determine whether the file should circulate further. The larger Admissions Committee has delegated responsibility to the admissions office to make a wide range of decisions on our own. These relatively "easy" decisions generally don't circulate to the committee. Once we're through, the borderline or difficult files begin circulating among the seven members of the committee, each of whom will make a series of written comments and then a particular recommendation. Once the file has circulated, if the recommendations come back unanimous, then that's the decision. If the decision recommendations are not unanimous, then we will meet as a committee and discuss the file.

So every person on the committee reads every file?

If they're around. Yes. Every file that circulates goes to every member of the committee.

What are the possible decisions available to a reader? Is it just admit, deny, or wait-list?

No, it's more narrative, and there are more gradations. Weak admit, strong admit, hold but could be persuaded—you know, that kind of thing. You basically write a paragraph or so on each file. Every member of the committee during the week will get these files, and there's probably twenty to twenty-five at a time. You review them, you write your paragraph, you pass it along to the next person. And then they all come back to me. I look at them. If they're unanimous, that's the decision. If they're not unanimous, then we have a meeting.

What happens at that meeting?

A freewheeling discussion usually ensues, during which you see all of the views that you hope you would see. The committee is intentionally composed of very different people with different opinions on things, but the common goal is to admit people who are going to show up every day, work hard, and contribute a unique perspective, background, or something else to the fabric of the class. And each person on the committee sees those things through a different prism. So that's where the give-and-take gets very interesting. Some members of the committee may have very different views of what is appropriate preparation for law school. Is a music major, for example, going to do well in law school or not? Was a particular candidate's overseas program a semester vacation, or did the student challenge himself with the semester abroad? How do we weight grades for a student who attends a school that allows you to decide whether to show your grades as pass/fail after your grades come out? So it's a very, very freewheeling process, and there are certainly no shrinking violets on the committee. But despite that, the cases are very, very rare when we cannot reach consensus on any particular candidate.

Okay, let's get specific now and break down the application into its component parts. Let's start with the personal statement. When you sit down to read a file and you read the personal statement, what is it that moves you about someone's statement?

I think writing an effective personal statement is a very, very hard thing to do. And it does not happen by accident. The very best ones are carefully crafted, and that's why they're so good. So the first thing I can say is that, like any important writing project—take your time, give it all the attention you can, and apply all of the tools that any good writer would use. Start with an idea, hone in, organize, start putting your thoughts down on paper, then put it away for a while, focus the theme, show it to a friend, and keep improving it incrementally. I think the thing that makes the best personal statement is the process rather than the actual topic. I see a lot of promising topics that are executed poorly, and on the other hand, I also see a lot of modest ideas that are executed well and become wonderful statements. So the thing I would emphasize is that the process is the most important part of crafting a good personal statement. The other thing I'd say is to try not to bite off more than you can chew. If you try to write an autobiography covering all the bases from the time you were in nursery school until the time you decided to apply to law school, it's not likely to work out. You need to just take one or two things that you would like the reader to know about you and concentrate on those. I always tell people to think of it as an interview. Say you had a short interview with somebody on the admissions committee for twenty minutes—half an hour at most. You would go into that interview knowing that you're not going to be able to cover everything you'd like to cover. So what you will probably decide to do is talk about the one or two things that most define you and leave that with the interviewer to remember. I think if you approach the personal statement exactly that way, you'll be most successful.

Moving on to letters of recommendation. What do you think is the best way to pick a recommender, and what is your view of the VIP recommendation versus a recommendation from a teaching assistant?

Well, first of all, I think the overriding thing I can say about recommendations is that it's virtually guaranteed that almost all of them are going to be positive. It's the rare recommender who will happily agree to write a recommendation and then, once you leave the room, decide to get back at you for repeatedly sleeping through his class by writing you a lukewarm recommendation. So the vast majority of recommendations are, by definition, positive. What do you do with that? The thing that helps us most—especially for applicants who are current students or recent students—is a recommendation from a faculty member who taught you, who knows your work well, and who has seen you in as many different circumstances as possible. And by faculty member, I mean that broadly. It doesn't mean it has to be a chaired professor; it could be a teaching assistant. But keep in mind, I also said someone who knows you and your work well. So your teacher from your large intro biology course is probably not going to be able to say anything too meaningful about your work. Ideally, your recommendations would come from a TA or faculty member in an upper-level class, seminar, or some other setting that was conducive to that person actually having the chance to get to know you and your work well. So pick that person, and don't pay any attention to what the person's title is. Pay attention to what they know about you and your work. Now, having said that, it does help to have the recommender be able to draw comparisons between you and other students he or she has taught, so the very best recommenders are those who have taught lots of students and can speak about you from that perspective versus someone who is teaching their first seminar and can only tell us that you were the best student out of the twenty that he had in class that semester. The larger the sample, the better.

You often hear stories about experienced recommenders using "code" in their recommendations to distinguish between students. Is this urban legend, or is there something to it?

Unless we know for sure that someone is using a code, and the only way I've ever figured that out is by getting many letters from the same person, we don't assume anything about language. In other words, we don't try and determine whether there is an intentional difference between somebody who says, "So-and-so gets my warmest recommendation," versus somebody else who says, "So-and-so gets my most outstanding recommendation," or, "So-and-so is recommended without reservation." What we try to do is focus on the substance and make our judgments based on that.

How many should you send, and is there ever a good reason for sending more recommendations than the admissions office asks for?

I think you have to use your judgment. If you think about it and you conclude that you have a good reason for adding a recommendation, then go ahead and add it. A good reason might be if there's something that you really want to tell us about yourself that isn't covered by your other recommendations. In general, what we're looking for is academic recommendations, but we want to know about your character too. We want to know what kind of classmate you're going to be, so that could be a reason to add a recommendation. If you had a particular working experience that's not covered, that could be a good reason for a supplemental recommendation. But if you can't come up with a good reason, don't just add another recommendation for reinforcement. We'll get it the first time.

Earlier on, you alluded to the care with which your committee reviews undergraduate transcripts. What is it you're looking at on these transcripts?

We look at the number of courses someone takes, the difficulty of these courses, trends in grades . . . a transcript can tell you a lot about someone beyond just the raw numbers. People should know that it's never bad to be adventurous about the classes you take. I say this to young college students who may be reading your book in anticipation of applying to law school down the road, and who may be wondering, "Should I take the safe track, take the minimum number of courses necessary, or take some gut courses to try to engineer my grades?" These people should know that we're a lot more impressed by people who are willing to venture out of their comfort zone and challenge themselves—because that's what they're going to be asked to do when they're in law school—and as you know, that's what you're going to have to do when you practice.

What about how people choose to spend their summers? Is that important to you, or even considered?

We do like the fact that people have interfaced with the world at large because that contributes to the law school experience. But how someone chooses to do that is entirely up to them. Just don't be a felon [laughs]!

What position do you have on people who apply to law schools directly out of college versus those who take some time off? Is there a preference given to one or the other? And if someone takes time off, do you scrutinize how they used that time off? Or is it just sort of a nonfactor?

I think it's a nonfactor in terms of the actual assessment in the selection process. However, this may vary a little bit among different people looking at the file. As a general matter, what I tell people is, go to law school when you are good and ready to go to law school. And if that means you want to take a little bit of time off before going to try something else out, or if you want to take a break and travel or relax before going—by all means do it. The last thing you want to do is arrive at law school and spend the first six weeks second-guessing your decision. You want the pedal to the metal when you're there. The law school application process has this sort of insidious quality, I think. You take the test, you get yourself all geared up, you apply, and if you apply wisely, you're going to get in somewhere. Next thing you know, the conveyor belt sort of carries you along, you roll through your three years, you get a job, you pass the bar, and a number of years later, an awful lot of people end up looking back and saying, "Whoa, I always thought I was going to do such and so with my life, how did I end up here?" So this decision about applying to law school needs to be taken seriously.

I have a lot of friends who are already in that boat. . . .

And you know, for those people, it might have been a better idea to take some time off and explore different career choices or life goals rather than following the herd into law school. For others who know that this is what they want to do, there is certainly no disadvantage in applying directly.

One of the questions that I get a lot when I'm out talking to people is why are law schools so reticent to interview? Why are interviews not more of an important part of the admissions process, given the daily human interaction that law involves? Med schools interview all of their applicants and so do business schools? Why not law schools?

I don't know why law schools don't interview more. Cornell is actually one of the few law schools that does incorporate interviewing in a modest way in our process at two different points. But there are very few, only maybe one or two law schools that are interviewing even half of their applicant pool. I think it has to do with the size of the applicant pools in relation to the size of the entering class, and what schools can support institutionally in terms of an admissions process.

Undergraduate schools have more resources than even the largest law schools to accomplish this kind of thing. The law school applicant pools are so large now that it's hard to do it in any sort of fair way. There is also literature out there that suggests that interviewing is not necessarily good for the process because you don't necessarily make good choices when you interview. One of the problems is that interviewers tend to favor applicants who are like the interviewer. So that puts a lot of importance on who you're using to interview. You don't want to disadvantage whole categories just because an interviewer doesn't like them. I think in the law school environment this may be even more important given the dynamic educational environment. You want the widest possible range of viewpoints you can get.

So how does Cornell use interviews, then?

We use interviews in two stages. In the first stage, we look at the group of people whose applications we know we are going to be spending a lot of time with, the people who look strong based on the numbers. We know we're going to read them, we're going to reread them, agonize over them, and eventually we are going to have to make distinctions between them. So we take a cross section of those people and see if we can't improve our selection process in those tough cases. We pick out 250 to 300 people whom we invite for an interview on this basis. We say it can be either in person or on the phone—no preference either way. We give them half an hour or forty-five minutes. And then we make that a part of the process. It works to most people's benefit. It always helps us flesh out the things that we have questions about. So that's the first point at which we interview people. The second happens once we have developed a waiting list. We give anybody on our summer waiting list a chance to have an interview. So during the months of June and July we will be interviewing a fair number of people. We also follow up with people every year because we have particular questions about their application materials.

What would be an example of that?

Well, here's a particular example. You have somebody who is making an argument for a trend in their grades. They started off slowly, but now they've really found their niche and are showing their true potential. But all you have are their grades through their junior year. And it just happens that they spent their junior year abroad. So in that case what I might do is contact that person and ask them to send along their fall-term grades to see if that trend is still holding up. Sometimes I'll even ask for spring-term grades. Or let's say that a recommender says something that piques my interest. I may follow up on that. I may call the applicant and talk to her for a few minutes, or I may even call the recommender. Occasionally we'll also see something in an application that just doesn't add up, like someone with C-pluses on their senior thesis getting honors from the department. So I'll make follow-up calls about discrepancies like that and try to get that clarified.

Obviously you're aware of the University of Michigan cases. Can you tell me how issues of diversity factor into the admissions calculus at Cornell?

I think diversity in law school really does matter a lot, diversity of viewpoint, diversity of background, diversity of ethnicity—those things do matter both in terms of the richness of the discussion and, more broadly, in view of the fact that our profession serves the interests of justice in our country and in the world. So we look for factors that are going to enrich our student body, and we do give those factors some weight. It's not a quota. It's an individualized decision that we make about every file. We'll say, "We want this person here because of something special about their background." It might be outstanding academic performance; it might be outstanding leadership; it might have to do with the cultural or ethnic environment in which they were raised, obstacles they had to overcome, discrimination they have experienced—

all of those things factor into the equation. No one of those things turns out to be determinative, but they all carry some weight because they all matter.

How do you let a school know that they are your absolute top choice without having it seem disingenuous?

I don't think there's any good way because it always seems self-interested. I suppose the best way to do it is indirectly. If it comes through a recommender, and we don't have reason to think that the recommender has been seeded to tell us this, then it has some credibility. Sometimes actions speak louder than words. Has a person visited the school? When they were here, how excited did they seem about the place? Were they talking to students? Did they stop by the office to say hello? Have they supplemented their application? There are ways of indicating that a school is your top choice without saying it directly.

In your years as the dean of admissions, you must have some great war stories. What are some of the most memorable mistakes you've seen made on applications? The last time around, Dean Austin at Penn talked about getting a sneaker sent in the mail with a message that said something like "Now I've got my foot in the door."

I remember that [laughing]. I think we got the other sneaker from that applicant! We get some pretty good stuff too. Videos come all the time, but a particularly weird one was a video of the person reading their personal statement to music that they had composed as background for their personal statement. One time, we got a body painting with an application.

Come again?

It was a body that was painted. It was to show the applicant's talent at doing this. We didn't actually get a body, but we got a large picture of the body that had been painted. That got quite a bit of attention around here.

Do these things ever work? I mean, do they show creativity?

Most of the time I think they show bad judgment. I always tell people, don't let the form of the statement get in the way of the message. If you want to convey your creativity, there are lots of ways to do that . . . and you can do it effectively without writing your personal statement in quatrains. If it seems contrived, people are going to see right through it, and it isn't going to work for you. You don't want that kind of attention. People have had enough worthwhile experiences by the time they apply to law school that they don't need to do crazy things to distinguish themselves. Their record, a couple of good recommendations, and a thoughtful and well-executed personal statement should be enough to distinguish them. And if it isn't, none of these tricks is going to help anyway.

What are some of the other more common mistakes you see on applications and how can they be avoided?

I am always amazed at some of the same mistakes I see. People are paying serious money to apply to law school, and yet, when you read their application materials, there are typos and flagrant grammatical errors. How does that happen? That should never happen if you take the time to proofread your materials and have someone you trust look them over before you send them in. An application that comes in with these kinds of mistakes tells me a lot about what kind of student lies behind it. The other humorous but incredible mistake I see every year is the personal statement, sent to me at Cornell, that ends with the line "Gaining admission to Penn would help advance those goals." Needless to say, my reaction to that application is "Well, good luck at Penn, then, because you're not getting into Cornell!" So it's really the simple things—editing and proofreading—and taking the time to make sure that the face you're putting forward represents your very best effort.

So let's talk for a minute about the decisions the larger committee makes on an applicant's file. First of all, what are they?

Admit, deny, or hold. By "hold," what we're saying is "Please hang in there; we need a little more time to make a decision about your candidacy." We're just not yet in a position to make a decision up or down on those people at the time their files are read.

Is there anything that those people can do to better their chances of eventually getting in?

Well, first of all, we already talked about the ways that you can express interest. If you want to supplement your application, by all means you should do that. At some point we look at the hold group again; and from that list, we deny some people, we take some people, and we create the smaller group that ends up as our summer waiting list. Those are the people who are then offered an interview.

How long would you advise someone who really, really wants to come to Cornell to hang in there on the wait list?

To the last possible minute. You may think this sounds really obvious; but if you're on the waiting list, the most effective thing you can do to increase your chance of getting admitted is to hang in there as long as possible. When we get to a point where we're filling a few seats very late in the process, we're going down the list looking for the person who we know is going to say yes.

So that is the time for someone to get in touch with you or someone in the admissions office and say, "It's June first, I'm going to be traveling in Europe and may be unreachable, but Cornell is my first choice, and if you pull me off the wait list, I'll definitely come"?

Sure. There's never a downside provided you don't go completely overboard and call every day. I don't think anybody thinks that doing that is offensive in any way provided you're polite. To hear from somebody every week or two as they start to get down the home stretch, just a quick call to inquire if anything has changed and to let us know that they're still interested—you know, we write all of that down, and we keep track of it. You don't want to call every day, but as long as you exercise some judgment, checking in every couple of weeks in the summer is fine.

Let's say that you're sitting with your son or daughter and you have a couple of minutes to give them the best advice you can about how to succeed in the law school admissions process. What would you tell them?

I think it very much depends on when you're answering that question. If my son or daughter came to me as a senior in high school or a freshman in college and asked me that question, I would tell them, don't engineer your college education solely with an eye on what you think you want to end up with for a career. Think in terms of your passion, your interests, and then apply yourself completely to those things without reference to where you think it is going to lead you because you can't possibly know that, and even if you did, you probably couldn't control it. You know what you like, you know what makes you excited—pursue those interests and do it with all the vigor that you can possibly muster. And then come back and talk to me when you're a junior or senior in college and we'll see where you are.

Okay, so let's say that your son or daughter has done that and comes back to you in the spring of junior year in college. Now what do you tell them?

Right, so after that advice, my daughter comes back to me, having been a music performance major, and says, "Dad, you know, I'm really interested in law school" [laughing]. No, but seriously, at that point I would suggest that we make sure there's sort of an inventory of basic skills. I'd look to see that she had done some serious research and writing, and that she'd taken at least a couple of courses that had pushed her in terms of her ability to analyze and deal with abstract ideas—no matter what field she was in. I would also want to make sure she'd had a chance to get to know something about the legal profession and what lawyers do. And if she had done that and reached the conclusion that she wanted to be a law student, then, in terms of applying, I'd encourage her not to focus initially on a particular region of the country and limit herself in terms of locale, but to try to find a law school that was a match with some of the things that had allowed her to thrive as an undergraduate student. For example, if she had thrived in a large university setting with an incredible range of opportunities, I'd tell her to look for that kind of a setting again in law school. Or, on the contrary, if she'd thrived in a really small university setting where she got some close attention, then she should make that her perfect law school. Start with those parameters first. Look at the things in your past that have allowed you to thrive, and make those things a focus in your application process. Then we'd need to look at her credentials and see if there was a match between her academic credentials and the people who would be competing with her for seats in the class, and make sure there was relationship there. And then I'd tell her to go out and prepare diligently for the LSAT.

And that brings us back to where we started. So the last question I have is, how would you advise someone to figure out whether they should go to law school at all? What criteria should be part of that analysis, from your perspective?

I think there are a couple of things that are good general indicators. One is if you find yourself being uncomfortable with just accepting simple answers or explanations for things. If you do, you probably have the intellectual makeup to thrive in the law school environment, where you are always grappling with complex issues or balancing interests and where a simple answer is rarely found. And I think the other thing is that if you feel a yearning to have an impact on the way our society works, law is a great, great way to do that. It is essentially a license to improve people's lives every day. And that is a very powerful thing.

Dean Geiger, I'd like to thank you very, very much on behalf of my readers for taking the time out of your very hectic schedule to share your thoughts with us. I think your words will bring some comfort to people facing this increasingly daunting process.

It's my pleasure. I wish everyone luck—and remember, don't make more of this than it is. If you work hard, follow your passion, and become informed about the process, you'll do fine.

Additional strategies

There are a few primary strategies that you may want to employ in planning your law school applications. As with everything else in this book, these strategies are culled from personal experience and will help you avoid some of the critical mistakes we made.

Strategy 1. Try to decide where you want to practice before you apply

I know, I know, you don't have any idea what you want to do with your life, so how are you supposed to know where you want to live? Well, guess what? If you read the first two chapters of this book, you should already have an appreciation of the importance of foresight and planning in determining the success of your law school career.

Hey, if you get into Yale or Harvard, that's great. You can keep this book around for some humorous bedtime reading and cease to worry about any of this stuff because you'll pretty much have it made. But the rest of us might want to heed this advice: Try to figure out where you want to settle down before you apply to law school.

Why?

It's simple. If you don't get into one of the top fifteen or so law schools in the country, it's going to be pretty hard to get a job outside the region where your law school is located. If you already know where you want to live, however, you can file applications with the top law schools, then hedge your bets by applying to the better regional law schools near the city where you hope to practice. This strategy has several advantages. First, you can virtually neutralize the placement problems associated with attending a regional law school because you'll want to practice in the region to which your regional law school primarily places its students. Second, in applying to that law school, your desire to stay and practice in the region can make a compelling case for your admission. Third, if you are admitted, you'll greatly reduce your stress during recruiting season knowing that before you even started, you've maximized your chances of getting a job in the city or region of your choice. We'll talk much more about the role regional preferences should play in your application process in chapter 5.

"I wanted to stay in the Boston area because that's where my family was located, so I applied to five local schools," Yvette recalls. "Plus, the Boston area has so many great schools to choose from, I didn't feel limited."

Strategy 2. Apply to schools as soon as possible

Dean Geiger made a pretty clear point in his interview earlier in this chapter—the Early Action pool produces a high yield of accepted offers and matriculating students. As a student, that should tell you two things: (1) as an early applicant to a law school, you are signaling a preference to attend that law school and, with competitive numbers, may increase your odds of admission; and (2) if you send out your applications late in the application season, many of the seats in the class may already be filled. There is no need to mince words here—you must file your applications as early in the application season as possible to maximize your chances of success. This process is competitive enough without putting yourself in a hole out of the gates. Apply Early Action wherever possible; and where such a program is not offered, aim to have all of your applications completed by November 1.

"I sent in all of my law school applications right at the deadline," Shruti warned. "I would advise future law school applicants to get their applications in as soon as possible instead of waiting for the deadline since many law schools admit students on a rolling basis. The earlier you send in your application, the earlier you will find out whether you were admitted, and the sooner you find out about what financial aid and scholarships the school is willing to give you."

Strategy 3. Make sure your application makes a coherent and compelling case

Admissions offices know well that law school is often a "default choice" for good or ambitious students who haven't figured out what they want to do with their lives. This often manifests itself in an application that fails to make a coherent case as to why you should be admitted to law school, as distinguished, for example, from business school or graduate school in some other discipline.

Before you submit an application, take a step back and ask yourself, "Does this application make a coherent and compelling case about why I want to get a law degree?" If it doesn't, retool an essay or some responses to short-answer questions to make the case.

"The theme of my law school application essay was goals, and how goals evolve over time as we mature and experience new things," Megan remembered. "I began the essay at the beginning of my freshman year and explained candidly that I really did not have any meaningful goals at that time. I went on to describe how my goals evolved as I made my way through my undergraduate career, ultimately ending at the choice to attend law school. I felt that this essay not only made the case that I wanted to go to law school, but explained how I had arrived at that decision, while simultaneously describing other happy, fun, sad, and difficult experiences that I'd had along the course of making that decision. I chose this topic because I felt it allowed me to tell my story, demonstrate that I was a real person who had made hard choices, battled through them, and in the end learned from them."

"I dedicated most of my college years to volunteering for the world's largest student-run philanthropy, Penn State's Dance Marathon (THON)," Lindsay noted. "THON raises money and awareness for pediatric cancer patients and their families and culminates in a forty-six-hour no-sitting, no-sleeping dance marathon. Even though THON has nothing to do with law school, I chose to write about my experiences with THON—and how the pillars of this philanthropy shaped me into the driven leader I am, how they will help me as a law student and a lawyer, and how my volunteer work reflects the type of law I want to practice. There's no 'right' answer to a law school essay, but it will be beneficial to write about something that you are passionate about—something personal that sets you apart. In fact, the dean of admissions at my school even e-mailed me the weekend of THON and commented on my work with the philanthropy! This just goes to show that you never know when your interests and essays will spark something in those reading your essays."

Strategy 4. Proofread everything

Yeah, I know I'm being redundant, but Dean Geiger couldn't have been clearer about this. Typos and sloppiness can kill your chances of admission. If it isn't absolutely perfect, don't send it out.

Strategy 5. Visit your top schools and keep in touch with the admissions office

Remember, you need to stand out. Visit your top-choice schools and figure out why it is that you want to matriculate there. Does something about the school's general philosophy draw you to it? Do you hope to study a certain subject in depth with the tenured faculty member who is the acknowledged expert in the field? Do you want to participate in a dual-degree program that is better at that school than elsewhere? When you visit the campus, drop into the admissions office and introduce yourself to the director of admissions. Don't brownnose, but don't be afraid to make that person aware of your attraction to the school and the reasons for that attraction. If you do get to speak to the admissions director, send a note a few days later thanking him or her for the time spent talking to you. Later, try to reference your campus visit and reinforce your reasons for applying somewhere in your application.

"I think visiting schools is very important," Megan observed. "Each school has its own personality, and through visiting, a prospective student can learn whether his personality meshes well with that of the school. Will he be happy there? Does he fit in with the other members of the student body? A general discomfort with your surroundings, when added to the discomforts, stresses, and challenges already associated with being a 1L, can be game ending."

About four weeks after you send out your applications, drop a quick letter in the mail to each school highlighting any recent achievements or accomplishments, enclose any subsequent grades you have received, reiterate your interest in attending the school, and express a willingness to discuss your candidacy further at any time. Include a phone number and e-mail address just in case.

These are all ways to keep your name fresh in the minds of the admissions offices at your top-choice law schools, which, as Dean Geiger suggested, can be helpful to your chances of success in a largely faceless process.

Be sure to respond immediately to any requests by admissions offices for more information, and don't even consider turning down an interview if you are lucky enough to be offered one. Finally, if you are wait-listed, open a line of communication with the admissions office and stay in touch until a decision is reached on your candidacy.

Supplement your application with anything new or relevant, and be sure that the admissions office knows, every couple of weeks during the summer months, that you are still holding out for a seat. Spots in first-year classes open up until the first week of classes. The longer you can hang in there, the better your chances of getting the call.

CHAPTER 4

Toward a New Philosophy in Legal Education

A practical education must prepare a man for work.
—DRUCKER

THE TRANSITION DURING THE EARLIER DECADES of the past century from the apprenticeship/mentorship model of legal education prevalent in so many other countries, to a model that viewed the study of law as an academic science to be conducted in the university setting, gave rise to an escalating conflict between academic and practitioner. Most commonly, this conflict presents itself with partners in American law firms and judges in American courtrooms lamenting the newly minted lawyer's (even, and sometimes especially, the newly minted lawyer from a top law school's) inability to write clearly, succinctly, and persuasively, to draft a lease or a simple business contract, to have some facility with drafting and serving a complaint or a subpoena or with the rules of procedure and evidence, or even knowing where to sit in the courtroom.

The Honorable Linda Stewart Dalianis has served as a justice on the New Hampshire Supreme Court for the past ten years and became chief justice in 2010. Prior to being elevated to the New Hampshire Supreme Court in 2000, Chief Justice Dalianis served for nearly twenty years as a trial judge in the New Hampshire Superior Court. With that kind of experience in the trenches, she has a unique perspective on the preparedness of young lawyers to serve clients in the real world, and her time on the bench convinced her that the system of legal education in the United States needed reform. Fortunately, Chief Justice Dalianis did not just opt to sit on the bench and chastise ill-prepared and ill-equipped young lawyers. Recognizing that the problem was not with the lawyers themselves, but with the education they had received, she opted to do something about it.

"It wasn't just about what I was seeing in my own courtroom, although some of that certainly horrified me," she observed. "Thinking back on my own experiences coming out of law school, if I had been thrown out on my own, I wouldn't have had any clue about how to do even the most basic things either. So that was the first thrust behind this effort."

Now, through her efforts over the past fifteen years, Chief Justice Dalianis is leading a renaissance in legal education, having developed, along with a committee of other interested parties, a legal education program known as the Daniel Webster Scholar Honors Program, at the University of New Hampshire School of Law, that may well revolutionize how law is taught in the United States in the years ahead. Chief Justice Dalianis and Professor John Garvey, a former longtime litigator and mediator in private practice who is now the director of the Daniel Webster Scholars Honors Program, join us for a discussion in the second half of this chapter about why understanding this trend is important to you, the prospective law student.

First, though, a little background to set up the issue.

Practicing lawyers looking back on their law school experiences commonly express the opinion that their law school education left them deficient in many practical skills that they were then forced to learn the hard way—in the real world—often by trial and error. With the wisdom of hindsight, practitioners often view much of the academic focus in law school classrooms, and the scholarship being performed by law professors, as increasingly irrelevant to the realities faced in the day-to-day *practice* of law.

In response, law professors, many of whom have never actually practiced law themselves, respond that law schools are not intended to be trade schools, but "centers of scholarship and learning," where students are "taught to think," not "taught to practice." It is not at all clear, however, at least to this author, when law schools were given license to subjugate their duty to impart a solid working knowledge of the practical skills needed to practice law to law professors' theoretical or academic interests—but that is my bias as a partner in a law firm and a practicing litigator. What is certain is that law schools seek to increase their national reputations by the scholarly "reputations" of their faculties, which in turn helps to attract many strong students who want to study with those professors. Those students, in turn, continue to perform strongly academically and, thus, reel in some of the best jobs upon graduation. That placement record then helps to drive the ranking numbers in *U.S. News & World Report,* which, in turn, draws even more of the best students to a school, and the cycle begins anew.

The real-world problem with this ongoing philosophical debate is that the majority of law students graduating from law school actually go on to *practice* law, and the student—caught in the middle of this struggle to define what should properly constitute a legal education in America—often graduates from law school having taken a full complement of theory-based classes, knowing how to think and reason like a lawyer, how to do legal research, and how to make good public-policy arguments, but with little to no idea how to actually do any of these things in practice. The biggest losers of that struggle are not the professors (who are largely isolated from it and insulated from being held accountable for it), nor the students (who will eventually learn by trial and error), but the American legal system, which is forced to endure the lag.

Hanging helplessly in the balance of this philosophical struggle, but, ironically, rarely mentioned in the discussion, are the actual *clients* whose dollars pay to keep much of the legal system running, and who suffer the most immediate consequences of the new lawyer unprepared to offer them practical, real-world advice and competent service.

In the real world, this problem takes one of two forms. For the client serviced by a larger firm, this means putting up with the redundancy and cost of overstaffing, as firms commonly staff files with a senior partner, a junior partner, and at least a couple of associates of different experience levels who are actually being trained how to practice law in real time while working on these real-life files. This is the old apprenticeship model in its modern form, and as long as the often overworked junior and senior partners do actually train these underlings, instead of focusing on their "more important" day-to-day concerns such as making their own billable-hour requirements, developing business, collecting accounts receivable, managing client relationships, and trying to balance work with their personal lives, the model can and occasionally does still work.

Up to 50 percent of all newly graduated lawyers will, however, never benefit from this redundancy and will instead hang out their own shingle and start to transact business on behalf of clients all by themselves. These lonely souls are often forced to cast about looking for a senior member of the bar to serve as a sounding board, or to rely on advice and form documents found on the Internet.

Either way, clients, and the American legal system, clearly suffer greatly under these models. Our legal system, which relies on the advocacy skills of opposing parties to function properly, is, as the mantra goes, only as good as the people who practice in it.

So why am I showing you some of the system's dirty laundry in the fourth chapter of this book, perhaps even before you've made the decision to go to law school? Because at this point in the book you are thinking about which schools to choose, and we want you to be aware of these issues, think about them, and figure out how they might guide the choices you make about your legal education, whether now, by choosing which school to attend based on the *availability* of a reasonable balance of practical classes, or later, in choosing your own curriculum.

The MacCrate Report

More than twenty years ago, Justice Rosalie Wahl of the Minnesota Supreme Court, then the chair of the ABA Section of Legal Education and Admissions to the Bar, urged legal educators to "recommit themselves to teaching students how to learn systematically from experience and simultaneously to educate them in a broader range of legal analysis and skills than have traditionally been taught" and mused whether we had ever really "tried to determine what skills, what attitudes, what character traits, and what qualities of mind are required of lawyers?"

In 1989, Justice Wahl convened a task force to respond to these questions, and after gathering information, holding hearings, and conducting extensive discussions for nearly three years, the task force, in July 1992, issued its report, which was designed to attempt to evaluate and close the perceived "gap" between the theory-based legal education being delivered in American law schools and the practical needs of the graduating law student heading out to actually practice law. This report, known in shorthand as the MacCrate Report,* highlighted the ten fundamental lawyering skills and the four fundamental values of the legal profession that the committee felt should be imparted to all law students, as follows.

Fundamental Lawyering Skills

1. **Problem solving**
    - 1.1 Identifying and Diagnosing the Problem
    - 1.2 Generating Alternative Solutions and Strategies

*American Bar Association Section of Legal Education and Admissions to the Bar, *Legal Education and Professional Development: An Educational Continuum, Report of the Task Force on Law Schools and the Profession: Narrowing the Gap* (ABA, 1992).

1.3 Developing a Plan of Action
1.4 Implementing the Plan
1.5 Keeping the Planning Process Open to New Information and Ideas

2. Legal analysis and reasoning

2.1 Identifying and Formulating Legal Issues
2.2 Formulating Relevant Legal Theories
2.3 Elaborating Legal Theory
2.4 Evaluating Legal Theory
2.5 Criticizing and Synthesizing Legal Argumentation

3. Legal research

3.1 Knowledge of the Nature of Legal Rules and Institutions
3.2 Knowledge of and Ability to Use the Most Fundamental Tools of Legal Research
3.3 Understanding of the Process of Devising and Implementing a Coherent and Effective Research Design

4. Factual investigation

4.1 Determining the Need for Factual Investigation
4.2 Planning a Factual Investigation
4.3 Implementing the Investigative Strategy
4.4 Memorializing and Organizing Information in Accessible Form
4.5 Deciding Whether to Conclude the Process of Fact-Gathering
4.6 Evaluating the Information that Has Been Gathered

5. Communication

5.1 Assessing the Perspective of the Recipient of the Communication
5.2 Using Effective Methods of Communication

6. Counseling Clients

6.1 Establishing a Counseling Relationship that Respects the Nature and Bounds of a Lawyer's Role
6.2 Gathering Information Relevant to the Decision to Be Made
6.3 Analyzing the Decision to Be Made

6.4 Counseling the Client About the Decision to Be Made
6.5 Ascertaining and Implementing the Client's Decision

7. Negotiation

7.1 Preparing for Negotiation
7.2 Conducting a Negotiation Session
7.3 Counseling the Client About the Terms Obtained from the Other Side in the Negotiation and Implementing the Client's Decision

8. Litigation and alternative dispute resolution

8.1 Litigation at the Trial Court Level
8.2 Litigation at the Appellate Level
8.3 Advocacy in Administrative and Executive Forums
8.4 Proceedings in Other Dispute-Resolution Forums

9. Organization and management of legal work

9.1 Formulating Goals and Principles for Effective Practice Management
9.2 Developing Systems and Procedures to Ensure that Time, Effort, and Resources Are Allocated Efficiently
9.3 Developing Systems and Procedures to Ensure that Work Is Performed and Completed at the Appropriate Time
9.4 Developing Systems and Procedures for Effectively Working with Other People
9.5 Developing Systems and Procedures for Efficiently Administering a Law Office

10. Recognition and resolution of ethical dilemmas

10.1 The Nature and Sources of Ethical Standards
10.2 The Means by Which Ethical Standards Are Enforced
10.3 The Processes for Recognizing and Resolving Ethical Dilemmas

Fundamental Values of the Profession

1. Providing competent representation

1.1 Attaining a Level of Competence in One's Own Field of Practice

1.2 Maintaining a Level of Competence in One's Own Field of Practice
1.3 Representing Clients in a Competent Manner

2. Striving to promote justice, fairness, and morality
2.1 Promoting Justice, Fairness, and Morality in One's Daily Practice
2.2 Contributing to the Profession's Fulfillment of Its Responsibility to Ensure that Adequate Legal Services Are Provided to Those Who Cannot Afford to Pay for Them
2.3 Contributing to the Profession's Fulfillment of Its Responsibility to Enhance the Capacity of Law and Legal Institutions to Do Justice

3. Striving to improve the profession
3.1 Participating in Activities Designed to Improve the Profession
3.2 Assisting in the Training and Preparation of New Lawyers
3.3 Striving to Rid the Profession of Bias Based on Race, Religion, Ethnic Origin, Gender, Sexual Orientation, or Disability, and to Rectify the Effects of These Biases

4. Engaging in professional self-development
4.1 Seeking Out and Taking Advantage of Opportunities to Increase His or Her Knowledge and Improve His or Her Skills
4.2 Selecting and Maintaining Employment That Will Allow the Lawyer to Develop as a Professional and to Pursue His or Her Professional and Personal Goals

The Carnegie Report (2007)

In 2007, fifteen years after the publication of the MacCrate Report, the Carnegie Foundation for the Advancement of Teaching published a report entitled *Educating Lawyers: Preparation for the Profession of Law.* This report illustrated that while the MacCrate Report had produced a flurry of study and discussion, not much practical change or real progress had actually been made in the implementation of its recommendations. The 2007 Carnegie Report continued to criticize legal education for its lack of focus on practical and ethical-social components, calling out the current system's continued "lack of attention to practice and the weakness of concern with professional responsibility."

The Carnegie Report proposed that legal educators adopt an "integrative strategy," comprised of cognitive, practical, and ethical-social components "in support of the larger goal of training competent and committed practitioners." The cognitive component would focus students on the substantive knowledge and way of thinking needed in the profession. The practical component would focus students on the forms and styles of expert practice shared by top practitioners. Finally, the ethical-social component would focus students on the purposes, attitudes, and values for which the profession is responsible.

Best practices for legal education

Around the same time of the Carnegie Foundation's 2007 report, the Steering Committee for the Best Practices Project of the Clinical Legal Education Association issued its report on the state of legal education in the United States. The Best Practices Committee, convened in 2001, was intended to "provide a vision of what legal education might become if legal educators step back and consider how they can most effectively prepare students for practice." According to the Best Practices Committee, while it "may not be possible to prepare students fully for the practice of law in three years . . . law schools can come much closer than they are doing today."

The key recommendations coming out of the Best Practices Committee were that (1) the primary goal of legal education should be to develop competence, defined as the ability to resolve legal problems effectively and responsibly; (2) law schools should integrate the teaching of theory, doctrine, and practice and teach professionalism pervasively throughout all three years of law school; (3) law schools should employ context-based instruction; and (4) law schools should assess student learning through various methods of assessment, including multiple formative and summative assessments.

Recent developments

The issuance of the 2007 Carnegie Report and the 2007 Best Practices Report led to another concentration of activity around legal education reform. This time the effort seems to have gained critical mass, as a number of law schools are developing promising initiatives to better integrate traditional legal instruction with training in skills and values.

In December 2007, the Carnegie Foundation for the Advancement of Teaching and Stanford Law School convened a meeting to discuss strategies for implementing change in law school curricula. This group included three representatives from each of the ten law schools (CUNY, Georgetown, Harvard, Indiana [Bloomington], NYU, Southwestern, Stanford, University of Dayton, University of New Mexico, and Vanderbilt) that comprise the Legal Education Analysis and Reform Network (LEARN). The group also included individuals from other schools identified as leaders in legal education, including Professor Garvey from the University of New Hampshire School of Law. Coming out of these meetings, the group decided to focus on (1) the structure of the law school curriculum as a whole; (2) the teaching enterprise as practiced by individual law faculty members; and (3) assessment of student learning. LEARN has also announced a series of projects intended to further these efforts including (1) a follow-up to the 2007 Carnegie Report to be published in 2010, which will examine the curricular developments that have taken place since the 2007 report was issued; (2) collaborations among faculty who teach doctrinal courses and those that teach practical skills courses; (3) a study of the use of interactive classroom technology; (4) an assessment of the use of periodic written assignments and/or examinations in lieu of the one-exam model currently used; (5) an assessment of the potential for the use of simulations as teaching tools in the classroom; and (6) an assessment of alternatives to the traditional bar examination.

While many law schools are now offering more courses in legal writing, trial advocacy, and negotiation, and making these courses full-credit graded courses so they are taken seriously by students, at least four law schools have developed significant, longitudinal curriculum initiatives in an effort to move toward the reforms suggested by the MacCrate, Carnegie Foundation, and Best Practices reports. One such initiative is the CaseArc Integrated Lawyering Skills Program at Case Western Reserve University School of Law. The CaseArc program begins with an intensive, weeklong orientation centered around a criminal case in which the students assume and attempt to carry out all of the fundamental roles in the case. Over the first two years of law school, students then take CaseArc courses that are integrated with substantive subjects and focus on different fundamental lawyering skills. The program, which relies on simulations, evaluates students formatively and substantively. The University of Idaho College of Law has commenced strategic planning with the aim of creating a program of study informed by the Carnegie Report and Best Practices Report. Similarly, Harvard Law School faculty are experimenting with a first-year problem-solving course that would integrate real-world problems, skills exploration, and analysis of substantive law and legal theory.

However, one program has led the way toward the educational reforms encouraged by the MacCrate, Carnegie Foundation, and Best Practices reports—and an examination of that program and how it works is the subject of the second half of this chapter.

The Future Model of Legal Education?: Profiling the University of New Hampshire School of Law's Daniel Webster Scholar Honors Program

In 2005, after years of study, the University of New Hampshire School of Law (UNHSL) (formerly known as the Franklin Pierce Law Center, or Pierce Law) launched a pilot program known as the Daniel Webster Scholar Honors Program. Intended to be an alternative bar licensing mechanism, the program was conceived and championed by Justice Dalianis on the principle that "there must be a better way to prepare students to practice law."

Leading a coordinated effort among the New Hampshire Supreme Court (which administers the New Hampshire Bar Examination), the New Hampshire Board of Bar Examiners, and the dean and faculty of the University of New Hampshire School of Law, Justice Dalianis created a committee to study and consider a curriculum-based alternative bar licensing program. This program, designed around the MacCrate factors, was intended to improve the quality of new lawyers by focusing on the practical skills needed and would function, in essence, as a two-year practical evaluation of a candidate's fitness to practice law and replace the bar exam.

The program was built using certain courses already offered by the law school, then adding a number of practice courses discussed below. These practice courses were designed to be small, taught in real life, and to emphasize the MacCrate skills and values. The program, which was initially implemented by the New Hampshire Supreme Court as a three-year pilot program, opened to students in January 2006 and graduated its first class of thirteen students in May 2008.

To keep the program sufficiently small and flexible during its developmental "pilot" phase, it was initially limited to fifteen students per graduating class. Based upon its early success and student demand, it was expanded to twenty students per class in 2008. Students apply to the program in March of their first year of law school and are selected in June by a committee composed of professors and graduated Webster Scholars. Selection is based on a personal interview and an evaluation of each applicant's academic, professional, and interpersonal skills. The committee attempts to select a balanced and diverse group from the pool of qualified applicants.

Daniel Webster Scholar Honors Program: Requirements and Sequencing

(as of July 2010)

GPA: Must *graduate* with a cumulative GPA of at least a B (3.0)

DWS Courses: No grade below a B- (2.67) in any DWS-designated course

First-Year Credit Requirements (required for *all* UNHSL students): 30

Upper-Level Courses (required for *all* UNHSL students):

Administrative Process (3)
Criminal Procedure (3)
Professional Responsibility (3)
Writing Requirement (3)
Subtotal: 12

Additional Upper-Level Courses (required for Webster Scholars):

Evidence (3)
Personal Income Tax (3)
Business Associations (3)
Wills, Trusts, and Estates (3)
Clinic/Externship (6)
Subtotal: 18

DWS Required Courses:

DWS Pretrial Advocacy (also satisfies 3-credit upper-level writing requirement) (4)
DWS Miniseries (2)
DWS Negotiations (2)
DWS Trial Advocacy (3)
DWS Business Transactions (3)

DWS Capstone—Advanced Problem Solving and Client Counseling (3)
Subtotal: 17

Total Required Credit: 77
Minimum Additional Elective Credits to Graduate: 8

Required Sequencing:*

2nd Year, Fall: DWS Pretrial Advocacy (4); Personal Income Tax (3)
2nd Year, Spring: DWS Trial Advocacy (3); DWS Miniseries (2); DWS Negotiations (2)
By the End of 2nd Year (Either Semester): Business Associations (3); Wills, Trusts, and Estates (3); Evidence (3)
3rd Year, Fall: DWS Business Transactions (3)
3rd Year, Spring: DWS Capstone—Advanced Problem Solving and Client Counseling (3)
By the End of 3rd Year: Clinic/Externship at least 6 hours total (including course work) (plus any prerequisites)

*DWS courses must be taken at time indicated; timing of non-DWS courses may be subject to modification by individual Webster Scholar request, primarily based upon scheduling conflicts.

Webster Scholars participate in the program during their last two years of law school and must meet all of the standard law school curricular requirements in addition to a series of requirements specific to the program. Thus, during the first year of law school, students take the normal core curriculum, taught by regular law professors outside the program, to ensure an adequate grounding in the necessary substantive law school courses. In their upper years, Webster Scholars are also required to take substantive courses in Administrative Process, Criminal Procedure, Professional Responsibility, and a Writing Requirement. Starting with the first semester of the second year, Webster Scholars must also take four additional courses that are elective to the rest of the student body, including Business Associations; Evidence; Wills, Trusts, and Estates; and Personal Income Tax.

From there, Webster Scholars take six specifically designed Daniel Webster Scholar (DWS) courses including Pretrial Advocacy, Trial Advocacy, Negotiations, Business Transactions, and a miniseries of courses in Client Counseling, Commercial Paper, Conflict of Laws, and Family Law taught by faculty members, adjunct faculty who are top practicing lawyers in their fields, and federal and state court judges. The last semester of the program also includes a capstone course: Advanced Problem Solving and Client Counseling, which integrates and builds upon all of the skills that students have learned throughout the program, placing particular emphasis on fact gathering and witness interviews, legal analysis, problem solving, and client counseling, and introducing a subject almost never covered in law school, law office management.

"They have to keep accurate track of their time, prepare time sheets, and handle client billing," Chief Justice Dalianis explained. "That was another thing I had no clue about when I started practicing law. Nobody ever teaches you about that."

"With the capstone course, we're trying to give students an academic and practical experience that ties everything together," explained Professor John Garvey, the program's director. "We develop client intake interviewing skills and explain the eight elements that you look for in a successful client interview. It's not like sitting in tort class, where even in a hypothetical, you know you're looking for a tort of some kind. This client comes in and is a client with a problem in a shoebox, and it all comes spilling out. Some of them are set up to be angry and unreasonable, and the students have to deal with that. Some of them are really reticent and have to be drawn out. Some of them are white-collar criminals who don't want to admit that they have made a mistake. So the students get lots of different scenarios where they have to evaluate legal claims while managing the client's personality and drawing the necessary facts out of that client.

"The Pretrial Advocacy course is like a trial advocacy course on steroids," Garvey said. "We try to emulate real life. We use actors who follow a rough script, so the students are not dealing with people they know. And by design, some of the characters are designed to be completely obnoxious."

"Just like life," Chief Justice Dalianis quipped.

"We also try to build in ethical issues where something is not quite right with discovery or client issues. So it's not that students can master these things by the time they get out of the course and graduate, but they are so much farther along than the typical student that graduates from law school with a lot of theory but no reality training," Garvey added.

Students must obtain at least a B- in all of their DWS courses and a cumulative B average in all of their courses to remain in the program. Most important, students create and maintain cumulative portfolios of their ongoing projects, including videos of their witness interviews, depositions, and trial work, and the cycle of assessment is continual.

Each semester, students create work product that is reviewed first by professors for a grade in the course, and then by bar examiners to determine progress toward competency to practice. Students are trained through simulations with actors posing as clients, with real judges and court stenographers, and are placed in real-world teaching environments common to practice, including client intake interviews, fact gathering, witness interviews, taking depositions (sometimes with unwilling or combative witnesses), and motion practice in real courtrooms before real judges. They also negotiate and mediate using particular fact patterns, then compare results.

Students then evaluate their experience and performance in each course with a reflective paper, which becomes part of their portfolio. Professors provide benchmark assessments and written feedback on each student's work, and a written summary of each student's overall performance in the course, which is also included in the student's portfolio. Each semester, the student meets with a bar examiner to review the student's portfolio of work and discuss the strengths and weaknesses of the work produced and the student's progress toward practice competency.

Compare that experience with simply getting a letter grade in an exam blue book at the end of a semester or a year's worth of academic work in the ordinary, theory-based law school teaching environment.

"The students in the second-year Pretrial Advocacy course are broken up into law firms and litigate a case against each other," Chief Justice Dalianis explains. "They send interrogatories and document requests, they take depositions using real court reporters, they examine witnesses, argue before real judges in real courtrooms, and go through the whole thing as if it were the real experience in the way the real experience would be. The program certainly requires a lot more of a law student than does the 'curl up in the corner with your books for the semester' curriculum—but it also gives a whole lot more back to them in terms of the value added to their familiarity with the process, their confidence, their ability to become employed, and to their basic understanding of how it all works."

Which teaching method do you think teaches you more? Which method of assessment do you think provides you with a better understanding of what you have mastered, and where you could use more work?

Upon passing the character and fitness check and the Multistate Professional Responsibility Examination (MPRE), students who successfully complete the two-year Daniel Webster Scholar Honors Program are certified as having passed the New Hampshire Bar Exam without actually having to take the traditional exam and are admitted to the New Hampshire Bar.

Yes, you read that correctly.

Because the program is, in essence, a two-year assessment of a student's capacity to practice law, and because the program has won the support of the New Hampshire Supreme Court and the New Hampshire Board of Bar Examiners, graduates of the program *do not have to take the traditional bar exam.* That means no eight weeks of summer lost studying for a bar exam, no expenses incurred in preparing for the exam, and no stress associated with taking the exam. It also means you are licensed to practice immediately upon graduation, so you can immediately get to work paying off those law school loans.

Can there be any doubt that the two-year Webster Scholar Program, with its practical approach and technologically advanced teaching tools, provides a better assessment of a student's capacity to practice law than a two-day multiple-choice and essay exam?

"We believed on our committee that having your own private bar examiner who was putting you through the test by evaluating your actual work product over the course of two years, discussing it with you, and forcing you to do it over again if it wasn't good enough would be a better indicator of what capabilities you have when you graduate from law school," Chief Justice Dalianis explained. "Our little group just thought that the old methods of admitting people to the bar were not necessarily producing good lawyers. I know any number of people who were able to pass the bar exam that nevertheless should not be practicing law, and I know a handful of people who haven't been able to pass the bar exam because they simply don't do well on standardized tests who I believe would make excellent lawyers. So why not try something new?

"I think it is very difficult, and getting more difficult all the time, for new lawyers to become really capable skilled lawyers because there is so much that they will be expected to know and won't even know that they don't know," Chief Justice Dalianis noted. "So it seems to be that if legal education can continue to evolve toward the model that we are advancing here, those new lawyers may have an easier time."

Writing this now, from the perspective of a partner with ten years of litigation practice behind me, I wish a law school offered this kind of intensely practical educational program when I was looking at law schools. Knowing what I know now about the skills needed for the real-world practice of law, I cannot endorse this approach strongly enough.

So what is the point of my including all of this in this book?

Because I am betting that what we are seeing here is, at least in some form, the future of legal education, and I want you to be aware of it, and to thoughtfully consider it as you think about where to apply to law school. Ten years from now, I'm betting that the purely intellectual, theory-based programs of study popularized in classic movies such as *The Paper Chase* and books such as Scott Turow's *One L*—programs that have populated the top law schools around the country for decades—will be a thing of the past. Practitioners, judges, clients, and now, even law students themselves, are simply demanding something better, such as law school graduates who are actually ready to be good lawyers rather than just good law students. Graduates who, in the parlance of the Webster Scholar Program, are "client-ready."

In April 2010, I was invited to attend and speak at a one-day symposium entitled "A Performance-Based Approach to Licensing Lawyers," which was aimed at examining and challenging the way law students are taught and licensed. The symposium focused at length on the MacCrate skills, and on designing a program of study aimed at making law students more client-ready when they graduate from law school. The symposium was attended by Supreme Court justices, trial judges, bar examiners, state bar leaders, and law school professors and personnel from a variety of states. Speakers included the chief justice of the New Hampshire Supreme Court, other New Hampshire Supreme Court justices, current New Hampshire trial judges, practicing lawyers, bar examiners, law professors, hiring partners from major law firms, and current and former Daniel Webster Scholars. At the end of the program, there was a lot of excitement to explore replicating the Daniel Webster Scholar program and two-year bar exam assessment program in other states, which, I am excited to report, has begun to occur.

One of the presenters at the symposium was Lloyd Bond, a retired Senior Scholar at the Carnegie Foundation for the Advancement of Teaching and an author of the 2007 Carnegie Report. Professor Bond, who previously taught skills measurement and assessment at the University of North Carolina and the University of Pittsburgh, made the following observations, which serve as the perfect capstone on this chapter:

> As many of you are no doubt aware, the Carnegie Foundation, as part of its series on education in the professions, published *Educating Lawyers* in 2007. . . . In the book, we called upon law schools to rethink the way they educate aspiring lawyers. We called for nothing less than a sea change in the way lawyers are prepared. More realistically, what we hoped for was to nudge

> legal education in the direction of preparing students to be competent lawyers rather than competent law students.
>
> Quite independent of our book, the University of New Hampshire School of Law has done just that, and much more. Never in our most optimistic moments did the Carnegie authors envision a school bringing . . . real stenographers, real paralegals, real lawyers, and, yes, real judges into the training program. We can only hope that other state Supreme Courts will seriously consider the Webster Scholar method as an alternative approach to training and licensing.
>
> When I studied the program in depth three or so years ago, I said that it fused instruction, assessment, and practice in such an integrated way that the three became indistinguishable. The Daniel Webster Scholar Program . . . exemplifies the sea change we had in mind.

Be aware that you are considering law school at a time when the very question of what a legal education should mean is being seriously revisited. Our hope is that you will let the exciting developments discussed in this chapter guide both your choice of school and your curriculum selection, and that once you get to law school, you will continue to drive this debate yourself.

CHAPTER 5

Choose Your School Wisely

The first step which one makes in the world,
is the one on which depends the rest of our days.
—VOLTAIRE

FOR MOST OF US, the choice of where to go to college depended first and foremost on the availability of sufficient funds. If the funds weren't there, the state university provided an adequate solution and, in a great many cases, provided a better-than-adequate educational experience. If funds were available, we made our decisions about which school to attend based on school size, interest in potential major programs of study, availability of sports teams and recruiting, and proximity (or lack thereof!) to home. Choosing a law school, however, is an entirely different enterprise and properly involves a much different thought process than choosing an undergraduate institution. The good news is that the number of relevant factors in choosing a law school is much smaller. The bad news is that with far fewer factors to consider, each takes on far greater significance. I run through each of these factors, in order of their importance, below.

The school's regional and national reputation

I'm sure you're familiar with the *U.S. News & World Report* "ranking" system for graduate schools. Published in April of every year, "The Best Graduate Schools" issue lays out where each of the 188 accredited law schools falls on the all-important continuum from "first to worst." These rankings are often quite controversial, and because the law schools know how much emphasis prospective students place on them, law schools frequently try to "massage" their numbers in a way that raises their relative ranking. Relative rankings are accurate according to the criteria used by *U.S. News*, but those criteria may not be the ones you should use.

So how should you use this information?

First of all, there is usually not much disagreement about which law schools are "Tier One." These schools are often referred to as the "T-14" schools. If you look back over the past few years, the same names are always there: Yale, Harvard, Stanford, Chicago, Columbia, NYU, Berkeley (Boalt Hall), University of Pennsylvania, University of Virginia, Duke, University of Michigan, Cornell, Northwestern, and Georgetown. Forget (for now) where any of these schools ranks within the T-14—as they frequently tie or move up or down a slot or two from year to year. The bottom line is, if you get into one of these top-tier law schools and perform respectably, you'll be positioned to do just about anything you want to do. You should know, however, that even among these very top schools, only Yale and Harvard are not subject to some regional bias with respect to placement. Students at those two schools are sought after with identical vigor by firms and judges all over the country. After Yale and Harvard, however, regional preference begins to play a role in impressions about a school. For instance, lawyers and judges on the West Coast refer to Stanford as the "Harvard of the West" and often prefer its graduates to those from any other top school. Similarly, Duke is often called the "Harvard of the South," and its students are the gold mine for firms in the large cities of the South, while students from the University of Chicago, the "Harvard of the Heartland," are the top draw in the Midwest.

In other words, the majority of students from Duke tend to stay in the South or mid-Atlantic region as far north as D.C., where lawyers and firms lust after them. Students from Penn tend to roam the I-95 corridor from New York City to Washington, D.C., where their placement numbers are strongest, and many students from the University of Chicago stay in the bigger cities across the Midwest.

So what does all of this mean to you? It all depends on your desired outcome, which is one of the reasons why we've been hammering on you to have at least some clue what you want out of law school before you apply.

"The degree to which the *U.S. News and World Report* rankings should play a part in your decision-making process really depends on where you ultimately want to work. If you have dreams of working at a large national firm or of doing a clerkship at a federal circuit court of appeals, then I think you need to pay pretty close attention to the

T-14," Megan noted. "For someone like me, though, who was more concerned about where I ended up geographically than I was in working for a national firm, it may be better to choose a well-regarded regional school that is geographically located in the area that you wish to work in. Local firms tend to pay attention to highly qualified applicants from local schools, so if you know that you want to stay in a particular area, you may be better off choosing to attend a lesser-ranked school in that area and working hard to establish yourself there. Excellent grades and law review membership at a lower-ranked but local school can sometimes get you further than mediocre grades at a higher-ranked school outside of the region."

> I went to the best school I got into. Sounds simple, right? It's not. Deciding which school is the best for you involves many, many considerations, some of which you may not even know about yet. First, you should think about what you want to get out of your degree, which you've hopefully already done in selecting which schools to apply to. If you want to be an academic, you should consider going to the most prestigious schools, ones that will give you many chances to interact with professors and develop your ideas into scholarship. If you're interested in doing public-interest work, you should determine which schools have the most extensive clinical programs and most generous loan-forgiveness options. If you're interested in a particular specialty, you should seriously think about going to the school that is strong in that area. On that last point, however, I wouldn't get too wedded to a particular field of law before you even begin. In my experience, what seems most interesting in law school are those fields you never even considered before entering.
>
> Second, you should visit all the schools you are serious about. It can be expensive, but to my mind, it is worth it. Each school I have been to has a vibe, a slight note of tension, or of enthusiasm, or of indifference. The atmosphere of a school is incredibly important. You're going to be there for three years and, probably, spending long hours there. If there's a constant tension, it's not a place you want to go to. When you visit, you should have the admissions office give you the standard tour, but make sure to do a little touring on your own. Sit around any cafés or snack bars at the school, have a cup of coffee, and observe the students and professors. Is anyone talking to one another? Do you hear laughter? Eavesdrop a bit. What are people talking about? Do those conversations sound interesting to you?

You get the picture. Also, walk around the school. Don't worry if you get lost. It's a good thing: you can see how people treat you when you ask for directions. Besides, you'll inevitably get lost the first few days of school anyway. Finally, be sure to include enough time to tour around the surrounding city or town. You'll be living there for three years: Is that something that excites or horrifies you?

—John-Mark

Pay the greatest attention to a school's placement record

The number you should be most concerned about is the school's "placement record"—that is, what percentage of its graduates have gone on to gainful employment, and more important, where? You can find the overall number in the *U.S. News* survey, although some schools have been known to lump any gainful employment, whether law-related or not, into these numbers. You may have to make some calls to get the more critical numbers.

And what are they?

Every law school placement office keeps records of what percentage of its graduates have gone to each region of the country—the number that is most critical in your decision about what law school to attend. You may be proud of your acceptance to the East Boise State Law Center, but if their placement record reveals that 98 percent of its lawyers stay in Idaho and the other 2 percent go to Montana, and you know you want to practice at a large Boston firm, you're setting yourself up for a titanic struggle.

Does this mean you could never go to a Boston firm from East Boise State? No, of course not, but you could win the lottery tomorrow too, and then all of this would be irrelevant. If you know you eventually want to work in Boston, you'll have a much better chance to achieve that goal if you go to a good regional school in or around Boston than you will coming out of a good regional school on the West Coast. Like it or not, this reality plays itself out in every region of the country, every year, to the disappointment of countless law students. As the quote at the top of this chapter suggests, your choice about which law school to attend will likely carry with it consequences about where you'll end up practicing and living for your first few years out of law school. Don't make that choice uninformed.

"As I mentioned before, I knew I wanted to stay in the Boston area, and Suffolk had a lot of diversity, especially because of its evening program. I was impressed that there were international students and students of color on journals and moot court. After visiting other schools, which had equal or better numbers in terms of minority matriculation, I was impressed with the achievements of the minority students at Suffolk. They seemed to be integral, as opposed to tokens," Yvette observed.

"My plan all along was to go away to college, but then return home for law school," Lindsay stated. "I strongly recommend going to law school in the area in which you want to practice. Your school's reputation will be stronger in that geographic area, and there will likely be a loyalty at least among some employers to hire from the local area's law schools."

The harsh reality

What I'm about to say is probably the most controversial thing you'll find in this book. Few professors or law school placement officers will ever admit this to you (for obvious reasons), and no other "how to do law school" book will tell you this either, but based on the experiences of the *Law School Confidential* mentors and a number of other law students we've known, it's one of the most important pieces of advice you could possibly have as you think about applying to law school. Based on some of the careless misreadings and amusing misinterpretations of this advice I've read on the Internet since I first provided it in the first edition of this book ten years ago, it is also one of the most misunderstood pieces of advice in this book—so please read it carefully.

If your goal in going to law school is to work for a law firm, and you don't get into one of the top fifteen to twenty law schools, *and you are not interested in practicing in the region where the non–Top 20 law school that you got into is located,* you're better off reapplying and trying again.

Here are some examples to illustrate the point.

You know you want to go to a large firm in New York City, and the best school you got into is Cornell Law School. Yup. You're all set. (Yes, that was an easy one.)

You want to go to a large firm in New York City and the best school you got into is Duke Law School. Yes, you're still all set. Duke is a well enough known Top 20 school to afford you a good chance, if you perform well academically, to crack the New York market. Note, however, that Duke's placement numbers into New York will not be as strong as those of some of the other Top 20 schools located closer to (or in) New York. So if your choice is a close one between comparably ranked schools, consider making a school's historical placement record your tiebreaker.

Ready for another one?

You are committed to practicing entertainment law in Los Angeles, and the best school you got into is Suffolk Law School in Boston (and no schools in California). Answer? You have an uphill battle ahead of you, even if you do amazingly well. Unless you network the hell out of the Suffolk Law School grads working in Los Angeles, you're not likely to get a lot of job offers out there. Impossible? No—nothing is impossible. But unlikely? Yes. Highly unlikely.

In providing this advice, we're trying to increase your odds of success at ending up with the job you want (or at least think you want based on your best guess right now), not put you in the position of having to be the one-in-a-hundred candidate who overcomes the odds. In this case, if you know you want to practice entertainment law and know you don't want to live on the East Coast, then you should at least consider releasing your offers and reapplying the following year.

If you want to end up practicing entertainment law in Los Angeles, think T-14, a regional law school with a killer entertainment law program, or a local law school in California with a good entertainment law program and a good placement record into Los Angeles.

Now, if you got into Suffolk and want to work in Boston or anywhere in New England? You're good. Most of the firms in Boston and up here in New England have Suffolk Law School grads successfully working in them, are familiar with the school, some have adjunct faculty at the school, and they are more than happy to interview and hire its grads.

See how it works?

Let's do one more. You want to practice hospitality law at a firm in Florida, and the best law school you got into is the University of Wyoming School of Law (and no schools in Florida). Again, you have an uphill battle ahead. If you want to practice oil and gas law (or any of a number of other interesting specialties) or just want to practice law in the West, you're good in Laramie. But you're not likely to end up in Florida from there—at least not easily. To end up in Florida, go to a T-14, a well-respected regional school in the southern United States with good placement records into the Tampa, Orlando, and Miami marketplaces, or a Florida-based law school.

Got it?

I am *not* saying that if you don't get into a T-14 school, you might as well hang it up and try again next year. What I *am* saying is that students should have a two-part strategy in applying to law schools. The first part of that strategy is to apply to the T-14 if your GPA and LSAT scores place you close enough to their medians to justify the attempt. Second, though, apply to the regional schools in the geographic area where you hope to settle down and practice. This is why it is so important to know enough about yourself and the world to know where that is *before* you apply to law school. If you know that you want to settle down in the Boston area after you graduate, then, yes, apply to the T-14, but also to Boston College, Boston University, Suffolk, Northeastern, the New England School of Law, the University of New Hampshire School of Law, Vermont Law School, the University of Maine School of Law, Roger Williams University School of Law in Rhode Island, and the University of Connecticut. Checking those schools' placement numbers, you will discover that all of them are, to varying degrees, easier to get into than the T-14 and also place a fair number of their graduates into the Boston legal market. For someone who knows that she wants to live and work in the Boston area, this is the best hedge to ensure that outcome. With this range of schools, chances are that an offer of admission will come from somewhere, and the chance of ending up in Boston at the end of it all is maximized. For the student who wants to live and work in Dallas–Fort Worth after graduation, however, the list of regional schools on a smart application list would look very different.

This advice and these examples are provided as general guidance and are not intended to substitute for your own due diligence. As we note throughout the book, you owe it to yourself to closely examine the latest placement numbers of every law school you are considering applying to. Each law school's career planning and placement office maintains its historical numbers and will be more than willing to share them with you. In addition to the education that you will receive, remember that this placement record is part of what you are buying. Ignore it at your peril.

If you follow the advice in this book, you should apply to a range of schools broad enough to ensure that you only need to apply once. If, however, (1) your interests do change between the time you apply and the time you need to make your decisions, and (2) you end up mismatched and don't want to change either your intended type of work or your newly intended geography, then don't be afraid to refuse the offers you get from mismatched regional law schools and try again next year. Try to raise your LSAT score, work for a year or two as a paralegal or a legal intern with a public-service organization to gain some law-related experience, then reapply. The numbers simply do not support you if you're planning to make the leap from a small regional law school to a New York megafirm. If you don't believe me, check the numbers yourself. Jump on the Web site of any big-city firm and examine the list of law schools where last year's associates came from.

"In applying to law schools, you should really be thinking about where you want to be living down the road," Joel observes. "Obviously, you won't be forced to live in the same city or area of the country that your law school is in forever, but there is no denying the regional control that every law school has. It is easier for a Harvard graduate to get a job in Boston than in San Francisco, and the opposite is true of Stanford graduates, and this state of affairs is magnified tenfold for graduates of less prestigious schools. Don't think of going to Kent if you can't see yourself settling down in the Midwest, or to American if you have no interest in living and working in D.C."

"Unfortunately, the *U.S. News* rankings are important enough in the hiring process that you really should consider them in choosing a school," John-Mark advises. "Keep in mind, however, that people on the outside (i.e., hiring partners) think in categories, not rankings: top schools, good schools, everything else. In my experience, they don't distinguish between the number seven school and the number nine school, but they do know the difference between the number seven school and the number thirty school."

I know far too many people who got good grades at regional law schools, passed bar exams in various states, and still had an extremely difficult time finding jobs. In getting rejection after rejection, each of them was given the same reason: "No one at our firm has any firsthand experience with anyone who has graduated from your law school." Remember, lawyers are risk averse, and with few exceptions, they're going to choose the known commodity. They're not willing to give you a chance unless you have a compelling story to tell.

Why put yourself through this?

"In the same way that your LSAT score puts you in a range of law schools in the rankings, your law school's reputation puts you in a range of firms that will review your application seriously and grant you an interview," Patrick advises. "Once you have the interview, then it's all about your personality and how well you connect with the interviewer . . . but it can be very difficult for students at lesser-known or lower-ranked schools to get that chance."

"If you go to a top law school, your résumé will stand out in the pack. That said, it's certainly not everything. I've been involved in numerous hiring decisions in which the candidate from the top school with okay grades and an unremarkable background loses to the candidate from a lesser-known school who excelled and/or seems like they would be an interesting person to know. Also, the reputation of a school is often employer-specific. It could be that a particular employer has had good experiences with graduates of a particular school. I have also seen the opposite. A general rule of thumb, though, is that the more renowned the school is, the easier time you will have getting a job," John-Mark observed.

The take-home message here is this: If you're going to accept an offer from a regional law school, make sure you're committed to practicing for at least a couple of years in that region. Forget the exceptions. There just aren't enough of them to make the chance worth taking.

Philosophy

The last of the "Big Three" concerns that you should consider is the prevailing "philosophy" at a school and how this philosophy meshes with your own. Is the school widely known to be an unfriendly, overtly cutthroat, and competitive place where people hide books and refuse to work cooperatively? (There are a few well-known examples of such places—just ask around, they're easy enough to discover.) But let's put some concrete examples behind this label of a "cutthroat" school. Legendary stories aside, here are some questions to ask to determine whether a school is cutthroat or not:

- Are grades posted on the hallway walls by name or readily ascertainable numbers for everyone to see, or are they distributed confidentially?
- Does the school compute and publish grade point averages and class ranks each term, thereby encouraging students to openly compete with each other for numbers?
- Are positions on law review determined strictly by grades, or can some people write on every year?
- Does the career placement office (1) assign employment interview slots by class rank, or (2) allow the employers to select which students to interview according to class rank, or (3) do the students get to choose which employers to interview with?
- How often do books needed for common assignments go missing? (You'll need to call the head librarian to get the answer to this one.)
- Do students share outlines and willingly help each other out?
- Do students socialize after class in intramural sports leagues and other extracurricular activities?

- Are there regular law student Happy Hours and other events?
- Is there an active social committee at the law school?
- Is there a student union or other area where students go to hang out with each other between classes or after class?

If you decide to attend a law school with a reputation for being cutthroat, realize what you're getting yourself into before you enroll. Aside from the more difficult social interactions you may experience with your classmates and the increased stress associated with open competition for grades, your performance on single-day exams may prevent you from involvement with a host of other experiences that open doors to your future. For example, getting on your school's law review is the gateway to getting a judicial clerkship. If your school seats people on its law review only on the basis of grade point average, one bad exam could compromise both your chance to make the law review and your chance to get a clerkship!

On the other hand, a school where the law review considers a combination of grade point average and performance on an independent writing and editing exam, or simply lets some people "write on" based on their high performance on this writing and editing exam, creates a much more student-friendly environment. Ditto for job screening interviews. If your school lets the employers pick you, they may screen you based only on your grade point average, which increases the stress level associated with grades and decreases students' willingness to cooperate with one another. If the school uses a random lottery or lets you choose which employers to interview with, that situation is diffused.

> The biggest factor in my ultimate decision was the atmosphere of the schools. I took tours of the schools, and I spent a lot of time talking to students. I asked about the atmosphere, the stress levels, and the general sense of the relationships that the students had with one another. Talking to the students that were already going to the schools I was considering was a big help in deciding which place was right for me. While administrators and books can tell you a lot about a school, nothing beats the firsthand information you can get by talking to the students who are already there and asking them the right questions.
>
> —Steve

Make certain that you know your school's philosophical stance on these issues before you decide to enroll. In some cases, it may help you make decisions between schools. How you weight this factor with the other factors you need to consider (reputation and placement success) is entirely personal. Each choice carries consequences, and it's up to you to decide what is most important.

But what about . . .

Whether your law school is in the middle of an urban war zone or located in a pastoral country landscape? What the climate is like? Whether the law school is near the rest of the university or not? How close it is to the beach, the mountains, and good skiing? How attractive are the people there? Whether you'll be able to bring your dog with you?

Yeah, I know you're thinking about these things. I certainly did. Just don't let them cloud your judgment. Worry about the Big Three factors discussed above. After all, you're going to professional school, and as I've illustrated above, the choices you make are going to have a dramatic effect on your life and career. You're not going on vacation, and this is not college anymore. Let these other issues intervene to influence your choice only when the schools you are choosing between are otherwise indistinguishable based on the more important Big Three factors.

> The academic strength and reputation of the schools I was considering was priority number one. You go to law school to get a good job, and if you attend a top law school, you'll get one.
>
> —Allan

A final word. Be incredibly wary about choosing a law school based on its proximity to a girlfriend or boyfriend. Law school is a disruptive experience and a supreme test of the strength of relationships. If yours doesn't survive and leaves you marooned somewhere you don't want to be, you're going to be very, very unhappy.

CHAPTER 6

An Investment in Your Future: Funding Your Legal Education

If you would know the value of money,
go and try to borrow some.
—BENJAMIN FRANKLIN

OKAY—so you've thought carefully about applying to law school, chosen your schools wisely, filed perfect, carefully crafted applications, and beaten the LSAT. For all your trouble and accomplishment up to this point, you'd think that you'd be in line for some sort of reward, right?

Yeah, well, think again.

Once the jubilation of having actually beaten the odds and gotten into the school of your dreams wears off, you'll need to welcome yourself back to reality. The cost of your law school education, including tuition, room and board, books, study aids, supplies, transportation, and personal expenses is about to set you back as much as $160,000, depending on your choice of school.

> I went to law school because I wanted to be a prosecutor, but starting salaries for assistant district attorneys in Massachusetts were about $27,000 when I got out of law school. I'm going to be paying about $1,100 a month for the next ten years in student loan payments, and after taxes that salary would barely cover my student loans. I didn't go to law school to get rich, but I didn't expect to get poor. I think it's disgusting that to get the degree to get the job I wanted, I had

to take on a debt load that precluded me from accepting that job.

—Bess

A great deal of financial aid is available, in scholarships, loans, grants, fellowships, and work-study programs. Most of your classmates will be depending on some sort of financial assistance to help get them through the door, and you'd be foolish not to explore whether the kitty might hold some assistance for you. Unless you're independently wealthy or were blessed with incredibly generous parents, you're going to need to get the money from somewhere, and you're going to have to pay it back. Here's what you need to know.

Sources of funding

Many different sources of financial aid are available for law students. The larger private law schools—those with sizable endowments—offer generous financial aid packages to top students. Other law schools may offer low-interest institutional loans. Many other private scholarships, fellowships, and grants—often targeted toward specific groups of applicants, including minorities, women, residents of particular states, children of veterans, or students who are committed to practicing in the public sector after graduation—are available from foundations, corporations, benevolent associations, local bar associations, social clubs, religious or business organizations, and veterans' organizations. Several different federal loan programs are available, as well as private institutional loans from banks and other financial institutions for students with good credit histories. Finally, the federal work-study program may be an option in your second or third years to help bridge the gaps in your aid package.

How do you decide which route is the best for you? Without a doubt, the financial aid offices of the law schools that admit you will be the best resources for information about how to fund your legal education. Inquire about the most common ways that students at that particular law school fund their legal education. Ask for any information and paperwork the financial aid office can provide you. At the very least, a discussion with your prospective school's financial aid officer should get the ball rolling for you.

General suggestions

If you know that you will need financial aid to fund your legal education, do not wait until you have been offered admission to begin applying for financial aid. In December of the year in which you are applying to law school, get a copy of the Free Application for Federal Student Aid (FAFSA) from your university's financial aid office, from one of your prospective law school's financial aid office, or online at www.fafsa.ed.gov. This form was developed by the U.S. Department of Education as a general need-analysis tool for use by all law schools you designate to receive it. Contact the financial aid office of each school to which you are applying no later than December 31 to verify each institution's financial aid filing requirements. Many schools require additional documentation (such as copies of your tax return or additional institution-specific paperwork) to the FAFSA.

As soon as possible after January 1 of the year in which you are applying, complete your federal income tax return. Keep a copy, as many schools will request a supplementary copy before determining your need package. Using the information from your tax return, complete the FAFSA form by providing all the information it requests and send it in. Completed FAFSA forms cannot be filed prior to the first of the year, but should be filed as soon as possible after January 1 to afford you the best chance of getting an optimal aid package.

The law schools you designate to receive the FAFSA will each make independent determinations on your eligibility for institution-based and federal financial aid. Because costs and expenses vary from school to school, the aid packages offered by different law schools may differ widely. As an applicant to graduate school, you will automatically be considered "independent" from your parents for the purposes of securing federal financial assistance.

Private law schools also typically use a specific institutional methodology to evaluate financial aid eligibility for funds under the school's direct control (unsubsidized loans, grants, and scholarships). Be prepared to fill out additional profile forms if you are applying to private law schools. When providing this additional information, you may find that some schools still require information about your parents' income. Note that you are required to provide this information even if your parents will not be making any contribution to your tuition. Many students mistakenly assume that since their parents are not going to be contributing to their tuition, they do not need to fill out these additional profile forms. This is incorrect! Failing to complete all financial aid forms sent to you will result in your financial aid application remaining incomplete and your being disqualified from receiving any aid award. Even if you think you have filled all of the necessary paperwork with the schools on your list, it is always a good idea to call each school's financial aid office and confirm that they consider your financial aid application complete.

When you begin to hear back from schools, do not be surprised if you receive a wide array of disparate aid packages. Each school has different methods of determining eligibility and different grant and scholarship capacities. Use the best of the financial aid packages you received to leverage the schools that have given you less desirable packages. Don't be obnoxious, but do call the financial aid office and speak to the financial aid officer in charge of your file. Explain your situation, express your preference to attend that school over the school that offered you the better aid package, and politely ask if they will reconsider your aid award. The earlier you make this call, the better the chance that you can convince a financial aid officer to sweeten your till.

Some terms they'll throw around in your aid package

Your "financial need" is the total cost of your law school education, including tuition, room and board, books and supplies, and living expenses (collectively known as your "student budget"), minus what you are able to personally contribute toward satisfying this amount. Your "unmet financial need" is your "financial need" minus any scholarships, fellowships, or grants you have received. Note that your "student budget" will vary from school to school, depending on the school-specific costs and cost-of-living differences from city to city, but it will never consider any personal consumer debt you may be carrying.

After completing its analysis, each law school's financial aid office will send you a financial aid package explaining your eligibility. Most students receive offers including several different types of aid in combination—often consisting of a partial scholarship, an institutional loan offer, and eligibility for federal loan programs. Once you receive each school's financial aid eligibility letter, begin the federal loan application process immediately.

Federal loan programs

Federal loan programs view law school applicants as independents. Even if you are still living with your parents when you apply to law school, the federal loan program still considers you an independent adult. Only the federal financial aid portion of a financial aid package assumes your financial independence from your parents (which usually works to your advantage). The rest of your aid package can, and usually does, depend on an independent evaluation by individual schools on your parents' ability to contribute to your education, even if they have no intention of actually doing so! Hence, the following discussion of federal loan programs may be of increased importance to you.

Stafford loans (formerly the Guaranteed Student loan)

There are two types of Stafford loans: subsidized (need-based) and unsubsidized (not need-based). The differences in these two types of Stafford loans are broken down in the chart below.

	Subsidized Stafford	**Unsubsidized Stafford**
Maximum amount you can borrow: (1) annually (2) in aggregate	 $8,500 $65,000*	 $20,500 $138,500
Interest rate	Fixed: 6.8%	Fixed: 6.8%
Interest due	None until you begin repayment schedule (see below)	Interest must be paid off each month or it will be added to the principal balance of the loan
Fee	1% to be deducted from each loan disbursement	1% to be deducted from each loan disbursement
Disbursement	In 2 installments generally, sent directly to the school. Extra loan proceeds over cost of tuition are paid to you directly or credited to your student account	In 2 installments generally, sent directly to the school. Extra loan proceeds over cost of tuition are paid to you directly or credited to your student account
Cancelable?	Yes**	Yes**
Repayment schedule	Generally 10 to 25 years, depending on your repayment plan	Generally 10 to 25 years, depending on your repayment plan

	Subsidized Stafford	Unsubsidized Stafford
Repayment plans	*Standard:* requires a fixed amount per month with a minimum of $50 per month *Graduated:* lower payments at first that increase every 2 years. Minimum payments must equal monthly interest accrued *Income sensitive:* bases monthly payment on a formula including your annual income and the loan amount	*Standard:* requires a fixed amount per month with a minimum of $50 per month *Graduated:* lower payments at first that increase every 2 years. Minimum payments must equal monthly interest accrued *Income sensitive:* bases monthly payment on a formula including your annual income and the loan amount

*If both subsidized and unsubsidized loans are taken, subsidized loans cannot exceed their maximum of $8,500 per year, and $65,000 in aggregate. Unsubsidized loans may then be stacked over the subsidized loans to their own limits, listed in column 2. Subsidized loan aggregate limit includes loans used for undergraduate study.

**After your school notifies you that it has credited the loan to your account, you may cancel your loan within fourteen days or by the first day of the payment period, whichever is later.

To be eligible for either of these Stafford loans, you must be enrolled at least half-time in an eligible program of study. Schools administer these loans either through the government's Direct Lending program or through banks and other private lenders.

Perkins loan (formerly the National Direct Student loan)

The Perkins loan is offered by participating law schools and, like the subsidized Stafford loan, is based on need. School financial aid offices use the FAFSA to evaluate student eligibility for the Perkins loan. Currently, the interest rate on the Perkins loan is 5 percent, and all interest is paid by the government during the period of your education. Repayment obligations begin nine months after graduation. The maximum annual distribution under a Perkins loan is $8,000, and the maximum aggregate distribution is $60,000. When repayment obligations begin, students are responsible for paying the school back, as the school is the lender on these loans (with funds contributed by the U.S. government).

The Perkins loan is extremely favorable due to the government-subsidized interest while you are in school and low interest rate.

Direct PLUS loans for graduate students

The PLUS loan is available through the U.S. Department of Education under the Direct Loan Program. This loan, like the Stafford and Perkins loans, requires that the student fill out a FAFSA. To be awarded a Direct PLUS loan, your credit history must be evaluated. The fixed interest rate is 7.9 percent. To apply, you must fill out a Direct PLUS loan application and a Master Promissory Note, which is a promise to repay. The maximum amount that you can borrow is the total cost of your school attendance minus any other financial aid awarded. A 4 percent fee is deducted each time a disbursement is made. Repayment begins sixty days after the final disbursement, but you may defer this repayment until six months after you graduate.

To learn more about federal loan programs and to get the most up-to-date information on rates and program changes, research these programs on the Web at studentaid.ed/gov or call the Federal Student Aid Information Center toll-free at 1-800-4-FEDAID (1-800-433-3243). You can also use this number to check if your FAFSA has been received and processed by the government.

Private loans

Private loans are personal loans from a bank or private lending institution. Of all the ways to finance your law school education, private loans are the most expensive, as they generally carry much higher interest rates and will come with a number of extra charges and insurance fees. Just as with unsubsidized federal loans, interest on private loans accrues during school.

If you must take out a private loan to bridge a financial gap between your expenses and your aid package, do everything you can to reduce the overall cost of these loans by shopping around extensively to find and secure the lowest possible interest rate. Having a cosigner on the loan or securing the loan with personal assets will reduce the bank's risk and may persuade a bank to lower its interest rate for you. If your family or the company you presently work for maintains a special relationship with a bank, that bank may be willing to give you a special rate. You will have to, and should, negotiate these points with a bank to determine the degree of flexibility they have with their rates. The overall cost to you of even a quarter of a point on an interest rate can be extremely significant over time, so make the effort to shop around and bargain hard for the best deal you can find.

When you begin your negotiation with a bank regarding a personal loan, a number of variables can be bargaining chips in that negotiation. In addition, information or concessions you receive at one bank can and should be used to negotiate with the others. Be sure to determine and negotiate the following:

- the interest rate, and how it is determined
- whether the interest rate is variable or fixed, and whether the rate is capped
- whether the loan can be paid off early without penalty
- the term of the loan (how long you have to pay it off)
- whether the loan has origination fees, and whether these can be waived
- whether the bank requires a cosigner, and whether having one can reduce your interest rate due to the decreased risk to the bank
- whether the loan needs to be secured with collateral, and whether doing so would reduce your interest rate
- whether interest on the loan is tax deductible

Making an appointment with a tax planner or a financial adviser can bring benefits here. Structuring loans in certain ways, or taking certain types of loans depending on your personal circumstances may offer tax advantages. Taking advantage of these tax breaks can bring significant savings over time, so don't blow this off.

Grants and scholarships

Financial grants are awarded based on need and, generally, only after all other forms of aid have been maxed out. In making these awards, financial aid officers typically focus on those students who have exhausted their federal Stafford and Perkins loan eligibility in order to help get these students "over the hump" in satisfying their unfunded educational expenses.

Scholarships, by contrast, may be awarded based on need or simply on merit to reward outstanding achievement. Most law school scholarships reward academic excellence, but some also recognize other things, such as a great commitment to community service. Some schools have particular scholarships set up by alumni to recognize traits or qualities that those alumni found meaningful. To learn more about the specific grant and scholarship programs available at the schools to which you intend to apply, contact each school's financial aid office.

During your conversations with financial aid officers, don't be shy about asking for each school's statistics regarding the percent of the student body that receives some type of financial aid, the percent of the student body receiving grants and scholarships directly from the school, and the average of each of these awards per student.

Finally, private grants and scholarships are also offered by a host of other institutions, businesses, and organizations. Devote some time to surfing the Web or doing research in the library to identify these sources. The largest online scholarship database, with more than 1.5 million scholarships worth more than $3.4 billion, can be found at http://www.fastweb.com.

Federal work-study

Given the rigorous demands of law school, particularly during the first year, financial assistance from the Federal Work-Study Program is best left as a last option during the second and third years of law school. Under this program, law students work on campus performing a wide range of school-specific services for which they are compensated. Information is generally available in any law school financial aid office.

Your day of reckoning

Unless you attend a well-endowed private law school, most of your financial aid will probably come from federal loans, and you will likely graduate with a large debt burden that may take you over ten years to pay off.

"Don't be afraid of borrowing. The real question, however, is the value to you of borrowing," John-Mark observed. "If it's important to you to be able to focus on your studies the first year (or all three years), and you would rather not work, borrow more. If you have some moral opposition to being a debtor (surprisingly common), work more or find a school that will give you a scholarship. Keep in mind that debt limits your freedom later. Thousands of dollars of school debts translates into hundreds of dollars in monthly payments after you graduate. That usually means you have to take a relatively high-paying job, which you may not want to have to do at some point in the future."

"I have over $100,000 of debt. Think about that. It's like a mortgage. It's a huge obligation. Even though salaries are great right now in the legal world, it still takes a great deal of time to pay off a debt like that. If you're going to go to law school on student loans, make sure that you really want to do it and make sure that you understand what being a lawyer is really like because you're obligating yourself to it for a long, long time. It's going to take me ten to fifteen years to pay off my loans," Steve warned.

Others agree. "Ten years, maybe seven or eight if I stay at a big firm and am really vigilant about paying them off," Alison added.

> Ten years at $1,100 a month.
>
> —Bess

> Ten years at $900 a month.
>
> —Joel

> My wife and I are allocating the majority of our incomes to paying off my student loans and will be for the next four or five years. Although we're making a good income, we have little to show for it.
>
> —Pat

"I obtained federal student loans for about 60K total. I was fortunate because I did not have undergraduate debt," Yvette recalls. "Plus, after college I moved back home with my parents and worked. I saved every penny, and that covered my books and some living expenses for my first year. I would recommend against working, definitely first year, and only if in dire need for the rest of school. I worked all throughout college and my grades suffered. I did not work during the semesters at law school and did much better and was happier throughout the experience without the added stress. As a summer associate at a big downtown firm in Boston, I made quite a bit of money and lived off of that one job for a while. But, again, living with my generous parents helped a great deal."

We're hammering home this point, and putting a real price tag on it, to force you to really think one more time about your commitment to go to law school and to reevaluate the practicality of your plans after law school. As Bess noted earlier, her debt burden is keeping her from doing the kind of work that drew her to law school in the first place. Steve experienced a similar reality: "While it is sad to say, my loans kept me from doing the kind of law that I wanted to do. I always envisioned myself as a prosecutor, fighting the bad guys and doing something that had meaning to it. The reality, though, is that there isn't any money to be made as a prosecutor, and the bank won't accept the meaningfulness of your work in lieu of the payment on the loans you owe them, so I entered the corporate world and am practicing asset securitization. Truth be told, I enjoy the work I'm doing, but if I didn't have my loans to deal with, I would be doing criminal work."

"I went to Rutgers to take advantage of the great in-state tuition while living at home to save money," Lindsay explained. "Obviously, that lifestyle choice isn't for everyone, but for me, it worked out perfectly. I knew I wanted a career in public interest law, where the paychecks would not compete with those I might get from a firm job, so I made a conscious effort to keep my law school loans and costs as low as possible to help make repayment more manageable. Rutgers's in-state tuition was around $20,000 per year, so I took out government and private loans to finance the cost of tuition, books, bills, and life. While I still walked out of law school with a massive amount of debt, it does not compare to that of some of my friends who went to law school in New York City, where one year of tuition equaled all three of mine, not including rent and other expenses!"

If you're still insistent, save as much money as you can before and during law school, and attempt to minimize your credit card and other consumer debt in anticipation of this reality. As a federal loan recipient, you will be required to attend an exit interview prior to graduation. During this interview, your financial aid officer will review your loans with you and help you develop repayment schedules and options to suit your needs. Keep accurate records of this meeting.

Income-Based Repayment (IBR) Program

If your dream is to work in the public sector, all hope is not lost. You can utilize an income-based repayment option for all of your federal loans, which includes any Stafford, Direct PLUS, or consolidated loan made under the Direct Loan or Federal Family Education Loan (FFEL) Programs. A student is eligible for the IBR Program if her debt is high compared to her income. Further, once you apply for this repayment option, if your monthly payment does not cover the interest on your loan, the government will pay any unpaid interest on subsidized

Stafford loans for up to three consecutive years after you enter the IBR Program. Working in public service and paying under IBR for ten years will entitle you to loan forgiveness. Short of that, if you pay under IBR for twenty-five years and meet certain eligibility requirements, any remaining balance of your loans will be canceled.

Other options

Some schools, particularly the better-endowed programs, offer school-specific or alumni-funded loan forgiveness or Loan Repayment Assistance Programs (LRAPs) to graduates who accept public-interest positions. These programs and their requirements vary widely. Call your law school's financial aid office or public service department for further information.

PART TWO

The First Year, They Scare You to Death

CHAPTER 7

The Ten Things You Must Do Before Classes Begin

A man who suffers before it is necessary
suffers more than is necessary.
—SENECA

RECALLING MY OWN EXPERIENCES, the weeks leading up to the first day of law school were filled with good intentions and fraught with anxiety. Knowing little about the intricacies of the law, I bought books about the American legal system and the U.S. Supreme Court and its justices and pledged to read them over the summer.

It never happened.

I dusted off the Constitutional Law casebook left behind from an undergraduate class and pledged to read a case a day, every day, to get one full subject ahead of the field.

You guessed it. On the first day, I made it about halfway through *Marbury v. Madison* (which, as you will soon discover, is the first case in just about every Con Law casebook ever published), and that was the end of that. I never read another page the whole summer. Never even finished *Marbury*. So much for good intentions!

After taking their bar review courses, many of your mentors noted that having a working knowledge of the framework of "black-letter" law* in each first-year subject at the beginning of law school would have been immensely helpful. Fortunately our wishes were heard and answered. Law Preview (www.lawpreview.com), a company founded by

*"Black-letter" law is the phrase used to describe the basic, fundamental legal concepts and settled decisions in a particular subject area.

a group of recent law school grads, has filled this need by developing a one-week boot camp to help incoming law students learn the fundamentals of the first-year courses before classes begin. Taught by professors top-rated for their teaching ability (which, as you will soon discover, isn't a given), the Law Preview boot camp offers a one-course-per-day overview of the basics of each first-year subject and an excellent set of accompanying written materials to help incoming law students grasp the overarching concepts of each course, and, as the old expression goes, "see the forest for the trees." By becoming familiar with the basic concepts of each course, when school actually begins, students should be more readily able to see the distinctions raised by individual cases and more easily grasp the progressions in an area of law, instead of wasting precious time trying to get the big picture on their own after classes begin. In this regard, Law Preview provides an excellent, long-overdue product and taking the one-week boot camp can help put you miles ahead of your uninitiated competition. It is unnecessary to spend the whole summer before law school trying to "get ahead," but if you can spend a week or so getting familiar with the first-year subjects before classes begin, your anxiety level will be significantly reduced, and you will enable yourself to study more efficiently and more effectively when classes begin. As you've probably noticed, I don't endorse many books, study aids, or programs in this book, but Law Preview's program is well worth your consideration.

"Try to enjoy your time before law school as much as possible," John-Mark advised. "The first semester, in particular, is stressful and tiring. It's good to come in well rested and at peace with yourself."

There are ten other things you should do before classes begin to make your life easier and to complete time-consuming preparations before time gets scarce. The following list is broken down into things you should do before you arrive at school, and things you should do after you arrive but before classes begin. Go through the list carefully and plan accordingly so that you'll have enough time to complete each item before your first day of class. Don't procrastinate! Once classes begin, any of these things will take valuable time away from your studies.

Before You Arrive on Campus

1. Read this book from cover to cover

You have in your hands a good compilation of wisdom to guide you through your three years of law school. It is a complete map of the landscape with all known pitfalls and obstacles identified, but like any other map, for it to be useful, you need to familiarize yourself with it ahead of time to know where you're going before you actually get there. Reading this book once through before you get to law school will assure you that you'll know enough of the lingo and vocabulary so you won't feel stupid at orientation events, and grant you the pole position at the start of the race. Plus, if you're anything like me, you'll be thirsting for all the information you can possibly gather about the experience that awaits you. It's all here, so drink up. Just leave the work sheets for the day when you're going through each chapter for real.

2. Arrange for housing

No later than early to midsummer, you'll need to start making arrangements for law school housing, and right away you'll have to make a critical choice. Do you want to live in on-campus housing (if there is any), where you'll likely be surrounded by classmates with whom you can study and commiserate, or would you prefer to strike out on your own? At many schools, you may have a third choice—opting to live in the off-campus apartment building or town-house complex preferred by students from your law school. Usually, a quick call to your law school registrar's office can reveal this location to you, since the registrar has every student's school address. Make this call so you'll have a complete set of information with which to make your decision.

> The biggest mistake I made in getting ready for law school was arriving in Philadelphia the day before orientation. I should have moved in a few days earlier, set things up, and spent some time getting to know the city and the campus. Instead, I spent three weeks traveling in Costa Rica, moved out of New York City in a rush, and stumbled into Philadelphia at the last minute. That was a bad idea because I never caught up with all the things I wanted to do to get ready.
>
> —Carolyn

Living on campus certainly has its advantages, including ease of acquisition and proximity to classes and the law library. Renting graduate housing space will spare you the need to search for an appropriate apartment and, perhaps more important, will spare you the potential headache of dealing with a landlord. Many graduate dorms will come furnished or at least provide major appliances, and should anything need repair, you can count on your university's custodial services to attend to your problems promptly. Many law schools also offer convenient nine-month leases, which will save you the hassle and risk of having to sublet your apartment during the summer. You should also not underestimate the convenience of rolling out of bed at 8:55 a.m. in time to make your dreaded 9:00 a.m. class, or having the ability to go back and forth from home to class and the library with ease. At many schools, up to half of the first-year class will opt to live on campus.

Students in the law dorm tend to bond readily. Friendships form easily out of the mutual misery of the long hours spent studying in close quarters. Mixers, happy hours, poker nights, and other social events also typically originate in the dorms. Study groups will form out of these friendships, and consequently it will be easier to find course outlines and to learn about good hornbooks and study aids if you live in the dorm. Living on campus during your first year of law school is not a bad idea if you think you'll be able to stand being around your classmates all the time . . . but that's a big if.

The closeness of the living quarters can also breed competition, anxiety, and stress. You may get up to use the bathroom in the middle of the night, look out the window, and discover that many of your classmates are still up reading. How will that affect you? In the dorm, there is always talk about how late people stay up, how many pages ahead in the syllabus certain people are, who is brilliant, and who seems to be struggling. There's always one jerk who will try to whip the class into a frenzy by passing along false information, or try to rattle individual members of the class, and unfortunately he always seems to live in the dorm too. Finally, you'll need to consider whether you'll be able to disconnect yourself from the stress overload that will electrify the doom come exam time. Everyone will talk about exams. People will stop by to ask questions that may unnerve you. People may experience nervous breakdowns.

> The biggest mistake I made in getting ready for law school was living in the dorms. The absolute worst, worst, worst! To feel like a person, I needed a real apartment, and the dorm was also a rip-off financially.
>
> —Alison

> I'd recommend living off campus. You'll soon be immersed in law school, and your head will be filled with new ideas. You'll find that while walking down the streets, you'll involuntarily start to identify potential torts. At law school parties people will

actually talk about consideration and illusory promises. Quite quickly you can develop law school tunnel vision. Living off campus with a roommate who knows nothing about law is a good way to keep your perspective, especially during exams. Inevitably, going to law school will change the way you think about the world, but at least you want to be able to step back and realize what is happening.

—John-Mark

As for dealing with an unknown, off-campus landlord, to pervert a Latin legal standard—*caveat rentor.* Living away from the law school will certainly afford you some space and the peace of mind to be able to remove yourself from the fray. Distance can certainly lend perspective. If your chosen law school is in a rural area, you may be able to rent a house, bring your dog, and build a low-stress law school life that few others will experience. If you're in the city, apartments are likely to be larger and cheaper than your on-campus housing. In either case, however, there are other important factors to consider.

First, living off campus means that you'll have to find a suitable place. Do you have the time or the inclination to spend several days setting this up? If you do, remember that you'll be traveling to and from class every day—often late at night. How close is the nearest public transportation? How safe is it, and how often and how late does it run? Are you willing to put up with this inconvenience in order to get some space? Second, if your pipes leak, the radiator bangs and whistles all night, or the water heater breaks down, it might be a while before it gets fixed. How willing are you to put up with the crapshoot of an unknown landlord? Finally, pay attention to the noise level around the apartment and, if at all possible, visit any potential living space at night to determine whether it is quiet enough to study there. Is the apartment located above a bar that will keep you up all night? Do the neighbors in the apartment next door practice the piano every evening or host opera recitals in their living room? Is the neighbor's TV on so loud you can't concentrate? Will there be early-morning truck traffic or loud deliveries to wake you every morning at dawn? Don't laugh—each of these scenarios is drawn from a mentor's sad-but-true real-life experience living off campus. If you opt to live off campus, research your choices carefully, because once you sign the lease, the place is yours for at least a year.

Actually, I made another big mistake. If I had spent more time, I would have chosen a more modern apartment. The building I chose was very old, and it took a lot of calls and a lot of work just to regulate the temperature and to get things fixed when they broke.

—Carolyn

On balance, I think living in the dorm was a good choice for me during my first year of law school. It was where the majority of my classmates at Penn lived, which made it easy to develop friendships and feel like part of a group. Although law school is not college and should not be expected to resemble it, living in the dorm first year did invoke some memories of college, which was comforting to me.

"I think choosing to live in the dorms was the best thing I did in preparing for law school," Allan agreed. "It was a great way to meet people and make friends. It was also advantageous to always have fellow classmates around to discuss classes and share outlines with."

Whatever you decide, spend as much as you can afford to assure yourself a comfortably large and quiet living space. Finally, and perhaps most important, be wary of taking on a roommate in law school, even if that roommate is an old friend living and working in the city you're traveling to or studying in another graduate program. The last thing you need in law school is a clash of schedules, conflicting work or sleep habits, or someone with annoying quirks or an antisocial personality. It seems that most of the law school horror stories you hear arise out of these situations. Take this advice to heart. Many times in law school you'll just want to hide behind closed doors and be alone. If you must take on a roommate, find a medical student. They're never home anyway.

Once you've decided where you're going to live, two more critical things need to be done. First, call the appropriate sources in advance so the phones will be working, the power will be on, and the cable and the Internet will be hooked up upon your arrival. There's nothing worse than having to wait three weeks for phone service. Finally, if you're moving into an apartment, check with the management company to see if you have to schedule a move-in time. Many city buildings require you to use freight elevators that are key-operated and scheduled well in advance. Forewarned is forearmed.

3. Use the summer to get in shape

No, I'm not kidding. The long hours of reading and thinking that you'll be doing in law school take stamina, and a daily workout can refresh you, clear your mind, keep you alert, and make your days more productive. You don't want to deal with the soreness and adjustment associated with a new workout program once law school begins, and you'll want to capitalize on the many benefits of being in shape from the first day—so start now! Load up your iPod with upbeat music and begin a physical workout program in June or July so that it will be a regular part of your routine and easy to continue once law school begins. Many of us made time in our daily schedules to run, blade, bike, shoot hoops, play tennis, or participate in yoga, and those of us who did swear that it made a difference.

4. Read now, sign up later

Beginning in late May or early June, you'll start getting inundated with mailings, pamphlets, and brochures. There will be note-taking services and "buy now and save" offers. There will be the pickup and deliver weekly laundry service, and the weekly dorm-room linen service. There will be offers for meal plans and "exclusive" graduate-student-only "dining clubs." The campus computer center will urge you to buy a computer. There will even be bar review organizations trying to get you to sign up for their classes three years in advance! Everyone will be hawking something. So how do you wade through this blizzard of materials and separate the necessary from the wasteful? How do you know what you need?

It's really quite simple. As each of these "Act now!" offers comes in, log it in on a list, throw the brochures and order forms into a big manila envelope, and wait. I'll let you in on a little secret. Almost all of these "But you must act now!" offers are miraculously extended for "one week only" during the first week or two of classes. When you get to campus, talk to your upper-class mentor or other 2Ls and 3Ls about the various items on your list. Scope out the typical patterns of behavior at the law school and then buy. Other than a computer (see below), which may be offered at an unbeatable price, these organizations are selling nothing that you can't wait to purchase until you arrive on campus. The last thing you want to do is sink $2,000 into the "prestigious graduate-only dining room" only to discover that it is a long, inconvenient walk from the law school, and that you have just condemned yourself to three meals a day with two hermits from the physics lab and a horde of arrogant business school students networking their heads off.

Remember the simple lesson of this section—read now, buy later. It will save you much money and aggravation.

5. Get an up-to-date, Windows-based laptop computer

Because most people today can type faster than they write, and because most word processors now have automatic outlining programs, taking a laptop to lectures and typing your notes in outline form can be a big time-saver. The great thing about taking notes this way (and we'll get more in-depth about this in chapter 9), is that at the end of each class, you'll have a rough outline of the material you covered, which you can then go back and easily supplement with material from your hornbooks and commercial outlines. Then, with a simple click of a button, you can have a fresh, clean, updated copy of an outline in-progress. Remember, getting the edge in law school is about making little distinctions—doing things just a little bit better than your classmates do them. Why waste time writing notes into the margins of your casebooks only to later find those notes illegible and disorganized? Do yourself a favor and make sure to get a copy of Microsoft Office installed on your laptop before you get to law school so that you can begin outlining and taking notes on your laptop in class right away.

You'll also want to have a computer to access LEXIS and Westlaw, the online legal databases that you'll need to conduct research.

As for choosing between Apple and Windows compatible computers, it's best to contact your law school to find out what platform(s) they support. As of this writing, most law schools are presumptively Windows-based. Although most law schools do not discourage the use of Apple computers, many schools do warn students that technical support available to Apple users is limited. Some schools have software that allows Apple users to take exams on their computers, but other schools still don't. If you do stay with your trusted Apple, you should at least make sure it is running on the OS X operating system (or later).

I was a devoted Apple user for my entire pre-law-school life and dragged my Apple desktop and laptop off to law school with me. I quickly discovered, however, that the entire law school environment was Windows-based. Networks were configured for Windows-based computers, the latest versions of legal research software were released first in Windows-based platforms, most available outlines were Windows-based, and most of my classmates had Windows-based systems—all of which made trading class notes and outlines and opening attachments from professors more difficult. The law review and other journals were also all running on Windows-based systems. Suffice it to say that for purposes of convenience, study-group coordination, and your own sanity, if your law school is Windows-based (which it will almost certainly be), and you haven't yet purchased a computer, you're better off buying a Windows-based laptop. Can you live with the Apple you already have? Sure. I did it for all three years, and I made it through just fine . . . but I have a Windows-based laptop now. Needed it for my clerkship because the U.S. federal court system was Windows-based, and so is my law firm.

As for what "toys" to get along with the computer, it is still best to get one with as much RAM as you can afford, as some of the current research software is vast and cumbersome to run on slower computers. A fast internal modem, wireless Internet capability, and a durable, reliable, laser-quality printer are also essentials. The fast modem is for convenient, rapid, and reliable downloading from online research networks, and to speed up your Web surfing on often overcrowded university networks. You'll need the laser-quality printer because many professors now expect nothing less.

Campus computer sellers generally offer competitive prices, but usually only on certain brand names, and their "bundles" rarely feature the most updated technology. I hopped on the Net, went directly to my manufacturer's Web page, had a system custom-built for my needs, and had it in my hands in ten days. If you don't already have a computer, you can also call the manufacturers directly or use any of the reputable computer mail-order companies to order a system. Any of these methods are safe and reliable and tend to get you the most computer for the least amount of money.

6. Check in with the registrar

Trust me, you'll be thanking me out loud for this piece of advice. Among the piles of paperwork you'll receive during the summer before law school will be a form from the registrar's office. It's standard issue at just about every educational institution nowadays, and chances are you'll remember running around with your parents trying to track down everything for the one you filled out for college. On it, you'll have to provide a complete, updated list of your vaccinations, medications, and any health conditions your school should know about. Many schools will also ask for a copy of your Social Security card and/or birth certificate for your file. During your law school career, you'll need many other "important papers" as well, so here's a time-saver that will spare you serious frustration.

Get yourself a folder—and if possible, pick one that is brightly colored so you'll never misplace it. In it, place one copy each of your birth certificate, your Social Security card, your medical history (including a complete and updated history of all inoculations), and your driver's license or state-issued ID card. Then get three certified copies of your undergraduate transcript (you'll need to request this in writing from the registrar at your undergraduate institution and pay a small fee for it); one uncertified photocopy of your undergraduate transcript (which, obviously, you can make by photocopying one of the certified copies); one certified and one uncertified copy of a transcript for each graduate degree you carry, if any; and one photocopy of each of your undergraduate and graduate diplomas—and add these to the file. Finally, toss in your original, current passport.

Some of these items, such as your medical history and two forms of identification, will be required before you are allowed to register for classes. Others, such as certified copies of your undergraduate transcript, may not be required to matriculate, but will certainly be required by employers and/or judges during employment recruiting, or judicial clerkship season. To graduate, you'll probably need to provide copies of your undergraduate diploma to your law school registrar. As for the passport, more than one person I know had a partner come into his office during a summer associateship and say, "I need you to fly to London with me to help with these depositions I'm taking. We'll be leaving on Wednesday."

Don't be the schmo who has to refuse the trip because you don't have a current passport. Remember that under the new laws, if your passport is within six months of its expiration date, many countries will not allow you entrance. So take a look at your passport, ensure that it is current, and put it in the folder. It might also come in handy for your spring break in Tahiti (after you've made real money during a summer associateship, of course), or conversely, when you make your first really big blunder during said summer associateship and need to rapidly flee the country.

After You Arrive on Campus

7. Set up "headquarters"

By this stage, you've probably picked up on my "law school is a battle" analogy, and at the risk of belaboring that symbolism further, I raise this vitally important point. Every general needs a headquarters, and so will you. If you've been paying attention thus far, it should also go without saying that once law school begins, you need to hit your stride as quickly as possible.

"The biggest mistake I made was thinking that law school was just an extension of college," Steve notes. "Don't kid yourself. It's not. College was a lot about fun, and most of the people spent more time having fun than working hard. Law school was not like that. It was much more intense much more quickly than I thought it would be. There were a lot of older people there, and a lot of serious people too. What I failed to realize was that the people in law school all had a pretty easy time in college, and that they viewed law school as a stepping-stone to top job placement. I wasn't expecting that people would come in from day one taking everything so seriously, and that was the hardest adjustment I had to make."

Once classes begin, there may not be time to take a weekend off to shop for furniture, build more shelf space, or unpack and get yourself organized. Think about the recommendations that follow before you get to campus, so that once you're there, you can efficiently and effectively set up a well-provisioned and properly outfitted headquarters for yourself.

Depending on where you fall on the anxiety scale and whether you're moving into an empty apartment or a furnished dorm room, accomplishing this mission might take you an afternoon or a week. Start by remembering the fundamental premise of this book: You're looking for little edges on the competition . . . and being organized and ready to go on the first day of classes is one of the biggest of those little edges.

So what do you need? Start with the most critical item. You must have a good bed.

Huh?

That's right. A bed. I know, I know . . . you were expecting a desk, a good reading chair, or some secret hornbooks*, right? All of those things are coming. Let me explain, however, why a bed deserves the top spot on the list.

When the battle begins, you may be working eighteen-hour days with regularity. The only way you can pull that off for any length of time and stay sharp is to sleep really well when you finally do get to sleep. On many, many days in law school, the only thing separating the hundreds of pages of reading and outlining that you'll be doing seven days a week is the time you spend sleeping—refreshing your body and your brain. So forsake the rickety iron frame and saggy foam mattress likely to await you in your dorm room and invest in something com-

*A "hornbook" is a supplemental study guide to a subject area, often written by a professor, which (theoretically) provides helpful commentary to aid you in your understanding of how the cases fit together, or how legal concepts developed and evolved.

fortable. Many law students choose large futons that can convert into couches, or actually spring for real beds. After so many years in dorm rooms sleeping in dorm beds or mattresses on the floor, you might have forgotten what it's like. Getting a good bed is one of the biggest favors you can do for yourself, as a restful night's sleep is truly one of law school's most precious commodities.

The next absolute "must" is a good fan, or two if you hate moving them around. Remember that it will still be summer when law school begins; and no matter where in the country you are, it's hot in August. Since tossing back too many cold ones might disrupt your concentration, you'll need to find another way to beat the heat, and your fan will likely be the best way to do it. Then, when summer fades, the dormitory heating system roars to life and you discover that your dorm room thermostat doesn't actually do anything, you'll have two choices: (1) open the windows (which, at least in Philadelphia usually produced noisy distractions such as street fights, gunfire, and blaring sirens, not to mention pollution); or (2) voilà—turn on your fan and enjoy the cool air and white noise. Having fans is a key to both comfortable studying and restful sleep. Trust me.

Now we get to the desk.

When shopping for a desk, avoid anything fancy that doesn't provide you with a sprawling top to spread things out on. Little antique desks just won't cut it here. You don't need lots of little drawers, compartments, and cubbies. You're not trying to please Martha Stewart or your mother. Many nights, you're going to want to have three or four books and your laptop computer open on your desk at the same time. Plan accordingly. For your purposes, a flat door on cinder blocks or a large table will provide a better workspace than the most elegant antique rolltop. It's all about flat space—and the more the better.

Next, you'll probably want to consider investing in some species of file cabinet. For about $50, I went down to the nearest office supply superstore and got a rolling, two-drawer wood file cabinet, which doubled as the stand for my laser printer. (Remember, think space—this got the printer off my desk and up off the floor.) I got a bunch of hanging folders to put inside the cabinet and created a file for each of my classes to store the syllabi and handouts. I started separate files for recruiting correspondence, writing samples, résumés, bank and credit-card statements, paid bills, and a few other things. I also placed my yellow "important information" folder in the file cabinet for safekeeping. Again, staying organized is the key. This categorized catchall system proved an easy way to keep paper organized—off my desk, but at my fingertips if needed.

You'll also want to be sure you have adequate shelf space. Your law books and hornbooks will accumulate faster than you'll believe, and you'll need a good place to keep everything. Invest in a sturdy bookcase or build some solid shelves so that you can keep your books and hornbooks in good shape and close to your desk.

If you're not a desk reader (and I'm not), you might want to commandeer a comfortable reading chair from home and throw it in the U-Haul or otherwise start staking out the secondhand furniture stores, flea markets, or yard sales for a chair that you can call your own. Pick something with good back support that you can sit in comfortably for hours. If you plan to read in your dorm or apartment rather than in the library, you'll be logging hundreds of hours in that chair.

Finally, make sure that you have proper lighting. Those fluorescent overhead lights in your law dorm room or the in-ceiling lighting in your apartment aren't going to cut it. Think about springing for a desktop banker's light, or some other form of desktop halogen reading light. The law books will cause you enough eyestrain—trust me. Have a good lamp on your desk, and another one next to your reading chair.

Other items that you'll probably want to have to outfit your headquarters include a TV and DVD player, a microwave, your iPod dock and speakers, a dorm-size refrigerator, or whatever you need to outfit your kitchen if you have one. Don't plan on having time to cook elaborate meals though. Simplicity and speed are of the essence.

Oh—and make sure you have a reliable alarm clock or know how to use the one on your cell phone. You'll definitely need that.

8. Learn the "lay of the land"

Once you've arrived on campus and set up your living and working space, take an afternoon to wander around the city or town that you'll be calling home for the next three years. Get a feel for where things are on campus. Do you know the names of the different law buildings and how the room numbers work? Can you find the campus bookstore? The gym? The undergraduate library? Next, get a subway map and a bus schedule and start to figure out how the routes work. Determine how long it takes you to get from your apartment or dorm room to the law school. Do you know where you'll be able to get a taxi when you stumble out of the library at midnight and don't feel safe walking home? Figure it out.

Have you found the place where you'll get your morning coffee on the way to class? Mapped out a safe running or walking route that you'll use to let off steam? Found a clean and affordable gym near home or school that you can join to ensure that you'll work out regularly?

Do you know which bank you're going to be using? My advice here is to open a no-frills checking account with the bank nearest to your apartment. Make sure the bank has an ATM machine—and even better if it also has one near the law school. Over three years, those service fees for using someone else's ATM will add up. Don't spend time worrying about interest rates. You need to face the reality that you'll be wasting a lot of money to save time and satisfy your id over the next three years. Having a free ATM machine nearby is key.

Did you find a good grocery store that can supply you with the necessities of your diet? What about places where you can go to get a quick sandwich between classes, or a late-night snack after a long night at the library? Have you located a cool neighborhood bar to meet friends for a drink on the weekends or a bookstore to spend a stolen hour reading something other than law? What about the movie theater that will provide you with your most common form of entertainment during law school? Is there live music anywhere in the area to refresh your spirit? Have you found a sanctuary where you can go to be by yourself, get grounded, and regroup when the pressure mounts? Do you want to join a house of worship?

There won't be a lot of time available to find these places once classes begin. You need to do it now.

9. Update your résumé

You probably haven't even thought about your résumé since you finished filing your law school applications. Nearly eight months have passed since then. You have changes to add! For one thing, you're in law school, so you'll need to add your new school information at the top of the "Education" section with the designation "J.D. expected 20xx." Beyond that, at least your home address, phone number, and e-mail have changed, so take care of those. Did you graduate from college last May? With a degree in what? Any honors? Get it down. Did you work over the summer or just terminate your long-term employment? Update!

If you've made it this far, it's probably safe to assume that you have a résumé and know what belongs on it. What you may not know is what a résumé for a legal job should look like. Your career placement office will likely accept and review résumés starting sometime in October—a service you should take advantage of. But since you're doing this now, here's some preliminary advice about what your legal résumé should look like. First and foremost, remember your audience. You're writing for the heavy-starch, dark-tie-on-white-shirt Brooks Brothers crowd, so think "conservative." That means heavy white bond paper—the best you can afford, and coughing up the extra money for real laser printing. Choose a clean, crisp, and simple font from the Times family. Use a clear layout with separate sections for "Education," "Professional Experience," "Publications" (if any), and "Interests and Hobbies." Include lots of white space, and vary the typeface within the same font, using bold caps, underlining, and italics thoughtfully, but sparingly, to set off the different sections and draw the eye. You want your résumé to look friendly and invite the reader to continue.

Present in inverse chronological order, with your most recent accomplishments first. In the "Education" section, be sure to list your college degree and the date it was conferred. Add a list of academic honors and a carefully chosen list of college activities. The general rule for inclusion is, if something illustrates your skills and relevant interests or distinguishes you as a person, you'll probably want to include it. Sports, writing, drama, teaching, outdoor, and leadership activities are all relevant. That you were your fraternity's beer-pong champion, on the other hand, is best left for a night in the bar with your fellow associates once you're safely employed. You'll also want to keep your discussion of high school to a minimum. The name and city of your high school is sufficient unless you did something to particularly distinguish yourself there, either academically or in writing or legal-related activities. For example, if you were the valedictorian in a class of eight hundred, or the editor in chief of the national award-winning high school newspaper, those things would merit a line on a legal résumé. But nobody will care that you were the president of the bridge club. Mention bridge in your "Interests and Hobbies" section so that anyone interested in bridge can engage you on that subject.

Start "Professional Experience" with your most recent job. If you've been a perpetual student, the rule of thumb is to include summer employment for the past five years. If law will be your second career, legal employers will generally be interested in where you worked over the past decade. If you've only been out in the workforce for a year or two, use year designations (e.g., 2001–02) for full-time employment, and summer designations for summer-term employment (e.g., Summer 2005).

Include a "Publications" section only if you have any written publications you deem worthy of inclusion. Relax, relax—you won't be the only person who doesn't have any.

Last, include an "Interests and Hobbies" section at the end of your résumé to fill out the picture of who you are. Are you an avid hiker, golfer, or skier? Do you sail, run, or play an instrument? Do you write fiction on the side? Interestingly, the items in this section typically draw a lot of fire in employment interviews because you're liable to encounter interviewers who share your interests. Given that people are naturally drawn to people with similar interests, the power of these connections should not be overlooked.

As for the controversial topics of sexual orientation, race, politics, and religion, you're on your own, but unless you're adamant about joining a firm that closely reflects your religious and political beliefs, I'd avoid these hot-button topics. Keep in mind that the white-shoe world of law is no different from the rest of the world as to the way these topics will play. While your work on behalf of your religion, political party, or sexual preference may be admirable, impressive, and a vital part of who you are, recognize that if you include these topics on a legal résumé, you might end up alienating potential employers.

Finally, your résumé must be as tight as it can be. Practice verbal economy by challenging the necessity of every word. Use the most active, descriptive verbs possible, and be certain that there are no typos, misspellings, or stray marks. If, after you've strained to cut all the fat out of your résumé, it still stretches onto a second page (or even more if you're coming to law from another career), that's fine. If you're certain everything on your résumé is relevant to a legal employer or manifestly illustrative of you as an individual, then you can safely ignore everyone who tells you that your résumé has to be one page long. Trust me, I just spent five years as the Chair of the Hiring Committee for my firm's four offices. If you have enough *relevant* credentials to stretch to multiple pages, your potential employers will read them. Don't eliminate the "Hobbies" section to placate your placement office's directive to stay on one page.

So why, you ask, is all this talk of résumés stuck in the middle of this chapter? Easy. In this chapter, you're learning about the things you need to do before law school begins. You need to update your résumé now so that it will be sitting in a folder in your files ready to be sent out to employers come the beginning of 1L recruiting season in November. You see, the first-year employment rat race begins on November 1, which, by agreement of most accredited law schools, is the day that law school placement officers can begin working with 1Ls. The problem is, come November 1, you'll be swamped with work and heading into the most critical period of the semester. There won't be time for résumés then. In fact, most 1Ls will ignore the lure of recruiting until after their fall-semester finals in mid-December, when most of the plum 1L positions at firms and public-interest placements have already been claimed. But not you. Come November, you'll be ready.

10. Get your books, study aids, and other supplies

If your school is like most schools, your first-year class will be broken down into two or three "sections." Everyone in your section will likely follow the same schedule and have all of the same professors. At least three days before classes begin, and probably much sooner than that, your first-year professors will have posted your section assignments. They'll probably be posted on a class bulletin board somewhere in your law school. There will likely also be syllabi and course packets, handouts, or other materials. Get the packets and handouts, then take your syllabi directly to the bookstore. Be sure to bring along a couple of large backpacks to haul your materials home.

When you get to the bookstore, buy a new copy of each of the required books. In law school more than most other programs, it's important to buy new because you'll be marking your books up in a way you never have before, and working around a previous user's extensive notations can be frustrating and distracting. Be sure to buy the right edition, and to get any paperback supplements offered with the book. Often, an author will put out a paper supplement between editions to keep up with the most recent case law in a particular area. These thin pamphlets are easy to overlook.

If the professor "recommends" a particular hornbook, you'd be advised to pick up a copy—chances are the professor will either lecture out of parts of it or at least refer to it. It may also prove extremely helpful to your understanding of the subject.

Wait on anything the professor lists as "optional." These books are frequently either written by your professor or contain contributions by your professor. You'll probably never need anything "optional" for a critical part of the class, but your professor would be happy to collect the royalties if you want to oblige.

"Unlike college, where you get an entire 'syllabus week' and don't buy your books until the week after *that,* law school demands that you stay on track from day zero," Lindsay notes. "Therefore, make sure you purchase and receive all of your books at least a few days before classes begin to allow you time to look through them and your course syllabi."

Next, go to the stationery section. After you've loaded up on your favorite types of pens, binders, and legal pads, find the highlighters and follow these directions carefully. Buy at least six each of green, yellow, red, blue, and orange. Yeah, I know that's thirty highlighters.

Trust me on this. You'll learn what these are for in chapter 9.

Finally, head for the section of the bookstore where the legal study aids are kept. These are huge business for the bookstore, so they should be prominently displayed. Chances are, there are three or four choices for each of your subjects. So how are you supposed to decide which ones to use?

Consult the list below. Find the subjects that you are taking this term, and immediately buy the study aid(s) listed after the subject name. These are our consensus picks of the best study aids and commercial outlines available. If you can't find them all at the campus bookstore, hop online to your favorite online bookseller, and each of them will only be a few mouse clicks away. The most important thing is to get your commercial outlines immediately, since they will play a vital role in the way you study from day one.

Recommended commercial outlines

Civil Procedure:	Civil Procedure: Examples & Explanations (Glannon) Emanuel's Civil Procedure Outline Acing Civil Procedure (Spencer)
Torts:	Gilbert's Torts Outline Torts: Examples & Explanations (Glannon)
Property:	Gilbert's Property Outline
Contracts:	Emanuel's Contracts Outline
UCC Article 2:	Gilbert's Sale and Lease of Goods
Constitutional Law:	Emanuel's Constitutional Law Outline
Criminal Law:	Gilbert's Criminal Law Outline
Criminal Procedure:	Acing Criminal Procedure (Abramson)

Remember that you won't have time to consult more than one or two commercial outlines in a particular subject, so don't overbuy.

Bonus: Go to orientation!

Finally, go to the orientation events. Law school can be an extremely lonely and isolating place. The experience is made much more tolerable if you can find a trusted friend or two among the masses—and grabbing a beer at orientation and mingling with your classmates is one of the best chances you'll have to do this in a relaxed atmosphere. Once classes begin and conversations turn almost exclusively to the daily grind, it is harder to get to know people.

The two or three days of orientation events will probably be the most fun you have in law school until you're a third-year student. Go forth and enjoy the last days of unburdened time. It is frequently during these first few days at these orientation events that memorable conversations, important bondings, and the formation of study groups occur. But you have to be there to be included.

CHAPTER 8

So What Is a Tort Anyway? A Brief Overview of the First-Year Curriculum

It is enough if one tries merely to comprehend a little of this mystery every day.
—ALBERT EINSTEIN

BY NOW, you should have gotten the idea that many people apply to law school without the vaguest notion why they're doing so. Not surprisingly, this lack of information also extends to the first-year program of study, and the entire law school curriculum.

"Not me," you say. "I know a lot about law school. I've read the first seven chapters of this book."

Okay then, what's a tort?

"Huh? A tort? Uh . . ."

Most American law schools offer a standard first-year curriculum that includes courses in Contracts, Real Property, Civil Procedure, Torts, Criminal Law and/or Criminal Procedure, Constitutional Law, and a full-year course in legal writing. In some schools, one or more of these classes might be offered as a full-year course, pushing one of the others, often Criminal Law or Constitutional Law, to the second year. Further, one or more of a limited list of elective courses, often including Administrative Law, Labor Law, Legal Theory, Economic Theory, or Legal History, may be offered during the second semester to provide a bit of variety.

In this chapter, we harbor no illusions of providing an exhaustive analysis of the first-year subjects. That's why you go to law school. This chapter is included for the day during the summer before your first year of law school when your mind starts to wander toward the end of August, and you start asking yourself, "So what am I going to be studying, anyway?" It is just an overview—to both sate your summertime curiosities and whet your appetite for the study of law.

THE SUBJECTS

Civil Procedure

Affectionately referred to as Civ Pro by students, or simply Procedure by the professors, Civil Procedure is typically one of the most intimidating and most feared of the first-year courses. Admittedly, understanding some of its more abstract concepts such as subject matter jurisdiction and the infamous "Erie question" may be more difficult than memorizing the elements of common law robbery in Criminal Law, or negligence in Torts. This fear and intimidation, however, can be successfully dispelled by discovering and understanding the broader purpose of the course and studying the rules "in action" with a good hornbook—a strategy that will be discussed at length in the next chapter. By following this approach, you will discover that an elegant, sensible structure underlies the rules of procedure—and that the system actually makes sense.

A civil action is an action brought to enforce private rights and/or seek private remedies in which money damages or some other court order is sought. It may be easier to conceptualize civil actions through the use of a negative—a civil action is "any noncriminal case." Civil Procedure at its most basic level is the study of the rules, procedures, regulations, and process governing these noncriminal actions in state and federal courts.

Because the rules of civil procedure govern a broad spectrum of cases, from garden-variety contract disputes to high-profile First Amendment challenges, the first thing to realize when you're reading a case for Civil Procedure is that you're not really concerned about the underlying substantive law dispute. It's not the contract issue or the First Amendment claim you need to evaluate. Instead, in Civil Procedure, you need to be on the lookout only for the procedural questions underlying the case that the court was forced to decide.

Most national law schools teach Civil Procedure from a federal court perspective and consequently teach the Federal Rules of Civil Procedure—a compendium of eighty-six rules that governs every aspect of bringing a civil action in the federal court system. Most professors require you to own a copy of the federal rules, but even if yours doesn't, you should buy a copy, as reading the applicable rule will greatly aid your understanding of the case law precipitated by that rule. In addition to providing a complete list of the rules, the "rules pamphlet" or "rule book," as your professor will likely refer to it, will contain instructive Advisory Committee Notes, stating the intended function of each rule, and the purpose of any amendments thereto. Penned by the drafters of the federal rules, the Advisory Committee Notes often hold the key to ambiguous language in a rule, or even to an entire case!

If you go to a smaller state law school, your course in Civil Procedure may focus on the procedural rules of the state courts where your law school is located. Like their federal counterparts, state courts are also governed by rules of procedure. Unlike in the federal court system, however, where the same Federal Rules of Civil Procedure govern your case whether you're in federal court in Alaska or Florida, each state's court system has its own rules of procedure. Fortunately, most state courts' rules of civil procedure are closely modeled after the federal rules. Radical departures by state courts from the federal rules of procedure are uncommon.

So what, specifically, will you learn in Civil Procedure?

First, you will learn how to determine whether you can bring a case in state court, federal court, or both, and which courts within those systems are available to hear different cases. This question, which raises issues of "subject matter jurisdiction," "personal jurisdiction," "proper venue," and "removal," encompasses the first broad area of Civil Procedure—choosing the proper court to hear your claims and making sure that you don't run afoul of that court's jurisdictional rules.

From there, you will discover how lawsuits are shaped through the evidence-collecting procedures of interrogatories, discovery, and depositions, joinder of additional culpable parties after the commencement of the lawsuit, and supplemental jurisdiction over additional claims involving those parties. You will learn how courts can hear counterclaims and cross-claims between these parties, and you may even delve into the complicated world of complex litigation and class actions.

Once you have your court properly chosen, all necessary parties in the lawsuit, and all claims on the table, you will need to decide which law governs the case. Federal statutory law? State statutory or common law? If so, which state's law? In considering these issues, you will encounter (1) the infamous "Erie question," which requires you to determine whether the issues raised in a federal court case implicate federal procedural law or state substantive law, and accordingly, which law to apply; and (2) the choice-of-law conflicts that arise when citizens of different states appear in a federal court, each alleging that the law of his own state should govern the lawsuit. In trying to make sense of all of this, you will likely address the policy underpinnings of the Erie decision, and the troubling problems of horizontal and vertical "forum shopping," where plaintiffs seek the court that will apply the most favorable law to their claims.

You will then learn about how cases can be derailed and ended prematurely through the motion to dismiss, the motion for summary judgment, and the motion for judgment as a matter of law. Finally, you will learn how the concepts of res judicata (claim preclusion) and collateral estoppel (issue preclusion) can bar a plaintiff from relitigating events or particular issues that have already been resolved on the merits in a prior claim.

Civil Procedure is one of the most complicated but most enjoyable of the first-year subjects because it is your undeniable entrée into the world of law. In studying Civil Procedure, you learn the blueprint of the American legal system and slowly discover how our entire system of civil justice fits together. Working through the rules to the point of mastery can take a long time and be extraordinarily frustrating, but when the clouds do finally part, the elegance of the system of American civil procedure will be yours to keep.

Contracts

Anyone who has read *The Paper Chase* or has seen the movie probably lives in fear of Contracts. In reality, however, Contracts is one of the most practical and common-sense-driven courses you will ever take in law school. Contracts is the study of how the law protects an original understanding or agreement between two or more parties, as manifested in a contract, from the subsequent misfortunes, changes in circumstances, accidents, later-discovered misunderstandings, or intentional breaches by one or more of the parties to that contract.

You will learn the three primary components of contract formation: offer, acceptance, and consideration, and what is required of each component for a valid contract to be formed. You will learn about the defenses to contract formation, including the absence of mutual assent, lack of valid consideration, illegality of the underlying contract, and incapacity to contract. You will also learn the defenses to contract enforcement, including when to apply the statute of frauds (which bars the enforcement of oral contracts concerning certain subject matter, and all oral contracts that cannot be completed within one year), and when the principles of impossibility, impracticability, frustration, and unconscionability can bar the enforcement of a contract.

From there, you will address the rules of contract interpretation, including how to resolve disputes over contract language and how to apply the Parol Evidence Rule (which holds that when the parties have reduced a contract to a writing that is intended to be the full and final expression of their agreement, any other prior or contemporaneous written or oral expressions cannot be interpreted to vary the terms of the written contract). You may also discuss the rights and responsibilities of third-party beneficiaries of the contract.

Finally, you will learn what happens when a contract is breached, and what different kinds of damages and other remedies are available to the nonbreaching party.

Contracts is typically taught using both case law and Article 2 of the Uniform Commercial Code (UCC), a special set of codified rules that govern all contracts for the sale of goods.

Torts

Finally! So what is a tort anyway?

A tort is an act or omission, perpetrated by one individual against another, for which a civil remedy is available. There are intentional torts, such as battery; economic or dignitary torts, such as defamation; and torts of negligence, strict liability, products liability, and nuisance. You'll doubtless cover them all, but regardless of how obscure your professor tries to get with the doctrine—no matter how much cost-benefit analysis and economic theory he tries to teach you—Torts is still probably the most straightforward, black-letter subject you'll have during your first year of law school. Don't lose the forest for the trees here. Mastering Torts, for the purpose of your exam, is mostly about memorizing the elements of the torts you cover and any defenses applicable to them, and then being able to spot them in a long, often comical exam fact-pattern.

You'll probably begin by learning the intentional torts: assault, battery, false imprisonment, intentional infliction of emotional distress, trespass, and conversion, and the defenses to these torts, including self-defense, defense of others, defense of property, consent, privilege, and necessity. From there, you'll address negligence, the mother of all torts. During your treatment of this subject, you will discuss (1) the duties of care owed by professionals, business and property owners, homeowners, drivers, and parents; (2) what specifically constitutes a breach of those duties; (3) the difficult subject of causation—including actual and proximate cause and the foreseeability of the injuries produced by a particular act or omission; and (4) the potential defenses to a negligence action, including contributory and comparative negligence, and assumption of risk. You will then discuss the various theories of damages and the interplay of insurance in a negligence action.

Later in the semester, you will address the subject of strict liability torts—torts that impose an absolute duty of safety on the defendant, including the harboring of wild or known dangerous animals, and the perpetration of ultrahazardous or dangerous activities and their associated defenses.

Time permitting, you may delve into one or more of the "specialty torts." Among them, you might study products liability—examining when commercial manufacturers and vendors can be held liable for product-related accidents and what defenses apply in such actions; public and private nuisance and their defenses and remedies; and the torts at the junction of constitutional law, including defamation (including libel and slander), invasion of privacy, and misrepresentation, and the related defenses to these torts, including consent, truth, and privilege.

In summary, Torts is a rich and wildly interesting course encompassing a wide array of subject matter. Its cases often read like tragicomedy and are among the most entertaining in all of law.

Property

First-year Property is a strange amalgam of the past and the present. The course couples obvious, almost inaccessible nods to ancient English traditions (e.g., the Rule Against Perpetuities and the Rule in Shelley's Case) with modern landlord-tenant, real estate, and personal-property issues that many of us may have experienced in our own lives. The result, once you get past the arcane language and theory, is a largely black-letter and practical body of doctrine that many students enjoy because of its ready application to everyday life.

The course generally begins with a nod to merry old England and a lengthy treatment of "estates in land," including the different types of present possessory estates and possible future interests that a person can have in a piece of real property. During this part of the course, you will learn about the effects that death and failing to heed your forefathers' wishes can have on your ability to receive and retain an estate, and the effect that sloppy drafting can have on who takes possession of your land after you die. Amazingly, much of this arcane stuff still applies today, which unfortunately means that most of it will also be fair game for both your final exam and the bar exam.

The next broad, and immensely practical, topic in first-year Property is landlord-tenant law. You will learn about the creation and enforcement of leases, the duties of both landlords and tenants, and the remedies that each have at their disposal upon a breach of those duties, the law of assignments and subleases, the law of fixtures, and the assignment of tort liability between landlord and tenant.

From there, you may pause for a couple of weeks to discuss the only marginally related area of personal property (read: possessions other than land). During this segment, you will discover who has legal rights to lost or mislaid property, what a "bona fide purchaser" is, and who has the "more significant" right to a piece of property that was lost by person A, found by person B, stolen by person C, sold to dealer D, and bought by person E, when person A sees person E wearing her "lost" ring and demands its return.

Later in the course, you will reach real property's boundary with real estate law, when you take up the subject of easements, covenants, profits, and servitudes, or, in a phrase, the different active and passive rights that a person, a corporation, the city, or the public may have on the land of another. You will learn what language is required to create these interests, how they are passed with the land, how and when other people are adequately notified of them, and how these interests manifest themselves in everyday life. You will also discuss the concept of adverse possession—the way that someone who lives on a piece of your land for long enough can actually gain legal title in it.

From there, you will move into "conveyancing," or how to pass title in land from one person to another through land sale contracts, deeds, and wills. Among the topics you will address in this section is how to conduct a title search to assure that the piece of land you are buying or receiving is free from encumbrances, and how to properly record the interest you receive to protect it from later fraudulent conveyances.

Finally, if time allows, you may touch upon the area of natural rights incidental to land ownership, including mining and mineral rights, and oil, gas, and riparian (water) rights.

If you use a good hornbook or commercial outline to get you through the more arcane subject matter, property can be an interesting and highly practical subject. Many people who have gone on to specialize in landlord-tenant law, real estate, or oil and gas law trace their initial interest in their specialty subjects to their first-year Property course.

Criminal Law and Criminal Procedure

Depending on what law school you attend, criminal law and procedure may be taught as one course or as two separate courses. For purposes of this explanation, I will treat them separately.

Criminal Law, the stuff of movies and prime-time television, is a favorite of most law students. The cases are interesting, the subject has an obvious place in everyday life, and accordingly the underlying theory is accessible and readily applicable.

The study of criminal law typically begins with a philosophical discussion of the different theories and purposes for punishment. You will likely discuss the purpose and origins of the Model Penal Code (a codification of substantive criminal laws promulgated by the American Law Institute), and how it compares and interacts with the various state criminal codes. From there, you will learn about the general elements of criminal conduct, namely the *actus reus* (culpable physical action or inaction), and *mens rea* (culpable mental states).

With an understanding of the underlying theory, you will launch into a study of the crimes themselves. You will learn the different types of homicide, and the physical actions and mental states required for each of them. You'll address attempt crimes, and the physical acts and mental states required to constitute attempt. You'll then learn the principles of exculpation, including self-defense, protection of property, law enforcement, justification, duress, intoxication, diminished capacity, and insanity. You'll also learn about accomplice liability, and the physical acts and mental state required for culpability. You'll then run through the alphabet of other crimes and their required elements, including offenses against the person (criminal assault and battery, mayhem, kidnapping, false imprisonment, and the sex offenses), offenses against property (larceny, robbery, embezzlement, false pretenses, extortion, receipt of stolen property, and forgery), and offenses against the home (burglary and arson). Throughout your coverage of criminal law, you'll read hundreds of cases from different jurisdictions that will both help to define the boundaries of the different crimes and raise fascinating theoretical questions about the theories underlying the criminal justice system. Without a doubt, Criminal Law will be one of the highlights of your first-year curriculum.

Criminal Procedure, often called Constitutional Criminal Procedure, is largely a study of the Fourth and Fifth Amendments, and how the adversarial clashes between criminal defendants and law enforcement officials have played out in the courts. The course typically features extensive coverage of Fourth Amendment law, centering on the relationship between the warrant clause and the reasonableness clause, and includes topics such as when the police can search homes, cars, and people, what constitutes probable cause, and what is required to obtain search warrants. You'll learn about eavesdropping and wiretapping and when these activities are permitted. Fifth Amendment law protections against self-incrimination, involuntary or coerced confessions, and improper witness identifications are usually studied in depth, as are the Sixth Amendment rights to counsel and trial by jury. In each of these areas, particular emphasis is commonly placed on Supreme Court decisions and how the different courts (Warren Court, Burger Court, Rehnquist Court) have approached these subjects philosophically.

Depending on your professor's particular focus, you may also take up trial-related subjects, including the roles of the police, the prosecutor, the grand jury, bail and pretrial release, discovery, plea bargaining, sentencing under the Federal Sentencing Guidelines, and the development and recent curtailment of habeas corpus rights. Whether it is offered as part of the first-year Criminal Law class or as an upper-year elective, Criminal Procedure always generates passion and excitement among students and, when properly taught, is usually one of the most popular classes in the law school curriculum.

Constitutional Law

Summarizing Constitutional Law in a few paragraphs is nearly impossible. At its broadest, Constitutional Law is about how the U.S. Constitution, as the "supreme law of the land," (1) establishes an organized framework that equally distributes power to the three branches of government (legislative, executive, and judicial), (2) describes the general plan by which public affairs are to be administered, and (3) lays out the fundamental principles that are to regulate the relationship between the citizen and her government.

So how does this play out in the first-year course?

Nearly every first-year Constitutional Law course opens with a discussion of *Marbury v. Madison*, the case that established the function of the judiciary and the nature of the Supreme Court's authority as the ultimate interpreter of the Constitution. From there, discussion typically moves to the relationship between the states and the federal government through the commerce clause, the spending clause, and the federal government's power to tax. While much of this treatment will be historical, the principles underlying the commerce clause and the spending clause and the powers they provide empower Congress with the constitutional pathway that produces much of the federal legislative action that happens today.

At some point during the semester, a clear break will occur in the doctrine as you move from discussion of the structure of government to discussion about individual rights and liberties. This half of the first-year Constitutional Law course typically begins with a discussion of the Bill of Rights, the post–Civil War amendments, and the circumstances surrounding their adoption. Due process of law, equal-protection rights and levels of scrutiny for racial, ethnic, and gender preferences, and constitutional restraints on private conduct will be among the many interesting topics you'll discuss.

Depending on time and the interests of your professor, you may touch on the First Amendment freedoms of religion and expression to a limited degree, although these subjects are usually saved for an entirely separate course or courses on the First Amendment given as upper-year electives.

Constitutional Law is one of the most complex, fascinating, and intimidating subjects taught in the first-year curriculum. However, as the essence of American law, it provides the often-unseen but ever-present framework underlying every other subject in law.

Administrative Law

Although neither a mandatory part of most first-year curricula nor a required upper-level course at most law schools, Administrative Law plays such an important role in the way our society functions these days that I'm writing this section with the expectation that before long it will be a required course. If not required to, you should take it during your first year so you have at least a rudimentary understanding of how the complicated administrative system works and fits into the three branches of government.

Administrative Law is the study of the rules, regulations, orders, and decisions promulgated and issued by administrative agencies to help them carry out their regulatory powers. In the introductory course, you will not be studying the specific rules and regulations promulgated by, for example, the Environmental Protection Agency, or the Food and Drug Administration. That task is left to specific upper-level courses in, for example, environmental law, or food and drug law. Instead, in the entry-level "Admin" course, you will study how administrative agencies came into being, and how, despite the tremendous protestations about separation of powers and lack of direct political accountability that continue to this day, the legislative branch was allowed, in the name of "efficiency" and "economy," to get away with delegating so much of its power to these agencies.

Your study of Administrative Law will engage these issues as they were decided by the U.S. Supreme Court. In addition, you will learn about the controls exercised over these agencies by the other branches of government. You will learn the framework for agency rulemaking and adjudication, the process by which judicial review can be taken from agency action, and what damages are available against the federal government and its officers when an agency oversteps its bounds.

You need only peruse your law school course catalog briefly to grasp just how important a role Administrative Law plays in the landscape of American law. Environmental law, oil and gas law, food and drug law, energy law, securities law, labor law, tax, and trade are only a few of the areas of law influenced heavily by administrative agencies. Best get this subject under your belt early.

CHAPTER 9

Getting Out of the Gate—Applying the Lessons of Futures Past

Where there is no vision, the people perish.
—PROVERBS 29:18

IMAGINE that law school is a horse race. On the first day of classes, the professors pass out the syllabi, the gates spring open, and the horses (that's you) burst forth from the cages. In a real horse race, the thoroughbreds charge forward on a beeline down the track toward the finish line. In law school, however, when the gates open, the first-year students charge out of their cages and spray out in any number of directions in a zealous but aimless charge. Not surprisingly, after fourteen weeks barreling off in the wrong direction, many of these hapless 1Ls cross the finish line exhausted, frustrated, and completely confused. Worse yet, many of them end up bombing their first-semester exams—and their dismal results hang around their necks like albatrosses for the rest of their law school careers.

Your job is to do everything in your power to make sure this doesn't happen to you.

How?

Truthfully, it begins with a change of mindset. An admission that the glory days of high school, where you could walk into a test without studying and get an A anyway, are over. An understanding that you spent your last miracle in college when you partied the semester away but crammed successfully enough to perform well on your exams. In law school, there are no miracles, and there aren't any gifts. At the end of the road, it's just you, an empty blue book, three hours, and a class full of competitors looking to force you down the curve in order to get the spot on the law review, the judicial clerkship, or the plum job in the shining city.

> If I could do it all over again, I would have taken an entirely different approach to my study strategy during those first few months. I would have been more diligent about keeping up with the reading, forced myself not to get bogged down in the minutiae of cases, started using commercial outlines sooner, and started making my own outlines right away.
>
> —Carolyn

People can sugarcoat it all they want, and believe me, they'll try, but if your law school employs a mandatory curve as most do, the reality is, somebody is going to get the A's and somebody is going to get the C's. You're either the predator or the prey. This situation doesn't give you license to be an asshole to your classmates, but it should light a fire under you. You're in a new reality now. Heed this warning: If you approach law school as if it were an extension of college, when grades come out, you'll find yourself in a hole that you may be digging yourself out of for the rest of your law school career.

Here's what you need to know to get a clean start out of the gates.

Case briefing—their way

If you talk to ten law students about the best way to study law you'll probably end up with ten different answers. Some students will tell you that you can do well in law school by simply reading commercial outlines and hornbooks and not actually reading cases at all. My experience suggests that this is true to some degree. Commercial outlines and hornbooks (Glannon, Emanuel's, Gilbert's, etc.) are an extremely important element in your studying. I wholeheartedly endorse their use, and I will teach you how to use them for maximum benefit in the next section. Before you start relying too heavily on commercial outlines, however, you need to learn to develop the core skills of the lawyer—how to sift through facts, glean the law from carefully written judicial opinions, and synthesize the law. After all, you're not just in law school to do well in law school. You're in law school to develop the skills you'll need in practice.

On the other hand, many law professors and some students take the extreme opposite position, suggesting that "real students" should be purists, embracing the struggle for understanding by simply reading the assigned cases over and over until clarity comes, and briefing every case on their own, and that commercial outlines, like Cliff's Notes, are cheating and should be shunned. That advice is equally bad.

> Never brief a case. The entire first semester, I typed up elaborate briefs of each case while I read. Don't do that.
>
> —Allan

Somewhere in your orientation materials, a professor from your law school probably sent you an article on "how to properly brief a case." Read that article carefully, and do the sample case brief if one was provided. Now hear me on this. What you're going to do in that exercise is learn the rudiments of a process. You need to know how to walk before you can run, so follow the directions. Put down the name of the case, and learn how to write the citation in proper form even if you don't know what it means yet. Write down the procedural posture—in other words, how the case got to the court it's in. List the relevant facts, carefully frame the question presented, and answer it. Add a few lines to flesh out the court's reasoning, and most important, provide yourself with a hook. Why was this case significant? What did this case contribute to its area of law?

I'm not providing you with an example of a sample brief for two reasons. First, unless your law school practices some unorthodox, alternative teaching style, you'll get an assignment to brief a case in your orientation materials. Second, you won't be using this method much longer. *You must learn how to do it, however.* This is not a place to cut corners. The more time you put into learning how to brief a case properly, the faster and more skillfully you'll be able to brief cases my way.

Do the orientation brief now, without looking at the sample provided.

Now compare what you've written to the model your professor provided. How'd you do? Chances are, if you took it seriously, your brief is twice as long as it needs to be, contains a slew of unnecessary facts and reasoning, and probably took you over an hour. Sound about right? Don't worry. Things are about to change dramatically for the better . . . but you had to do at least one case their way in order to recognize just how much better!

Case briefing—my way
(The five-step plan to success)

You already read chapter 7, so this shouldn't be news to you. Two nights before classes begin, you should have a syllabus, a textbook or textbooks, the *Law School Confidential* recommended hornbook and/or commercial outline, and a three-ring binder for each of your law school classes. Now pick a subject, grab your syllabus, and let's get started!

Step One: Start each night with a lesson from your commercial outline

One of the most critical secrets of law school success is being able to put the hundreds of cases and case excerpts (often called squibs) you'll read for each law school class in some kind of context. The most efficient way to do this is to start with the commercial outline. Why reinvent the wheel struggling for countless hours to create a context when someone has already done this for you?

Law professors generally scorn commercial outlines. Some even ban them from their lectures. But in truth, for your purposes in law school, there is not an enormous difference between a well-constructed commercial outline and a good hornbook. In fact, some offerings—such as Professor Joseph Glannon's highly recommended *Civil Procedure* from Little, Brown's Examples and Explanations series—are a hybrid between a commercial outline and a hornbook. You're looking to put each night's reading in context, and consequently each night's reading should start with a reading of the relevant section of the applicable hornbook. Here's how you do it.

> If I could do it all over again, I would focus much more on the "black-letter" law—the holding and how each case advances the ball in that particular area of the law—because that's what's important at exam time. I tended to focus too much on facts because I was terrified I would look stupid in class if I couldn't remember what a case was about.
>
> —Keith

Grab your syllabus and determine what pages in the textbook your professor has assigned for tonight. Go to the textbook and see what the general topic heading is. If you're having trouble determining what it is, don't forget to check the table of contents of the book. When you've determined the general topic area, write it down.

Next, flip through the span of pages the professor assigned, and write down the name of every case that appears. There will be "major cases," the ones that are excerpted in edited form, and "squibs," the cases that are mentioned and discussed in a paragraph or two in the professor's linking text between major cases. Be sure to write down the names of these squib cases, too, as they often provide important interstitial developments between the major cases that can greatly assist your understanding. Once you have your list of cases for the night in that subject, put the casebook aside (for now) and consult one of the recommended commercial outlines. Go to the index in the outline and find the pages where the cases you've listed are discussed. Chances are, the cases will be grouped together in a section not unlike the one in your textbook. Read that section of the commercial outline for understanding, marking the holdings of your listed cases, and any explanatory text discussing how the cases affect each other, with a highlighter. Don't try to memorize things or write anything down yet. Just read and highlight sparsely. What you're looking for is an overview of the night's reading in that subject—a context in which to put the cases you're about to read. To employ a metaphor, think of the law as a series of somewhat linear lengths of chain. Each case you read adds another link to the chain and is dependent on the cases that preceded it to illustrate the development of the law. That's the magic epiphany you're striving for in each of the subjects you'll study in law school—to be able to follow the cases, link by link down the chain, until you finally grasp the big picture of how all the cases work together to develop and govern a particular area of law, where the unanswered questions remain, and what the next links in the chain might look like. This is a somewhat simplistic notion of the law, but it will work for now.

> The key to academic success in law school is good outlines. A huge mistake I made in law school was refusing to use outlines from former students and commercial outlines like Gilbert's and Emanuel's. Using these outlines is an integral part of studying for law school! It is not against the rules. But for some reason, I wanted to prove that I could do well on my own. And all I did was put myself at a disadvantage to everyone else by not using all of the resources available to me. After my first semester, I learned.
>
> —Steve

So what do you do if an assigned case isn't discussed in your commercial outline? One possibility is that the case is of minor importance, in which case it's probably in a squib, and thus you can take its holding at face value from that squib and move on. If you're really stuck on that case, you can always jump on the Internet or go to the law library and consult some of the other hornbooks in the subject area to see if they covered it, but my recommendation would be not to worry about it. We're using the outline right now for an overview, so complete coverage is unnecessary. Use the outline for what it can give you, and move on to briefing the actual cases, discussed in the next section. Getting 100 percent coverage of cases discussed in your textbook in your commercial outline is rare. Don't worry about a missing minor case or two on any given night. The questions to ask yourself are, do you know what you're going to be reading about tonight, and do you have some sense about how the law has developed in the area? If you can answer yes to these questions, you're ready to proceed to the next step.

Step Two: Brief in Technicolor

If you followed the instructions in chapter 7, you should have an ample supply of green, red, yellow, blue, and orange highlighters on hand. Open up each of your casebooks to the inside front cover and reproduce the following key inside:

GREEN:	facts
YELLOW:	critical legal reasoning
RED:	holding; court; judge; procedural posture
BLUE:	important precedents cited and their holdings
ORANGE:	important dissenting remarks

From now on, you won't be writing any more case briefs. You'll be briefing your cases in your casebooks, in color, as you go along. Here's how to do it.

First, skim the case completely from beginning to end. Just read. No pen, no highlighter, nothing. Force yourself not to get too bogged down in minutiae. Just get a sense for how the case is organized, what the case is about, what the holding is, and how much good supporting reasoning is provided. Resist the urge to mark anything. An average-size case should take you ten to fifteen minutes to get through.

When you've finished skimming the case, you're ready to start briefing it. Remember the one cardinal rule about this method of case briefing—highlight *sparingly.* Mark the court, writing judge, procedural posture, and holding in red, the most relevant facts in green, the most persuasive or historically important reasoning in yellow, significant case precedent in blue, and any notable reasoning in the dissent in orange. *If you find yourself passively painting the text as you go, rationalizing that you'll come back to this later, you're missing out on the benefit. Force yourself to read, highlight, and mark the text actively and critically—bringing out only the most crucial aspects of each case.*

When you've finished that, skim back over the case and write a word or two in the margins next to each highlighted section to flag important concepts. For example, in a contracts case, you might write "consideration" next to the part of the case where consideration is discussed, or "three-part test" next to the place in a constitutional law opinion where a three-part test is applied. Just a word or two here or there to trigger your memory. That's all you need.

Finally, go back to the top of the opinion and draw yourself a simple picture to remind you what the case is about. I don't care that you got a C+ in seventh-grade art, just draw a picture that will trigger your memory. No one else will see it but you.

So what's the benefit to this method? There are several. The first is time. This method saves a lot of time that you'd otherwise spend copying passages of an opinion into a notebook or typing them into a computer. The words are already on paper in a safe, organized, and bound volume. Why re-create the wheel? Spend the time you save by not having to write out your briefs in analyzing and thinking about the law. Figure out how each case fits into the framework you discovered in the commercial outline.

> Spend more time figuring out the black-letter law. The professors tend to emphasize the methodology (i.e., how to think about the law) and don't emphasize the black-letter law. However, when it came time to take exams, I found that the key was the black-letter law.
>
> —Pat

Critics of my suggested method will argue, correctly, that people don't remember things as well when they highlight them as they would if they wrote them down, and that studies have shown that highlighting encourages passive study and postpones learning and commitment to memory. They're right—and that's why briefing in Technicolor is only a *part* of your overall study method. If you do this correctly, while your classmates are writing their briefs for every case, you'll have time to make at least two more passes through the material—the first in class when the material is discussed, and the second when you're constructing your own outlines for each class. You'll be writing those outlines yourself, and that final step will be your act of engaging the material actively, which will help to crystallize and structure your understanding of how the law fits together. But we're getting ahead of ourselves. First, go ahead and do your first case brief for class following the method I just discussed and come back when you're done.

Finished?

Great. Now quickly flip back through the case. You should see a lot more black-and-white, unmarked passages than you do highlighted sections. Do you? You must resist the urge to highlight too much, because when you're preparing your outline of the material, you'll be coming back through the case looking just for the major points—and you won't have the time to reread everything! Highlighting too much will make you your own worst enemy. Less is more!

Okay, so I promised you that my system had several benefits, but so far I've only told you that it saves time. What about the other benefits?

Flip back through the case again. If I ask you to stop on a dime and tell me the holding of that case, how long does it take you to find it? Go ahead—find it. Look for red.

Got it?

Great! How long did it take you? Five seconds? Congratulations. You now have an effective shield against the fear and paralysis caused by the Socratic method.

How?

An example:

You're sitting in Contracts at 9:00 a.m., and your first cup of coffee is just starting to raise the fog. Then suddenly, and completely without warning, it happens. "Ms. Reader [that's you]," the professor blurts out, "what happened in the case of *Hadley v. Baxendale*?"

You're overcome by fear and start to panic. You didn't even have your book open yet. You did your Contracts reading two days ago. A dead silence falls over the classroom as you furiously flip to the right page. There, staring you in the face at the beginning of the case, is a badly-drawn picture of a mill wheel with a line through it. Now it all starts to come back to you. In the next moment or two, you've found the green highlighted text, and you're ready to recite the facts.

"Uh . . . there was a mill, and the crankshaft broke. The mill operators sent out the crankshaft to have it fixed, but the delivery of the new shaft was delayed, resulting in lost profits to the mill operators because the mill couldn't function while they were waiting."

"Not exactly eloquently stated, but good enough, Ms. Reader," the professor chides. "And what did the court hold about those lost profits?"

She wants the holding. Just look for the red highlighting and read it.

"Umm . . . the lost profits weren't reasonably foreseeable as a consequence of the breach of contract and shouldn't have been taken into consideration in estimating the damages."

"Excellent, Ms. Reader. What was the disposition of the case?"

"The disposition of the case?"

"Yes, Ms. Reader. How did the court rule?"

Oh-oh. Didn't highlight that, did you? Don't ever forget to highlight the disposition of the case (affirmed, reversed, remanded, vacated, etc.). It's part of the holding, so it goes in red too, and it's almost always in the last three lines of the opinion before any dissents. For those of you playing along at home, the answer is that a new trial was ordered. It's right there in the last paragraph.

Highlighting in Technicolor goes a long way toward improving your performance in the Socratic sweepstakes because you'll never totally freeze up. It will take the fear away from speaking in class when you get called on. Best of all, it is much, much faster than writing your own briefs for each case, which will free up more of your time to study smarter by writing your own outlines for each of your courses, as we will discuss below.

Step Three: Supplement your notes and tab your statutes in class

A third benefit to briefing in Technicolor is that it permits you to concentrate more intently during lectures. Personally, I hated taking notes in classes—there were always gaps in the notes I took, and while I was distracted by the necessity of getting everything down, I would always miss important comments made during the lectures.

Not anymore.

By briefing this way, you'll already have marked 90 percent of the material the professor will bring out during the lecture. No need to frantically write down holdings, procedural postures, or important reasoning—you've already captured it.

Sure, the professor will point out a few things in class that you won't have marked in the text, and that's why you should bring a set of highlighters to class and simply mark those passages in the casebook in the appropriate colors as the professor hits them. You may also want to date the cases as the professor discusses them such that, at the end of the semester, you'll know what cases the professor discussed in class and on what days. That way, if you need to clarify a point, you'll know what day to consult in your friend's notes. I also liked to star the passages that the professor noted were particularly important.

The same goes for statutes, rules pamphlets, and advisory committee notes. Time is usually short in the law school exam room, so one of the biggest favors you can do yourself before you enter the exam room is to have your permitted materials as well organized as possible. There is no reason, in a Civil Procedure or Contracts exam, to waste precious time flipping through your Federal Rules pamphlet or the UCC aimlessly looking for a particular provision.

Go to your campus bookstore or nearby office supply store and purchase a few sets of stick-on flags that you can write on. Bring them to class with you every day, and every time a professor discusses a particular rule or code provision, highlight the relevant portion of the provision, write anything the professor says about it in the margin next to the provision, then flag it in the statutory compilation with a stick-on tab with the number of the provision and a brief description written on it. This way, come exam day, if the section is implicated on your exam, you'll not only know exactly where to find it, but you'll have an instant index of everything the professor said about the provision right where you need it.

Finally, most professors like to make a summary comment or two about a case or statute—often putting it into context with the other cases and statutes you've studied or placing it in a particular historical or political context. You'll want to capture those comments, but don't write them down on loose-leaf paper or in a notebook—put them right in the margins. That way, you'll have everything in one place! It will make outlining simpler, and once you are out of law school, after your notebooks and loose-leaf paper are long gone, those notes will still be right there at your fingertips.

A fourth advantage of this method of case briefing is how much it will increase your concentration. When you get into class, look around during the middle of the lecture. As the professor goes over a case, most of your classmates will have their heads down, typing furiously, trying to take a stenographic record of every word the professor says. They won't succeed, so they'll get frustrated and confused—distracted from the critical conveyance of information going on in class. They may even mishear things and record misinformation in their notes. Later, they'll spend countless hours trying to reconstruct and decipher these notes—if they even use them at all.

You, on the other hand, will be watching the professor—intent on the discussion and stopping only to highlight a few passages here and there and make a few marks in the margins as class progresses. You'll already have captured the critical material, so you'll be free to concentrate on what the professor is saying or eliciting from your classmates.

Learn the material by actively listening instead of trying to take a stenographic record of the class in your notes.

This is, of course, not the only way to succeed in law school, and it is not the only way to study. But this system worked really well for me and has worked well for many students that have followed it. It all but eliminates the fear of the Socratic method and frees up the time that your classmates will spend writing briefs for each case for you to spend working on the next section—which is the biggest advantage of all.

Step Four: Write your own outlines

This is unquestionably the most crucial step in the learning process and also the hardest step, because it requires the most discipline. Every day after class, for every class you had that day, you need to consolidate your knowledge into a concise but comprehensive outline summarizing that day's material. If you don't actively keep up with this step, then you will not derive the advantage that this system has over briefing cases.

> Every semester, my friends and I would say, "This semester we'll start outlining our notes right away, and that way we'll be done by reading period and we can just study." And every semester we would fail miserably and spend the last few weeks in utter hell living at the library.
>
> —Bess

Here's how to do it.

Go somewhere quiet where you can spread out your materials and plug in your laptop. Start just as you did last night—by typing in the names of the cases you read in chronological order. Be sure to include the name of the court and the date of the decision to aid understanding and avoid possible confusion. Now, taking each case one at a time, refer to your casebook and, after scanning for green highlighter, plug in one to four sentences of the most relevant facts. Anything more, and by the end of the semester you'll have produced a new casebook—so don't do that. Keep the facts short and simple—only the critical ones to the opinion. You may want to set off these facts in italics to make them more easily distinguishable.

Next, go back to the casebook, and after looking quickly for red, plug in the holding. You may want to set this off in bold to distinguish it from the facts, or skip a line between the facts and the holding. Force yourself to make the holding as succinct and clear as you can.

Next, go back to the casebook and see if the professor had anything interesting to say about the case historically, politically, or contextually. What, if anything, did you scribble down in the margins? Skip a line after the holding and plug it in.

Finally, go back to the commercial outline where you started last night and remind yourself of what it had to say about the case. What did you highlight? Did the outline help put the case in a framework by linking it to the cases that preceded and postdated it? Did the outline make any other remarks that your professor didn't? If so, add these notes from the commercial outline right after your professor's comments.

Do this for every case you covered, in every subject you had that day, during every day of the semester. It will probably take you about an hour, on average, to update your outline for each class. That is a heck of a lot less than it would take you to brief every case, and the advantage is that you are both actively engaging the material and incrementally building your blueprint of the course for the exam. If you brief every case, all you're left with is a pile of briefs, and then you'll *still* need to assimilate them into an outline. Study smart! Assuming that you have three classes a day, you'll be spending three hours every day developing your class outlines. This is absolutely crucial to your mastery of the material, however, and it is by far the most valuable time you'll spend studying. If you keep to this schedule daily (which requires a great deal of discipline), at the end of the semester you'll have a 60–120-page outline for each of your classes that will represent, in one neat, concise package, everything you need to worry about for the exam. And because of all the active learning you've been doing in creating these outlines, chances are you will already have a good understanding of the subject.

Learn from what your mentors are telling you here.

> If I had it to do over again, I would have kept reviewing material from earlier in the semester as the semester wore on. I kept up with my reading and always went to class, but nevertheless found that by December, I had forgotten virtually everything we learned in September.
>
> —Joel

When you get near the end of the semester, we'll address the final step to the plan, where we'll take your outlines and distill them into a series of case-chain "maps" or short bullet point outlines—the deadliest weapons in the armory for conquering exams. We'll get to those in chapter 13. For now, though, your job is to religiously develop your outlines for each class. Force yourself to do it every day as the end-of-semester benefits of your discipline will be enormous.

Determining your work schedule

It is vitally important to your success in law school that you develop an effective routine in the early days of the first semester and stick to it. In law school, time is your most precious commodity, and managing it wisely is critical to your success. A brief look at the schedule that awaits you makes it obvious why this is so.

The average law student will take four classes per semester and have three lectures a day. Assuming that each class lasts roughly one hour, that's three hours of in-class commitment every day. Pursuant to the strategy we just discussed, when you get out of class, you'll need to spend approximately one hour per subject consolidating last night's highlighting in your casebooks and commercial outlines, and anything you added to them from today's lectures, into your outlines. That's three more hours. Then there's tonight's reading. Assuming that you have three classes tomorrow, and an average reading load of twenty pages of cases per class—at a reading rate of ten pages per hour, that's another six hours. Three hours in class, three hours of outlining, and six hours of reading and briefing for tomorrow's classes equals twelve hours of work. Throw in an hour for lunch, an hour for dinner, a couple of hours for your afternoon workout, and you're looking at a sixteen-hour day.

Even if you spill some of your outlining hours over into your weekends, as you'll almost certainly have to do on occasion, it should be extremely obvious that you don't have much time to waste! Your daily schedule will look something like this—the schedule that I eventually settled on:

7–9 a.m.	breakfast/read for class three
9–10 a.m.	class one
10:30–11:30 a.m.	class two
11:30–12:30 p.m.	lunch
12:45–1:45 p.m.	class three
2–4 p.m.	workout/break
4–6 p.m.	outline classes one and two

6–7 p.m.	dinner
7–11 p.m.	read for classes one and two
spillover to weekend	five hours outlining for third class each day

You can move things around as needed, but the take-home message is the lack of free hours in each day. If you choose to sleep late in the morning, you'll have to either cut your workout down, stay up later to make up the hours, or push more of the outlining off until the weekend. You can't put it all off, though, because that's fifteen hours, and you need four hours on Sunday to read for Monday.

Find a schedule that works for you and stay dedicated! You're going to fall a bit behind here and there, but struggle every weekend to stay current. Every now and then you'll catch a break when a professor gives a shorter reading assignment or fails to get all the way through the material you prepared for that day, and you'll end up with bonus hours you can use to stay as close to caught up as you can. You must, at all costs, avoid the crush at the end of the semester. If you arrive in December nearly on schedule, you'll have a tremendous advantage over your classmates—and you may be able to avoid the crippling stress that many of them will succumb to as exams near . . . which means better grades for you. You have to get through all the material—and it's now or later. Do it now.

A word about study groups

Some people swear by them, others won't go near one. I never consistently participated in a study group because I found them frustrating. People often showed up late, and without their promised materials prepared. We wasted a lot of time gossiping about classmates, bantering about professors, and planning meeting times. When we did finally get down to work, the focus of our discussion had to be divided among everyone's questions—which meant that we spent considerably more time going over things I already knew than on things I needed clarified. Given the tight schedule I just illustrated for you, I found study groups to be more of a hindrance than a help, and if you stick to my system, you probably won't ever need one anyway.

"I have mixed feelings about study groups," John-Mark noted. "They can be very time-consuming, and talking to several people who are all confused about a case or issue is often worse than being mixed up by yourself. Study groups also have the tendency to descend into gabfests that accomplish nothing."

"I tried doing the study group thing for the first semester of law school, but it wasn't working," Shruti explained. "Instead, a good friend of mine and I would sit together while writing our own outlines and discuss topics if either of us needed clarity about something."

That said, many people like to bounce ideas around with others, and to have someone around to test their understanding of the material. If you're one of these people, you might try to find a study "partner," someone you can count on to do the reading, keep up with outlining, and discuss the law with you. Finding someone like this can also be helpful in forcing you to stay on schedule. I did this, and it worked out well. Someone was always there to discuss the material, but with no bureaucracy, fewer distractions, and no time wasted discussing things we both knew.

"My first-year study group was vital. I had the same group, three people in total, in all my classes. We met every Saturday morning to review outlines to make sure no one had missed anything and to go over difficult cases and rules of law. Sometimes my group helped me understand rules I could not figure out on my own or from class," Yvette said.

"I'm a big proponent of study groups too, especially for first-year courses," Lindsay agreed. "I was in a study group of about five people that worked out very well for all of us. Individual reading and studying are obviously important, but study groups will keep you on track and offer other perspectives and approaches. My study group set up weekly meetings throughout the semester to go over what we learned. As finals approached, we met every day. We set deadlines when outlining should be done and kept each other honest to the deadlines. Since we finished our outlines weeks before exams, we spent the last few weeks working on practice exams, which gave us plenty of time to work on problem areas. I strongly recommend joining a study group for 1L year—they don't have to be your best friends, and in fact, it's probably more productive if they aren't. Find people who are reliable and hard-working, and you should be successful."

"My study partner and I were best friends in law school. We would do outlines separately and then compare them to make certain we had covered all the territory. Then we would work through prior exams, compare answers, and augment our outlines as necessary. It sounds very systematic, and it was. We both did well in law school, and we both think that working together was the most important part of our success," Patrick noted.

It's your choice, but think it through carefully. Once you commit to being in a study group, you can't change your mind without angering the other members of the group and at least potentially damaging those friendships and your own reputation. This is an issue to consider in the first few days of law school, because once school starts and these groups begin to form, you'll need to decide right away whether you're interested in participating.

CHAPTER 10

The Unspoken Code of Law School Etiquette

So it is that the gods do not give
all men gifts of grace.
—HOMER

LAW SCHOOL IS A kind of intellectual boot camp. It is likely to be as strenuous and draining as anything you've ever experienced in your life. With this new experience comes a new set of social norms—a canon of ethics to govern your behavior and social interactions during the next three intensely competitive years. The problem is, in most schools, the canon is unspoken. You have to figure it out as you go along, which can be extremely stressful, deeply humiliating, and even permanently destructive depending on which mistakes you make, and when and how you make them.

Consider this chapter to be your "Federal Rules of Proper Law School Behavior," a codification of the dos and the don'ts collected from your *Law School Confidential* mentors. When these rules are followed, you end up with a school where class materials, knowledge, and understanding are generally freely shared among students, where in-class discussion is vigorous but respectful, and where the study of law is made just a little bit more humane. When the rules aren't followed, you end up with places (if you've done your research, you know the schools I'm referring to) where needed books disappear from the library shelves, every word spoken is contested and challenged, your classmates try to bring you down, and the educational experience seems to degenerate into cannibalism.

Regardless of what school you go to, becoming familiar with these rules will help to ease your assimilation into the confrontational, competition-laden law school culture, help to ensure that you remain in the good graces of your classmates, and, consequently, assure that your law school experience will be as civil and collegial as possible.

Things You Should Do

It is your duty to follow the honor code

At some point during the summer or during your law school orientation, you received a copy of your law school's honor code, or code of ethics. If you haven't already done so, read it from cover to cover and make certain that you understand the expectations it places on you.

Some of the things in there are probably pretty harsh, but there's a reason why most law schools make you a culpable party if you see someone hide a book, lie on a résumé, or cheat on an exam and fail to report that student to the dean. That reason is called civility. Law school is competitive enough. With a mandatory curve forcing a large percentage of the class, most of whom are used to getting A's all the time, to get B's and C's—and with those grades perhaps causing rejection by law journals, judges, and employers, and ultimately taking money out of people's pockets—most law school student bodies exist in an uneasy if not perilous equilibrium. All it takes is one well-known case of a person successfully cheating his way to success to throw off the balance and create an atmosphere of every man for himself.

On the other hand, if cheating is reported by students, is thoroughly investigated by the school disciplinary board, and severe punishments are meted out and announced to the student body, the equilibrium is strengthened. At a place where everyone has an equal chance to succeed, and where cheating carries a supreme price (normally suspension or expulsion and a permanent letter in your files sent to all future employers), an atmosphere of civility and cooperation can flourish.

Permit me an example. During my years at Penn, I was elected to represent my class on the law school's disciplinary committee. In my first semester on the committee, we heard the case of a student who had been turned in by a fellow classmate for using a commercial outline in an exam where the use of such outlines had been expressly forbidden by the professor. The student (who had gotten an A on the exam) admitted to using the outline, knew that it was cheating, and defended his choice by referring to the pressures he felt to do well. We gave the student an F in the course, expelled him for a year, and ordered a "letter of reckoning" placed in his file for all future employers to see. We then announced our decision to the student body.

The result was remarkable. After the decision was made public, more than two dozen students in my class approached me before first-semester exams to clarify which materials were permitted and which were forbidden. Everyone wanted to be sure he or she was in compliance with the code.

A level playing field was assured.

Unfortunately, which result ultimately prevails depends on the attitude of the student body as it is passed down from upperclassmen to 1Ls from year to year. The deans and professors aren't going to catch the cheaters in the majority of cases.

You are.

Or, you'll decide that you don't want to be a rat, turn the other cheek, and ignore it, and the cheating will go unpunished to the detriment of everyone, including you, and the atmosphere of the school as a whole.

At some point during orientation, the dean will probably make some high-minded speech about how you must keep people who are willing to cheat in law school out of the profession by reporting them. He'll say that if they're going to cheat here, they'll cheat to win in practice too and bring disgrace upon the profession. He'll probably also talk about reporting cheating to preserve the law school atmosphere of civility and cooperation—a point that I've just addressed and I think is extremely valid. But for those of you who still aren't convinced and are out there shaking your heads saying, "I'm not going to rat out a friend," I'll appeal to your basic, utilitarian instinct. Do you want to let that person next to you get away with using notes in a closed-book exam and push you down the curve? Positions on the law review are routinely decided by fractions of grade points. Whether you make the law review substantially affects your chances of getting a judicial clerkship, and whether you get a judicial clerkship significantly affects your employment opportunities. One grade can matter. The cheater knows that, or he wouldn't be taking the risk.

Don't let him get away with it. If he does, he'll enter practice and likely be the lawyer on the other side of your case who hides or destroys documents and lies to you and the court. How will you feel then?

A final word on the subject. Make sure you understand what obligations the honor code puts on you. If you're unclear about what you're allowed to bring into an exam, ask each of your professors to clarify the rules. Make sure you know what constitutes plagiarism in law school, and whether your professors intend the rules of plagiarism to apply during your written exams. This is particularly relevant in long take-home exams. Be sure you understand the rules of proper citation and attribution when writing papers and journal articles. You will be expected to know what the rules are, and you may pay a high price for your ignorance.

Last, remember that no situation that you find yourself in is so desperate that you have no alternative to cheating. If you ever find yourself (and most of us have) feeling so overwhelmed and outgunned that you start rationalizing about cutting corners—stop. Take a night off. Go see the dean. Extensions can be given. Exams can be postponed. Maybe all you need is the dean's reassurance that everyone feels the way you do. Just don't cheat and throw away all that you've worked so hard for. The pressure is real, but it's passing. The consequences of cheating and getting caught, however, will in all likelihood be permanent.

Share your class notes, hornbooks, and outlines with anyone who needs them

You don't have to put posters up advertising that you have the best Civil Procedure outline known to man and that you'll gladly make copies for anyone who asks, but if someone in your class needs a hand, be willing to provide it. The operative rule here is "what goes around, comes around," and building up some "favor equity" in your classmates is advisable. You never know when you'll miss some classes and need notes or fall far behind and need to borrow an outline to catch up. Resisting the urge to be cutthroat will earn you a solid reputation among your classmates, win you some friends, and make your law school experience much more enjoyable. Take the time to notice when the person sitting next to you is missing. If she is, and there's a handout or revised syllabus distributed in class that day, pick up an extra copy for her, slide it into your notebook, and give it to her in the next lecture. Do your part to make the law school atmosphere more cooperative.

> The reality is that law school attracts competitive people, and the way the system is set up really encourages people to be competitive. My father, who was a partner at one of the biggest law firms in New York, used to say, "Hierarchies don't select for nice." That may be true, but my feeling is, life is short, and the

world is a much more pleasant place when people are nice to one another. Be decent to people. Don't belittle others to make yourself feel better, and don't refuse to help someone because you think you'll do better if they do poorly.

—Carolyn

I agree with Carolyn. Sharing class materials never cost me a grade in law school. Try taking the collegial approach. I think you'll agree that the benefits far outweigh the negligible risks to your GPA.

Phrase in-class comments as questions, not statements

Assume, for the sake of example, that the topic of the day in Torts is proximate cause, and your professor has just given you the famous hypo about the guy in San Francisco who accidentally spills a drum of gasoline down a hill. The gas flows down the hill past a service station, where a spark from a mechanic's torch ignites a raging fire that destroys the service station. Assume that after a confusing Socratic exchange, it is established that the gas spill was the proximate cause of the fire, and that the guy on the hill is found negligent and responsible for the damage to the service station because the potential damage to the service station was foreseeable (a requirement of proximate cause). Now assume that you have no idea what the professor is talking about because you can't understand how a fire at a service station that far away could possibly have been foreseeable to our hero on the hill (trust me, you wouldn't be alone in your confusion on this point), so you decide to try to clear up the point. You raise your hand, and the professor recognizes you to speak. Observe the following subtle, but significant difference in phraseology, and the different effect it will have on the professor and your classmates.

The wrong way to make a point

"Well, I don't think it's foreseeable to the guy on the hill that his gas spill would cause a fire that far away, especially since it was the spark from the mechanic's torch that ignited the fire."

You've raised a good point, and no doubt it's one that a lot of people in the class were probably pondering. But a few people in the class are probably also now mumbling under their breath about you. You know why? Because they don't care what you think, they just want to know what the law is! If you make enough of these "I think" or "I don't think" comments, people will start resenting you for taking up their class time with your opinions. People will start rolling their eyes at you when you raise your hand, whispering to each other as you speak, and not listening to the comments you make, because they'll assume that you're just expressing more of your opinions again.

I know your intentions were good. You were just trying to clarify the point, right? Well, how about doing it this way instead?

A better way to make the same point

"Professor, I don't understand this. I'm confused as to how it's foreseeable to the guy on the hill that his gas spill would cause a fire that far away, especially since the spark from the mechanic's torch ignited the fire. Can you explain that?"

Now your classmates are nodding in consensus with your question instead of muttering under their breath because you expressed your opinion. They're paying attention and waiting for the professor to clarify his point in response to your query. They may even come up to you after class, reassure you that they had the same confusion, and thank you for raising the issue. Over time, this subtle nuance makes a big difference in the way you are perceived. Try to limit your use of the word *I* when speaking in class.

Understand that when you express confusion and ask the professor a direct question, she's more likely to break the Socratic dialogue and respond with a direct answer rather than another confusing hypo. People like direct answers in law school, and they'll appreciate your taking class time to ask the question and elicit a clearer answer. Your opinion, though, they can do without.

Remember that.

"The most respected students in law school were the ones who showed respect for others," Yvette recalled. "They had humility, weren't afraid to admit their confusion, and understood that they were not in law school to show everyone else up. They never belittled others for being lost or asking a so-called stupid question . . . and they had the ability to laugh at themselves."

"The most respected students were the strong, silent types," Lindsay recalled. "The best students tended to be the ones who worked hard, were on point when they were called on, but otherwise shut up."

When you're speaking, speak up, and when you're not, shut up!

Even if you're not the type to speak out in class, at some point you too will be a winner in the Socratic sweepstakes. Like it or not (and most don't), when your day comes, the rest of the class has to be able to hear you to learn from the responses you give the professor. The soft talker is not welcome in law school. Your classmates are going to have a tough enough time deciphering your comments as it is. Don't make them struggle to hear what you're saying. Speak up!

When you don't have the floor in the lecture, close your mouth and open your ears. Talking to your friend next to you about how much you disagree with so-and-so's political views, how attractive so-and-so is, what exactly the professor just said, or what you're doing for the weekend is rude. So is texting your friend or surfing the Internet. It's rude to the professor (and he might just embarrass you to make that point), rude to your classmates around you who are trying to listen to and take notes on the in-class exchanges, and on top of that—it's against your own interests. While you're busy prattling away, you're missing what's going on in class, and you can't afford to do that.

When referring to cases or statutes, provide page or section numbers

This is an often unspoken but major pet peeve of many students. When you refer to cases or statutes while making comments in class, either in response to a professor's question, or in asking one of your own, always provide page numbers and paragraph or section references so that everyone else can follow along with your comments. You'll all be teaching each other through your comments and questions. Offering page and section references communicates a spirit of collegiality to your classmates and fosters a more cooperative atmosphere.

Rein in your electronics

Most law students now take notes in class on a laptop computer. Not all laptops are made alike, however, and many of us like to customize our laptops with various downloaded apps, some of which make sounds. Random buzzes, beeps, quacks, or whatever other sounds your laptop makes can be extremely distracting to your classmates. If you're going to take your laptop into lecture, disable your sounds ahead of time, and if your lecture hall isn't modern enough to have a plug at every seat, make sure you have a fully charged battery so you don't have to scuffle around to charge it or change it out in the middle of the lecture. It is also considered proper etiquette to check with the people assigned to the seats around you to determine whether your typing bothers them. Some people just can't concentrate with all that clicking going on. If they object, see the professor and ask to have your seat moved. You're the one making the noise, so it's your problem, not theirs.

Don't surf the Net in class. It is distracting to your neighbors, disrespectful to your professors, and, unless your professor is truly horrible, detrimental to your understanding of the subject matter. Remember that professors usually tip their hands and hint at likely exam questions during lectures. If you are playing online poker instead of listening to what your professor is saying, you can easily miss these important hints.

One last point on electronics. For everyone's sake, silence your cell phone when you're in a lecture and resist the urge to text people during class, even if you can do so silently. There is no quicker way to draw the ire of the professor and your classmates than to have your cell phone chirping at you during class. No law student is so indispensable that he cannot get through class out of cell phone contact. Get over yourself and leave the phone in your bag, on vibrate, for the duration of the lecture.

Maintain a sense of humor

Law school can be a deadly serious place, and the best way to cut through that atmosphere is to slip in a well-placed witticism or a little dose of self-deprecating humor during Socratic questioning. You don't want to force it in there heavy-handedly, but if the professor gives you the opportunity, go ahead and let it fly. Remember, you're paying for the flogging you take every day. The least you can do is attempt to enjoy it.

Things You Shouldn't Do

Resist the urge to make unsolicited, tangential, politically charged, or absolutist comments during lectures

Sometimes, in trying to do the "right thing" in law school, you feel as if you're walking through an unmarked minefield. Law is essentially about policy decisions, and policy decisions beg to be argued about. So why, then, am I counseling you to try to hold your tongue?

Every section in every law school has at least one "talker" or "gunner," a person who egregiously violates this rule. Within a week or two, everyone in your section will have identified this person. It's a blowhard who speaks before he thinks his points through carefully. It's the knee-jerk liberal or the gun-toting conservative whose position on a point of law is predictable before it's uttered. The people who feel that no lecture—no topic of discussion—is complete until they've offered their opinion.

People don't like that. Not in law school, and not in life.

Don't be "that guy."

It can start innocently enough, early in the semester. The class is discussing something that you know something about. You raise your hand and the professor acknowledges you. You speak strongly and make some good points. It feels good. People seem to be listening to you. Your confidence increases, and as the days go by, you find that you have a lot of things to say. Soon, however, your classmates begin to wonder why you think that your opinion is important enough to express three or four times per class, every class, every week. Shortly after that, they'll stop listening to you. If it gets bad enough, you may even hear audible groans the moment you put your hand in the air.

"I really disliked it when the same people spoke in class over and over," Carolyn recalls. "There were some people who seemed to take every opportunity they could to express their political views or general ideas about the world. It really made me angry when people took up class time to express these views when they had nothing to do with illuminating the doctrine we were all trying to learn."

Elizabeth agrees. "Those who were to be respected the most were those who spoke the least. There is at least one person in every section who could not let a class go by without hearing themselves talk. You will identify him or her quickly as the person who raises his or her hand every time a professor asks a question, or even when the professor doesn't ask a question, and often gives a long-winded, politically charged response that is often completely off base. In one of my classes, our frustration about this was validated one day when this person raised his hand, as always, and the professor said, 'Anyone? Anyone? Anyone else?' "

So what? you say. You're an individualist, and you don't care what other people think? Fine. Just don't go asking to join your classmates' study groups, or to borrow their notes or outlines, or hope to get a good word from them someday if you end up trying to move to a firm they work at, or expect to get any client referrals from them in practice.

The legal world is smaller than you think, and a negative reputation most definitely can and will follow you around.

"Always ask yourself, before you speak, whether your comments are likely to illuminate the doctrine. While it might be fun for you to talk about your foray into the Greek jail or the time you were sexually harassed, it is not likely to help anyone else in the class understand the law," Patrick advises.

This "rule" has two corollaries. First, don't ever try to "show up" a classmate during a lecture. If a classmate is struggling with the answer to a question from the professor, and the professor asks if anyone else knows the answer, don't be the guy who shoots his hand up to prove how smart he is. No one likes a know-it-all, especially when it comes at the expense of a classmate. If you're going to challenge what a classmate is saying in lecture, be civil and polite. Don't lead with an opening like "That's ridiculous!" or "That's completely baseless." Instead, lead with a question like "But isn't it true that . . ." or "But I thought that . . ." Remember that you're trying to trigger a worthwhile conversation about the issue, not trying to make it personal.

Second, if you're having a problem understanding a concept during a lecture, it is perfectly acceptable to raise your hand once and ask for a clarification. Chances are, if you're confused, others are too, and they'll appreciate your efforts to get the issue resolved. If the professor stops to explain the issue, and you still don't understand, however, don't belabor the point in lecture. Wait until after class, then follow up with the professor, either at the podium or during his office hours. The purpose of the lecture is not to resolve your own difficulties with the material, and people will start to resent it if you try to turn the lecture into your personal tutorial.

Don't boast about your study habits

Another readily identifiable "annoying person" in law school is the one who leans over before lecture three weeks into class and tells you that she was up until 4:00 a.m. working on her Contracts outline, which is already two hundred pages long. Similarly, you don't need to tell anyone that you're one hundred pages ahead in your Civ Pro reading, that you put in one hundred hours on your Legal Writing appellate brief, or that you had tea and a fantastic philosophical discussion about *mens rea* with your Criminal Law professor yesterday afternoon. People just don't want to hear it. If you loved the topic you were working on enough to stay up all night with it, good for you.

Just don't tell anyone else.

"People like that used to really make me roll my eyes," Elizabeth recalled. "I had a classmate who took great delight in trying to unnerve her fellow students before exams by saying things like 'Did you study the latest revisions to the Uniform Commercial Code? . . . No? Really?' Gasp for breath. 'Oh, well, I guess you still might pass.' "

"The 'gunners' [students who were blatantly competitive with one another] were definitely the least respected people in the class. Competitiveness, when allowed to get out of hand, begins to affect social skills that are critical to practicing law successfully," Megan warned. "You should never talk about all the things you have to complete in order to demonstrate to others how busy you are and how your schedule is that much more taxing than that of anyone else in the school, as if he or she with the most miserable existence is somehow the winner? No one wants to hear how busy you are. We're all busy, and we all have a lot to do."

Safeguard your reputation

Yeah, it's a euphemism, and you probably know what I'm getting at here, but in case you're really a wonk, let me spell it out for you. Your social life at law school will be . . . well, put it this way: Remember high school? Bingo. Except you don't have to sneak around to drink, you have your own place, you don't have a curfew, and sex probably isn't as much of a mystery anymore.

On the other hand, you're back in an environment with two hundred to three hundred people who all take the same classes and are forced to spend almost every waking hour together. You'll see these people every day, like it or not. You have a locker again. People will be cliquey and catty just as they were in high school. And even though sex probably isn't a big deal anymore, people in law school will still whisper and gossip as if it were.

Before you enter law school with the intent to make up for the opportunities lost when you were a dork in high school, remember this: It's a small environment, with little privacy. With the long, grueling hours of tedious work and frequent feelings of hopelessness, people get worn down and seek comfort in different ways. Among people with nothing but law to discuss otherwise, gossip spreads quickly. A couple of early mistakes can earn you a reputation for the duration, and a damaged social reputation can easily carry over into the academic environment, and into your future as a lawyer.

The moral here? Exercise discretion, and treat people with respect.

> In law school and in your legal career, your reputation is your most valuable asset. Once you've lost it, it's really, really hard to earn it back, and you may never be able to outrun it either. You never know where the road ahead of you will lead to, and the legal community is smaller than you think. The people you mistreat today might be in the position to remember those acts one day.
>
> —A mentor

Oh, in case it needs saying, it's never a good idea to get romantically entangled with a professor. You never seem to hear any story with that premise ending happily.

Adhere to your school's recruiting guidelines

The National Association for Law Placement (NALP) disseminates, through your placement office, a list of guidelines for students at member law schools to follow during recruiting season. These guidelines regulate how many employment offers a student can keep open after certain dates in the recruiting season and are meant to free up job opportunities for other law students. In addition to the NALP guidelines, your school may have its own set of rules about recruiting, such as whether you are allowed to put your class rank and/or grade point average on your résumé.

You must inquire about these rules and guidelines in advance, and be sure that you adhere to them throughout recruiting. If your school does not compute class rank and GPA and forbids you from computing your own GPA and putting it on your résumé, don't even think about doing it. Schools that do this are typically trying to prevent employers from comparing their students on the basis of numbers alone. You ought to appreciate this effort. Once one overly competitive student computes a GPA and includes it on a résumé at a school that bans this practice, employers will start asking all students at that school about their GPA, and why theirs isn't on their résumé. If you are discovered doing this, you will face stiff penalties from your school, and even stiffer ones from your classmates.

The same advice applies to keeping too many employment offers open after stated deadlines. The most recently enacted NALP guidelines (www.nalp.org) allow you twenty-eight days to respond to an offer from a firm you haven't previously worked for, and to keep five offers open at any time. Obviously, no one can keep track of every law student's open offers, so you are largely on your honor here, but that is true with a lot of things about legal practice. Become familiar with the most current NALP guidelines by consulting the NALP web site or checking with your placement office and respect them. There should really almost never be a reason why you can't whittle your choices down to five firms at any one time. Remember that somewhere out there, another law student is waiting to hear from the firms you turn down.

Imagine that student is you.

Avoid all postmortem discussions about exams

Law exams are anxiety-inducing. More often than not, they test the gray areas of the law or inquire about the "next link in the chain" of a particular doctrine and force you to apply the law you learned during the semester to reason out an outcome to the exam questions. In most cases, there isn't going to be one right answer to a law exam question.

When the exam is over, there will be winners and losers. Some people will feel great about their exam; others will feel like hurling themselves off the nearest bridge. The funny thing is, there is often no correlation between how you feel about an exam when it's over and the grade you ultimately receive. Too many variables are involved to accurately predict your grade. If you feel like a winner, that's great. Work off your euphoria on your afternoon run, or in the nearest bar. If you feel as if you've been beaten up, take solace that, unless you left your exam book blank, your grade is still largely unpredictable.

Either way, you may feel an overwhelming urge to "check" or discuss your answers to the exam with your classmates in the exam room or hallway immediately afterward. Resist every temptation to do this. It is a major no-no of law school etiquette.

Why?

Because nothing good ever comes of it. No matter whom you talk to, it is a virtual certainty that either you or the other person (or both of you) will end up feeling bad. Because there is typically no right answer to a law exam question, people can arrive at acceptable, full-credit answers in different ways. How are you going to feel when your classmate reveals the brilliant public-policy argument she threw in, or the directly on-point advisory committee note she found in the back of the Federal Rules of Civil Procedure that enabled her, in two paragraphs, to answer the question that took you ten pages to reason out? And how is she going to feel when you start talking about an issue raised by the question that she didn't even notice?

See what I mean? Nothing good ever comes out of such discussion. When an exam is over, it's over. You can do nothing about it, so why dwell on it? All you're going to discover is that your classmates had things in their answers that you didn't include, and it's going to upset you. They're going to discover that you had things in your answer that they didn't include, and it's going to upset them. Soon, you all end up feeling that your performance could have been better, then people start fretting about how much damage their omissions will do to their grade in the course.

Furthermore, some people just hate discussing exams after they're over, and they'll get upset with you for talking about exams in their presence. Don't ever start a discussion of exam answers before you've identified whether you're talking to one of these people. If you absolutely must share your thoughts about an exam, do it only with an equally willing group of people away from the exam room.

Never discuss grades

Finally, we come to the number one rule of law school etiquette, which I've saved for last for emphasis. Never, never, *ever* discuss your grades in public. Not even if people ask you about them.

Why?

Again, because nothing good can come of it. If you have better grades than the person asking, that person is going to be made to feel bad. If she has better grades than you do, you might be made to feel bad. Of course, all of this depends on whether you're both telling the truth, which is no small consideration where grades are concerned.

Gary Clinton, the University of Pennsylvania Law School associate dean for student affairs, who wrote the foreword to this book, once told me, "There are a lot more students walking around here with straight A's than there are students walking around here with straight A's."

Don't play this game. The correct and only answer when someone asks about your grades is "I don't discuss grades."

Period.

CHAPTER 11

The T-Minus-One-Month Checkpoint: How to Arrive Ahead of the Competition

In fair weather, prepare for foul.
—FULLER

THE MOST IMPORTANT THING that you can do in law school on a day-to-day basis is to maintain your focus. With thousands of pages of reading to complete during a semester, and four months to get through before you're held accountable for any of it, it's easy to spin your wheels. At one point or another, you'll find yourself overreading and overanalyzing individual cases, spending more time on the subjects you like at the expense of the ones you don't like, and excusing frequent lapses in your studies by deluding yourself with the thought that you have plenty of time to catch up. In law school, there's no such thing as plenty of time. Let this chapter be your wake-up call—the last checkpoint separating you from disappointment on exam day.

In most schools, November 1 is the target date—putting you about five weeks away from your first set of exams in December. If you attend a school that schedules exams after winter break or only at the end of the year, this chapter is no less applicable to you. You can use this chapter now as a measure of how well you've maintained your focus and kept up-to-date during the first two months of the semester, then come back to it again when you're five weeks away from your first set of exams.

So how are you doing? Starting to feel the pressure mounting? Have you noticed that the library is getting more and more crowded? Have you fallen behind? Are you feeling overwhelmed?

Don't worry. All of those feelings are par for the course during your first year of law school. Everyone is feeling the same way, even though they're not admitting it openly. Let's see where you are, though, so we can evaluate what you need to do during the next five weeks to prepare you for those exams!

Remember, your goal is to arrive in your last week of classes with up-to-the-minute class outlines. If you're like most students (I'd say about 98 percent), you're not up-to-date today. You've tried your best, but the pace we set for you in chapter 9 was tough. Some days your reading took longer than expected . . . days after you broke up with your significant other when you were too distracted to stay focused on your work . . . and some days you were just too tired and fed up to outline. That's okay. The key now is to start fresh from here. You have a month until exams, and you know what your goal is. You must get those outlines finished, and it's time to decide how you're going to get there from here. Find the heading below that is most appropriate for you and follow its directions.

I've missed a couple of classes, a couple of reading assignments, and I'm two weeks or less behind in outlining for each class

Good news! Compared to the rest of your classmates, you're in pretty good shape! Most of your classmates are further behind than this, and many of them aren't ever going to catch up. Don't get complacent, though.

The first thing you need to do—this weekend—is get those missing class notes from a friend and make up your reading assignments. Stay in Friday night and Saturday until you get that done. As for your outlining, it's time to do some simple math. Figure out exactly how many classes behind you are on each outline, and budgeting one hour per class, figure out how much time it's going to take you to make it up. You have four weekends left with Friday nights and Saturdays unscheduled. Plan your makeup time on these days, and force yourself to stay disciplined so you don't slide farther behind. You're almost there! Come finals, you're going to be in a relatively painless position with plenty of time to take sample exams, taper your studying, and rest up properly to be in optimal condition when your exams arrive. You may even get Thanksgiving weekend off if you really focus! Have that as your target, and if you're caught up by Thanksgiving, take the four days off to relax knowing that you're in perfect position as you approach your endgame strategy.

I've fallen way behind in my outlining—what do I do?

Listen closely. All the reading and color-coded briefing that you've been doing isn't going to do a thing for you if you don't actively engage in the process of structuring it. Law school isn't like college—just doing the reading isn't going to be enough. There's too much of it, and the distinctions tested are too subtle to rely on the memory of what you read twelve hundred pages ago to carry you through. It's time to take some fairly drastic measures to ensure that you arrive on December 1 with four complete outlines of your own creation. Creating your own outlines is the best way to struggle through the material and get it organized in a way that you can understand. If circumstances warrant it (and they're beginning to in your position), you might have to cut back on everything else that you're doing to ensure that you get the outlines done—and that includes actually reading all the cases.

Yes, you read that correctly.

I'm not endorsing your cutting corners regularly, and I'm not suggesting that you'll learn as much from the experience (you won't), but if it comes down to a choice of skipping reading or not finishing your outlines, my recommendation is to finish your outlines, regardless of what your professors or anyone else may tell you. You must have a sense of the big picture—how all the law fits together—at the end of the semester, or you're just not going to perform the way you want to on your exams. It is that simple. Here's how to extricate yourself from the hole you've put yourself into to still be in decent shape come exam time.

> You have to realize that the key to being successful is not necessarily being prepared for class, but rather focusing on your outlines and on learning the black-letter law in preparation for your exams. Don't worry about being prepared for class.
>
> —Pat

The first thing you need to do is to figure out exactly how far behind you are. Remember, plan for one hour of outlining per class for each day behind you are in that class. How many hours will it take you to catch up? If you're three weeks behind in your outlining for each class—that's four classes times three days a week for each class times three weeks times one hour per class to outline, or thirty-six hours total. At nine hours a day of outlining on top of the rest of your workload, that backlog will consume the final four Saturdays of your semester—including the one during Thanksgiving break.

I think you can see that if you're any farther behind than this, something's going to have to give for you to stay on schedule. If you are, pick a class to jettison. Make it one of the classes for which you have a good commercial outline that can pull you through on its own. If I were in your position (and I was), I'd probably pick Torts and rely on Gilbert's to carry me through the rest of the semester. Stop reading for that course and use the extra two hours you gain three times a week during the month of November (two hours times three times a week times four weeks, or twenty-four hours) to catch up on your outlining. Those hours will buy you two weeks of outlining in each of your four classes. Add to that the hours from the Saturdays you have left (four Saturdays times nine hours a day, or thirty-six hours), and you have three more weeks of outlining for each of your four classes. That's five weeks of outlining—nearly half the semester—for each class. If you're farther behind than that, you really need to be reading the next section.

Panic button

I'm sure you have your reasons for being in this position, but you need to realize the dire nature of your circumstances. This far behind in your preparation, you're in considerable danger of registering a potentially irreparable semester, unless you take some affirmative steps, now, to right your course.

First, you need to figure out whether whatever has been distracting you is still a distraction. If you've been troubled by family problems, illness, financial issues, or other personal matters that continue to plague you, it's probably time to schedule an appointment with your dean of student affairs. He may offer to postpone your exams or suggest that you take a voluntary leave of absence, straighten out your problems, and start fresh in the spring term. Yeah, you might have to graduate a semester later than your classmates, but that's a hell of a lot better than taking four horrendous grades on your first-semester exams and paying the price in lost opportunities for the rest of your legal career. Too much rides on your first-year grades. Don't gamble with them.

If your distractions have been resolved and you don't want to talk to the dean about getting a postponement (or if he denies your request), you need to decide today what method of damage control to adopt to try to salvage the semester. It's too late for you to start writing your own outlines, so you're going to have to proceed on faith. The following method should be enough to earn you some form of B in your classes, and while B's aren't exactly going to wow employers, earn you a seat on the law review, or qualify you for a judicial clerkship, they will keep you in the middle of the pack and prevent your law school career from falling into an irreparable shambles. Let me hasten to add that this method is for emergency use only. I do not endorse its use for routine study.

Read Legalines to catch up, and find four good student outlines for your courses

Something has to go, and if you're trying to save your grades this semester, it has to be your daily reading assignments. There is a set of commercial outlines called Legalines, which are essentially Cliff's Notes for law casebooks. They boil down the long cases into simple, one- or two-page briefs that you can easily skim in a couple of minutes. Get the edition of Legalines specific to each of your textbooks and read the cases you've missed. At least you'll get the most important facts, the holding, and some basic reasoning from this.

Next, try to find someone in your class who sympathizes enough with your predicament to be willing to give you copies of the four outlines he or she has prepared for the classes. If your reasons are compelling enough, someone might be compassionate enough to bail you out. In that case, simply take over, starting today, where those outlines leave off and force yourself to stay current for the rest of the semester.

More likely, though, you'll have to settle for copies of last year's (or older) outlines circulating among the 1Ls in your class. Upperclassmen are usually willing to allow you to photocopy their old outlines, so find a 2L you know and ask. Be sure that the person you ask had the same professor and used the same casebook that you're using.

Assuming that you do find appropriate outlines, spend several days reading each one carefully. Note the different sections each is broken up into and study the sections separately, examining the holdings of the individual cases and how they "flow" together to create the governing law in a particular area. If it helps you to focus, highlight the relevant parts of the outlines in the appropriate colors as if you were reading the cases directly.

This method will not provide you with the same depth of knowledge and understanding of the material, but this late in the game, you don't really have time for depth. What you're looking for is a basic knowledge of how the material fits together so you'll be able to apply the law you've learned to a new set of facts with a slight distinguishing twist or wrinkle. On your exams, the professor will be evaluating how you analyze those facts based on the law and underlying social policy you learned during the semester. Shoot for the basics.

"Focus on learning the material in an outline—not on catching up with your reading," John-Mark counseled. "Commercial materials can be very helpful; they present the doctrine in a clear, straightforward way. Use the outlines to get the big picture."

You're not likely to get many A's using this method—you simply won't have enough knowledge of the policy and reasoning underlying and driving the holdings—but you will probably be able to avert disaster. Given your situation, expect to get B's, and feel fortunate to have escaped your predicament without irreparable damage.

"If you had not gotten behind, you could spend time on subtle nuances, but when you are behind, you don't have time for such luxuries. Weed out the minor rules of law and focus on the big-ticket items," Yvette smartly advises.

Regardless of your situation, you now know what you must do during the next month to get ready for exams. Remember, the goal is to arrive on December 1 (or a week prior to the end of the semester if your school uses a different exam schedule) with four complete outlines of your own creation—one for each of your classes. In chapter 13, we'll discuss the fifth and final step of outlining "my way"—how to turn your outlines into concise, one-page visual "maps" of the law that will help you to spot issues, red herrings, and take you step-by-step through your first-semester exams in the most painless way possible. To be ready to map, however, your outlines must be finished—so get to it!

What Else Do I Have to Do Between Now and Exams?

Acquire old exams

Spend the dead time between classes this week in the law library making photocopies of at least three old exams, and model answers in each of your subjects. Do the best you can to find the actual exams that your professor has administered in the past, as every professor has a different exam-writing style, and different preferred areas of focus. If your professor is a visiting professor or new to your school, use your ingenuity, the Internet, and/or the telephone to find copies of the exams she administered at her prior law school. If you do this, you might even catch an unsuspecting professor administering an identical exam in her new law school. This has happened in the past, and the advantage of having worked through the exam and reviewed the model answer in advance is immense.

Resist the urge to work any of the exams, or even to read any of the model answers, until you've finished outlining. Much about your success in law school turns on confidence, and you don't want to undermine your confidence by prematurely addressing an old exam before you've learned all the material it covers. You'll only scare yourself. Wait until chapter 13. You've budgeted adequate time to practice sample exams there.

Clarify exam rules with each of your professors

No later than the first week in November (or a month before your exams), talk to each of your professors before class and ask them to address their exam restrictions with specificity. Will it be an in-class exam or a take-home? How many hours will you have to complete it? Will the format be multiple-choice, short answer, essay, or some combination? Will the individual sections be timed, or will you be responsible for your own pacing? And most important, what materials will you be allowed to bring with you into the exam?

Force your professor to be extremely specific in this area—will commercial outlines be permitted in the exam? What about hornbooks or outlines written by other students? Can you bring in a copy of the UCC, the Federal Rules of Civil Procedure, the Federal Rules of Criminal Procedure, or the Model Penal Code? Can those materials be tabbed and annotated by you? Is it okay if you've scribbled notes in the margins?

Forcing your professor to specify exactly what is allowed and what isn't accomplishes several things. First, it prevents your professor from surprising you at the end of the semester by telling you that your exam is closed book. Second, it alerts you to the materials you'll be allowed to bring into the exam room so that you can prepare them adequately (see chapter 13). Third, it puts everyone in the class on a level playing field and prevents the confusing and patently unfair scenario on exam day in which some students bring no supporting materials into the exam, while others bring an entire library of resources. Finally, it establishes, beyond doubt, the ground rules for purposes of the honor code. If the professor specifically says "no commercial outlines," and in the middle of the exam you notice that the guy next to you is using an outline composed of photocopied pages from a commercial outline, he's clearly and unquestionably cheating—and you have an ethical obligation to report him to the administration. As I've said before, if the ethical obligation doesn't grab you (though it should), maybe the utilitarian argument will. With the aid of that commercial outline, that guy is likely to kick your butt on the exam, force you down the curve, and cost you many hard-earned opportunities that you've worked for legitimately.

Send query letters to potential employers

Yes, now.

Recruiting season for 1Ls begins on November 1, and many firmsr make hiring decisions in December immediately after they've completed their 2L recruiting season and have a better sense of what their needs are. If you wait until winter break to get your letters out, the pool of scarce opportunities for 1Ls with law firms may be significantly reduced.

Thus, on the first weekend in November, you need to compile a mail merge and get your query letters out. Remember that résumé you worked up during the summer? It's in your filing system. Pull it out, and you are ready for the next chapter.

Chapter 12

Making Your Summer Plans: How to Win the 1L Recruiting Lottery

The die is cast!
—Suetonius

Around November 1, just at the time when you are becoming increasingly unable to take on more responsibility, you'll receive your first package of introductory materials from your school's career planning and placement office. Around the same time, placement officers and upper-level students may also start conducting informational question-and-answer sessions about first-year legal employment, often including one or more hiring partners from local law firms as panelists. All of a sudden, you have another monkey on your back. You'll start hearing about "summer associateships" with law firms, "internships" with judges, and "externships" with public-service organizations. How do you make sense of it all?

At this stage of my law school career, I seriously considered spending my 1L summer at my old job as a counselor at an overnight camp in the New Hampshire mountains. I figured that the rest and balance the experience had always provided would be ideal after the rigors of the first year. Several practicing lawyers I consulted heartily supported the idea and lamented that they hadn't been clever enough to come up with such a plan themselves. In the end, however, I got a summer associateship at a law firm and took it—and it proved to be the wiser choice.

Why?

When you enter the real recruiting market as a 2L, the screening interviewers and hiring committees you'll be dealing with are going to carefully scrutinize what you did with your first-year summer. They're going to ask you questions about it, and they're expecting to see something law-related. While you may occasionally find a New Age interviewer who will be supportive of your choice to spend your first-year summer hiking the Appalachian Trail or working with kids, most will immediately suspect that you couldn't get a job or didn't have enough interest in the law to pursue one. Yes, it's unfair. Yes, it may be completely untrue. But that's what many of them will think, and it will make it harder for you to get the job you want in the 2L market if you haven't had some form of real-world legal experience during your first-year summer. That's just the reality of it, so you best be aware of it now.

Because most schools subscribe to the general guideline prohibiting 1Ls from using campus recruiting services until November 1 (ostensibly because they want you to "settle in" at law school and worry about figuring out how to learn the law for a couple of months before you spend the next two and a half years trying to get a job), after that the process will kick into high gear. Fortunately for you, most of your classmates will be too overwhelmed with how far behind they are in their studies to make any efforts to secure 1L employment until after the end of first-semester exams. This presents you with an opportunity, if you're prepared to take advantage of it.

First, a reality check. Unless you go to Yale or Harvard, securing a paying position in a law firm after one year of law school is extremcly difficult. Many firms don't find it economically feasible to pay your exorbitant salary only to have you run off somewhere else during your second summer and then sign on with that second firm out of law school. Few of these firms deign to waste time accommodating the limited scope of legal knowledge and "rookie mistakes" so common to 1Ls. Thus, unless you come from one of the top-shelf law schools, the odds are against you. The strength of the legal market at the time you're applying will largely determine how successful you'll be. Of course, that doesn't mean you shouldn't try—just don't brand yourself a failure if you don't secure one of these plum jobs during your first summer.

> Don't expect to be paid during your 1L summer. Focus on finding great work.
>
> —Patrick

"Finding a paying 1L summer job is very, very hard," Steve notes. "Unless you have good connections, be prepared to put in a lot of hard work and suffer the whims of the current economic circumstances. If you are in the position financially where you can take a job that doesn't pay, then it gets a little easier. The best advice I can give is to be persistent. I sent out over five hundred résumés in order to find the job I eventually got. I started by sending them to all the big firms in New York, Philadelphia, and Washington, D.C. When that didn't produce any results, I started targeting smaller, specialized firms in those cities. After that failed, I started looking to larger firms in smaller cities. Eventually, I went to the small firms and solo practitioners in the smaller cities. I didn't get a job offer until mid-May, after finals had passed, when a solo practitioner in Wilmington, Delaware, finally offered me a paying job. As it turns out, most people didn't think to send résumés to solo practitioners, and mine was one of the only ones he saw.

"I ended up with a great job that summer that gave me not only an income, but some great experience, since the work I was doing with a solo practitioner was much more in-depth than the work summer associates at large firms saw. In the end, it was all about persistence and perseverance: There is a job to be had out there somewhere; it's just a question of how many résumés you'll need to send out in order to get it. For me, it was five hundred. But I got my job."

"After your first year of law school, many people are truly exhausted," Yvette recalled. "Find work that will energize you. Take the summer to explore other areas of law. Quench your curiosities. Challenge yourself in a demanding environment—it will make you a leaner and meaner law student."

The firm

A paid summer associateship with a law firm is definitely the position most coveted by the majority of law students contemplating summer job options. These positions are extremely scarce, however, and frequently taken by 1Ls from the nation's top-five law schools. Every year, however, other students manage to get these positions. So how can you be one of them?

> I mass-mailed my résumé to firms in D.C. and Boston in November, making sure to hit all the firms that had posted openings on our career services bulletin board. I got forty rejection letters for each positive response, but all you need is one good interview. Focus on a city or cities that you have some connection

to on your résumé. I got all my 1L callbacks from D.C., where I had lived and worked previously. And if you have any connection you think might be useful, use it.

—Joel

Most law firms complete their 2L recruiting in the late fall and impose an acceptance deadline of December 1 on the candidates to whom they've offered summer associateships for the following summer. In other words, as of December 1 each year, almost every law firm knows how many of its summer associate slots have been filled, and how many vacancies they have. Many of the large law firms save one or two spots for 1Ls, but the rest of the positions they ultimately offer to 1Ls derive from unclaimed 2L positions, or from an uptick in the legal market that has generated an unexpectedly heavy volume of work. If you want one of these positions, your résumé and cover letter needs to be floating around at these firms before the December 1 deadline, ready to be snapped up when a space opens.

You won't have grades yet—at most schools, grades aren't released until late January or early February—and although some of these firms will wait to see your first-semester grades before they offer you a position, others will take chances and hire you on the strength of your undergraduate résumé. If you can secure a job before your first-semester grades come out, it will take a lot of pressure off and make those first-semester grades somewhat less crucial. The only way this can happen, however, is if you get your résumé to these firms before December 1.

So, you ask, how do you find out where to send your materials?

A fantastic resource, produced by the National Association for Law Placement (NALP) and disseminated to 2Ls, called the *NALP Directory of Legal Employers,* can be found online at www.nalpdirectory.com. The online directory is searchable by state, city, employer type, and employer name. There's also almost certainly a hard copy of the most recent NALP directory in your law library and several in your placement office.

The first thing is to figure out what cities you'd like to explore, or ultimately to practice in. The NALP directory contains a listing of firms by city—so look those up. Find the ones that practice the areas of law you're interested in learning more about, then check each firm's chart to determine if they've ever hired 1Ls. While a track record of hiring 1Ls isn't mandatory, many firms have policies against hiring 1Ls and won't even read your materials, so why waste the postage? Conversely, by examining these charts, you can easily locate the firms that have hired 1Ls in the past and ensure that each of these firms gets your résumé.

Once you've targeted all of these firms, if you want to take a chance at a few firms with no record of 1L hiring, you can always add them to the list. Once you've finished with the NALP directory, however, your list is far from complete. Perusing the NALP directory should have produced a list of fifty to a hundred possibilities in at least three large cities. Now it's time to think closer to home.

Think of everyone you know who is a lawyer. Your girlfriend's mother, your next-door neighbor, Uncle Louie in Chicago, everybody. Make a list of these people and get their addresses. Do your parents have a lawyer? Did they ever use a lawyer for anything? Do they know any lawyers? What about your grandparents, uncles, aunts, cousins, friends, or your parents' coworkers? Do they know any lawyers? With so many lawyers around these days, it's a safe bet that most of these people can name at least one lawyer in their area. Get their names and addresses.

It doesn't matter whether the lawyers they know work for a megafirm, a small-town firm, or toil as solo practitioners. You have an "in" with these lawyers—a personal connection. If the lawyer your parent/relative/friend knows can't offer you a job for the summer, he's a member of a bar association and undoubtedly knows many other lawyers who might be looking for help.

Network shamelessly! You have to be willing to pull out all the stops, to call in every favor, and pull every string within reach to get one of these jobs. Hey, your classmates will be doing it, and the spoils of this game usually go to those people who are the most creative in their networking, and the most persistent in their efforts. I'd say at least eight of every ten people I know who got firm jobs during their first summer got those jobs by networking through someone they knew. This is no time for moral posturing. Gather these names and addresses, add them to the list, and be sure to personalize their letters to highlight your connection. When writing letters to people you know or have been networked to, always close with the line "Any assistance or suggestions you can provide would be greatly appreciated." People like to help, and if they can't help you directly, they might be able to point you to someone else who can.

Once you have your completed list of names, firm names, and addresses (try to list at least a hundred possibilities), learn how to do a mail merge on your computer or ask the people in your placement office to teach you how to do one. For the big firms that you culled from the NALP directory, direct your query letters to the named recruiting coordinator or hiring partner. If a personal connection has directed you to someone at a firm, send the letter directly to that person and be sure to personalize it (e.g., "Our mutual friend, Harry Helpful, suggested that I contact you").

When writing these letters, remember your audience! First, this is no place for flash, so save the fancy fonts, résumé folders, and chic denim paper for your casting interviews in case law school doesn't work out. When dealing with law firms, twenty-pound white bond and a plain font is the only way to go. Be brief! There's no reason to write a tome since the construction of these cover letters is almost boilerplate.

Introduce yourself, state what school you attend, and make your request in the first paragraph. In the second paragraph, explain why the firm and city you selected is of particular interest to you. Add a concluding sentence or two in the third paragraph, and you're done. Straight to the point, and nothing fancy. A sample cover letter follows. The selections in parentheses should be added only if you are networking to a known person at the firm.

Thomas One El
101 Law School Way
City, State, Zip Code, Phone
E-mail Address

Mr. Larry Lawyer, Esq.
Weemake, Bigcash LLP
1 Federal Street
NY, NY 10010

Dear Mr. Lawyer:

My name is Thomas One El and I am a first-year student at the XXX Law School. I am seeking a summer associate position with Weemake, Bigcash (and our mutual friend Harry Helpful, suggested that I contact you).

Although it is early in my law school career, I'm interested in becoming a litigator and pursuing my interests in civil rights and employment litigation. I'm particularly interested in your film because of its reputation as a specialist in these areas of the law. I'm also from New York City and look forward to returning there to practice law after graduation.

Enclosed please find an updated copy of my résumé and my

undergraduate transcript from XXX University. My first-semester grades from law school will be available in early February. If there is anything further I might provide, please do not hesitate to contact me. (Any assistance or suggestions you can provide would be greatly appreciated.)

Respectfully,

Thomas One El

If you used a mail merge, when you have all the letters personalized and printed, *double-check to be sure that the name and address headings match the greeting line* since an undetected error in your mail merge can doom your entire stack of queries. Make certain that the letters contain no typos or printing errors, and be sure that the right letters end up in the proper envelopes. Make a chart of all the firms and contact people to whom you sent queries so you can log the responses as they return. Then send off the letters and get back to the important business of your first-semester workload.

The rejection letters should start flowing in as soon as two weeks later. Don't be surprised by the number of these ding letters. A 1 to 2 percent success rate is considered good, and many people send out hundreds of letters before eventually landing a summer position.

Some firms may respond by expressing interest, asking you to send your first-semester grades when they become available, and reserving judgment until after they've evaluated those grades. At these firms, your first-semester performance will determine whether you are invited to interview. Other firms, however, may call you directly to offer an interview for the position. When that good news comes, refer to chapter 18, which addresses everything you need to know about law firm interviewing.

A final word about applying for firm jobs. Remember that getting one of these positions as a 1L is against the odds. Once you send your letters out, you'll receive a blizzard of rejection letters in response. Many of my friends made light of this humiliating experience by papering the walls of their dorm rooms and apartments with these letters, or having competitions to find the most obnoxious, callous, or comically written rejection letter. Your batting average will be abysmal, so be prepared for that. You may get a hundred rejection letters. You may get all rejection letters. Still, it only takes one yes, one door of the hundreds you knock on, to make you one of the few 1Ls that actually find first-year summer employment. Rest assured that finding this job is the hardest it's going to get for you in law school, but if you do find it, you'll have a crucial foothold that will dramatically increase your chances of success in next year's recruiting season and beyond. Fighting this battle is worth every ounce of effort you put into it.

"I realized early on that I probably wasn't going to get a firm position, and after realizing this, I looked for an interesting job in the legal field that would be challenging and would give me something to talk about in a job interview the following fall," Pat recalled.

"Use whatever connections you have, and spend as much energy as it takes to get a job in the legal field, whether it is paid or unpaid," Carolyn agreed. "It is very important that a 2L be able to talk about her first-summer legal experience at interviews during the fall of the second year."

"I was too cavalier about my first-year summer job because I didn't think it mattered that much," Keith noted. "As a result, I ended up interning for a criminal law judge even though I had no interest in ever practicing criminal law. In the long run, my résumé would have been more impressive had I taken the time to find a summer job in an area of the law in which I hoped to practice or at least wanted to explore."

Here's one more hint. My firm, Sheehan, Phinney, Bass & Green, routinely hires one or two 1Ls for our summer program . . . but we're looking specifically for 1Ls with a demonstrable connection to New Hampshire, or a sincere desire to practice law here. If you fit this description, be sure to get in touch with us in November or December of your 1L year.

Interning for a judge

Many federal judges (both circuit and district) bring on an intern or two during the summer season to help with their caseloads. Many state supreme court justices, and state appellate and trial court judges, also hire interns during the summer months. Although wholly voluntary (meaning that you're totally on your own for all of your expenses, including travel, and will not be paid anything), federal and state court internships are, nevertheless, highly competitive. In the more popular courts, or with better-known judges, fifty to a hundred applicants may be vying for the one or two available intern positions. Other judges, however, get no applicants at all. It's best to apply for these positions by February 1, and it's best to cast your net wide.

Start by trying to figure out which type of judge you're more interested in working with. Consult chapter 25 on judicial clerkships for a full account of the differences among clerkships in various chambers. While you shouldn't limit yourself to any one type of judge, you should have a working knowledge of the differences between internships in the various courts—and mention your interest in the particular internship you're applying for in your cover letters. In other words, in writing to a district court judge, you might add a line mentioning your interest in working with the entire span of a case, from pretrial motion practice, to mediation, to voir dire and actual trials. Conversely, in writing to an appellate judge, you should highlight your interest in working within the narrower confines and intricacies of appellate issues and the intellectual challenge of resolving gray areas of the law.

The point is, internships in different courts are very different and will make many different demands on you. Knowing what these demands are and the differences between them and identifying them in your cover letter will make you a much more attractive candidate.

So how do you start?

As usual, I'd start in your school's placement office or law library. Look for any good directory of federal judges. These directories are usually organized by circuit and state and provide the names, mailing addresses, and (depending on which directory you find) even short biographies of all the federal judges in the United States and the territories.

List the names and addresses of every federal circuit judge and federal district judge in your home state, and in the state and judicial district (if applicable) where your law school is located. These chambers will be especially fertile ground because in choosing interns, judges frequently favor locals—residents of the state or students at a nearby law school.

Next, get a directory that lists all the state supreme court, state appellate court (if applicable), and state trial court judges in your home state and in the state where your law school is located. Although finding this directory can be a bit trickier than finding one that lists federal judges, your placement office or law library should either have a resource providing these names on hand or be able to get one in short order.

By the time you've finished listing these judges, you should have more than fifty names on your list. To round it out, choose one or two other states to which you have some connection, such as the state where you did your undergraduate work or a state where you have interest in practicing after graduation. For example, if you've spent every summer since childhood vacationing in Wyoming, apply to the judges in Wyoming and mention this connection in your cover letter. Do not underestimate the power of local ties. If you go to a top-twenty law school on the East Coast and randomly send a letter to a federal district court judge in Wyoming, your application is likely to be greeted with "Why is this guy applying to my chambers in Wyoming? He must be doing a massive mail merge. . . . I'll save the position for someone more appropriate." But if you send this letter to Wyoming and explain that you spend every summer there, love the state, have left many footsteps in the Wind Rivers and the Tetons, and are considering settling there, you stand a much better chance.

Once you've compiled this list of judges, separate the names by the type of court they preside in (federal circuit, federal district, etc.). When you have the judges categorized this way, further subdivide them by state. Each separate pile will need a differently personalized letter, one that stresses your interest in the kind of experience particular to that kind of court and states your connection to the state where that court sits. If you have any common ground with the judge (same law school, same undergraduate school, love of bird-watching, etc.), you'll want to work that into your letter as well. You're looking for any edge that will distinguish you from the masses.

It is not disingenuous to tell one judge that you're fascinated by appellate work, and another judge that you're interested in learning the ropes in state trial court. Judges understand the high hurdles posed by the first-year employment search, and they're not about to hold your disparate interests against you. As long as you don't tell every judge that you write to that the "only thing I've ever wanted to do in my life is intern in your chambers," you're on solid ground.

So what should your query letter look like? All the basic rules about correspondence sent to law firms apply equally to correspondence sent to judges. Again, the letter is almost boilerplate, other than whatever personalization you can add. It's a three-paragraph letter. In the first paragraph, introduce yourself, your law school, and state your purpose. Express your interest in the type of work particular to that court, your connection to the state, and any common interests shared with the judge in the second paragraph. Reference your enclosures in the third paragraph, and end with a conservative close. Simple and to the point. No frills. An example follows.

Thomas One El
101 Law School Way
City, State, Zip Code
Phone
E-mail Address

Hon. Gavel A. Blackrobe
Federal Courthouse
55 Court St.
Concord, NH 03110

Dear Judge Blackrobe:

My name is Thomas One El and I am a first-year law student at the University of XXX Law School. I am seeking an internship in your chambers for the summer of 20XX.

As a future litigator, I am particularly interested in learning about the breadth of federal trial practice, from pretrial motions and mediation to voir dire and evidentiary issues. I am developing strong research and writing skills during my law school's full-year Legal Research and Writing course and would love to have the opportunity to develop and hone them further in the context of such an internship. Given my family's ties to the state and my strong interest in hiking and other outdoor activities, I am particularly interested in returning to New Hampshire to practice after graduation from law school. Accordingly, I am focusing my job search on opportunities to return to New Hampshire this summer.

Enclosed please find a copy of my current résumé and undergraduate transcript from XXX University. My first-semester grades will be available in early February. If there is anything else I can provide, please do not hesitate to contact me.

Respectfully,
Thomas One El

Note the important information conveyed by the letter. In paragraph one—the name of the law school you attend. If it's a nationally known school, the judge's alma mater, or an in-state school, you'll likely catch the judge's eye. In paragraph two—your justification for applying to his court, your connection to the state where the court sits, and any commonalities shared with the judge (here hiking and outdoorsmanship, which could be a common interest shared with the judge or a justification for coming to New Hampshire). In the final paragraph, you've worked in the name of your undergraduate school. Again, if it's a nationally known school, the judge's undergraduate alma mater, or an in-state school, it will help.

Make a chart of all the judges to whom you send letters so you can easily track responses when they arrive.

Working for a public-interest organization

A common misperception among first-year law students is that, should you choose to volunteer your time with a public-service organization, you'll have your choice of places to volunteer and can wait until the last minute to make the arrangements.

Think again.

Service organizations, like law firms, deal with real people and real problems. These organizations frequently feature tightly knit and highly energized work environments, and they tend to be careful about whom they hire. As with law firms and judicial internships, the most popular public-service internships—particularly those with the Department of Justice, the U.S. attorney, state district attorneys' offices, prosecutors' offices, or any well-known national organizations—are going to be highly competitive. Accordingly, query letters for these placements should be sent no later than winter break to ensure the best possible return.

So how do you know what options are available, and how to apply? Again, your first stop should be your law school placement office. They will likely have binders containing lists of public-service organizations offering internships, including contact names, addresses, required documentation, and deadlines. If you have a favorite professor, you might also want to ask him to recommend a good service organization for a summer internship.

Once you've compiled a list of contact names and addresses, you'll need to formulate individual query letters for each organization. Avoid using a boilerplate letter and mail merge for these letters as each of these organizations will be a distinct entity with a different mission that you should address individually. Follow paper and font guidelines as with firm and judge queries, but the text of these letters can be made more personal, expressing the reasons for your interest in the particular organization, your endorsement of their mission, prior related work you've done, etc. There is no one proper way to write a query letter to a public-service organization. Let your feelings be your guide.

"I knew I wanted an internship at a prosecutor's office, so I applied to all of the prosecutors' offices in south Jersey and Philadelphia,"

Lindsay advised. "One of my friends in law school mentioned that she came across a job posting for the Philadelphia District Attorney's Office, specifically for the Family Violence and Sexual Assault Unit. I applied, interviewed, and ended up landing the internship. My advice is to apply early and follow up with the internship contact person. I hadn't heard from the D.A.'s office within two weeks of submitting my application, so I e-mailed the contact person and ended up receiving an interview later that week.

"Public-interest and government agencies usually start accepting applications in the late fall and continue through the early spring," Lindsay continued. "Your professors are an often untapped resource for these 1L internships. Talk to your professors about the type of internship you are seeking and ask their advice. Chances are, they will reach out to their contacts for you."

Occasionally, you may find an organization that offers stipends for some positions, while other positions in the same organization are strictly voluntary. You'll want to make it clear which position you're applying for, and should you decide to apply for both positions, do so in separate letters sent under separate cover. It's hard to make a convincing case that the organization should give you a stipend if, in the next paragraph, you make it clear that you're willing to work for free.

Working for a public-interest organization can be immensely rewarding, both emotionally and intellectually, if you find a placement you're interested in and take an active role in seeking the kind of work you want. In the right situation, you will be given important and challenging work with immediate consequences on human lives.

Researching for a professor

In the weeks just prior to spring break, professors will begin deciding how to spend their summer months away from the classroom. Many professors will sign deals around this time to write a hornbook, edit or contribute to a casebook, or begin work on a law review article that they intend to write during the summer. Many of these professors will need research help, and some will be willing to pay for it. If you don't see any signs around the law school by the end of February, ask your favorite professor if he, or one of his colleagues, needs help for the summer. If he isn't writing this summer, chances are he'll know someone in need of help and can direct you to that person.

The opportunity to work for a law professor carries with it a number of benefits beyond whatever stipend is offered. The experience will likely offer you the rare opportunity to establish a close, one-on-one relationship with a law professor, a relationship that may help you to discover an intellectual curiosity in a particular area of the law, provide you with ideas for a "note" or "comment" if you make the law review or another journal, provide you with an important source for recommendations, and even give you a mentor on the faculty (something that few law students have, but nearly everyone wishes he or she had).

Research positions are probably the most overlooked opportunity for 1L summer employment, typically because they are perceived as the least prestigious option. Don't be guided by the misperceptions of your classmates, however. It's a position that may open more doors for you than any of the others.

Working it

Remember the take-home lesson from this chapter: Obtaining employment as a first-year law student will be difficult, and any of the positions discussed above will provide you with valuable experience to ground the knowledge you'll soak up during your first year. Just about the only rule of thumb to follow is to do something law-related. Accordingly, you may want to send query letters for many or all of these different positions. So how do you "work it" to afford yourself the maximum opportunity to get the position you desire?

If you're interested in law firms, those query letters should go out the first weekend in November. If you're on top of your course work and can also afford to write up letters to public-service organizations at that time, all the better. These letters, however, can also safely be sent out during winter break. Follow those letters with query letters for judges by February 1. Finally, start asking professors about research positions in February. Be persistent, and be resilient.

"I sent out a mass mailing to no avail," Allan recalls. "After that, I got bogged down with schoolwork and didn't start looking again until April or so, which was definitely too late. The best advice I can give a 1L would be to apply to firms and judges as soon as possible. As soon as you are allowed to start applying, you should do so."

"And be persistent," Pat adds. "I called up so many places telling them that I wanted to do volunteer work, but this didn't produce any job offers. I was amazed that after a full year of law school I couldn't even give my time away! But I kept at it, and the persistence eventually paid off in the spring."

Remember, all you need is one positive response.

CHAPTER 13

Your First-Semester Endgame

The true test of any man lies in action.
—PINDAR

THERE IS LITTLE disagreement that your initial first-year law examination is the single most unnerving experience you will face in your law school career. Sure, you've taken exams before, but chances are, you've rarely if ever faced a situation where a single four-hour examination will be the sole determinant of your entire semester grade. The experience will be unfamiliar, the setting can be intimidating, and unscrupulous classmates may even try to throw you off your game—a confluence of factors that can be a recipe for disaster.

We pick up the story one week prior to the end of your first semester, which, for most of you, should be around the first week of December. If you've been keeping up with the preceding chapters, you should at this point have a completed outline (minus the final week of lectures) for each of your classes. We're now in the endgame, the critical time of the semester that ultimately decides who gets the A's and who doesn't. Things should have started getting crazy some weeks ago, but the insecurity and the levels of stress among your classmates should be reaching fever pitch right about now. For you, this means only one thing . . .

It's time to find an off-campus location to study

That's right. It's time to leave. Take what you need with you and get yourself the hell out of the law library, and out of the law school.

Now is the time to seek sanctuary in your secret spot in the stacks of the undergraduate library, at the table in the never-visited map room, or even in your own apartment if you can stand being cooped up there all the time. Just don't even think about hanging around the law school!

Why?

Because anxiety is contagious, and you don't want to catch it.

Permit me a story. During my first year of law school, I lived in the graduate dorms at the center of the law student floors—basically right at ground zero for first-year anxiety and stress. I had created what I thought was the ideal sanctuary—incense burning, a collection of Windham Hill instrumental music playing on the stereo, and a steaming mug of herbal tea at my side. I was the picture of peace and tranquillity, and I was being productive.

Then, it started.

The phone rang—parents inquiring about my progress and wishing me well, friends calling to chastise me for being out of touch for months, and to finalize plans for our annual Christmas-week ski trip, and classmates calling to ask questions, ask for notes, or just to bitch about the whole thing. Then came the knocks at the door from classmates looking for notes, outlines, and study aids, or friends on different study schedules looking to take a study break. Then, there was always the game on TV, which required a score check every thirty minutes or so, and every time the computer beeped with a new e-mail message—well, it had to be answered promptly, right?

All of this distraction was, however, nothing compared to what happened a night or two later. Just before midnight, I was at my desk working on Civil Procedure. Suddenly, a bloodcurdling shriek came from the hallway just outside my room. When I opened the door to investigate, I found one of my classmates slumped against a wall just down the hall sobbing, on the edge of madness. As soon as she saw me, she ran over to me, clutched at my arm, and started babbling almost incoherently between sobs about jurisdiction, going on hysterically about last year's exam (which I hadn't yet looked at), and assuring me that she was going to fail.

So much for my little sanctuary. I could feel the blood rushing to my head, and my mouth ran dry. After talking to my frenzied classmate for a couple of minutes, I was completely stressed-out myself. I didn't understand half of what she was asking me about.

After she left my room, I called a friend downtown, packed my books and some clothes, and moved out of the dorm, not to be seen again until the beginning of the spring semester.

Avoid the maelstrom at all costs because once you get infected with anxiety, it's hard to get rid of it.

"The panic point for me in the first semester was Thanksgiving break," Steve recalls. "Everyone said Thanksgiving was when things got serious, so I knew that I had to be ready for the postholiday crunch. Despite that, when I returned from break, the pressure was there instantly. There were only a couple of weeks left until finals, and you start realizing how little you know . . . not just in the sense of what has been covered in the courses, but in the sense of what finals will be like. No matter how laid-back you are, there's no way to avoid feeling pressure, and you can't help but panic a bit. The thing is, there is no way to overcome the pressure and panic. You just have to work through it and cling to the thought that in a month it will all be over."

"Try not to worry too much," Allan notes. "Go at your own pace and don't let other people's study habits affect you. Once you've decided on an approach, stick to it."

Elizabeth agrees. "My most effective strategy was keeping to myself. I avoided study groups, avoided people who were panicking, and played by my own rules."

Okay, so you're somewhere else, away from your classmates and most potential distractions. Now what?

Now it's time to get busy with the fifth and final step of my five-step briefing method that I taught you in chapter 9. This week, you'll be distilling your outlines down to single-page "maps" or "bullet outlines" of the law you covered during the semester. This way, you can see exactly how the law developed and how it all fits together.

"My theory about law classes is that there are three stages one goes through in preparing for an exam," Carolyn explains. "Stage one is getting a superficial understanding of what the law is—like you could get from just reading a commercial outline a couple of times. Stage two is where you lose the forest for the trees by working through the detail and complexities of the cases in the area of law you are studying. Stage three is where you put it all together—where you have an understanding of the detail and complexity of the case law, and you also know how it all fits together. Obviously, it is ideal to be at stage three when you take an exam, but it is better to be at stage one than to be at stage two.

"The classes I did the worst in were those in which I got bogged down outlining and obsessing about details. When this happened, I would get into an exam and forget even the most fundamental black-letter law in the subject area. If you find yourself in this position a week before an exam, recognize that you are trapped at stage two, force yourself to stop outlining, and simply work through a completed outline. Master that outline and then work through some practice exams with it," Carolyn suggests.

Mapping out the law

At this point, you're probably thinking, "What? I've just spent the last three months writing these masterful outlines, and now he's telling me that I need to distill them down to the point where I might not even get to use them?"

Absolutely. Here's why!

Your outlines for each class are probably between 60 and 120 pages long and aren't in a format that you can glance at to quickly spot issues or to easily see how the different lines of cases fit together. Putting these outlines together, however, has forced you to synthesize and organize the cases you read into a comprehensible structure that you'll later be able to use and apply to the hypotheticals of new facts that you'll find on most of your exams. Naturally, writing these outlines has also forced you to understand the doctrines better and has given you a level of knowledge that you would never have had simply by reading the cases and going to lectures.

Your experiences up to this point have given you the raw materials. Now, however, it's time to hone the tools you need for serious exam success.

"Condense, condense, condense!" John-Mark advises. "I would always start off with a fairly large annotated outline that filed all the cases we'd discussed in class under the relevant legal concepts. Then I would take that outline and summarize it, and then summarize the summary, until finally, at the end, I had an 'attack' outline that was a good reference to make sure that I wouldn't miss anything."

Find your first-semester classes on the list below, and take note of the tools I recommend that you put in your arsenal for that exam. Then read on for complete instructions on how to create those tools for yourself.

Civil Procedure	map and bullet points
Contracts	map and bullet points
Torts	bullet points
Property	bullet points
Criminal Law	map and bullet points
Constitutional Law	map
Criminal Procedure	map
Administrative Law	map
Labor Law	map

How to create a "case map"

Tape together six sheets of blank, white 8½-by-11 paper to create a large, foldable blank map. Grab an outline for a class listed above that requires a map. Flip through your course syllabus, the outline, or the table of contents of the corresponding casebook or commercial outline to determine how the material is organized. For example, your Contracts outline is probably most broadly divided into five separate sections covering (1) offer, (2) acceptance, (3) consideration, (4) damages, and (5) equitable remedies. Consequently, your case map should be divided into separate case chains for each of these areas, with lines and arrows connecting the various sections of the chains as required. Go through your entire outline carefully, placing each case and its holding into its proper place in the chain. Limit yourself to a case name, date, court, a single line stating the holding of the case, and a number citing the page number in your outline where the case is discussed. Do not rewrite your outline on your map. Your map is visual, the outline is substantive. These two resources must work in conjunction, so there's no reason to try to make one a substitute for the other. A copy of one of my Criminal Procedure case maps follows.

Creating a bullet outline

A bullet outline is most useful for classes where general principles can succinctly be stated in a series of elements or steps, and where the development of the doctrine is somewhat less important than its result. Introductory Torts, for example, is a largely black-letter subject. In preparing for your Torts exam, it is generally more important to know that the elements of negligence are (1) a duty of care, (2) breach of that duty, (3) causation, and (4) damages, than it is to know details of the cases in your casebook that illustrate the particular tort. In Torts, theory is primarily relegated to questions of risk allocation and damage calculation. Most law school Torts exams thus usually consist of (1) some multiple-choice or short-answer questions addressing the elemental requirements of different torts, and (2) a large "issue-spotter" essay where you need to identify and evaluate as many torts as possible in the allotted time. If you attend a law school that emphasizes theory, your Torts exam may also feature a theoretical essay at the end. To perform well on an exam like this, having a list of torts and their individual elements will clearly be more helpful to you than a map of the development of the doctrine.

WHAT IS A SEARCH AND WHAT ISN'T?

4TH AMENDMENT SEARCH & SEIZURE

"The right of the people to be secure in their persons, houses, papers, and effects, against unreasonable searches and seizures, shall not be violated — and no warrants shall issue, but upon probable cause, supported by oath or affirmation, and particularly describing the place to be searched, and the persons or things to be seized..."

OVERVIEW

SEARCHES w/o WARRANT ARE PER SE UNREASONABLE UNLESS FALLING INTO ONE OF THE PERMISSIBLE EXCEPTIONS

Ask: (1) WAS IT A SEARCH; (2) WAS THERE A WARRANT (3) IF NO WARRANT – WAS THERE AN EXCEPTION?

Katz v. United States (1967) (7)

REASONABLE EXPECTATION OF PRIVACY TEST DEFINES "WHAT IS A SEARCH"

(1) govt conduct conflicts w/ citizen's subjective exp. of priv. (subj – abandoned)

* and (2) interest is one that society is PREPARED TO ACCEPT AS LEGIT (objective – now controls)

- privacy-centered approach replaces property-centered approach
- 4th Am. intended to protect people – not places

(• NO ELECTRONIC SURVEILLANCE of public phone BOOTH)

* 3 CATEGORIES OF LEGIT. INTERESTS *

1. freedom from physical disruption + inconvenience
2. freedom from forced disclosure of personal or embarrassing info which doesn't implicate crim. act
3. control over + use of property

NO REASONABLE EXPECTATION OF PRIVACY IN THINGS OPEN TO PUBLIC EXPOSURE

PLAIN-VIEW NONSEARCH

(1) Requires a PUBLIC VANTAGE POINT

- ANY viewing location to which public has LEGAL ACCESS – even through extraordinary means (Florida v. Riley SCT 1989) (54)

includes: sidewalks, front walks, driveways, neighbor's home

excludes: curtilage

* OVERFLIGHT CASES

Florida v. Riley – plurality says legal access becomes test – not ordinary access.

↓

ABANDONS KATZ SUBJECTIVE PRONG – if Court is prepared to accept interest as LEGIT – it applies to everyone, regardless of individual expectation

SENSORY ENHANCEMENT

United States v. Knotts (1983)[12] – if police COULD HAVE SEEN w/ naked eye, they can use surveillance instead (once expectation of priv. lost, form of intrusion irrelevant)

EXTENSIONS: flashlights, telephoto lenses

- as long as from public vantage point +
- same basic information available to naked eye

LIMITATIONS United States v. Karo (SCT 1984)[13]

search if "otherwise entirely unavailable to senses"

CANNOT "see through walls" (most often w/ INTRUSION INTO HOMES) → b/c subject specific judgments about VALUE of privacy

* close cases between Knotts + Karo – lower courts have applied KARO in telescope cases in residential settings (i.e. to determine if marijuana)

* Dow Chemical v. US (SCT-1986 bk 64) – overflight of chemical plant w/ special photo equip. WAS allowed under Knotts – but commercial setting narrowed holding

* no infrared device to look through fabric curtains under Karo – inaccessible to senses

ASSUMPTION OF RISK

(1) Requires a VOLUNTARY conveyance of information to a third person

- if informant is wired – STILL not a search – police only getting more accurate picture of what they would have had anyway
- SPLIT on documents: banks, credit card cos., post office, IRS
  1. deemed exposal to 3rd person – no search
  2. deemed INVOLUNTARY, so legit. expectation of privacy + no assumption

United States v. White (SCT-1971)[13] "Doctrine of Selective Exposure leaves you w/ NO REASONABLE EXPECTATION OF PRIVACY. If you speak "in confidence" – you lose expectation.

United States v. Miller (SCT-1976)[14] No reasonable expectation of privacy in bank records – voluntarily made accessible (govt wanted to check credit card records for upsurge in spending – ruled NO SEARCH)

ILLEGAL ACTIVITIES

(1.) NO LEGIT. EXPECTATION OF PRIVACY b/c per se NOT AN ACTIVITY society wants to uphold

- any device which can reveal ONLY an illegal activity CAN be used by police
  - ↳ canine sniffs if dogs trained only to search for illegal drugs – but probably not of person b/c too intrusive.

United States v. Pinson (8th 1994)[14] infrared heat detection device ALLOWED b/c seeks only infrared lamps growing pot.

Note: if dog alerts to luggage – can't open it immediately – usu. need warrant unless exigent exception.

OPEN FIELDS DOCTRINE

"Open fields are NOT the setting for intimate activities that the 4th Amendment was designed to protect"

- distinguished from public exposure b/c not necessarily plain-view or assumption. Open fields is a SEPARATE EXCEPTION.

Oliver v. United States (SCT-1984)[15] officer's search of field surrounded by chain link + locked gate NOT violation of 4th Am. search. MIGHT BE COMMON LAW TRESPASS / STATE LAW.

- Court wanted BRIGHT LINE RULE to set specific stds for police.
- note tension w/ Katz – here, back to textualist approach, not in Am., so not protected

"CURTILAGE"

United States v. Dunn (SCT-1987)[15]

4 FACTORS FOR DETERMINING CURTILAGE

(1) proximity to home
(2) whether area included w/in enclosure
(3) nature to which area is put
(4) steps taken to protect area from observation

↳ if 4th Am. implicated, you need a warrant, or an exception.

- entry into curtilage is a search
- any steps taken from lawful vantage point BEHIND curtilage (see plain view non-search) (jumping up + down behind fence, peering over it, using ladder to look over, etc. are all OKAY) are OKAY.

(rises vertically to level of FAA allowed airspace)

TRASH

NOT A SEARCH b/c "readily accessible to children, animals, scavengers + snoops" – so POLICE DON'T HAVE TO AVERT THEIR EYES.

Justification problems:

Karo: "not accessible to senses"

not really assumption of risk b/c then car on street is too...

Conveyance to 3rd person? but what about mail?

HARRIS says although Cts try to make plain view non-search it's really a separate exception

California v. Greenwood (SCT-1988)[17]

police CAN ask garbagemen to deliver your trash to them if they suspect you of narcotics use, etc.

PRISONS / SCHOOLS

- Hudson v. Palmer (SCT-1984)[16] (PRISONS) no constit. protected 4th Am. exp. of privacy in prison cell, or papers + property therein. Based on legit. institutional interests.

  BUT, no impunity for destruction of prop. b/c Due Process requires a remedy for wanton destruction of property.

- NJ v. TLO (SCT-1985)[16] (SCHOOLS) Court DECLINES to expand Hudson to schools. Kids don't waive all rights to privacy in school.

  BUT...

  reasonable expectation of privacy only 1st inquiry. IF FOUND, next question is, was gov't intrusion REASONABLE based on totality of CIRCUMSTANCES? Here, it was b/c school officials had reasonable suspicion that student was carrying contraband in [illegible]

- O'Connor v. Ortega (SCT-1987)[17] (gov't [illegible]) Court REJECTS idea that govt EEs never have a reasonable expect. of privacy in workplace. Desk + files there. Intrusions judged by TOTALITY of CIRCUMSTANCES reasonableness standard.

Accordingly, for an exam such as Torts, Property, or Criminal Law (if it is taught without Constitutional Criminal Procedure), we'll develop bullet-point checklists in lieu of a case map. These checklists will function the same way as a map, helping you to spot issues and address each of the elements of each tort. So how do you develop a checklist like this?

Once again, start with the index of your casebook or a good commercial outline. Using Torts as a continuing example, go through the index and first make a list of all the torts you covered in class. Under each tort, make a list of its required elements. Once you've done this, go through your outline and add in any clarifying information or illustrative examples discussed in the cases or the lectures for these elements. For the tort of negligence, then, you'd start by listing the tort and its elements (duty of care, breach of that duty, causation, and damages). But you won't stop there. Under the "duty" element, bullet out what you learned about what constitutes a duty and when you have a duty. Under "causation," bullet out what you learned about the doctrines of proximate cause, and last clear chance, and the law of the intervening actor. Under damages, you'd list the different theories of damages, and mitigating factors such as contributory and comparative negligence. Remember, you're not trying to re-create your outline. A bullet outline is purely for recall and issue-spotting. Cross-reference pages in your outline to point yourself to more detail so you'll have it at your fingertips if you need it. An example of a bullet outline for "piercing the corporate veil" follows on the next page.

Taking sample exams

Once you have all of these materials prepared and assembled for a class, you are ready to start taking sample exams. Try to take at least one exam under real testing conditions, so you'll get a sense for the timing required. Whenever possible, take a sample exam for which the professor has made a model answer available. That way, when you finish, you actually have something to compare your answers to. This brings us to a critical point, however. Do not expect to address everything that you'll find in the model answer. The model answer is just that, a "model." Typically, it is either an amalgam of the best student responses or an answer written by the professor with unlimited time and resources and his mastery of the subject at hand.

Don't freak out if you missed an issue or two. Instead, ask yourself how confident you felt answering the exam questions. Did you have a

"**PIERCING CORPORATE VEIL**" (PURPOSE: to hold ind. SH personally liable for corp. debts)

Four factors: (1) is case contract or tort – more willing to pierce in tort (voluntary creditor doctrine) p11

* (2) did Δ stockholders engage in FRAUD or WRONGDOING (draining assets) p11

(3) adequate capitalization – KEY FACTOR, but MAJ. VIEW says need this plus #2 or #4 p11

* (4) were corporate formalities followed?

* Cts more likely to pierce on behalf of gov't entity. Almost NEVER to benefit a SH...

- best chance for Π is to allege siphoning of assets (#2), failure to follow formalities (#4) AND inadequate capitalization, since most cts will require either #2 or #4 to pierce (Minton v. Cavaney) p12
- inadequate capitalization usually means inadequate INITIAL capitalization. If initially adequate, but intentionally drained, this can be FRAUD or WRONGDOING – may be actionable under state or Fed law allowing set-asides of transfers in fraud of creditors (Law of Fraudulent Conveyances) Courts NOT likely to find duty to replenish corporate assets drained by poor economic conditions.
- FAILURE TO FOLLOW FORMALITIES
  - shares never formally issued
  - SH + dir. mtgs never held
  - intermingling of corporate + personal property
  - proper corporate records not kept

PIERCING IN PARENT/SUBSIDIARY STRUCTURES (more likely than general piercing)

Veil will NOT be pierced as long as (1) proper corporate formalities observed
(2) public not confused about whether dealing w/ parent or subsidiary
(3) subsidiary operated in fair manner w/ intention of making profit
(4) no manifest unfairness

Factors LEADING TO veil piercing: (1) corporate formalities not followed / intertwined operations
(2) unified business – subsidiary undercapitalized (taxi fleet) p.14
(3) public misled about which entity handles which part of business (for K sake)
(4) intermingling of assets (undocumented transfers of funds, etc.)
(5) unfair operation (ex: sub forced to sell at cost to parent, so sub never makes profit – operation of subsidiary only for advantage of the parent)

ENTERPRISE LIABILITY: enterprise divided into # of separately incorporated pieces for sole purpose of reducing liabilities – if operating as single business, court may view various "pieces" (subsidiaries) as ONE – a single business from which creditors can collect ("one pot").

good idea of what the questions were getting at? Did the issues seem to jump off the page at you while you were reading the question? Did you identify and discuss most of the key issues? That's what you're looking for at this point. Don't forget to use your maps, checklists, and your outline during the exam. It's meant to be a realistic trial run.

"I wrote out answers to old exams, as a rule, in preparing for my exams," Patrick recalled. "It put me in the mind-set to write for the correct amount of time and forced me to formulate answers in the same manner as I would need to on exam day."

Don't worry too much if you find things in the sample exam that your professor didn't cover this year—or even if you find things in the model answer that seem to be dead wrong compared to what you learned in class—particularly if the exam and model answer are several years old. The professor may have changed the focus of the course, and the law may have changed too. Rely on your current outlines, not on what you read in a model answer.

> The classes in which I had the greatest success were those classes in which I had prepared my own outline, taken time to review the outline and become familiar with it, and then taken time to do practice exams using the outline, so I could get comfortable using it.
>
> —Carolyn

Finally, remember that a sample exam is just that—a sample. It's a noncounting dry run. Don't be rattled by the experience. Learn what you can from having taken the dry run. The only exam that counts is the one that you'll take in class.

Review sessions

To go or not to go. That is the question.

The answer depends, in large part, on your personality. Start with the premise that you will learn more substantive law by going to your professor's office hours and banging out all of your questions there than you will ever learn in a review session. If you want substantive questions cleared up, go to office hours, not to a review session. You go to a review session to attempt to steal the exam from the professor.

Yes, you read that right. If you go to a review session, listen carefully, and perhaps ask a probing question or two, you can often glean critical information about the structure and content of the exam, which can substantially simplify your preparation. Typically, during the review session, some eager student will ask the professor to discuss the format of the exam. By this time, your prof has probably already written the exam, so she'll inevitably be commenting on the actual exam you're about to take, and she may discuss it in some specificity. Listen carefully to everything that comes out of the professor's mouth about the exam, particularly her responses to students' questions. Little throwaway phrases like "Yeah, that's important" or "Good question," or any in-depth analysis the professor undertakes during the review session, may tip you off to material implicated on the exam. Conversely, if a student asks a question about a particular area of the law and the professor responds, "Don't worry too much about that," that should immediately translate to "Forget it, it's not on the exam." Pay particular attention to anything the professor writes on the board during a review session as it is likely to be important to the exam, and write down any hypotheticals she covers, as they may closely mimic exam questions.

It is also worth your while to know what particular areas of legal doctrine your professors are wrestling with in their own research and writing. Professors are notorious for trying out legal theories or principles, or hypotheticals based around those legal theories and principles, in law school exams. If your professor is interested enough in something to want to write about it, he or she will likely also be interested in seeing what you can do with the issue on an exam.

> Know your professor. Is there some theme she has mentioned again and again throughout the semester? If there is, there's an excellent chance you'll see it one more time—on the exam.
>
> —Joel

Finally, listen carefully to any suggestions the professor makes about how to structure your exam answers. If she tells you she prefers the answers to be written in black pen, be sure to write in black pen. If she tells you to print and skip lines, do it. I once had a professor state in a sparsely attended review session that he preferred "essay" questions to be answered in outline form, with lots of letters, numbers, and bullet points, because he had an answer key he was working from and it made it easier to check off points in an outline than points in prose text. Interestingly, he mentioned this only in the review session!

In the average law school class, fewer than half the students will attend the review session. Needless to say, that gives you an important advantage if anything significant comes to light, and remember the mantra of this book—success in law school is all about getting a little bit of an edge.

So, if this is true, you ask, why don't more students attend them?

First of all, most students are too far behind in their exam preparation to spare the time to go to a review session in the final week of the semester. Others have been frustrated by past sessions that didn't actually function as a "review," or where they couldn't get their questions answered because other students monopolized the questioning. In other words, these students went to the review session for the wrong reasons and ended up disappointed. However, if you go to a review session looking for exam hints, you'll rarely leave without gaining some insight.

In my mind, the only valid reason for *not* attending a review session is if you know that you are overly anxious about the subject and will be unable to sit through other students' questions without panicking. Remember that much of success in law school is about confidence, and the worst thing you can do before an exam is sabotage your confidence. If you fall into this category, try to remember that most people who ask questions are confused—and don't you listen to anyone except the professor. If you follow this advice, you should be able to overcome your anxiety.

The final hours

A few final words about preexam preparation. Don't discuss your preparation with anyone except a study partner or the members of your study group. Nothing will bring on self-doubt and paranoia faster than finding out that you have taken a different approach to preparing for an exam than your classmates have. There's no telling whose methods are better, and since you're the one using this book, forget about everyone else. Trust my advice, and trust yourself.

On the eve of an exam, gather all the materials you'll be taking into the exam room in one place. Be sure you have your exam ticket, photo identification, a watch, and a sufficient supply of pens. If the administration allows you to bring food and beverages into the exam, bring a PowerBar (or the like), a couple of rolls of Life Savers, and a bottle of water—each of which will give you a little boost when you need it most. You want to be as calm as possible on the morning of your exam, and the last thing you want to be doing is scurrying around looking for things.

Finally, and perhaps more important, stop studying around dinnertime the night before your exam. Acknowledge that you'll never master all the material. Think about how far you've come with the doctrine and how much you've learned about the subject since the beginning of the semester, then go do something fun and relaxing to take the pressure off. Take a long walk, grab a workout, or go to a movie—just don't study. Don't drink to excess or take anything to help you sleep, since you don't want to be groggy in the morning. Go to bed a bit early and try to make peace with yourself knowing that you've done all that you could possibly do.

Exam day

The big day has come.

Get up a little earlier than usual and collect yourself. Force yourself to eat a good breakfast. You'll be surprised how draining a four-hour exam can be, and you'll need the resources.

Get to the exam room at least twenty minutes before the exam is scheduled to start and scope out a good seat if you're allowed to choose your seating. The best seats in an exam are the seats that minimize distractions—typically the seats in the front and back corners of the exam room, and the seats farthest away from exit doors. Gather up a supply of blue books and scratch paper so you can use one blue book per essay response and so you won't need to get up during the exam, when every minute counts. Spread out your materials to make them easily accessible. Relax, and above all, don't talk to your classmates about any substantive law or eavesdrop on any such discussion. Block it all out. When ten minutes remain before the start of the exam, take a precautionary bathroom break to stave off any need to leave the exam room during the next four hours.

Examsmanship

Perhaps the most important piece of advice I can give you about taking a law school exam is to budget your time. The most common and most destructive exam mistake made by first-year students is spending too much time on any one question, and coming to the end of the exam with only ten minutes left to respond to an equally weighted final essay. Do not let this happen to you. Be disciplined! The second important rule of first-year examsmanship is that you need not spend all of your time writing. In fact, you shouldn't. These two rules, working in concert, can help to ensure that your exam-room performance is as relaxing and productive as possible.

When you first get your exam and the proctor gives you the green light to begin work, take a deep breath, sit back, and read. Just read. Let the questions wash over you, and let your subconscious mind begin working on the answers. When you've read through the entire exam once, determine how the points are allocated between questions, determine the order in which you want to attack the questions (remembering that there is no requirement to do them in order), then physically write down on the exam itself at what time you have to move on to the next question. For example, for a three-hour exam with twenty-five multiple-choice questions worth one point each, five short-answer questions worth five points each, and two essay questions worth twenty-five points each, you should devote forty-five minutes to the multiple-choice questions (or slightly less than two minutes each), forty-five minutes to the short-answer questions (nine minutes each), and forty-five minutes to each essay. You must force yourself to stay on this schedule no matter what. When your time on a particular section expires, wrap up and move on.

Continuing with the same example, and assuming a three-hour exam that begins at 9:00 a.m. and that you're taking the sections in the order given above, write 9:45 at the top of the multiple-choice section, 10:30 at the top of the short-answer section, 11:15 at the top of the first essay, and 12:00 at the top of the second essay. Start working the multiple-choice questions. Bang them out in order and skip any that you can't answer. Remember the technique you used on the LSAT and cross out any clearly wrong responses as you read them so you won't waste time rereading wrong responses on your second pass-through. Remember that you have less than two minutes to respond to each question. At 9:45, guess on any questions you have not yet answered and move on to the next section, regardless of how many questions you have left. Begin attacking the short-answer questions, remembering that you have only nine minutes to spend on each question. Don't fall into the trap of spending fifteen or twenty minutes on the really tough question you're almost certain to find in this section. It's a trap for the unwary, designed to keep people from getting to the essay questions, and thus to make the grades easier to distinguish from each other. Hit and move on. Include as much relevant information as you can, but when the nine-minute interval has expired, force yourself to keep moving. Remember that no one will get the full number of points on the exam, so you won't need full credit on every answer to do well.

At 10:30, decide which of the two essays you want to deal with first, and reread it. As you read, spot issues and mark up the text of the question accordingly. When you've finished doing this, take a deep breath, sit back, and carefully read the paragraph(s) at the end of the question where the professor lays out the question(s) he wants you to answer. Take time to think about and sketch out a brief outline of your response to the question(s). It is perfectly acceptable to spend the first fifteen to twenty minutes of a forty-five-minute essay reading the question carefully, spotting the issues, and organizing your response. A well-thought-out, well-organized response will almost always outpoint a rambling, disorganized answer with cross-outs and arrows drawn all over it.

"Outline your exam answer before you begin to write," Yvette suggested. "Write big, and write legibly. Anyone who has ever graded a written exam knows that the 'look' of the exam can make the job of grading it a lot easier or a lot harder. To that end, I used erasable pens so that my exam books would always look neat and used a highlighter to highlight key terms in my responses."

Use headings whenever possible to help guide your professor through your response, and don't waffle or equivocate. If the question requires you to take a position, take one—and remember that on most law school exams, it's not the position you take, but how you defend that position with applicable law and policy, that determines your grade. If you must equivocate, or if the outcome of a question is seriously in doubt, take what you perceive to be the stronger position in your heading, then add a sentence or two of potential alternative outcomes at the end of your response. Adopting this structural approach to answering essay exams will make your exam read more clearly and look more professional—attributes that almost always translate into higher grades.

> Remember to go through your analysis in logical steps, from beginning to end. The order in which you present your ideas is more important on a law school exam than it ever was in an essay or on a term paper. Include only those facts and issues which are relevant, but don't exclude basic principles because you think they are too obvious.
>
> —Elizabeth

A couple of final pieces of advice. First, answer only the questions the professor asked you to answer—don't waste your time with extraneous issues or go off on a tangent for the sake of getting more of what you know down on paper. Chances are, if it's not on the professor's grading sheet, you're probably not going to get credit for it. Finally, if you perceive a problem with the question or must make any assumptions prior to giving a response, be sure to note your assumption at the top of your response to make the professor aware of the perceived ambiguity.

Focus on what you're doing and ignore everyone else. Some people will finish a three-hour exam after two hours, and some people will write two blue books for every one of yours. It can be hard to keep from getting nervous when you see people doing such things, but just get back into the questions and plug away.

"Tune everyone out before the start of the exam," Megan advised. "Listening to the chatter in the exam room will only lead to stress and confusion right at the time when it is most crucial to be relaxed and confident."

> Keep track of time. Use only the time allotted for each question and then move on. There is a natural tendency to try to finish a question, even if it is time to move to the next question. Resist this temptation. Believe me, any extra points you pick up will be at the expense of many more points you will forfeit by not having adequate time to answer the final question on the exam.
>
> —John-Mark

But wait . . . my exam is closed book!

Few compelling arguments favor the administration of a closed-book law exam. With the exception of think-on-the-fly evidence questions in a deposition or in trial, you will almost never have to respond to a legal question without the aid of some resources. Consequently, in a perfect world, closed-book exams should rarely be given. Occasionally, however, you will run into a hardheaded professor who doesn't conform his teaching to the realities of legal practice. If you're faced with this, your preparations should be identical to your preparations for an open-book exam, with an additional day or two budgeted into your study time to allow for mnemonic development and memorization.

Rest assured that students' answers on a closed-book exam will be of a significantly lower quality than the answers given in an open-book exam where case names and other information is accessible. Don't be dismayed if you draw a blank on a case name, or if one of your mnemonics fails you in the exam room. Don't be a prisoner to memorization. When all else fails, remember that you wrote outlines and case maps and spent a long time working with the doctrine before you memorized anything, so think back to the general themes of the course and the way the law developed and work from there.

The doomsday scenario

It's virtually guaranteed that you will face the doomsday scenario at least once during your law school career. For me, it happened during my first-year Contracts exam. The three-essay (each with multiple parts) exam was slated to last four and a half hours. I had prepared my own extensive Contracts outline and knew the cases from the class cold, but I did not prepare the bullet outline that would have spared me this brush with disaster. I got the exam, read over the three essay questions, and began to outline the first question, but quickly got stuck. I moved to the second essay, worked through part of that one, and got stuck. Now, about forty-five minutes into the exam with nothing to show for my effort, I began to panic. I moved to the third essay, read it, and couldn't even spot an issue in it. With classmates writing furiously all around me, I sensed the walls beginning to close in and felt a lump rising in my throat. I checked, and rechecked, and re-rechecked the time, and went back to the first essay, but after flipping through my outline, I couldn't resolve my mental block.

A full ninety minutes had passed, and I still didn't have a word written down in a blue book. I was looking at certain failure, and with this growing realization, I became incapable of even reading the words on the paper in front of me. We're talking a complete mental meltdown. Then I made the move that almost certainly saved my skin on the exam.

I got up and walked out.

Yup. I left the exam hall, went to the bathroom, took some deep breaths, and splashed some cold water on my face. I imagined skiing in Colorado over winter break and inhaling the crisp winter air. Knowing that I was facing a disaster in progress, I calmed myself down, rechecked the time, and realized that I had two hours and fifteen minutes left to answer all three essay questions—or forty-five minutes per question. I then reentered the exam room, sat down, pushed my outline aside, and resolved to just write down what I knew.

Two hours later, I had written what I felt was the bare minimum on the three essays, and left the exam room feeling thoroughly beaten and humiliated—but I had at least managed to beat the mental block and get something down on paper for each essay. Outside the exam room, panic and distress were in the air as exasperated students expressed their dismay at the difficulty of the questions. It seemed that I was not alone in my confusion. My spirits were somewhat lifted by hearing this, but I was still gravely concerned about reeling in a C or worse.

When grades came out, however, I was pleasantly surprised to discover that my resuscitation efforts had earned me a B on the exam—hardly a stellar grade, but a pretty good "save" considering the dire circumstances I'd found myself in. As bad as the situation seemed at the time, it proved not to be the end of the world.

I share this story with you to arm you for your inevitable confrontation with the doomsday scenario. If an exam has you on the ropes, remember this story and don't be afraid to take a walk to clear your head and refocus your resolve.

"I have a story of a 'save' that I made on an exam that I thought I was going to fail too," Megan recalled. "It was my Federal Income Tax exam, and I had gone in feeling unusually unprepared. I had tried hard to study and to understand the concepts, but the amount of information was immense. In addition, numbers were involved, and numbers are always bad for me. The exam involved one big essay, and in answering it, I made one big mistake early on, which affected the remainder of my analysis in a big way. I noticed the mistake as I was reading over my answer just as the proctor announced that we had one minute remaining. I had just enough time to write on the very top of the exam booklet that I noticed the mistake, that it changed my analysis and numbers, and that I had no time to fix it. Miraculously, I got an A in the class. I assume I got the grade because that one sentence demonstrated that regardless of how incorrect my answer was, I understood the material."

The Performance Self-Examination: Part One

Immediately after you take each exam, no matter how tired, fed up, or anxious you are, you need to force yourself to sit down for a few minutes and indulge in the following exercise.

In the table that follows, fill in the name of each of your first-semester classes in the space provided, then, as soon as you finish an exam for a particular class, answer each of the questions in the table in the column for that class. Be as complete and as honest as possible. Put your responses right here in the book, in the spaces provided. Spill over into the margins if you need to. Remember, this is your book, and you only do law school once, so scribble at will.

After you've taken all of your exams, the notes you put here will be a testament to your preparation for and execution of each exam. Then, when your grades come out next semester, you'll put those into the chart and be able to compare how you did in each class to the way you prepared, in the hopes of making some distinctions about what worked and did not work for you.

First-Semester Performance Evaluation: Part One

Name of class				
Grade received				
Number of lectures skipped				
Statute/code/rules–based class or case law–based class (e.g., tax-code based vs. Con Law based)				
Percentage of reading assignments completed on time				
Duration of class period and time of day it met				
Professorial style (Socratic/lecture)				
Male or female professor?				
Seat location (front/mid/back)				
Did you sit next to friends or other distractions during class periods?				
Brand of commercial outline/hornbook used				

First-Semester Performance Evaluation *(continued)*

Did you use the commercial outline as directed by chapter 9 of this book?				
Did you participate in a study group?				
Number of times you went to office hours				
Did you attend the review session?				
Did you make your own outline?				
Did you make your own bullet-point outline, map, or checklist? Which?				
How many sample tests did you take?				
Was exam open or closed book?				
Was exam essay, multiple-choice, or mixed?				
Was exam a take-home or in class?				
How did you spend the night before the exam?				
How many hours of sleep did you get the night before the exam?				
Did you wake up feeling well rested?				
What did you have for your preexam meal?				

First-Semester Performance Evaluation *(continued)*

Did you eat or drink anything during the exam?				
Where did you sit in the exam room?				
Were you bothered by any distractions in the exam room?				
Did you take a bathroom break to clear your head?				
Did you take time to read the questions carefully and outline a response before you began writing?				
Did you organize your exam answers well with headings, letters, and numbers as in a memorandum?				
Did you write in blue or black pen?				
Did you skip lines and write on only one side of a page?				
Did you print, type, or write legibly?				
Did you have problems with time?				
Any other thoughts				

Now for each class, consider what you brought with you into the exam room. What did you depend on the most? The least? What did you never look at? What would have been helpful to you if you had it in the exam room? How might you have been better prepared for the exam? Should you have known more policy and theory? More case names? Should you have spent less time with individual cases and more time on the big picture? Write down your responses to these questions in the space below.

CLASS ONE: ____________________

____

____

____

CLASS TWO: ____________________

____

____

____

CLASS THREE: ____________________

____

____

____

CLASS FOUR: ____________________

____

____

Good.

Now you have a permanent record of things while they are fresh in your mind. When your grades come out, come back to this chart, put them in at the top of each column, and try to make some distinctions based on your results.

For now, though, go home and relax. Have a good time. Indulge yourself in the holidays, the company of friends and family, bad television, trashy novels, sun, skiing, or whatever else suits you. Don't dwell on your exams—they're history now, and there's nothing you can do to change them. You'll take part two of this performance self-exam on the day your grades come out.

CHAPTER 14

Looking Behind and Looking Ahead: Assessing the Damage and Charting the Course for Your Second Semester

An error gracefully acknowledged is a victory won.
—GEORGES GASCOIGNE

SO YOU SURVIVED your first semester of law school. You arrived home craving nothing more than sleep and several days of mindless television, but were instead forced to tolerate Uncle Bernie's incessant questions, and your mother's annoying references to "my son/daughter, the budding lawyer." But somewhere, alone in the dark, however briefly, you probably found yourself smiling in tacit recognition of what you've just accomplished. Although the worst is only half over, you're a survivor. Whether you're anything more than that will be determined by a slip of paper with four letters on it that you'll receive sometime in late January.

Your grades.

The only commemoration of the war you waged against yourself during your first semester of law school. The fruit of nearly four months of arduous labor. The cold, hard truth.

So what do you do if the news is bad?

First of all, we need to discuss what standards we're using to evaluate performance. This is not college, and although law schools definitely still practice grade inflation, getting straight A's in all four first-semester classes is rare in most law schools. The majority of students receive a mix of grades. Starting with that as the realistic standard, let's evaluate your first-semester grades.

Every school uses a different grading system and inflates grades to varying degrees. Some schools use a strict B– mean, while other schools scale up to B or B+ mean. You may already know what the mean grade at your school is, but if you don't, look on the walls near the registrar's office for the compiled grade distributions from last semester's exams. Specifically, check the grade distributions in the sections taught by the professors you had. Almost every law school compiles these grade distributions section by section to assess the reliability of grading between sections, and to assure that one first-year professor is not grading radically easier or harder than another. As I discussed earlier, to encourage this result, many law schools employ a strict bell curve for first-year grades, assuring that each section has 20 percent A's, 40 percent B+'s, and 40 percent B's and B–'s, or some such arrangement. If you can't find the distributions posted anywhere, ask the registrar for the information.

So what does it look like? Where are your grades compared to the grades of the people in your section? Glance at the headings below. Determine which one is most applicable to you, and read on.

I got straight A's, mostly A's and B+'s, or I am ahead of the curve in most classes

If your first-semester grades fall into this category, you are now in the pole position in the race to secure a job during your 1L summer, a seat on the law review or one of the other journals at your law school, and the plum interviews with employers next fall. You are also at a huge psychological advantage given that you found a formula that worked at getting you the grades you want and deserve. Congratulations on your outstanding results, but don't rest on your laurels. The hallowed halls of law school are littered with the broken dreams of students who got off to great starts their first semester, but then became cocky or complacent.

Flip to the middle of this chapter and take part two of the performance self-evaluation. Try to concretize the formula you used to achieve success in the classes where you met with success, so you can go back to that formula again and again this semester and beyond.

HOW TO SPIN THESE GRADES: You won't need to spin anything. You're in position to attract maximum attention from employers looking to hire 1L help. Be sure to send a photocopy of your grades and a brief cover letter to any employers you contacted back in November that haven't already rejected you. Prepare to get some favorable attention. Remember to practice humility and not to discuss your grades with your classmates. When asked, just say, "I did okay."

I got a mix of grades, some ahead and some behind the curve

If you got a mix of grades, perhaps something like A–, B+, B, B, you are part of the perplexing group that includes most first-year law students. Ahead of the curve in one or two classes, dead at the mean in a class or two, and behind the mean in the last class, you wonder what caused the discrepancy in your results.

That's precisely what you need to find out, and that's what we'll be doing in part two of the performance self-examination later in this chapter. Don't worry too much. You're probably right in the middle of the pack, within striking distance of making law review with a good second semester, and with grades that aren't going to scare off potential 1L employers. Spend some time with the performance self-examination. With a mix of grades, you have the most to learn, and the best opportunity to draw distinctions between strategies and approaches that worked for you, and those that didn't.

HOW TO SPIN THESE GRADES: Because a combination of grades is common, they won't hurt your chances of getting summer employment—they just won't get you any additional attention. If you went to an outstanding undergraduate institution (such as an Ivy League university or its equivalent), graduated with an excellent GPA, and have a strong résumé, wait for potential employers to contact you to request grades. Some employers may hire you on the strength of your undergraduate record without waiting for your first-semester grades. Since your grades aren't anything to be ashamed of, send your transcript immediately to any employer that requests it.

If you went to a second- or third-tier undergraduate school or had an average undergraduate record, you may want to be a bit more proactive and send your grades out to your top-choice potential 1L employers without waiting for them to contact you. The operative rule here is, getting a 1L position is extremely difficult. If you think your first-semester grades improve your overall record, send them out right away. If they detract from a sterling undergraduate record, wait until employers solicit them.

One grade is widely disparate from the others

Hopefully this means three A's and a B–, but even if it means three B's and an A, you are in a great position to learn something about why one class worked out so differently from the others. Go to the performance self-examination later in this chapter and compare your preparation for the disparate class with the others in an effort to make distinctions to help you in the future.

HOW TO SPIN THESE GRADES: If you got three A's and a B– (or a close equivalent), you had a bad day. You misread or mistimed a question. The professor tricked you with a tough question. You are almost certain to be asked, either this year in a 1L employment interview or next fall in 2L recruiting, "What happened?" in the disparate class. Don't run and hide from a bad grade. Embrace it, and discuss it candidly. Few law students escape law school without at least one low grade. Almost every law firm recruiter will have a war story of his own. Tell yours, and laugh about it.

If you have one good grade and three mediocre ones, is it because you were really interested in the subject you did well in? Is it because late in the semester you figured something out about law school and applied it in that class with great results? Figure out a way to show a potential employer that you learned something from first semester and are excited about the distinctions you made. People know that first semester can be a difficult period of adjustment. If you can show both that the experience didn't destroy you, and that you are actively pursuing ways to improve, you might impress an employer enough to take a chance on you.

All grades are at or below the mean

You are probably somewhat depressed about this outcome, and after all the work you put in during the first semester, that's understandable. But did you really put in the time? Were you really disciplined? Did you follow the advice of the earlier chapters in this book, preparing your own outlines, staying current in your reading, and not missing classes? Or did you party too much, spend too much time with a new love interest, or underestimate how hard you really have to work to do well? When you complete part two of the performance self-evaluation, spend some time thinking about how you spent your first semester, day by day. Be honest with yourself. Did you really put in your time? Get your exam responses and look them over. Compare them to any model answers the professor might provide.

If, after honest introspection, you feel that you worked as hard as your classmates did, you followed the advice in the previous chapters, and you are at a loss, it's time to take the next step. Make appointments and talk to each of your professors from last semester. Ask them for their advice on ways you might improve your performance. Do not allow your bitterness or embarrassment to stop you from turning this seemingly negative experience into a positive chance to learn something. Speak candidly to each professor. Ask each of them for their advice. Although one or two of them might brush you off, chances are you'll find one or two of them will want to help you. Listen carefully to what they say, and write down any suggestions they make. By opening up to a professor, you might establish the rapport necessary to turn one of these professors into a mentor.

HOW TO SPIN THESE GRADES: Getting four B's (or worse) during your first semester puts you into a bit of a hole. Those grades aren't going to attract 1L employers, and they're going to make it pretty hard for you to grade onto the law review, even with a sterling second semester.

So should you just pack up and go home?

Of course not.

First of all, you need to spring into action the day you first find out about these grades. Chances are, you'll get your grades first by calling the automated grade retrieval system or looking them up on your law school Web page. These grades are still unofficial and can occasionally be changed if errors in the curve or errors in grading are subsequently discovered. It will likely be a couple of weeks before you receive "official" notice of these grades from the registrar.

In the meantime, call in every favor you can. If anyone you know well works for a firm that you've queried, particularly in your hometown or home state, it's time to make a frontal attack on that firm with everything you have. Call them immediately to determine the status of your query. Offer to come up and interview at your own expense. Make them refuse you on the phone before you give up. If you are asked about your first-semester grades, tell them that you'll be getting official notice from the registrar in a couple of weeks. This may buy you the critical time you need to get the firm to make you an offer. What you're hoping for is that they'll hire you on the strength of the personal relationship you have with the person there, on the strength of your undergraduate résumé, or because they have a need they are impatient to fill, without seeing your first-semester grades. If the firm wants to wait to see your first-semester grades, there is nothing you can do about that. Under no circumstance should you ever lie about or misrepresent your grades.

Grades are critical, and without good grades you will have a much more difficult task in securing 1L summer employment. Don't give up. Somewhere out there is a judge who will bring you on as an intern, or a public-service organization or a professor in need of free research assistance. Keep asking around. Use the professors you talked to as networking resources. Go to your career placement office and ask for advice.

When you do get an interview for a position, don't apologize for your grades, and don't hide from them. They're out there, and you're going to be asked about them. Have a well-thought-out response ready. Explain what you learned from first semester. Tell the interviewer about the distinctions you've made, and how you're applying them to improve this semester. Be self-deprecating, but be confident. It is, after all, only one semester. If your credentials were impressive enough to get you into law school, you still have a proven track record to build on.

"In college, I had become accustomed to a steady stream of A's and A-minuses with an occasional B, but in my first year of law school, I got a steady stream of B's with an occasional A or A-minus," Joel notes. "I was unhappy, but I don't have many words of wisdom here except to say that law school is hard—it's full of smart people, and the curve is generally steeper than the curves in college. Don't be defined by your grades, and don't think that your occasional answer in class or your comments in study group aren't worth making because you didn't get straight A's during your first semester. Your grades are not you—they're just your grades."

THE PERFORMANCE SELF-EXAMINATION: PART TWO

Go back to the table in the last chapter and write in the grade you received for each of your classes. Whether your grades were perfect, perfectly awful, or anywhere in between, you have something to learn from the following exercise. Answer the following questions as truthfully and completely as possible.

If there were differences among your grades, look at the different variables in the table and highlight any differences between the classes you did well in and the classes you struggled in. What do you notice about the classes you did well in? What did you do differently in the classes where you faltered? Answers to these questions might not be immediately obvious. There might not seem to be any correlation. That's part of what makes law school so frustrating—sometimes, it just seems as if the grades were handed out randomly. But perhaps something is hiding in this chart you've just filled out. Look for any distinctions you can draw. Remember that to succeed in law school, you only need to be a little bit better than everybody else.

I had two midterms first semester because my Contracts and Property classes were full-year classes, whereas Torts and Criminal Law were only one-semester classes. I bombed both my Contracts and Property midterms. I think I got a C in both. I was devastated. I understood all the rules of law, concepts, and issues. I had met with both professors throughout the semester to review my outlines and practice exams. I was really baffled with my C performance since it seemed as though I had done everything I was supposed to do study-wise. Fortunately I did well on my Torts and Criminal Law finals. Not only did my GPA not suffer greatly, but I was able to compare those A exams to my C exams. When I examined my answers side by side, I truly saw a difference. My A answers were straight to the point, very precise. I simply identified the issue, the applicable rule, and applied my analysis. My C answers were full of tangential thoughts and what-ifs and contained a fair amount of BS, not because I did not understand or know the answer, but because I thought I needed to write more. By doing this comparison, I learned to tailor my answers to the distinct question posed. I focused on the major issues and learned to become as succinct as possible.

—Yvette

So now you face a new semester, clean textbooks, and a fresh start. Take one more look at the chart you filled out in the last chapter and remind yourself what you learned and the new approaches you are going to bring with you into the new semester. Don't fall into the same traps that caught you last semester!

"I stopped briefing cases and concentrated on doing all the reading and making some notes in the margins," Allan states. "I think this system was much more efficient. You get used to reading cases and what you're looking for, so you absorb a lot more."

"Second semester, I picked the two classes I really wanted to master and decided early on that I wanted to prepare my own complete outlines for those classes. I prepared outlines for both of these classes and shared them with my study partner in exchange for his outlines for the other two classes. This system worked really well," Carolyn notes.

"My biggest lesson after first semester was that my writing style needed to change," Elizabeth adds. "If you were an English major or a history major, or a major in a similar subject, yours may need to change too. I discovered that I could no longer write in a flowery, free-flowing style. Legal writing is crisp, brief, and to the point."

So what are the things you are going to change about your approach to the new semester? Write them in the space provided below so you can refer back to them and so you don't forget what they are.

____

____

____

____

____

____

You may have the choice of one or two elective courses during your second semester. If you do have such a choice, choose wisely. In law school, you have a limited number of credit hours at your disposal, and you can't afford to waste any of them. Every choice should be made for a reason, so before you take a course, ask yourself what purpose the course will serve in your "grand scheme." This is a good time to begin thinking what approach you want to take to the rest of law school. To get a head start, jump ahead to chapter 17 and read about the different philosophies you can take to your upper years in law school.

"I took a practical-skills type of class rather than another big doctrinal course. This was a good strategy for me because it was a change of pace from the rest of the first-year offerings," Joel recalls.

"I tried to take the courses with the professors I heard were the best," Alison adds.

Finally, with a semester of law school under your belt, you may start to feel restless and drawn toward some public-service work or some of the various extracurricular activities at the law school or in the larger university community. My advice is to wait a few weeks until you get a feel for whether your schedule is actually any lighter this semester. Remember, this is still the first year of law school, and grades remain crucial. During the recruiting season next fall, employers will be scrutinizing your second-semester grades, both to look for trends, and to determine whether you were able to adjust and improve your performance after one round of exams. This is not the time to commit to anything except your studies.

> Although I felt okay about my grades, I was bored with law school, and the whole scene made me depressed and unhappy for most of second semester. I was sure that I didn't want to be a lawyer. Obviously, that would change later on.
>
> —Alison

There will be plenty of time for public-service work and other extracurricular activities during your upper years of law school. In the first year, your first priority, indeed your only priority, should be getting the best grades you can. If, after two or three weeks of class, you feel that you have a couple of free hours a week to commit to an activity, then go for it. Anything more demanding than that should be deferred until next year.

CHAPTER 15

First-Year Endgame: Succeeding in Exams and the Law Review Competition

There is a tide in the affairs of men,
which, taken at the flood,
leads on to fortune.
—SHAKESPEARE

ALTHOUGH IT SEEMS like only yesterday, it has been nearly a full semester since your first set of grades arrived. Whether the news you received that day was positive, positively abhorrent, or somewhere in between, another opportunity is coming.

What are you going to do differently this time? Look back at the performance self-examination you completed at the end of last semester. Hopefully you have been implementing any distinctions you were able to draw from that comparison with respect to study habits, but what additional distinctions can you draw about exam day itself? Compare the classes where you did well with the classes where you didn't. Where are the differences?

Assuming that you feel you were equally well prepared for all of your exams, you need to try to give yourself a little edge. Did you get more sleep the night before the exam where you did well? Did you eat a better breakfast? Did you eat something during the exam to stave off fatigue?

What did you rely on in the exam room? Where did you sit? Did you print in pen and structure your exam answer like a legal memorandum, with headings, letters, and numbers? What else can you see as potential differences between the exams where you scored well and those where you didn't?

I developed the performance self-examination after my third semester of law school. Comparing my first three semesters' grades, I noticed that I got better grades on pure essay exams (exams without multiple-choice sections), on exams where I'd sat in the very first or very last row or in the corners (where distractions from other classmates were significantly minimized), on exams where I'd relied on the case maps I'd developed, on exams where I'd relied heavily on Emanuel's and Little, Brown's Examples and Explanations study aids, and on exams where my essays were printed or typed, double-spaced, written on one side of the page, and organized in legal-brief format with headings. I did best on open-book and take-home exams.

I can almost hear your skeptical groans from here, thinking that I've gone completely off the wall, that these findings are just coincidental, and that I'm wasting my time and yours highlighting these differences.

Well, maybe, but once again I remind you that success in law school is all about finding and capitalizing on the little distinctions that will make you just a bit better than the person in the seat next to you. It may be coincidence, but I never got worse than a B+ in the six classes where I used case maps, never got worse than a B+ in the seven classes where I sat in the back corner of the exam room to shield me from in-class distractions, and got a B+ or better in five of the six classes where I used the relevant Emanuel's commercial outline throughout the semester.

My worst grades in law school came on multiple-choice exams, exams where I failed to follow the timing suggestions the professor provided, and exams (during my first semester) where I did not have a bullet-point outline or case map in addition to my outline.

Great, you say. So I'll sit in the back corner of the exam room and follow some of the other suggestions in this book. But how can I avoid taking a multiple-choice exam?

Glad you asked.

Take a look through your course-selection book next time you're picking courses. See if you don't find at least a couple of sections of the same class taught at different times by different professors. Now read the course descriptions. Chances are, you'll find at least a couple of courses where you'll have the choice between a take-home final and an in-class final, or a multiple-choice final and an essay final. At least three times that I can remember during my law school career, I chose one section of a course over another section based entirely on what kind of exam was to be given at the end, with great results. This should not be the only factor you consider when choosing classes, but it deserves thought.

The law review competition

In most law schools, at the end of the second semester, often immediately following the conclusion of the last first-year final examination, you will be confronted with a great challenge.

If at any point during your first year of law school you've found yourself wishing you could start over with a clean slate, kicking yourself for not working harder, or feeling as if you've bought yourself a nonexchangeable, nontransferable seat in mediocrity class, then this is the answer to your prayers. An opportunity, for one week, to wipe the slate clean, to forget about the grades you've posted to date and stand on a level playing field once again to confront the "great equalizer."

The law review/law journal writing competition.

At most schools this includes a writing component and an editing component. Although you are likely to be in no mood for such things right after exams, if such a competition is offered at your school, it can be more important to your future than any law school exam will ever be.

In the "bad ol' days," membership on a school's law review was determined by grades alone, and only the true elite, usually the top 10 percent of a law school class, were offered membership. At most schools, however, the system changed as the powers-that-be recognized that many excellent writers and legal thinkers were slipping through a grades-only filtering system. Accordingly, a new system began to emerge, using a combination of first-year grades and a score on a writing and editing test to select journal members.

> My law school had no grade-on slots; that is, law review membership was determined strictly by a writing competition. I did participate, and it was difficult. They made the competition packets available right after the last exam. So you just finished your last exam of your first year of law school and you want to celebrate, yet you have a week to write a twenty-page case note. Not fun. However, I can honestly say, it was worth it. It is definitely a plus to have the law review, or other journal experience, on your résumé. It indicates to people that you are a hard worker and a good writer.
>
> —John-Mark

> Our competition was eight days long, right after finals. I started the day I got it and worked diligently, eight to nine hours per day on it, with a half day off in the middle to do something fun and relaxing. My main advice is to start as soon as you get the

competition. If you procrastinate for two or three days, there is a good chance that you will either give up, or not do as well as you might have done, since you'll have to work longer hours in the remaining time to make up for it, and there is no way that your twelfth consecutive hour of subciting will be your sharpest. My method worked, as I made the law review entirely on the strength of my writing competition.

—Joel

While these systems vary from school to school, and the exact formulas used are often closely guarded secrets, this is typically how such a system works. The registrar assigns a code number to each student entering the competition, and a copy of that student's first-year grades with name removed and code number added is submitted to the law review editorial board. A grade point average or other numerical equivalent is then computed to represent that student's grades, and the coefficient representing the percentage that the law review decides should be assigned to first-year grades is multiplied with the grade point average to determine a "grade value score." Some law reviews offer automatic membership to the students with the top five or ten grade value scores without considering performance on the writing competition. Others don't.

The editing portion of the writing competition is typically a grueling exercise in "bluebooking"—that is, using the legal style manual (*The Bluebook*) rules to correct an unedited law review article section containing hundreds or even thousands of errors in its text and footnotes, using a large photocopied packet gathering the relevant sections of the original source materials. Your job will be to carefully mark up the manuscript, checking every quote, citation, and footnote for stylistic, grammatical, content, and bluebooking errors.

Take a few hours off after your last exam. Watch TV, drink a beer, unwind. Then give the package a look-over later that evening. Then, as much as it hurts, start working on it diligently the next morning. Set yourself a work schedule and stick by it; you probably won't have to put in exam hours, except near the deadline. Of the people who begin the competition, a fairly large percentage fail to complete it. Set a schedule you can live with and submit a completed piece and you have a good chance of getting on.

Also, read the directions carefully and review a sample submission if one is attached. I can remember grading for the competition the year after I got on, and it was surprising to me the number of people who ignored the directions. There were people who tried all kinds of crazy fonts and spacing to flout the page limits. There were also people who ignored the format and wrote legal briefs instead of case notes. A lot of law review work is making sure authors stick to accepted editorial and publication rules; if you demonstrate that you don't pay attention to such rules, you won't get on the law review!"

—John-Mark

At Penn, the competition was held in three large classrooms at the law school, which were open from 8:00 a.m. to 11:00 p.m. every day for the nine days of the competition. Students were free to come and go as they chose, but no materials were allowed to enter or leave the room. As sick as it sounds, most students spent at least fifty hours during that week editing that manuscript.

About 80 percent of the class signed up for the competition. However, the apparent absurdity of the exercise, combined with the frustration and exhaustion in students who had just completed the rigors of the first year and yearned to escape Philadelphia for the summer, produced a dropout rate of about 20 percent. Other students remained in the competition, but turned in lackluster efforts. A select core of students, maybe 30 percent, churned away day after day, morning to night, in search of the elusive invitation to join the law review.

The edits were then collected and scored, page by page, against a list of the errors intentionally written into the manuscript by the editors. Generally, for every error discovered, you get some fraction of a point, and for every error properly corrected, you get some additional fraction. Your entire edit receives a raw score.

For the writing component, at Penn and many other schools the editors of the law review select a general topic (drugs, education, crime) and gather hundreds of pages of sources on the topic, including law review articles, legal cases, commentaries, editorials, book chapters, and the like. Your job is to develop a thesis, then write a piece of persuasive writing, usually ten to twenty pages in length and in proper *Bluebook* form, using only the provided materials as sources. This essay is then graded by the editors for quality of writing, persuasiveness of the argument, grammar, style, content, and bluebooking and assigned a raw score.

BU gave us two weeks to prepare a ten-page article based on a package of materials that we were given. There was also a technical bluebooking assignment. Then, from a mystical combination of your grades and your perceived performance on the competition, you were offered a position on one journal at the school. (I think we ordered our preferences when we handed in the writing sample.) I was placed on the second-best journal at BU—everyone who is not on law review says they are on the second-best journal. I hated it. I hated the bluebooking assignments; and because my journal was limited in scope (health law), I didn't enjoy writing my note. I left the journal after one year. I have mixed feelings about my departure. While it freed up more time for me to do other things, including moot court competitions, I think it hindered my applications for clerkships.

—Patrick

Time is often a factor in the quality of student performances on the journal competition. If your school's competition includes a writing segment, make sure you get to it with enough time to do a good job. It doesn't do you any good to turn in a sterling edit if you turn in a sloppy essay.

"I killed myself on the editing part, and by the time I got to the writing part, I was completely spent and did a bad job. I made a journal, but I didn't make the law review. I really wish I had better divided my time between the two parts," Alison counsels.

"I worked hard and methodically revised my paper several times before handing it in," Keith remembers. "If I could recommend one approach to the writing portion, it is revise, revise, revise."

"I approached the competition like an exam because it is certainly as important, if not more important, than an exam," Bess adds.

"Getting on the law review is definitely worth it for the doors it opens," Megan noted. "Succeeding in the write-on competition is not a hard task. It is a task that we are all smart enough to complete—it just involves extreme determination and patience. The students who get on the law review tend to have superior legal writing skills and also those who pay close attention to detail—both skills that employers really care about."

Depending on the particular practices of a school's law review, the writing and editing raw scores might be combined or assigned separate coefficients. Assuming that they are kept separate, each student's grade scores, writing scores, and editing scores are then totaled up, and a rank order is established. Journal membership is decided from this final rank order.

To fully comprehend the critical importance of the writing competition, consider the following hypothetical example. Student No. 1, whom we'll call Arrogant Andrea, has the first-year grades A, A, A, A,

B+, B+, B, B—certainly a solid effort, but probably not enough to simply "grade-on" to the typical law review. Using the common numerical equivalents (4.0 for an A, 3.5 for a B+, etc.), Andrea's grades add up to a 29 raw score. Student No. 2, whom we'll call Earnest Erin, had a rougher time of it during her first year. Her grades were A, A, B, B, B, B, B, B–, for a numerical equivalent of 25.67.

In approaching the writing competition, however, Andrea got cocky, feeling that her grades were probably good enough that a minimal effort in the competition would suffice to earn her a seat on the law review. Her essay earned only 7 out of a possible 10 points, and her edit, a 122/200. Erin, realizing that she was fighting an uphill battle, wrote the essay of her life, earning a 9.5 out of 10 points, and did extremely well on the edit, netting a 178/200.

Assume that the hypothetical law review in question values grades at 50 percent, the edit at 30 percent, and the essay at 20 percent in determining its members, and that the scores are normalized using coefficients to put each of the individual scores on a scale with a top score of one hundred. Accordingly, raw grade scores are multiplied by 3.125, the edit score is multiplied by 0.5, and the essay score is multiplied by 10. Each score is then multiplied by the percentage weight assigned to it by the editors of the law review.

Take a minute to work through the math so you understand what I'm talking about.

Got it?

Now, on to the fate of our two competitors. Follow the math below.

Andrea's total score is the sum of each coefficient × section score × weighted percent of the section, or $(3.125 \times 29 \times .50 + .5 \times 122 \times .30) + (10 \times 7 \times .20)$ or 77.6 out of a possible 100 points. Erin's total score is $(3.125 \times 25.67 \times .50 + .5 \times 178 \times .30) + (10 \times 9.5 \times .20)$ or 85.8. Erin, whose grades were decidedly worse than Andrea's, gets the seat on the law review.

As the example above illustrates, the law review competition can provide a "back door" to journal membership for individuals whose grades wouldn't get them in the front door. For the truly determined, this competition can be a one-week cure-all to a semester's worth of disappointing grades.

So should you do it?

What's so important about being on the law review anyway? Does it just mean that you'll be part of an elitist "club" and have to spend a lot of time doing the same kind of mind-numbingly boring editing that you did in the competition for two more years, surrounded by some of the most arrogant, annoying people in your law school class?

Yeah, maybe. That depends on how your law review selects its members. But you might want to be on the law review for a lot of other reasons.

First of all, it's a tremendous honor, among the biggest you can get in law school, and everybody knows it. Employers know it and covet members of law reviews, sometimes providing a sizable bonus to incoming associates who were members of their law review in law school. Judges certainly know it, as membership on a law review is almost a prerequisite to getting a high-level clerkship with a federal district or circuit court judge. Law schools know it—check someday to see how many of your professors made the law review at their respective schools. Even clients know it—being able to put "law review" on your résumé and your firm biography singles you out for distinction, even though few clients have any idea what a law review really is. There is just no ignoring that membership on your school's law review opens important doors for you, and in this business, the more doors you have open to you, the better.

How important journal membership is to getting prime job interviews and offers depends largely on the reputation of the various law schools. Generally, at the top ten or fifteen law schools, it is less critical than it is at other schools.

"At a school like Harvard, journal membership is relatively unimportant to getting the best job offers," Joel notes. "Journal members do very well during interview season, but many nonmembers also get excellent offers, and virtually everyone who isn't a psychopath or a chronic drooler gets a respectable offer."

Carolyn agrees. "At Penn, journal membership seemed to be only one of many factors that firms considered in deciding whether to hire someone. I don't think that it was overwhelmingly important. But at Penn, we also got to pick the firms we wanted to interview with—the firms weren't allowed to pick us—and that makes a big difference."

"At Boston College, being on the law review was really important to getting the prime job interviews," Bess recalls. "When the school posted the interview lists for on-campus interviews, the lists for the employers all included substantially the same people—all law review and other journal members. This was frustrating for people who weren't on a journal. You might not make the cut for an initial interview solely because you weren't on a journal because the firms get so many résumés that many of them make the cut based on this distinction."

Everyone agrees that being on the law review, or at least being on some journal, is critical if you plan to seek a federal clerkship or a prestigious state court clerkship after graduation.

"Pretty much crucial," Keith notes.

"It's really important in the clerkship process," Joel counsels, "since the process is extremely competitive and most judges were journal members themselves."

"If you're at all interested in getting a prestigious clerkship after graduation, being a member of the law review, or at least some reputable journal at your law school, is virtually a prerequisite," another mentor added. "Many judges won't even consider applicants who weren't on a journal."

But what about the substance?

There is no denying that certain aspects of law review membership are mind-numbingly boring. You do have to cite-check and bluebook professors' articles, which can often be tangles of nearly incomprehensible argument, impenetrable language, and sloppy citation. On the other hand, you get to write a "Case Note" or "Comment" of your own, generally on a subject of your choosing, and have a chance to get that note or comment published, an impressive credential that again helps you with employers, judges, and clients. You also get a lot of firsthand contact with professors, which can help you establish the rapport needed to find a mentor on the faculty and get the most out of your law school experience. You'll be on the front lines of the law, reading articles espousing the newest legal theories and policy arguments. Finally, with all the writing and editing you'll be doing, you'll be honing your legal writing and editing skills to razor sharpness—skills that will serve you well for the rest of your days in the law.

Law review membership is not for everyone. It is grueling, tiresome, inconvenient, time-consuming, and often incredibly frustrating. To me, however, given how it is perceived and used as a differentiator in the marketplace, its benefits far outweigh these drawbacks in the mind of the long-term thinker.

Think carefully before passing up this golden opportunity.

Finally, before you leave law school for the summer, stop by the placement office and provide them with your summer mailing address. During the summer, the placement office will need to send you a lot of important correspondence regarding recruiting season, and you'll want to be in the loop.

CHAPTER 16

Working for Free or Working for Pay, Your First Summer Paves the Way

The world is always ready to receive talent with open arms.
—HOLMES

WHETHER YOU ARE working for a firm, interning with a judge, or doing public-interest work, your goal during your first summer is quite simple. You're looking for a valuable, worthwhile experience, and you want to make a great impression.

Even if your experience is not all that you hoped it would be (and many first-year positions aren't because, depending on the economy, you may have to take what you can get), your first-year position will inevitably lead you somewhere. If you love the position, perform admirably, and prove to be a good fit for the firm or organization where you spend your first summer, your first-year position may lead to permanent employment. This is pretty unusual, however. More likely, your first-year position will expose you to new areas of the law, will help you determine what areas of law motivate you, and will, consequently, suggest areas of interest to focus on during the upper years of your legal education. Be on the lookout for these things as you proceed through your first summer.

> The most important thing I learned during my 1L summer is how important it is to be able to write well. At Penn, like all lLs, I took the legal writing course. The course was pass-fail, though, so a lot of people did not take it seriously. I was glad that I did.
>
> —Carolyn

"You learn a great deal more about law and lawyering during the summer than you do in school," Bess suggests. "I learned more about the law in ten weeks of a summer job than I learned during an entire school year because you learn the most by doing."

"I did research, wrote memos, and even wrote a few briefs," Allan adds. "Pretty much the same thing I do as an associate today, so it was a good barometer."

"The most important thing you discover is how everything you learned during your first year of law school applies in the real-world practice of law," Pat concludes.

> I worked in the Criminal Division of the United States Attorney's Office in Boston, Massachusetts. This experience was among the most influential I have had. The people who work at that office (and U.S. attorney's offices, generally) are among the brightest, most enthusiastic lawyers I have ever encountered. And, in a profession where so many people find themselves saying that they'd rather be blueberry farming in Maine or cleaning toilets in Penn Station, enthusiastic lawyers are difficult to find. I was able to assist in briefing appeals for the government, attend court every day, and participate in lectures from the FBI, the IRS, and former AUSAs who had gone on into private practice. This experience charted my career course.
>
> —Patrick

In addition, your first-year position can be valuable in helping you to judge your affinity for a particular city or geographic region of the country, the size of the firm or organization you most want to work for, or, even more broadly, whether you enjoy practicing law at all. As Joel discovered, "I learned that I didn't want to spend a career working in the ultrapolitical atmosphere of Washington, D.C."

Most important, your first summer experience will earn you important contacts in the legal community to support your candidacy for future positions. Contacts are crucial in the legal profession. Lawyers move around a lot, and chances are, wherever you end up during your first summer, you'll find people who have already been where you want to go who can help you get there.

To take full advantage of all of these possibilities, keep your eyes and ears open, do good work, and make people want to help you. Here are some strategies about how to survive and thrive in your first summer position in order to achieve the maximum benefit from it.

For those clerking for a judge

You have two ultimate goals to achieve from your position this summer. First, you want to cultivate the judge as a mentor. Judges are typically seasoned veterans of the legal wars with a wealth of advice to provide to law students, but they don't always just volunteer their advice. You have to ask for it, and the judge is more likely to provide you with his best wisdom if he likes you. Makes sense, right? So how do you make the judge like you? We'll get to that in a moment.

The second goal of your summer internship is to earn the judge's enthusiastic reference. Remember, every judge on the bench once worked somewhere else, and a recommendation to his old law firm to hire you will virtually assure you of success. Similarly, no matter what kind of judge you are interning for, chances are he knows a fair number of people in the local bar association who have the power to hire you. Finally, if you do an exceptional job for the judge and the two of you hit it off well, you stand an increased chance of getting hired by that judge for a full-time judicial clerkship after graduation. Although many judges say that they avoid hiring former interns as judicial clerks because of just such an expectation, I know at least three people who are presently clerking for judges they interned with as 1Ls. So the take-home message about your judicial internship is to (1) do the best job you can, and (2) try to develop a relationship with your judge. But how do you do that?

At the beginning of your internship summer, you will probably be given a couple of case files to work on. These files will typically be relatively straightforward cases containing one or two discrete issues. Alternatively, the judge or his law clerks may simply give you individual issues upon which you will be asked to draft "bench memos." The judge and his clerks rely on these memos when drafting legal opinions, so the accuracy of your work and the clarity of your writing is of paramount importance. Be certain to read cases carefully before citing them, and always cite-check everything before you turn it in.

Depending on the trial schedule in your court, you may have opportunities to watch trials. Ask the judge every couple of weeks whether something interesting is coming up that he thinks would be worthwhile for you to observe. Remember, however, that first and foremost a judicial internship is an academic position, and you will be expected to help shoulder some of the written workload in the chambers during the weeks you are there. The most respected judicial interns are humble, arrive at the office on time, perform careful research, write clear and well-organized prose, confer with the judicial clerks and the judge and ask questions when doctrinal questions arise that they don't understand, and generally help to reduce the workload for the chambers. The less well-respected judicial interns view their internship as a "summer off" or take the attitude that since they aren't being paid, they don't have to work hard. These interns typically spend a lot of time surfing the Net, talking on the phone, socializing with other interns, clerks, or court staff, or sitting in the courtrooms watching trials, but complete little substantive work. The diligent intern not only gets more from his experience, but will almost certainly get more in the way of advice and assistance from the judge. Work hard and consistently prepare high-quality product, and long before you'll find yourself in the good graces of the judge. Take the other road, and you'll waste an opportunity.

For those going to a firm

For those of you heading to a law firm during your first summer, you should have one of two primary goals in mind: (1) perform admirably and be personable enough so the firm invites you to return during your second summer (and then perhaps permanently); or (2) perform admirably, get exposed to the firm's different practice areas, get some good experience, and parlay that into the job you want for your second summer. Although we'll discuss a number of subsidiary goals in a moment, be clear that one of these is the main objective for your first summer in a law firm. A lot of first-year students lucky enough to end up with firm jobs during their first summer fail to fully capitalize on the experience, either because they know going in that they're not interested in joining the firm permanently, or because they're not focused on what they need to take from the experience.

We discuss summer associate life in a law firm in detail in chapter 24. If you will be working for a firm during your 1L summer, however, you should flip ahead and read that chapter before your summer begins. The advice and suggestions contained in chapter 24 apply equally to 1L and 2L summer associates, with the caveat that as a 1L summer associate expectations of you will be somewhat lower, and you won't be facing the prospect of a permanent-employment decision at the end of the summer.

Your subsidiary goals as a 1L summer associate, however, can be much different. During your 2L year, assuming a robust economy, you'll probably experience a seller's market and have some choices about what positions to pursue and which offers to accept. As a 1L, however, if you managed to land a position in a law firm, it might not be the firm you want to end up at. It might not be the right size, it might not practice the kind of law you're interested in, and it might not be in the right state or even in the right region of the country. Nevertheless, there will always be lessons to learn from your 1L position if you are aware of the opportunities to make these distinctions. Accordingly, after you've read chapter 24 and have a good understanding about how to succeed and thrive as a summer associate in a law firm, and after you've identified which of the primary goals you're working toward, consider the following.

If you think the firm you're at is the place that you'd like to end up after you graduate, make an effort to get to know as many people at the firm as possible. Don't brownnose or walk around pressing flesh like a politician, but take every nonawkward opportunity to introduce yourself to people you haven't met. This includes support staff, associates, and partners. Spend some time with the firm directory and do your best to learn and remember names. Find the associates and partners that do the kind of work you're most interested in, take the initiative to express your interest to those people, and inquire if they have any work that they'd like you to do. If they offer something to you, you're in business. If they don't have anything at the moment, ask them to remember you when they do, and let them know how long you'll be at the firm.

Remember, people who take polite initiative get what they want. There is a difference between sycophantic groveling and a sincere expression of interest in pursuing a line of work. The above strategies constitute the latter and should readily be employed.

If you discover that you have no interest in returning to the firm you're at, you can still do a lot to make the experience worthwhile. First of all, no matter what firm you're at, the people have contacts that could prove useful to you. Cultivate these potential contacts by doing a great job on the assignments you are given, being a team player, and learning about the partners and the associates and where they've come from. Ask a lot of questions during the summer social events to get to know these people better. If you've done a great job but decide not to stay, these people will know you, like you, and will be willing to offer enthusiastic endorsements of you to their friends in the places you are more interested in staying long term. Even in the largest metropolises, legal communities are well connected, and people move around so much that contacts are plentiful. Whether you will have access to these contacts depends on how you come across as a 1L.

You should also use your first summer to explore the city and the geographic area where your firm is located to determine whether you want to consider the area in your 2L job search. If you have no interest in staying in the area next summer, figure out why. Is the city too big or too small? Is it too congested? Does it lack character or culture? Is it too far away from a large metropolis? Not enough young, single people in the area to socialize with? Forcing yourself to answer these questions will help you to eliminate similar geographical areas during the fall recruiting season just ahead.

Next, consider the firm itself. What has made you decide that you're not interested in staying with them long term? Consider the following list of questions, and/or add your own thoughts.

- Is the firm too big or too small?
- Has the firm seemed poorly organized to you?
- Does it lack the practice areas you want?
- Are the partners and associates hostile toward each other or toward you?
- Did you notice any camaraderie among the partners and among the associates?
- Is the firm too much of an ol' boys' club for your tastes?
- Has the firm made any effort to provide you with work you are interested in, or have you been more like slave labor to the firm's "dog cases" and scut work?
- Did you get enough guidance on your projects and enough feedback on your work?
- Did people at the firm have time for their outside interests and families, or did it seem as if the law trumped everything else for the majority of people?
- Is the firm a sweatshop where people seemed to work around the clock?
- Did people at the firm generally seem happy or miserable?

Finally, we come to the big question. What if the reason you don't like the firm is because you just hate practicing law? Does this mean that you should quit law school now, save yourself the rest of your tuition money, and find something else to do?

The answer to this question is necessarily too much of an individual choice to be answered generally. Several people involved in this book, knowing what they know now, would not go to law school if they had it to do over. Others of us, however, would have quit after our first summer, but are now happy that we made it through and are putting our law degrees to good use. If you despise everything about law school and the practice of law, you have thoroughly explored the different options for legal practice (e.g., firm practice, in-house counsel, permanent law clerk, prosecutor, public defender, public-service work), you have thoroughly examined the different ways a law degree can advance other careers (e.g., anything business-related, consulting, agenting, editing, and/or writing), and you still see no benefit to continuing, then you should probably make an appointment with the dean of students at your law school to discuss your future. If you haven't thought these things through, however, don't even think about dropping out until you do. You've simply come too far to make a rash decision.

As you proceed through your 1L summer, write down your thoughts and the answers to all of these questions while they are fresh in your mind. The observations you make now will greatly aid your employment search this fall, both by helping you to avoid ending up in a similar place next summer, and by providing you with certain questions to ask during your screening and callback interviews. Space is provided at the end of this chapter to note these impressions so they will be available to you in one place when you need them next fall.

For those going into public-interest jobs

Our discussion in this section must necessarily be general because the breadth of possible jobs in this category provides innumerable different experiences and challenges. A few things can be said, however, about how to maximize your summer working in one of these organizations.

First of all, display initiative. It is easy, particularly if you are working in a larger organization such as an urban district attorney's office, or a large urban service provider, to get lost in the shuffle. Often overburdened with work and understaffed, these places can appear to be disorganized and frenetic, and if you wanted to, you could spend a large part of your summer sitting around watching things happen around you. Accordingly, in many cases it will be up to you to step up and take the initiative. Volunteer to help someone on a project, or find out which people are overworked and ask them to delegate some work to you. Law students who are proactive in this way tend to have great experiences in these positions. Those who wait to be spoon-fed will often go hungry.

Second, cultivate a mentor, and try to get that person to take you under her wing. Summer internships in service organizations can often be less structured than law firm summer programs, but popular opinion has it that if you have a good mentor, you'll have a great experience. Find time at the beginning of the summer to sit down with someone within the organization to discuss roles and goals. If no mentor is assigned to you, target one yourself. Be clear on what you would like to do with your summer, then ask your mentor whether your desires are realistic, and what he or she recommends that you do to have an experience as close as possible to the one you want.

Finally, be a team player and be enthusiastic. As with judicial internships and firm associateships, even if the experience ends up being somewhat disappointing, you can always gain things from it. Work hard, do a good job, be sociable, and get to know people and their backgrounds. That way, when the summer is over, if you decide you're not interested in a repeat engagement with the organization, people will be happy to provide contacts for something more like what you're looking for.

"I did an unpaid internship with a legal services clinic, and I learned that I was really comfortable in the public sector," Yvette recalled. "The atmosphere was so dynamic, and everyone was committed to providing quality service to indigent clients. My colleagues were intelligent, and we were constantly challenging each other to think faster and harder and to provide better service more efficiently. Even though it was summer, the clinic was always moving at a fast pace, and I thrived."

It is easy, if your first summer position is disappointing, to simply write off the experience, rest up, do as little work as possible, and count down the days until you can go back to law school. As I have tried to illustrate in this chapter, however, it is not good for business. Every experience you have links into something else. The exact pathway may not be clear to you yet, but someday, you might be able to call on the contacts you made at a prior stop. With this in mind, do the best job possible and trust that your efforts will eventually pay dividends.

Thoughts about your 1L summer

___

___

___

PART THREE

The Second Year, They Work You to Death

CHAPTER 17

Charting a Course for Your Upper Years

In life, as in chess, forethought wins.
—HENRY BUXTON

AT THE END of your first full-year cycle of law school, if you're not completely confused, disenchanted, or disillusioned, you may be thinking about the best way to dedicate your remaining four semesters. With most of the required courses now out of the way, you'll have the luxury to choose what to take and when to take it. But should you choose the practical over the philosophical? The useful over the interesting? Only the courses you'll need for the bar exam?

How do you decide which approach to adopt?

This chapter proposes and explores several different general approaches to your upper-years curriculum to help you decide which approach best fits your needs. While you will no doubt want to dabble a bit in the different courses your law school offers, you do have a limited number of credit hours to spend, and only two years to take what you can from the diverse offerings of your law school curriculum. A general philosophical approach can help dictate the majority of your course selections and ensure you an enlightening and meaningful educational experience.

> When I first went to law school, I thought I wanted to practice international law. I used many of my second-year electives to take things like Public International Law, International Business Transactions, and other such courses, only to decide it wasn't for me. I became more and more interested in litigation, so in my third year, I loaded up on trial advocacy classes.
>
> —Elizabeth

First, some general comments. In planning your upper-years curriculum, remember that in law school, as in college, course formats will vary. Be sure to avail yourself of seminars, and smaller, non-Socratic, discussion-based classes in addition to the large, Socratic lecture classes that characterized your first year. If your law school is part of a larger university, don't dismiss the possibility of cross-registering for a couple of classes at the business school or the undergraduate college if doing so will enhance the approach you choose. When you find your niche, explore the possibility of doing a one-on-one tutorial with a faculty member in your area of greatest academic interest. Finally, make every effort to take at least one intensive research and writing experience, since these are the skills you'll rely upon most in whatever field of law you ultimately practice.

> I took classes that fell into three categories. First, there were the "you must take these to pass the bar exam" courses, which included Trusts and Estates, Corporations, Tax, and Criminal Procedure. Second, there were the "I think I like that area of the law," including Criminal Procedure, Antitrust, and Labor and Employment. Third, there were the "this professor is awesome" classes. I hate antitrust law, and the professor makes all the difference. Take as many classes as possible from the professors at your law school whom all the students love—there is a reason why. When I think back about laughing in Federal Taxation because the professor was so hysterical, it makes me feel like a dork, but I remember federal taxation really well too. In the end, I learned that I was going to learn everything that I needed to know for the bar exam during my BARBRI bar exam prep course, so taking courses for that purpose ended up being unnecessary.
>
> —Patrick

With this in mind, let's explore the different approaches that you might take during your upper years of law school.

The bar exam preparation approach

I've put this one first because I think it is the easiest approach to dismiss and is probably the least beneficial strategy to employ. Although you don't know it now, you're going to learn everything you need to know for your bar exam in your bar preparation course. That six-week program will teach you all the black-letter law (the rudiments of a particular subject) you'll need to master for each subject covered on your state's bar exam. In law school, however, you learn theory and policy, follow the law through its historical changes, and learn much more than you'll ever need to pass a bar exam.

Taking classes in law school solely because you need to know the subject for the bar exam is overkill. By the time you get to the bar exam, you'll have forgotten half of what you learned, and if your law school emphasizes theory and policy over black-letter law (as most of the top law schools do), there's no guarantee that you'll even cover everything you'll need to know for the bar exam.

Take my advice—let your bar review class teach you what you need for the bar exam. Use your time in law school to adopt another approach. You can always take a couple of nonrequired, broad survey courses (see the survey approach below) in frequently tested subjects such as income tax and corporations if waiting until the bar review course to see these subjects for the first time is just too unsettling for you.

The survey approach

Adopting this approach depends, in large part, on the vision you have for your future. In large-firm, big-city practice, the days of the "lawyer as generalist"—moving effortlessly from a tax question to a torts question to a constitutional law question—are gone. For the most part, attorneys in the large firms that populate the big cities have become specialists in a particular area of law (labor law, real estate, tax, etc.). Many of these lawyers have developed further subspecialties such that their entire practice revolves around one or two sections of the tax code or the securities regulations, and the progeny of cases developing from them. On the other hand, law school graduates who flee the big city and hang a shingle in smaller towns or rural areas still need to be generalists to put food on the table. These lawyers may still do a will in the morning, a real estate transaction at lunch, and argue a torts case in the afternoon. Those who go to small or midsize firms may find their experience to be somewhere between these two extremes.

No one expects you, as a beginning second-year law student, to know that Rule 10 (b) (5) of the securities regs is going to be your bread and butter. But you'll need to know something about your interests before you start going to recruiting interviews because you'll be seeking firms that have active practices in the area(s) of your greatest interest, and you're likely to be asked what your interests are, at least generally.

I can see you now, shaking your head and wondering out loud, "But what if I have no idea what area of law I'm most interested in? All I've done is take required courses for a year."

Not a problem. If that sentiment applies to you, then the survey approach is where you belong, at least for this semester. But don't just go into it blindly. Think about which courses you enjoyed during your first year, and which ones you hated, and look for trends.

Did you enjoy the structure provided by working closely within the provisions of the UCC in Contracts and the federal rules in Civil Procedure, or did you prefer the wide-open, theoretical concepts of Constitutional Law? Were you more interested in the legal aspects of human drama found in Torts and Criminal Law, or the business-related themes of Contracts and Property? Did you enjoy the research, writing, and oral argument in your first-year Legal Research and Writing seminar? Were you relatively comfortable responding to the challenges of the Socratic method, or does speaking out in class make your stomach turn? Do you see yourself more as a litigator or a corporate lawyer?

Well?

Yeah, I know these are tough questions, so take some time right now to think about them. Sketch the classes you liked and didn't like into groups and look for similarities. Take as much time as you need to get a better sense of what your interests are in the law. Don't read on until you've done this exercise.

No, I said don't read on until you've finished the exercise! Did you do the exercise? The next paragraph will still be here when you finish.

Okay. Now that you have some idea where your motivations are, it's time to think about which survey courses you should take this semester.

If your interests were more on the business and/or financial side of the law, look for the general, introductory survey courses in corporations, commercial paper, federal income tax, corporate tax, antitrust, securities regulation, and bankruptcy. Don't even think of taking them all in the same semester, because if you find out your interests really lie elsewhere, you'll be in for the roughest ride of your life. Generally, Corporations, Commercial Paper, and one of the introductory tax courses is where most business-law-oriented students cut their teeth. Take two of these courses to start. If your interest in this area is still viable after those courses, you can take the others next semester, then move into the major approach in a couple of these areas during your third year.

If your interests were more in litigation, your scope of choices is even wider. Perhaps the first choice to make is whether you're more interested in criminal or civil practice. Keep in mind that while criminal work may seem sexier right now, this choice generally narrows your options upon graduation to (1) state or federal prosecutor (positions that pay much less than the going rate for private practice and are still extremely hard to get); (2) the public defender's office (which generally pays little and may raise a number of moral issues for you); or (3) specialized criminal defense (which you can do in a firm). If any of these choices interests you after the introductory courses in criminal law and constitutional law, look for courses in constitutional criminal procedure and advanced criminal procedure, and evidence. If your interest continues after these courses, you can further specialize (see the major approach below).

If your litigation interests are in the civil arena, after the introductory courses in civil procedure, torts, contracts, and property, consider taking the survey courses in evidence, federal courts, First Amendment law, administrative law, labor and employment law, family law, or real estate. When you find an area that you're interested in, you can further specialize (see the major approach below).

> I tried to mix together tougher, code-based classes like Tax, Commercial Credit, and Securities Regulation with common law classes or classes in a particular area of law that were easier to grasp.
>
> —Alison

While it is possible to stay with the survey approach for the entirety of your law school career in order to get a broad view of the legal landscape, most law students eventually like to graduate with one or two areas of advanced expertise. Accordingly, if you can move from the survey approach to the major approach by the beginning of your third year of law school, you'll be in great shape to launch your career come graduation.

The major or career-focus approach

The major or career-focus approach begins for most students with at least a semester in the survey approach—until such time as you are clear about what areas of law you are most interested in pursuing. Once you've made the general decision between corporate law and litigation, and if you've chosen litigation, between criminal and civil litigation, you're ready to specialize.

Why is this helpful to you?

If you think you're headed for big-city or large-firm practice after graduation, you'll eventually be asked to specialize, so it's not a bad idea to develop an expertise in law school. Even if you're looking to a midsize or smaller firm, you won't be practicing every kind of law, so develop some more thorough knowledge in the areas in which you're likely to practice. For example, if you know that your life's calling is going to take you to your uncle's five-person firm in Peoria, you probably don't need to take too much time developing a specialty in oil and gas law, but you might want to know something about wills and trusts. Perhaps now you're beginning to understand why I've been preaching about having a vision for your future before you get to law school!

> It's great if you can identify early on what area you want to practice in, because you can then structure your course load accordingly and begin to build a transcript that your prospective employers will really notice.
>
> —Keith

Although every school is different, a chart of some of the more common majors undertaken by today's law students follows. Other possible majors are not on this list, but this representative sample will get you started. Below each major is a sampling of courses you might take to develop your specialty.

Majors

Business/Finance/Commercial Law

- Accounting
- Corporate Tax
- Partnership Tax
- Closely Held Corporations
- Corporate Finance
- Antitrust
- Commercial Paper
- Mergers and Acquisitions
- Securities Regulation
- Bankruptcy

Constitutional Law

- Administrative Law
- Federal Courts
- Constitutional Criminal Procedure
- Constitutional Litigation (Section 1983)
- Education Law
- Employment Discrimination
- First Amendment
- Conflicts of Laws
- Immigration Law
- Any upper-level seminar on specialized topics in constitutional law

Criminal Law

- Criminal Procedure
- Constitutional Criminal Procedure
- Evidence
- Mental Health Law
- Death Penalty Law
- Habeas Corpus
- White-Collar Crime
- Topics in Criminal Law Theory

Family Law

- Family Law
- Wills
- Trusts
- Estate and Gift Tax
- Estate Planning
- Mental Health Law
- Welfare Law
- Education Law

Health Care Law

- Health Care Law
- Administrative Law
- Antitrust
- Insurance Law
- Law and the Elderly
- Mental Health Law
- Advanced Topics in Health Care Law

Intellectual Property

- Copyright Law
- Patent Law
- Trademark Law
- Computer Law
- Internet Law

International Law

- Conflicts of Laws
- Comparative Law
- Comparative Constitutional Law
- Comparative Labor Law
- International Business Transactions
- International Environmental Law
- International Human Rights
- International Trade
- Uniform International Sales
- International Civil Litigation

Labor and Employment Law

- Labor Law
- Employment Law
- Employment Discrimination
- Federal Courts
- Constitutional Litigation
- ERISA
- Sports Law

Public Interest Law

- Federal Courts
- Constitutional Litigation
- Employment Discrimination
- Family Law
- Education Law
- Health Care Law
- Immigration Law
- Welfare Law
- Local Government
- Civil Practice Clinic
- Public Interest Externships

Real Estate

- Real Estate Transactions
- Environmental Law
- Administrative Law
- Construction Contracts
- Land Use
- Local Government
- Zoning
- Federal Income Tax
- Estate and Gift Tax
- Wills and Trusts

Tax

- Federal Income Tax
- Corporate Tax
- Partnership Tax
- Estate and Gift Tax
- International Taxation
- Tax Policy
- Advanced Specialized Topics in Tax

The clinical approach

The clinical approach is designed primarily for those students with a future in litigation. Law school classes can be frustratingly theoretical, and professors often pay little or no lip service to how different concepts play out in real-world practice (in many cases because the professors never had any real-world practice!). If you are like I was, you're probably sitting out there reading this with no idea about how to draft interrogatories, what you can and cannot ask in a deposition, or what a "speaking objection" is. You took Civil Procedure, you took Evidence, and still you feel as if you would have no command over these subjects in real-world practice.

Sound familiar at all?

If so, you might want to consider making room for some clinical experience in your law school career. A good course in trial advocacy, for example, typically takes you through a hypothetical civil trial from the client interview through the jury verdict—illustrating the interplay of the rules of evidence and procedure in drafting and responding to interrogatories, conducting depositions, assembling affidavits to support a motion for summary judgment, and the like. You won't get these things in a regular law school course, and without such a course you could easily graduate from law school with no idea whatsoever about how to handle a civil case in the real world. A course in trial advocacy is a must if you're going to be a litigator.

Pro bono or legal aid clinics offer similar, real-world practical experience with real clients with real problems. If you are willing to make a large time commitment, an experience with one of these clinics could allow you (with the aid of a more experienced supervisor) to handle a whole case from beginning to end, affording you exposure to all the intermediate steps. Internships and externships with judges or public-service organizations (see chapter 23 for more information) can provide similar practical experiences to ground your theoretical legal knowledge.

There is much to be said for devoting a semester, later in law school after you have developed a working knowledge of the core litigation subjects, to trial advocacy or a clinical practicum. Doing so will illustrate how the legal system actually works in practice in a way that none of your theory-based classes ever will.

Other considerations

Finally, you may want to take some classes simply because you heard the professor is great. You never know what the professor's love of a subject might do for your own interest in it.

"Just as I would strongly recommend that you avoid taking any class taught by a professor who is widely regarded as a bad teacher, I would try to take classes taught by professors who have reputations as excellent teachers," Carolyn notes. "I decided not to leave Penn without taking Constitutional Litigation because I had heard how excellent the professor was, and it turned out to be the best thing I did in my three years of law school. Professor Kreimer was one of those rare teachers who, through his own enthusiasm for and knowledge of the subject matter, inspired a classroom full of students to push themselves harder intellectually than they ever thought they could."

"Cross-register once or twice too," Joel adds. "Take a business school or public-policy school class if the schools are good and the subject matter interests you."

"It also pays to take easier and/or more mainstream classes during the first semester of your second year because of recruiting," Steve suggests. "Interviewing for a 2L summer job is very important, and very time-consuming. You'll be in and out of town on callbacks, and ultimately everyone ends up blowing off classes for the first few months to focus on the job search. Sooner or later, though, you're going to have to go back and figure out what you missed, and it's a lot easier to do that if you are taking Corporations, where there are ten different commercial outlines and fifty different outlines prepared by former students floating around, than if you are taking the Feminist Perspectives on Intellectual Property Law seminar, for which no study aids are available."

CHAPTER 18

Your Survival Guide to Recruiting Season

Make hay while the sun shines.
—ENGLISH PROVERB

WELL, THIS IS IT. For many of you, this is what law school has been all about. For well over a year, you've put in the long hours, endured the journal competition, and positioned yourself with an at-least-somewhat-calculated employment decision last summer, all with an eye toward this day.

The day it all begins to pay off. Literally.

Whether your law school allows employers to select whom they want to interview, whether it uses a lottery system, or whether you are traveling to a regional recruiting event, a number of strategies and tactics can radically increase your chances of surviving the screening interview. But let's not get ahead of ourselves. First, a word about how this whole process works.

Whether the employers come to your campus, or you travel to a regional job fair or similar recruiting event, the process has two stages: the screening interview, and the callback or flyback interview. The screening interview is usually a twenty-to-thirty-minute, one-on-one interview conducted by a single representative of a firm or organization. During this interview, you will generally be asked about your résumé, your grades, your practice interests, your law school experience, and anything else the interviewer picks up from the materials you submitted. You can do a lot to prepare for these screening interviews, and prepare you should, because although a screening interviewer doesn't usually have a fixed quota of students to call back, the number of students invited to a firm for a second round of interviews rarely exceeds 25 percent. To earn one of these prized callback interviews, you need to make yourself stand out from the crowd.

How will you know whether you've succeeded?

Generally, a firm or organization will call you within a week to ten days of your screening interview to set up a callback (also called a flyback) interview at the firm. But we're getting ahead of ourselves again. Let's start at the beginning.

How to decide where to interview

As I touched on earlier, depending on which law school you go to, interview opportunities may be predetermined by employers, decided by lottery, or open to your preference. Given the importance of this process, I would make every effort possible to attend a law school that uses one of the latter two systems.

In schools where employers determine whom they want to interview, you have little choice. If you are selected, you go to an interview. Period. In a school using one of the latter two processes, however, you'll need to research firms and submit a preference list to your placement office—probably during your 1L summer.

You'll do most of this research in the *NALP Directory of Legal Employers,* an online compendium of information about nearly every law firm in the United States. The directory contains the mailing address, contact person, and a one-page synopsis of the practice areas and other relevant information about each firm.

"I did the on-campus interviewing thing," Shruti noted. "But I also sent my résumé out to numerous firms around the country that I identified an interest in and did not participate in our on-campus interviews. The firm I ended up working for was one of those—they initially interviewed me on the phone and then flew me in for a callback."

"I chose an area of the country I wanted to explore a bit," John-Mark recalled. "Because I was interested in a smaller market, there weren't as many firms from there interviewing at my school. I could interview with all of them and get a good sense of the differences between firms. I chose my firm based on the personalities of the people I met and the quality of work available. At Davis Wright, everyone had interesting lives outside of the practice of law, they were interested in finding out about what I was like as a person, and finally many of the lawyers were doing very interesting work. It made for a great work environment."

"I wanted to stay in Boston where all my family and friends were located," Yvette said. "I ultimately chose Foley, Hoag because I had lunch with a black partner who really made me feel that the firm wanted to reach out to minorities and support their careers.

"I would not bother with big firms if you are confident you are not interested in that environment. While I learned a lot from that summer, I think I already knew that I didn't want to work at a big firm. I went more because it was expected, rather than listening to my own instincts."

How to prepare yourself for the screening interview

Is there any magic formula to guarantee success in a screening interview? Well, a résumé including a high grade point average from an Ivy League university and a law school transcript with straight A's during your first year at a top-ten law school, coupled with an affable personality, would probably ice it for you.

What, you don't have all of these attributes?

Well, relax, because most people don't—so let's talk about what you can do with the record you have to maximize your chances of securing the largest percentage of callbacks from the firms at the top of your list.

"My 2L job search again concentrated on the public sector," Lindsay noted. "I highly recommend staying in touch with the contacts you made during your 1L summer internship. Then, when you reapply and set up your interview, reach out to those contacts! Let them know how school is going and remind them of the work you did together and how much you enjoyed working for them. Ask them if they have any advice to offer you. Most of the time, they will offer to pass on your résumé and write a recommendation to the person or committee making the interview selections and doing the hiring.

"The attorney I worked with during my 1L summer became my mentor and helped me through every step of the applying for my 2L internship," Lindsay added. "In fact, she even popped in on my 2L internship panel interview 'just to say hi.' "

Know your audience

Remember when your seventh-grade algebra teacher told you that "the only dumb question is the question that you don't ask"?

She was wrong—at least in the context of law firm recruiting. In this game, the only dumb question is the one that is readily answered by a law firm's publicity materials. Know why it's a dumb question? Because it makes you look as if you didn't give too much thought to the firm you're interviewing with.

Between the NALP directory, your law school placement office, the Internet, the *Martindale-Hubbell Law Directory,* and the telephone, there is little general information about a firm and its lawyers that you can't find out ahead of time. As soon as you know you have a screening interview with a firm, you should begin gathering this information.

So what, at a minimum, should you know?

I would know approximately how many lawyers the firm has, in what cities it currently has offices, what its practice areas are, and what its specialty areas of practice are. I would find out who the firm's largest clients are. If the firm is large, I would know where the firm ranked in the city and in the country in the annual poll of associates' satisfaction, and where the firm ranked in the annual poll of summer associates. I'd find out the latest information about starting salary, bonus structure, vacation time, partner track, and billable-hour requirements, and how those numbers compared to the numbers of comparable firms in the same city. I'd also want to know whether the firm has a multitiered partner track. Finally, I would go to the placement office a day or two before the interview, get the name of the lawyer conducting my interview, then find out a few things about her from Martindale-Hubbell. Determine where she went to college and law school, how long she has been with the firm, what areas of practice she is involved in, and what a couple of her interests are. I'd put all of this information down in a notebook or journal and take it into the interview with me.

Then, I'd formulate at least three questions about the firm that I would like to have answered and that I am reasonably sure are not answered by the firm's other materials, then write them down in the same section of the notebook or journal with room for answers. Things such as whether the firm makes an effort to direct specific kinds of work to the associates most interested in doing that kind of work; how easy it is to move between practice groups at the firm; and what kind of training and feedback the firm provides to first-year associates. See the section "What you should ask" below for more ideas. You want to have these questions ready when the interviewer inevitably asks you, "So, do you have any questions for me?" or to jump right into at an appropriate point in the interview.

"After my first summer working in the public sector, I wanted to try out working for a law firm. I was interested in living in the Pacific Northwest so I targeted firms based in Portland and Seattle. That generally was a good strategy. While most of my friends and colleagues were killing each other over firms in San Francisco and LA, I was one of only a handful of students interviewing with firms outside the large markets. The most significant hurdle I faced was convincing the firms, especially the smaller ones, why I wanted to relocate to the Northwest," John-Mark recalled.

"As far as interviewing strategies, my approach has always been to be dead honest. I wasn't sure what type of law I wanted to practice, so I just said as much. From what I've heard, that can be a turnoff to some interviewers. My attitude has always been, however, that if I have to create a persona to get a job, it's not one I want.

"I made sure I knew something about each of the firms I interviewed with. You should have an answer for why you want to go to the firm you're interviewing with. Candidates who know little about a potential employer do not rise to the top of the résumé pile. Look at the firm's Web site, find out the firm's strengths, or talk to 3Ls from your law school who've worked there."

Be prompt and polite

You'd think this advice would go without saying, but firm recruiters have told us that it is not uncommon for law students to arrive late and out of breath to a recruiting interview. Plan to arrive at least fifteen minutes before the time your interview is scheduled to leave yourself enough time to review your notes and your list of questions for the firm you're about to interview with. When the interviewer greets you, be confident! Smile and introduce yourself with a firm handshake. While you will, no doubt, be nervous, remember that (1) the recruiter is just a human being like yourself and probably had to endure a similar interview, and (2) first impressions count.

Dress conservatively

As I just said, first impressions count. While your classmates might think it wonderful that you've maintained your individuality in law school by wearing tie-dye to lectures and following Phish around the country during winter break, the law firm recruiting interview is not the time to wear anything controversial. At least not if you want to get a callback.

If you're a guy, lose the earring and any excessive jewelry, and cover up your tattoos. Regardless of your gender, leave the nose ring and any other unusual piercings at home. Get a conservative haircut, and save the wild ties for another occasion. Finally, refrain from wearing any political pins, emblems, or identifying symbols on your clothing. (Mind you, none of this is a value judgment on my part—just advice about how to survive a screening interview.)

For the men, an ironed and starched white shirt, dark tie, and dark suit (yes, a suit, and, no, khakis and a blazer is not appropriate) is your best choice. Don't have one? Buy one. You'll need at least a couple of them for work anyway. For the women, a white blouse under a freshly dry-cleaned dark business suit, a pair of tasteful matching shoes, and a conservative necklace and earrings is the proper choice. Any deviations from this boring but professional standard are made at your peril.

So what are they going to ask me, anyway?

Every interviewer is different, but an interviewer can ask you only so many kinds of things. Questions during a screening interview will generally come from among nine substantive categories: (1) general questions; (2) questions about your background or the experiences listed on your résumé; (3) questions about your choice of law school; (4) questions about your grades; (5) substantive questions culled from your writing sample; (6) questions about your substantive legal interest; (7) questions about your interest in the city, state, or region where the firm is located; (8) questions about your interest in the firm; and (9) the "stunners." I address each of these areas, briefly, in turn.

> Be confident but not arrogant. Try to come off as a person that the interviewer could tolerate spending seventy-two hours in a row with.
>
> —Allan

General questions can be as broad as "Tell me about yourself," and as narrow as "What is the one thing you'd like to be remembered for when you're gone?" Spend some time thinking about what your strengths and weaknesses are, what your proudest accomplishment has been, and what the biggest obstacle in your life has been so far and how you managed to overcome it. Think about what you'd like to be doing in five or ten years, how you plan to balance work and family, and what your most important value is. There are many more questions like this, but hopefully you have some sense of what is in bounds.

For questions about your experience, know your résumé cold and be prepared to discuss anything on it in detail. Often, interviewers will seize on something you wouldn't expect (such as your interest in rock climbing or oil painting) in lieu of the real accomplishments on your résumé. Be prepared to address everything. The most common question in this area concerns what you did last summer—so be sure you have some insights ready.

Questions about law school may be as broad as "So, how do you like law school?" Try to resist the urge to say, "Pshaw—it sucks," and instead come up with something substantive to say about the subjects you like and why, what your biggest accomplishment in law school has been, or how you've struggled to maintain your identity amid the rigors of the schedule. You might also be asked to describe your favorite professor, and why she's your favorite, what your most rewarding experience has been, how you like your classmates, or how you would respond to a particular situation (such as seeing a friend cheat on an exam).

So what about grades? Yeah—they can ask you about them, although in my experience and the experiences of the mentors in this book, employers asked about grades less than we thought they would. The most important thing to remember about grades is not to apologize for them, no matter what they are. If you are asked something like "Wow, what happened in Contracts?" go ahead and chuckle as you remember getting drilled on the final, but then take a deep breath and come back with something like "Yeah—it was pretty ugly, but you know what? I learned a lot in that course," then tell the interviewer about what you learned from the experience. Knowing how to diffuse a potentially tense situation with some self-deprecating humor is an incredible skill to have as a lawyer and will serve you well if you are asked about grades. Most of the people who will interview you bombed a course or two themselves and should find your ability to find humor in the situation an asset.

> I wanted to get a job at a large New York law firm so I went through the "blue suit, hotel, fifteen minutes of discussion, *change*!" drill. It was fine. I like to chat with people and that was all it was. My suggestion is to let the interviewer talk. As you meet more lawyers, you will find one common trait—they like to

talk about themselves. If you let them do that during an interview, they will remember liking the experience and, derivatively, liking you. Trust me, it works.

—Patrick

Know your writing sample. This is an often-overlooked area for potential questions, but I got a substantive legal question about my writing sample, and I bombed it. Couldn't even remember what the damn thing was about, much less answer a jurisdictional question relating to it. Didn't get a callback from that firm either. Hmmm . . .

Be prepared to talk about your areas of substantive legal interests—as they relate to the courses you've taken, the subjects you still want to take, and any interests that were triggered by the work you did last summer. You'll also want to tailor your interests to the strengths of the firm you are interviewing with, so if you love First Amendment work, but the firm you're talking to doesn't do any, you'll want to save that one and talk about some of your other interests that the firm does feature. If you can't find any, then guess what? You probably aren't a good fit at that firm.

One of the most critical questions you might be asked will concern your interest in the city, state, or region where the firm's office is located, and you better have a good answer ready because this question can be fatal. If you grew up in New England, went to high school and college in New England, have family and friends in New England, spent your 1L summer working in New England, and then, out of the blue, are interviewing with a San Francisco law firm, what do you think they're going to ask you about? Why San Francisco? And you know what? An answer like "I really want to try something different" isn't going to cut it. The firm is going to be looking to see where your ties are. You need a more compelling reason to relocate, such as a fiancée from the region, a spouse attending graduate school in the region, relatives in the area, a history with the area (such as spending summers there as a kid, or going to high school or college there), or a particular practice group (such as high-tech start-ups) that is concentrated in the region. Comments about the climate, the atmosphere, the culture, the people, and the outdoor activities can help if they are well thought out, but they probably won't be enough on their own. So figure out why you want to be in the city or region of the country that this firm is from and come up with a compelling answer to this question, which is almost certain to be asked of someone in those circumstances. Of course, if you are talking to a New England firm and you fit the bill described above, then you have your compelling reason right there—you're returning home. Just don't forget to make this point clear to the interviewer even if you aren't asked about it.

You may be asked to describe your interest in the firm you're talking to, what made them stand out to you, or how you feel you might contribute to the firm. Here, the interviewer is probing to determine how well thought out your choices are, and once again a bad answer can be deadly, so be ready. Preparing a one-page summary sheet on every firm should help you make distinctions about them, but exercise caution here. You don't want the firm's only distinguishing characteristics to be that they have the highest salary and lowest billable-hour requirement in the city. Look for practice areas, firm philosophies, or reputation as possible answers here.

Finally, we come to the "stunner" category—the questions that make your jaw drop and your heart race faster as you struggle to find a suitable answer that is confident but not cocky, humble but not meek. Questions like "Aren't you really just using our firm as a stepping-stone to go to . . ." or "I could fill my entire recruiting class with people from Harvard Law School, why should I choose you?" The best thing to do here is to take a deep breath and make a remark like "Wow—let me think about that for a moment," while you consider an answer. Don't be afraid of silence. It's better than putting your foot in your mouth. When you are asked a stunner, it's usually more to see how you'll react to it—so think before you speak.

"At one screening interview, the interviewer came right out and said, 'Well, I can see from your grades that you're no legal eagle, so why should I hire you?'" Carolyn remembers. "Even though the question made me mad, instead of getting defensive, I just sort of laughed off the comment and told the guy that while I got off to a somewhat average start in law school, my grades were steadily improving, and I was confident that they would continue to improve. I also drew his attention to my writing sample as an indication that I write well, and to my résumé as an indication that when I commit to something, I get the job done, and done well. I don't think the interviewer really cared about my grades that much. I think he was testing me to see how I would react to his question because he offered me a callback and the firm made me an offer."

When an interviewer goes over the line

Once in a while, you hear a horror story about a partner (usually one of the older ones) making an off-color remark or asking an inappropriate question. If this happens to you, the best approach is the calm, rational approach. Don't pop off and start condemning the behavior. First ask to have the comment or question repeated to assure yourself that you heard it correctly. If you did, and it is inappropriate, it is perfectly acceptable to respond by saying, "I'm sorry, Mr. So-and-So, but that question is out-of-bounds." Inquiries about marital status, sexual orientation, religious persuasion, ethnicity, political beliefs, and offers from other firms are regarded as inappropriate. If the interviewer makes an off-color remark about race, sexual orientation, religion, or the like, and you are bothered by it, politely call him on it by saying, "Excuse me, Mr. So-and-So, but what exactly did you mean by that comment?" That should be enough to get the interviewer to move on—and will probably be reason enough to get you to look elsewhere for employment.

What you should ask

If you've followed my advice, you should already have two or three questions prepared for each firm based on the research you've done. But what are some other questions you might ask? Ask about plans for the future of the firm, and any potential areas of growth. Find out what factors led your interviewer to decide to work at the firm, and what it is like to work there—including questions about how work is assigned, how much supervision is provided, how projects are staffed, and how feedback is provided. Find out what traits are shared by the best associates at the firm. Ask about what the social life is like, and how satisfied, overall, the interviewer is at the firm. You'll probably only have time for one or two questions, so ask the ones you are most curious about, that are the most critical to your continuing interest in the firm, or the questions that were triggered during the interview but not sufficiently answered.

Many law students struggle with whether to ask tough questions of an interviewer. If a firm's summer associate program ranked last in the city last summer, or the firm ranked low in the annual poll of associate satisfaction, or the firm recently experienced a bloodletting and fired a number of people, or was implicated in an ethical scandal, you're going to want to find out about those things before you accept an offer from the place. You owe it to the firm and to yourself to put those questions to the firm's front person—and for your purposes, that's your interviewer.

"Remember that you are interviewing the firm too," Elizabeth noted.

Although most law students worry that asking tough questions will be insulting to the interviewer, in the vast majority of cases the result is just the opposite. Asking tough questions of an interviewer shows that you have done your homework about the firm, and that you are concerned about those things—as you should be. It also shows the interviewer that you are seriously considering the firm as a place of employment. So when the interviewer inevitably asks, "So, do you have any questions for me?" ask away. If you are still squeamish, give the interviewer a softball like, "I couldn't help but notice that you guys ranked last in associate satisfaction last year. I'm sure it won't happen again, but what changes have been implemented to try and improve the situation?"

Don't cower from asking the tough questions.

The things you should avoid

It should go without saying that no matter how comfortable you feel with a particular interviewer, you should never forget that you are still the interviewee. Vulgarity, off-color jokes, and political humor can only get you into trouble in an interview, so avoid these things at all costs. Equally important to remember is never to bad-mouth another interviewer or another firm during an interview, no matter how terrible your experience or impression may have been. You don't know all the players, and you might step on a mine. Finally, stay away from all questions about salary, bonus structure, benefits, and vacation time until after you have been extended an offer by the firm. That's the only time these issues become relevant.

A few horror stories to calm you down

Every now and then, you'll end up with a particularly salty character on the other side of the desk, and things will take an unfortunate turn. Maybe it's the end of the day, and the interviewer is tired. Maybe it's the beginning of the day and the interviewer is tired. Maybe the interviewer is tired of being a lawyer. While you'd think that firms would not roll out their nastier characters on these occasions, sometimes the people who make the decisions at these firms don't think the way you and I do. On these rare occasions, things like this can happen:

"I was interviewing with a major law firm that has offices all over the world, and the interviewer did not ask me any questions!" Elizabeth recalls. "He just sat there and read my résumé while I sat silently in the chair on the other side of the desk. This went on for some time until I finally broke the silence by mentioning that I love Italy and asked what opportunities I would have to work in the firm's Rome office. The guy then looked at me like I was the stupidest person he had ever seen and abruptly told me that no associate would ever have such an opportunity, much less someone at the bottom of the ladder like I would be."

"I had a screening interviewer from a firm in a smaller market, which happened to be my hometown, close the door, put his feet up on the desk, and say to me, 'Now don't try to bullshit me. You know and I know that you're just using this interview as a trial run for something better, so why should I take you seriously?" one mentor recalls with a smile. "I knew this was the firm I really wanted to work at, so no joke, I looked right back at him and, without batting an eye, said, 'Because if you don't, you'll be making one of the biggest mistakes of your life.' I think he was trying to intimidate me, but I didn't let him. It must have been the answer he wanted because he made me the offer, and I'm still there today."

And finally, there is this gem.

"I know someone who had an interview with someone who closed the door, started crying, and said, 'Don't come here—it's a horrible place that just sucks the life out of you,'" Bess recalls. "Needless to say, he took a job somewhere else!"

CHAPTER 19

Everything You Need to Know About Callback Interviews

You can fool some of the people all of the time,
and all of the people some of the time,
but you can not fool all of the people all of the time.
—ABRAHAM LINCOLN

IN THE REALM of law firm recruiting, popular opinion says that if you get a callback, the offer is yours to lose. While this is not entirely accurate, the recruiting coordinators and hiring partners we canvassed said that in a typical year between 60 and 80 percent of the candidates invited on a callback interview will eventually be extended an offer.

So if all is going well, it is September or October of your 2L year, you've been to a bunch of screening interviews, and now you're starting to accumulate some callbacks. Only problem is, you don't really know what a callback is.

So what the heck is a *callback* anyway?

A *callback,* or at some schools, a *flyback,* is just the fancy name for the second round of law firm interviews. A callback interview means that you won the screening-interview lottery, and that the firm is interested enough in you to fly you to their city, put you up in a hotel, take you out on a lavish "recruiting lunch," and have four to six more attorneys at the firm talk to you. This usually takes the better part of a day and will culminate in either an offer of employment during your 2L summer or a ding letter (polite rejection).

The process begins with an invitation from the recruiting coordinator at the firm to make an appointment to come to the firm for a morning or afternoon interview. This invitation is almost always made by telephone and can come as soon as the same day that you complete your screening interview. Thus, as soon as you start screening interviews, double-check your cell phone to make sure that your outgoing message is professional and clearly identifies who you are.

Callback interviews typically take place in the city where the firm is located, almost always at the firm itself. Unless the firm is in the same city as your law school, that means traveling, but don't worry—the firm will reimburse you for your travel expenses as long as you don't make outrageous arrangements (see the section on fiscal conservatism in "Scheduling appointments" below). If the city is far enough from your law school to make traveling back and forth in the same day difficult, you will also be entitled to charge a hotel room, meals, and related expenses to the firm.

When you get to the firm, you will usually be greeted by the recruiting coordinator, who will likely provide you with a schedule of the partners and associates you'll be meeting with, and the times you are expected to meet with them. In the typical callback interview, you will meet with four to six lawyers, probably a mix of associates and partners. Don't worry that you haven't had time to "study up" on each of these people in Martindale-Hubbell. They won't be expecting you to know their life histories. The schedule you'll be given by the firm will probably tell you whether the people you are meeting with are affiliated with the corporate or litigation side of the practice and may also include their areas of specialty or practice group affiliation. If it doesn't, don't sweat it. It makes a perfectly good question to ask during the interview.

In the typical callback interview, the recruiting coordinator will then hand you off to the first person on the list. The individual interviews during your callback will be a lot like the screening interview, so if the nine common question areas are not fresh in your mind as you are reading this, you might consider going back to the last chapter and brushing up. When your designated time with each person runs out, he will take you to the next person, and so on, until you've interviewed with everyone on the list. From there, someone you met with will probably ask you to join them, and several other members of the firm, for lunch (if you had a morning interview), or for drinks or dinner (if you had an afternoon interview). Don't be lulled into complacency by this "social time," however. You're still very much under the microscope for these people, just in a different way. We'll address the finer points of handling recruiting "social time" below.

That's the callback interview in a nutshell. Now let's discuss the important things to remember about the different parts of a callback and develop some strategies for each part.

Scheduling appointments

It is a good idea to schedule your callbacks as soon as possible, both to assure that the day and time you want is available, and to maximize your chances of getting an offer. During hiring season, the hiring committees at most large firms meet weekly or every other week to make decisions about callback candidates. This process is akin to rolling admissions, and consequently, the earlier you complete your callback interview, the more open slots the firm will have.

When you call the firm to schedule your callback, ask to speak to the recruiting coordinator, and treat that person the same way you would treat a partner at the firm. Be polite and as flexible as possible. Remember that administrative assistants and recruiting coordinators often wield unexpected power in hiring decisions. One negative word about you can sink your candidacy. One former hiring partner I talked to told me that at his firm the partners paid particular attention to the way prospective associates treated the administrative staff, and the first sign of disrespect or derision guaranteed rejection of that candidate.

When scheduling your appointment, if you'd like to speak with any particular person at the firm, or if you would like to meet with the members of a particular practice group or groups, you should indicate that preference to the recruiting coordinator. Firms will almost always attempt to accommodate these requests. If you will be traveling to another city, you may also need to make travel arrangements and overnight accommodations. Before making flight arrangements or hotel accommodations, however, ask the recruiting coordinator if the firm gets a preferred rate at a particular hotel that they'd like you to use, and whether they would prefer to book your flights or have you do it. Asking these simple questions shows fiscal responsibility and is always appreciated. The general rule is that if you cannot make the round-trip for your interview comfortably in one day, an overnight stay is warranted. If there is any doubt in your mind about the propriety of an overnight stay, consult the placement director at your law school for advice.

Once you know you'll be traveling to a particular city for a callback, if you had screening interviews with any other firms in that city but have not yet heard from them, it is acceptable to call your screening interviewers at those firms for a status report. The best way to handle this is to (1) tell the screening interviewer that you will be traveling to her city for a callback interview at another firm, (2) that you are still interested in her firm, and (3) that you were wondering if you could get a status report for scheduling purposes. If a decision has already been made, she will probably tell you what it was. If a decision has not been made, the news that "the competition" is after you and that you called to inquire about your status may get you the nod in close cases, so don't be afraid to inquire.

If you have two or more callback interviews in the same city, do everything you can to schedule them on back-to-back days. This will enable all the firms to divide the airfare and the cost of your accommodations, exhibits fiscal responsibility on your part, will save you a lot of unnecessary travel, and will curb the necessity of your missing too many classes. While the thought of jet-setting around the country to law firms may sound romantic and exciting, it is incredibly draining and will quickly become tiresome after one or two canceled flights or long airport delays.

"Since I traveled to interview, I packed as many interviews as possible into a few days," John-Mark noted. "It made for an uncomfortable experience. Having two callbacks in one day, ten to twelve interviews, is a draining experience. I would recommend pacing yourself a bit more than I did."

Finally, practice fiscal conservatism during your callback layovers. While it is fine to order room service, and unnecessary to restrict yourself to the cheap chicken entrée, you should not be ordering the $49 twin lobster tails, expensive wines, or entertaining a spouse or significant other on the firm's tab. Cabs are fine. Limousines are not. And if you want a Swedish massage at the hotel after your interview, you'd better pay for it yourself. You might think that since law firms simply expense these charges out, they don't matter. Think again. Some firms don't look these expense reimbursements over, but you don't know which ones do. If a firm is watching and your charges look extravagant compared to those of other callback candidates, it will call your judgment into question.

Tackling the callback interview

Arrive ten or fifteen minutes early at the firm. Travel to the firm by cab unless it is a short walk from your hotel and you know exactly where it is. This is no time to get lost. Dress conservatively, and remove any controversial accoutrements.

Read the best paper in the city on the day of your callback. I got a lot of questions that I couldn't answer about what had been on the front page of *The New York Times* that day.

—Alison

While you will not be expected to know anything about your interviewers individually (unless you specifically requested one or more of them), that doesn't mean that you can't ask them questions about themselves! Before your callback, consult the list of questions you had for the screening interviewer at the firm and see if any of those questions are still relevant. Then try to develop two or three additional questions that are firm-specific or practice-group-specific. Remember the two psychological axioms central to interviewing: Interviewers prefer the people they like, and the more good questions you ask and the more you get the interviewer to talk about his life and his experiences at the firm, the better that person's impression of you will be. That doesn't mean you should duck his questions and try to ask ones of your own. It just means that you'll want to ask two or three good questions of each person you meet with, and you don't need to wait until the end of the interview to do so. If the opportunity presents itself, jump right in with your questions.

But what about those hard questions? The real zingers like "Why do you think the firm ranked last in the city in associate satisfaction last year, and what is being done to remedy that situation?" or "I noticed that the firm is currently involved in a high-profile gender-discrimination lawsuit. I know you can't talk about the specifics of the case, but can you reassure me about the way the firm views its female associates?" Should you ask these questions in a callback interview?

Absolutely.

If you are interviewing at a firm that has recently received some negative ratings or publicity, they'll be prepared to answer questions about it. Just the same as in the screening interview, if you don't ask about it, the firm might wonder whether you looked at them carefully enough to become aware of the problem, or they may conclude that you were simply too timid to ask about it. Timidity has no place in the practice of law. This doesn't mean that you have to go after the firm with both barrels on a sensitive issue. Simply pose the question frankly to your interviewer, then listen intently to his response. Never be afraid to ask the tough question. Just ask it professionally.

Be sure to ask a lot of questions about the firm. There are two reasons for this. First, it gives the interviewer a chance to talk, and it is a lot easier for an interviewer to answer questions than to ask them. Since I now work for a smaller firm, I've had a chance to be the interviewer, and based on that experience, I can tell you this—the interviewer is not going to like you much if you make her work too hard to come up with questions to ask you. Second, by asking insightful questions, it makes it clear that you are really interested in the firm and have done your homework about it.

—Carolyn

Joel agrees. "Talk to some 3Ls who worked at that firm last summer and get some questions from them. Your career services office should be able to give you some names. Read about the firm in *The Insider's Guide to Law Firms*. Check out the firm's Web site."

If you are interviewing with five different attorneys at a firm, you don't need to have fifteen different questions. It is perfectly acceptable to pose the same questions in each interview. The consistency or inconsistency of the answers you receive from the various interviewers can be quite instructive! As with the screening interview, you should not ask during a callback interview about salary, benefits, and vacation time. Save those questions until after you have been extended an offer.

Finally, if the firm you are talking to is your first choice, make that clear to every person you talk to. Preferences like that count a lot.

How to handle the recruiting meal

If the thought of the recruiting meal conjures images in your mind of that scene from *Pretty Woman* where Julia Roberts's character flings escargot across the restaurant and fumbles haplessly with the silver, you are not alone. For many 2Ls, recruiting lunches and dinners may be among the most formal dining experiences they will have had. Here are some general suggestions.

When you sit down, don't forget to place your napkin in your lap. It's an easy thing to forget when you're on edge. People at the table may be asking you so many questions that you won't have time to look over the menu before the server comes to take your orders. That's par for the course. If one of the partners encourages you to order first, beg off, tell him that you haven't had a chance to decide yet, and ask to choose last. This gives you the added benefit of seeing what everyone else is ordering. Try to follow the pattern. If everyone else orders an appetizer, a salad, and an entrée, you should feel comfortable doing the same. If no one else orders an appetizer, you should skip it also.

> The recruiting meal is what I refer to as the "social testing segment" of the interview. The opportunity to dine with someone gives people at the firm a chance to observe what you are like as a person in a more social setting, including how you treat the waitstaff and what your table manners are like!
>
> —Elizabeth

If you aren't immediately certain what you want to order, it is a nice gesture to ask your companions for a recommendation or two. Again this is calculated, but it won't seem like it. People love to be asked for their advice, particularly when you appeal to their taste and experience, so do it if you can.

If everyone else has a glass of wine, you can too, but otherwise, avoid alcohol. As the old Latin adage goes, *in vino veritas*. As a recruit, you may not want too much *veritas* spilling out during the meal, so watch yourself here.

Remember to be polite to the server. They may be watching for that, and even if they aren't, it's still the right thing to do.

Try to keep asking questions of people during the meal to keep the conversation from lagging. Throw out a question about the city, where everyone grew up, or what people typically do for fun on the weekends. Keeping it light during the meal is fine, but you'll want to make sure you sustain the conversation. Above all, remember that the recruiting lunch is still that—a recruiting lunch. Let someone else tell the questionable joke or make the political slam. You should stay on the safe topics and refrain from heading into dangerous territory (politics, religion, firm bashing).

Finally, when the meal is over, as you are rising to leave the table, be sure to make a general comment to everyone thanking them for having you.

When the callback is over

If you have the opportunity, ask the recruiting coordinator when you might expect a decision. Be sure to keep all your receipts together and send them as soon as possible to the firm with any paperwork they gave you for reimbursement. If some expenses, such as a plane flight, are being divided between two or more firms, make copies of the receipts and put a note on them to indicate how things have been divided. Finally, if you made a personal connection with anyone at the firm, a hand-written thank-you note (no, not an e-mail) to that individual is appropriate. Otherwise, a brief thank-you note to the recruiting coordinator asking that person to convey your appreciation to the other attorneys you met with will suffice. Yeah, I know. Somebody probably counseled you against sending a thank-you note, right? I think that's baloney. Use some common sense here. It is never a mistake to express your appreciation for another's hospitality, and I'm quite certain I never lost anything by doing so.

Some horror stories to calm you down

"At one of my callbacks, I met with a senior partner who asked me why I was interviewing with his firm," Allan remembers. "I told him I was there because the firm emphasized 'lifestyle' where the associates tended to have lives outside the office. The guy then went off on me, telling me that any large firm, his firm or any other firm, would make me kill myself, and that my expectations were unrealistic."

Fortunately, Allan's story is relatively rare. Most horror stories are more like the following:

"It was my first callback, the day was cold and rainy, and I really wasn't feeling well," Alison recalls. "I went through each interview getting more and more nauseous until I could barely keep my head up. All I could think about was how I was going to get through lunch. When lunch came, I left the table and threw up, and the associate I was with had to have his food wrapped up to go. I went home in a cab, half crying, half sleeping, sure that I would never get a job."

"I got food poisoning during one of my callbacks and had to excuse myself from the table before throwing up in the bathroom of a very upscale restaurant," Shruti recalled.

Finally, there is this beauty.

"An airline lost the luggage of a somewhat heavyset friend of mine on his way to an important interview," a mentor recalls. "He had to go to the interview in the khakis he wore on the plane, and a borrowed shirt, jacket, and tie that were too small and looked ridiculous on him. Nevertheless he marched through the interview with confidence, poking fun at his misfortune instead of obsessing about it, and got the job offer. Callback interviewers want to like you. Let them."

CHAPTER 20

Everything You Ever Wanted to Know About Law Firm Hiring: An Interview with Douglas H. Meal of Ropes & Gray and David W. McGrath of Sheehan, Phinney, Bass & Green

Find a job you like, and you add five days to every week.
—BROWN

LAW SCHOOL CONFIDENTIAL interviewed Douglas H. Meal of Ropes & Gray, and David W. McGrath of Sheehan, Phinney, Bass & Green to get differing perspectives on hiring from the long-term hiring partners at a large, national law firm and a midsize, regional law firm. With a 135-year history, nearly six hundred lawyers, and offices in Boston, New York, San Francisco, and Washington, D.C., and an impressive roster of internationally known clients, Ropes & Gray is one of America's most highly regarded law firms. Sheehan, Phinney, Bass & Green, with approximately fifty-five lawyers and offices in Boston, Manchester, Concord, and New London, is one of the best-known and most well-respected regional law firms in New England.

First of all, on behalf of my readers, I'd like to thank both of you for taking the time out of your busy schedules to talk hiring and share some of your thoughts about the hiring process. . . .

Mr. Meal: You're welcome—it's a pleasure to do so.

Mr. McGrath: Happy to talk about ways law students can make themselves more marketable.

To start things off, how many 2L résumés do you receive in an average year and for how many spots, on average, in the summer program?

Mr. Meal: We typically receive between a thousand and fifteen hundred applications for our summer program. Over the last five years, the program size has pretty consistently been between fifty and seventy-five summer associates.

Mr. McGrath: On average, we receive over a thousand résumés a year. Our hiring needs tend to fluctuate somewhat with the economy, but we generally hire two 2Ls per summer. We take great care in deciding which 2Ls to bring on in our summer program because the expectation is that these 2Ls will go on to become associates, continue to develop, and then eventually make partner with us. Our associate retention rate is very high. We never bring on more 2Ls than we need with the idea that we'll just make offers to the best ones. Our approach is to go out and find the best ones up front, train them, and expect that they'll be with us long term.

What are your views on the on-campus hiring processes at the various law schools? Do you prefer certain systems over others? If so, which do you prefer and why?

Mr. McGrath: We don't actively participate in the on-campus interviewing process. Because we're only looking to hire a couple of people a year, we use our contacts at certain law schools to encourage students who have New Hampshire connections to apply with us. That strategy has proven very successful. We also screen hundreds of résumés. With that, and the screening interviews we conduct at the New Hampshire Legal Job Fair, we have an incredibly rich pool of applicants from which to choose. Because we are especially interested in law students who are ready to make a commitment to working in New Hampshire long term, this approach works well for us.

Mr. Meal: By contrast, the law school on-campus hiring process is really a fantastic thing for large law firms like ours. Thanks to the logistical support that the law schools give to the process, each of our on-campus interviewers can meet and interview between twenty and twenty-five applicants in a single day, which is an enormous advantage to large law firms, like ours, that year-in, year-out need to hire between 50 and 150 new associates. Last year our firm was able to do initial interviews with more than seven hundred applicants for positions in our summer program. A number of the people from that group who wound up receiving and accepting offers for our summer program never would have been interviewed by us had their application come to us through the lateral hiring process, given our extremely limited ability to do lateral interviewing. So when I say that the law school on-campus hiring process is fantastic, what I mean is that it creates an array of interviewing opportunities, from both the law firms' and the law students' perspective, that really facilitates the large law firm hiring process.

Having said all that, there are school-by-school differences in on-campus interviewing programs, and some of those differences are pretty significant. A number of schools have moved to the "early interview week" model that Columbia and NYU developed in the mid-1980s. Under that model, all, or virtually all, of a school's on-campus interviews are done over the course of a five-day period in the second half of August, before the law school academic year has even begun. The students then do their callback interviews and get their offers during the first part of September. I am not a big fan of the early-interview-week model for three reasons. First, under that model the students have to choose which firms they want to interview with by some time in early July, which is a shame because it prevents students from factoring into their selection process input they might receive on various firms (pro or con) once they return to school from fellow students who have just completed their summer programs. Second, the early-interview-week model inherently forces students to do far more on-campus interviews than they need to because the students have no way of knowing, until the week is over, how well they are going to do in terms of receiving callback invitations. So what often happens is that the stronger applicants do dozens of interviews during the early interview week and then receive dozens of callback invitations, many of which they wind up declining. The result is that these students—through no fault of their own, but through the fault of the system—take away both on-campus and callback interview opportunities that might have been beneficial to their peers. Third, the early-interview-week model is problematic because, as I mentioned, under that model the students usually receive their offers by the end of September. Under NALP rules, they have until December 1 to act on those offers. This results in an extremely drawn-out postoffer recruitment process for these students, which, though it may sound attractive in the abstract, I think most students wind up finding to be quite time-consuming and stressful in reality.

The other on-campus interview model, which I prefer, is the "fly-out week" model. Under that model, the school schedules on-campus interviews to occur over about a four-week period after school begins and then cancels classes during what is called fly-out week, during which students are expected to arrange their callback interviews—at least the ones that will occur out of town. Under this model, students can make much more intelligent decisions about how many, and which, firms they will see on campus. Also, from a law firm's perspective, it is advantageous for planning purposes to know that, for example, all of the Stanford callback interviews will occur in one particular week, and all of the University of Chicago callback interviews will occur in another particular week. For schools that follow this model, the offers are typically going out during October, which still leaves plenty of postoffer recruiting time prior to the NALP deadline.

In reviewing résumés, how important is the ranking of a candidate's law school in the* U.S. News & World Report *annual review of graduate schools?

Mr. Meal: The ranking of a candidate's law school winds up, indirectly, being a relatively important factor. I know from having interviewed over one thousand law students during the past three years and from having discussed this very issue with nearly every one of them, that the law school applicant pool relies very heavily on reputational surveys in choosing which law school to attend. While there are exceptions (most often in a situation where a law school having a lesser rank offers a significantly stronger financial aid package to the applicant in question), the vast majority of law school applicants choose to attend the "best" law school they are admitted to, as measured by the reputational surveys. Other factors—such as the geographic location of the law school or the particular features of the law school's curriculum—come into play only at the margin, when the choice is down to two or three schools that, "reputationally speaking," are more or less equivalent.

This phenomenon is a significant change from the way things were twenty years ago, when other considerations—particularly geographic ones—played a much more significant role in the applicant's decision-making process. For example, it once was the case that a law school applicant who wanted to live and work in the Boston area following law school, and who did not happen to get into Harvard, would routinely choose to go to either BC or BU, for example, rather than a "better" law school located outside of the Boston area. That is far less likely to be the case today for two reasons. First, the reality is that the law student pool of today is, as a whole, much less parochial in its geographic experience and hence much more open to different geographic alternatives than it was twenty years ago. Second, and I think more importantly, over the last twenty years virtually all of the "top" law schools—and I believe BC and BU are very good examples of this trend—have worked very hard and very successfully to build much more national student bodies than they did in the past in the hope that those student bodies will, eventually, turn into a nationwide alumni network for the school. In order to accomplish that goal, the law schools had to persuade students from other geographic regions that they could come to the law school and enhance, rather than diminish, their career opportunities outside the region where the law school is located. In order for that to occur, law schools had to persuade large law firms like ours that we could go on campus there and find a group of law students who would have a serious interest in coming to our geographic area.

This process took a long time to evolve, but looking at the market today, it certainly has succeeded. For example, up until the mid-1980s, our firm did not even go on campus at Columbia and NYU, which then, as now, were two of the top six law schools "reputationally" in the country, not because we didn't admire the talent of the students at those schools, but because our perception was that virtually everybody at those schools wound up staying in New York after law school so that we had no meaningful opportunity to recruit people from those schools to come to Boston. In the late 1980s, however, each school persuaded us to launch an on-campus interviewing program at the school; and over time, as the schools have succeeded in attracting more nationally diverse student bodies, we have succeeded in attracting a significant number of NYU and Columbia students to join our summer program each year.

All of this is a long-winded way of explaining why, today, if law school A has a better "reputation" than law school B, it almost invariably is able to recruit a stronger class of entering law students, from an LSAT and undergraduate GPA perspective. The *U.S. News & World Report* survey corroborates this point pretty dramatically as there is almost a perfect match between the reputational ranking of the law schools in the survey and their relative ranking in terms of the LSAT scores and undergraduate GPAs of their entering classes. What this means to a large law firm like ours is that, looking at law school student bodies as a whole, the student bodies at the top five law schools in the reputational rankings have a significantly stronger record of pre-law-school academic achievement than the student bodies at the law schools ranked between, say, fifteenth and twenty-fifth in those surveys. So, in the end, the "reputation" of a candidate's law school winds up being, indirectly, significant because it tells us something about the pre-law-school academic achievement of students at that school generally, which is a useful starting point—and I want to emphasize that it is merely a starting point—for evaluating any particular candidate from that school.

Mr. McGrath: It certainly is a relevant consideration to us, but it is not the be-all and end-all of our analysis. We have many lawyers at Sheehan, Phinney who have gone to top-fifteen law schools, but we also have some lawyers who have graduated from some of the solid regional law schools in this area that don't happen to be in the top fifteen nationally. Many of those lawyers have done exceedingly well in the profession. So while the reputation of a candidate's law school does matter, we also look at a number of other things, including the undergraduate institution you attended and your record there, both academically and otherwise; the range and breadth of your experiences; your demonstrated writing ability; and your potential to be an active member of the community here.

How important are the candidate's grades at that law school? Do you weight grades differently depending on what law school the candidate attends?

Mr. McGrath: Grades are important, and in evaluating grades we do take into consideration which law school the candidate attends. Some schools use different grading curves, and as such, grade inflation varies from one school to the next. We are pretty familiar with the grading policies in place at most schools. I know, for example, that Boston University School of Law has far less grade inflation than some other comparably ranked schools. We're mindful of that, and we take those differences into consideration when evaluating applicants. Assuming equivalence in grading schemes, though, do we give more weight to the candidate who has achieved a 3.5 at a top-ten law school versus the candidate who has achieved a 3.5 at a school that is ranked somewhere between twenty-five and fifty? Yes, we do. Those differences do matter. Keep in mind that we are trying to get a sense of a student's analytical abilities and work ethic. Grades are only one factor we consider in that process.

Mr. Meal: We do give significant weight to a candidate's first-year law school grades in evaluating the candidate, but for us there is no first-year law school GPA that is ever high enough to guarantee an offer or low enough to preclude an offer.

By the way, we pay little or no attention to second-year or third-year grades because we find that the second-year and third-year course loads differ so greatly from student to student, and in turn have such widely variant grading standards applied to them, that it is basically impossible to compare one student to another based on their second-year or third-year grades. As a result, we pay much more attention to what courses the student has chosen to take in his or her second and third years than we do to how the student actually performed in those courses.

We believe that success at our law firm depends on the degree of a person's intellectual and analytical ability and on how motivated and goal-oriented a person is. We think first-year law school grades provide us with some indication of a candidate's intellect and drive relative to his or her law school peers. Moreover, because we feel that some law schools have stronger student bodies, viewed as a group, than other law schools, as I've previously discussed, we do weigh a candidate's first-year GPA somewhat differently depending on what law school a candidate attends. For example, a first-year GPA in the top 10 percent of the class at one of the top five law schools, reputationally speaking, in the country is more impressive, standing alone, than a first-year GPA in the top 10 percent of the class at a law school with a significantly lower reputational ranking. Having said that, however, we look at other data beyond first-year GPA to evaluate a candidate's intellect and drive; and in evaluating candidates we look to other criteria, beyond intellect and drive, that a candidate's first-year GPA tells us nothing about. As a result, it is never the case that a candidate's first-year GPA, no matter how high or low it is, and no matter what law school the candidate is from, is in and of itself either conclusive or preclusive of an offer being made.

How important is the reputation of a candidate's undergraduate institution?

Mr. Meal: A candidate's undergraduate school, in and of itself, is relatively unimportant to us. Virtually all of our hiring is done from law schools that, according to the reputational surveys, are among the top thirty in the country. It turns out that the overwhelming majority of students at those law schools attended about fifty undergraduate schools that all have outstanding reputations. Thus, almost every candidate we interview went to an undergraduate school that has an outstanding reputation. Moreover, I don't have data that enables me to draw what I feel are meaningful or reliable distinctions between those undergraduate schools in terms of the overall quality of their student bodies. So the only situation in which we pay a lot of attention to a candidate's undergraduate school is in the relatively rare instance when we are not particularly familiar with that school. That will lead me to make some inquiry into the quality of the school and the candidate's reasons for attending that particular school, rather than going to what might be thought of as one of the "usual suspects." Oftentimes, that inquiry winds up reflecting quite positively on the candidate, so even in that relatively rare circumstance I don't think one could make any generalization about the undergraduate school's reputation, or lack thereof, having had a negative effect on the candidate's chances.

Mr. McGrath: A candidate's undergraduate institution is an important factor. It's not as important to us as the law school you attend, obviously, but it plays a role. We look at your undergraduate institution and your record and experiences there to round out the picture of who you are as a person. One of the ways we evaluate your undergraduate institution is by looking for individuals who have had some connection to the area and, thus, demonstrate a familiarity with the culture and lifestyle here—so we look favorably on candidates who have attended Dartmouth, or any of a number of other colleges and universities in northern New England—that may suggest a highly qualified candidate's preference for a more balanced lifestyle.

How important is a candidate's undergraduate record?

Mr. McGrath: Undergraduate grades do play a role in our hiring decisions. A lot of the superficial analysis is captured simply by the reputation of the law school you attend. If you're attending a top law school, I know you've done very well at your undergraduate institution. So I tend to look elsewhere on a candidate's résumé to determine how rigorous the applicant's course of study was as an undergraduate. What did the person major in? What was her thesis topic? Did he do any research or publish anything with a professor? We're also looking for people who have demonstrated commitment, initiative, and leadership ability, so I look for some evidence in the undergraduate record of those qualities. Finally, I look at the record as a whole and make a general determination about whether the candidate is someone that I have an interest in getting to know and spending time with—and, by extension, whether our clients would likely feel the same way.

Mr. Meal: We place a lot of emphasis on a candidate's undergraduate record because we feel that the undergraduate record, properly understood, can provide an insight into a candidate's intellect and drive that is both very reliable and very different from the insight one obtains from his or her first-year law school GPA. The key, in our mind, is putting the undergraduate record in proper context. Being magna cum laude at undergraduate school A can mean something very different from being magna cum laude at undergraduate school B. Indeed, even at the same school, an undergraduate GPA of 3.75 can mean one thing in one particular major and something very different in another particular major. I actually spend a fair amount of time educating myself as to those differences, at least among the fifty or so "core" undergraduate schools that the vast majority of our candidates have attended. With that background context, we are able to get a pretty good understanding of how strong, relatively speaking, each candidate's undergraduate performance was in the context of their particular school. That understanding can, potentially, tell you a lot about the candidate's intellect, how goal-driven he or she is, or the candidate's work habits. We use the interview process to explore the reason behind a candidate's undergraduate performance and thereby understand what that performance is really telling us about the candidate. But overall, the undergraduate performance means a lot to me because it is a four-year record of achievement—or in some cases, lack of achievement—as compared to the one-year record we have based on law school grades. Moreover, whereas first-year law school grades are usually achieved by means of a single exam administered in a single day, undergraduate grades are more often achieved, or not achieved, on the basis of longer term projects, such as term papers, that are much more akin to the kind of work that lawyers do in real life. So, to me, there is a lot of valuable information to be gained from evaluating a person's undergraduate record, once you put that record in its proper context.

I am also interested in the extracurricular activities the candidate has engaged in during college and law school. For me, the number of activities is much less important than the depth and quality of a person's commitment to the activities and, even more important, the candidate's reasons for having selected those activities. I'm also very interested in how people spent their summer after their first year in law school and their summers during college. Again, what interests me is not so much what the candidate did during those summers, but why he or she chose to do it and what he or she took away from the experience. I'm also interested in what things, outside of work-related matters, the candidate finds engaging. It doesn't matter to me whether the candidate is a bird-watcher or a baseball fan; what I want to know is how and why that particular interest became an important part of the candidate's life.

Do you have any particular view of candidates who took time off between college and law school?

Mr. Meal: That's a very interesting question, and one that is very difficult to answer. In and of itself, the fact that a candidate took time off between college and law school has no bearing on our evaluation of the candidate; that is to say, we do not mark candidates either up or down just because they either did or did not go directly to law school from college. Having said that, I think the reality is that candidates who took time off—particularly those who took two years or more off—between college and law school tend to be noticeably more polished and have much more developed interpersonal skills than candidates who did not. This enables them, as a general rule, to do better in the interview setting than candidates who went straight to law school from college.

Also, any candidate who has spent at least two years following college doing "something else" presumably did so for a reason. We believe that we can learn a lot about a candidate's affinity for law firm practice in general, and for working at Ropes & Gray in particular, by looking hard at what the candidate chose to do and, more importantly, why he or she chose to do it during the "time off." So the reality is, I think, that whereas sometimes our evaluation of a candidate can be negatively impacted by the fact that he or she took time off before going to law school, it is more often the case that the time-off period winds up improving our evaluation of the candidate. I say that, however, only based on intuition; I haven't ever done an empirical study of the matter, but your question makes me want to do one!

Mr. McGrath: Well one of the things I noticed in law school, although I don't have any data to support it, is that the people who took some time off between college and law school, either to work or to explore other interests, tended to perform better in law school than those who went straight through. There can be real benefit in exploring other interests, traveling, or even working for a couple of years after college to confirm your commitment to the practice of law. Those candidates who have gone through that process are almost always able to communicate much more clearly why they want to practice law. These individuals tend to have more poise and more confidence—and in a process like ours, where we're looking for only a couple of people a year, those things matter a lot. We expect all of our lawyers to interact well with other lawyers and clients. We do not have the luxury, for example, of dedicating lawyers only to appellate brief writing or other specialized areas of the law where good interpersonal skills are not crucial.

How important is a candidate's tie to the local area to you in making decisions to grant screening interviews and callbacks?

Mr. Meal: Our hiring process places no importance whatever on this factor. There are two reasons for that. First, our objective is to bring to our summer program, and ultimately to our firm, the most talented law students in the country. It would be inconsistent with that objective to turn down a highly talented candidate who has a marginal tie to our area in favor of a less-talented candidate with a strong local tie. Second, our experience is that these days law students take quite seriously the decision about where to spend their summer after their second year in law school. As a result, our recruiting history tells us that if we are able to persuade someone to join us for the summer, the likelihood is extremely high that, no matter how tenuous his or her tie was to our area before the summer began, the probability is extremely high that he or she will accept our offer at the end of the summer to become a full-time associate at the firm. So for us, at least, the specter that someone would spend a summer with us on a lark, all the while having the intention of returning to his or her hometown after graduating from law school, has proven to be far more imaginary than real, which has eliminated from our thinking any concern that we might once have had as to the necessity of weeding out, during the hiring process, candidates who lack a substantial tie to our geographic area.

Mr. McGrath: Since we are competing for talent against the high-profile firms fifty miles to the south in Boston, we need to be convinced that a candidate for our summer program has a real interest in not just spending the summer with us but in practicing here in New Hampshire for the long term. As I mentioned before, we carefully screen and then usually hire only two 2Ls per summer, with the expectation that these successful candidates will perform well, train with our attorneys, receive offers from us, return to our ranks after graduation, and eventually make partner here. Unlike many of the large firms in Boston and elsewhere, where only a handful of every class of sixty or seventy associates ever makes it to partnership, at Sheehan, our expectation is that, assuming diligent performance and development, there is a spot in the partnership for every associate we hire. Accordingly, if someone we hire as a 2L chooses not to return, we'll have a gap in our associate ranks that we'll likely need to fill through lateral hiring, which is not as desirable, unless we're dealing with a more experienced lawyer with her own book of business. So commitment to the area is very important to us.

That commitment falls along a continuum. Obviously we prefer to find candidates whose families are known in the area because, in addition to those candidates' intellectual talents, they are likely to also have contacts in the community that might make them significant client originators down the road. Short of that, we like to hear from people who spent their undergraduate years at Dartmouth or the University of New Hampshire, demonstrating some familiarity with and commitment to the area. Further down the list is the person who grew up in Massachusetts, Vermont, or Maine but has regularly spent time in New Hampshire—but we're looking for something more than "I went skiing there a few times" or "I spent some time on Lake Winnipesaukee as a kid."

So how does the candidate who doesn't have any connection to the area convince us that we're the place for them? It happens on a case-by-case basis and by a careful evaluation of the candidate's reasoning. We probe that issue carefully in the interviewing process, which helps us to get a sense for how honest the person is about their desire to practice in New Hampshire, how well thought out their choice of New Hampshire is, and where else they're applying. For instance, if I find out that the candidate I'm considering is also applying to large firms in Manhattan, I'm less convinced by their arguments that they want to practice in a smaller market and have a better lifestyle. On the other hand, if the candidate I'm considering is also applying to firms in Portland, Maine; Providence, Rhode Island; and Burlington, Vermont—or firms in her hometown of Portland, Oregon; or Raleigh, North Carolina—then I'm more apt to buy the lifestyle argument.

I'm sure we've lost a few qualified applicants based on the judgments we've made about candidates' commitment to this area. On the other hand, we have a number of attorneys on our roster who were not originally from New Hampshire but who did manage to convince us of their interests in practicing in New Hampshire and in having a more balanced lifestyle. A candidate who is not from this area but is sincerely looking for the sophisticated but balanced law practice that we offer needs to think carefully about the reasons why they want to come here and how to make a compelling argument about that to our hiring committee.

How important is the appearance of the résumé and cover letter? Are there any fatal mistakes that a person can make on a résumé or in a cover letter?

Mr. McGrath: I don't know if there are any fatal mistakes, especially if we're dealing with an extraordinary candidate, but there are mistakes that can be made on the cover letter that would make it a very steep climb for somebody to land a job here. Grammatical and typographical errors are always disappointing. If you can't get a cover letter right, what is your work product going to look like? I've seen our firm's name misspelled and my name misspelled. That just demonstrates carelessness—not a good thing to be exhibiting when you're trying to sell a hiring partner on your candidacy—since carelessness and the practice of law don't make a good marriage. I don't know that I've ever attended to the niceties and subtle differences in font or presentation in résumés. Don't send me colored paper or a glossy folder. I don't know if law schools are encouraging students to be creative, but lately I have seen résumés styled as pleadings in the form of motions to hire, replete with captions and numbered paragraphs. One application, trying too hard to convince us of his enthusiasm for the law, argued in his "motion" that he would deliver the eulogy for his deceased mother by telephone if the funeral services conflicted with a key deposition. Motion denied! I recommend you stick to the basics. Black laser print on white bond, in an easy-to-read font, and in a pleasant layout is what you should be shooting for. As I mentioned, we look at many hundreds of résumés every year; and while we look at each one, given that we have active law practices at the same time we're doing our hiring, we can't spend an enormous amount of time on each one. We focus on the big-ticket items—your law school record, your undergraduate record, your connection to the area, and any interesting and diverse experiences you may have had. Those things ought to be set forth prominently on your résumé.

I just want to add one other thing about the résumé. Sometimes I'll be interviewing a candidate during a screening interview or a callback and I'll learn something really interesting about her, something that would have made a significant positive impact on my decision to interview her in the first place, that wasn't on her résumé! If you have trekked Mount Everest—even at base camp—been a member of an ECO-Challenge, run a marathon, written a novel, traveled extensively, or done something else that is interesting, put it on your résumé! We want to know that you have other interests that make you a well-rounded person, so we definitely want to see those noteworthy activities prominently featured on your résumé.

Mr. Meal: I don't think that there are any truly "fatal" mistakes that one can make in this regard, except perhaps for mixing me up with the hiring partner at another firm, which does happen from time to time. In my view, however, people do make a mistake when they try to make either their résumé or their cover letter stand out from the pack, either by the way in which they format it or by the content they include within it. There is a pretty standard format for a law student résumé and for the cover letter, which any law student can easily obtain from the career services office at his or her school. When I review an application, there is certain information I am looking for that will be readily and easily ascertainable by me if the standard format is followed and the standard content is included. When someone chooses, for whatever reason, not to follow the standard format or not to use the standard content, all that does is slow things down from my perspective and raise questions in my mind both about the candidate's professionalism and about the candidate's confidence that his or her record is sufficient to establish his or her credentials for a position at our firm. So while I wouldn't characterize those out-of-the-ordinary applications as being "fatally" flawed, I certainly don't think that they are helpful to rate candidate's chances. Certainly, great care should be given to making sure that neither the cover letter nor the résumé contains any grammatical or spelling mistakes. Again, mistakes like that are not necessarily fatal but they do make people like me wonder about a candidate's professionalism, conscientiousness, and attention to detail.

What, specifically, do you look for in a candidate during the screening interview?

Mr. Meal: We evaluate every candidate, at each stage of the interview process, based on three separate criteria: intellect, interpersonal skills, and drive. There is information on each candidate's résumé that is potentially—and I emphasize the word *potentially*—valuable to us in evaluating each candidate in each of these three categories. We use the screening interview, and ultimately the callback interview, to get behind those items on the résumé and find out what those items are really telling us about the candidate in terms of each of those three criteria. For example, suppose the candidate had a 4.0 average at his or her undergraduate school. Was that because he or she has a brilliant mind? Or because he or she simply outworked everybody else in the class? Or because he or she structured his or her schedule so that it included nothing but gut courses, so that the candidate would have the credentials necessary to get into a top-tier law school?

Depending on which of those is the correct answer to that particular question, we've learned something different about the candidate in terms of our evaluative criteria and, as a result, in terms of his or her affinity for private practice and for our firm. So what we try to do during the on-campus interview, and during our callback interviews as well, is to drill down into particular items in the résumé that interest us and, through that drilling-down process, gain information that allows us to draw what we think are reasonable inferences about the strength of the candidate's intellect, interpersonal skills, and drive.

Mr. McGrath: Apart from someone who is clearly very bright, we're looking for folks who are poised, confident but not arrogant, and engaging. I'm looking for someone who shakes my hand confidently and looks me in the eye, but who can also relax and engage in a little bit of humor—even better if it is self-deprecating. Someone who we would be both comfortable and proud to put in a room with a client or out in the community at a social or political event representing our firm.

What do you think are the three most common mistakes made by candidates during the screening interview?

Mr. McGrath: One big mistake I see occasionally is overconfidence or arrogance. As I've mentioned before, our firm is populated by bright, able lawyers—many of whom were laterals from large metropolitan firms looking for a more balanced lifestyle or had the credentials to work at large, metropolitan firms but opted out of that life. So it amazes me when every now and then I'll meet a candidate who seems to have the impression that he is doing us a favor by interviewing with us. I don't know where those people end up, but that kind of attitude certainly doesn't fit into our firm's culture. I would also caution all applicants to know their résumés cold. If you have something on your résumé, particularly a law review note or article, or some other research project that you're working on, you have to be prepared to discuss it and to do so intelligently. You're going to be interviewing with five or six people, and at least one of them is going to be well versed in that area of the law; and because they're interested in the subject matter, they are likely to ask you penetrating questions about it. I am always disappointed when I find that a student is incapable of discussing in depth a legal issue about which he should be well versed. Finally, a limp handshake and lack of eye contact is unfortunately a common mistake. The way I look at it, if you can't look me in the eye during an interview and convince me of the merits of your candidacy, how are you going to inspire confidence in our clients?

Mr. Meal: The biggest mistake, by far, is that a lot of candidates have not thought very hard about, and as a result are unable to articulate in any convincing fashion, why they are sitting there interviewing for a position at our firm. The reality is that most law students wind up going to law school not out of any burning desire to be a lawyer, and certainly not out of any burning desire to practice law at a large firm like ours, but rather more by default, because it seemed like a path that left a lot of options open to them and that was being followed by a lot of the other top students at their undergraduate school who did not have a firm career plan in mind. Then, when the 2L interview season rolls around, most law students start interviewing like crazy with large law firms like ours, again not because they have any real idea of what large law firms do or why they might like doing it, but rather because that's what everybody seems to be doing. So the result is that most candidates who we see during the 2L recruiting season have no real idea what they want to do career-wise and hence no real idea why they might want to work at a firm like ours. Now, in and of itself, that is not fatal, because most applicants we see fall in that category, but we do see some candidates each year who have taken the time and made the effort to think hard about this question and who, based on that thinking, are able to articulate convincingly why they feel they are suited for large law firm practice and would find that environment engaging. Candidates who have both taken the time to develop a genuine understanding of what large law firm practice is like—perhaps they worked in a large firm the summer after their first year; perhaps they took the time to get acquainted with lawyers who work in large firms; perhaps they made the effort to read up on large-law-firm life—and who then have thought hard about how and why that sort of career would work particularly well for them, given their particular strengths, can distinguish themselves from their peers in a very dramatic fashion.

The second biggest mistake that applicants make in a screening interview is not understanding why the interviewer is there. Most large law firms do most of their work in teams. Thus, in conducting an interview, most interviewers are trying to envision the interviewee as somebody who they might be working with on a matter for a client somewhere down the road. In thinking about whether someone would be a good partner on a project, any interviewer would like the person to be intelligent, certainly, but it is just as important for the person to be cooperative, energetic, enthusiastic, conscientious, and determined. Almost every question an interviewer asks is an open-ended invitation to the interviewee to grab hold of the question and use it to demonstrate some positive quality of that sort about themselves, beyond his or her intellect. Too often, I think, interviewees fail to realize that the interviewer is looking for them to demonstrate those qualities and hence fail to take full advantage of those opportunities.

The third biggest mistake that interviewees make, in my view, is not being prepared to talk about some item that they included on their résumé. For example, I frequently ask interviewees about their college thesis. Such a question gives an interviewee great opportunity to demonstrate their intellect, their drive, and oftentimes—where they worked on the thesis in collaboration with a supervising professor—their interpersonal skills as well. I'm amazed how often interviewees, having put the thesis on their résumé and thereby made it fair game for a question, can hardly even remember the topic much less engage in an intelligent discussion of it. There really isn't any excuse for that. Interviewees should understand that any and every item listed on their résumé is something that, sooner or later, someone in the interview process is going to ask them about and expect them to be able to discuss thoughtfully.

How important is a candidate's physical appearance (style of dress, hair, accessories) during the screening interview? Is there any specific advice you can provide to candidates?

Mr. Meal: I think the interviewee is better off if he or she does not try to stand out from the pack in terms of his or her physical appearance during the interview. A job interview is an important business meeting and there is a fairly standard range of attire that is expected at an important business meeting. While it would not be fatal for a candidate to deviate from the normally expected range of attire, I can't really see such a deviation being helpful to a candidate's chances of success. Any candidate who chooses to come to an interview dressed in an unusual fashion presumably did so because he or she made a conscious choice and thus had a particular reason to look unusual. Now, while there isn't anything necessarily wrong with that, there is a good chance that the interviewer will be left thinking that the interviewee was trying to make a point with his or her attire and left wondering what that point was. So if a candidate were to choose to dress for an interview in an unusual or unexpected style, I assume the candidate would have some particular reason or point in mind in making that choice, and as a result I would urge the candidate to explain the point or reason for his or her attire during the interview. Otherwise, I'm afraid the point or reason will probably be lost on the interviewer.

Mr. McGrath: Our firm is business casual all the time unless you're meeting with clients or going to court. If a candidate is interviewing for a job at our firm, however, I would expect that he would show up in a suit and tie. Even though the trend in recent years has been toward more casual attire, I think that trend is starting to reverse itself now; and trends notwithstanding, law firms are still pretty conservative places. If you keep that in mind, you'll be fine.

Are there any memorable interview blunders that are worth mentioning?

Mr. McGrath: I remember one interview recently, which I conducted in one of our firm's conference rooms on the seventeenth floor. I noticed that throughout the interview, the candidate kept fumbling my questions and looking over my shoulder as if he were not paying attention to me. Eventually, he stopped one of my questions in midsentence and asked me if the bird hunting outside our conference room window was, in fact, a peregrine falcon. In fact, it was a peregrine falcon—they nest on a nearby building—but I was left with the impression that this candidate wasn't interested enough to maintain his focus on the interview. It was a very strange exchange.

Mr. Meal: Occasionally, in the context of the law schools that have the early-interview-week model that I discussed earlier, we'll run into an interviewee who is doing so many screening interviews during that one week that he or she is either completely uninformed about, or even forgets, which particular firm he or she is interviewing with in this particular interview. So, occasionally, we've had interviewees come in and start the interview by proclaiming how committed they are to spending the summer in Atlanta, or Houston, or Seattle, or some other city where our firm does not even have an office. Similarly, once in a while an interviewee will make a point of emphasizing that he or she has chosen to interview with us because he or she has one particular esoteric practice area that he or she wants to focus in—and the practice area turns out to be one that our firm does not even specialize in. Those situations, which do arise from time to time, can be pretty memorable, not only from the interviewer's perspective, but from the interviewee's as well.

What is the most important determining factor in deciding whether or not to give someone a callback?

Mr. Meal: For us, there is no one factor that is most important in determining whether or not to give someone a callback. As I discussed earlier, we evaluate candidates based on three criteria that we think are fairly distinct from one another—intellect, interpersonal skills, and drive. Callback invitations are extended to those candidates who we believe are the strongest candidates in the applicant pool, in an overall sense, in terms of those three criteria, and no one of those three criteria is any more or less important than the other two in terms of our overall evaluation of a particular candidate.

Mr. McGrath: For us it is a combination of academic achievement—intelligence and diligence—and a demonstrated commitment to the area. During the interview process we'll probe those issues further and will hopefully get a sense of whether or not the person is someone with whom we'd like to spend a considerable amount of time, not just as a summer associate, but down the road, as one of our partners.

What does it mean when someone does get a callback from your firm? What category does that put a candidate in? Can you put it in words?

Mr. McGrath: If you've gotten a callback interview from us, it generally means that you have satisfied our academic requirements and have emerged as one of the top eight or so candidates of the five hundred or so résumés we screened and twenty or so people with whom we did screening interviews. At our firm, the callback interview is an opportunity to get you in front of more of the partners and associates with whom you would likely be working and to get their impressions of you. It is, essentially, a fit interview. As I mentioned before, assuming appropriate performance and development, there is a spot in the partnership for every 2L we bring on—so we take this process very seriously. During the callback, the evaluation tends to focus on the more subjective aspects of your candidacy—how well you seem to fit in with the rest of the team.

Mr. Meal: The way the hiring process works at our firm, we rely on the on-campus interviewers to make recommendations as to who should, and who should not, receive callback invitations among the group of candidates that the on-campus interviewer saw at whatever law school he or she was covering. While technically I, as hiring partner, approve or disapprove of whatever recommendations the on-campus interviewer makes in this regard, in practice I follow the on-campus interviewer's recommendation well over 90 percent of the time. What I ask each on-campus interviewer to do, in coming up with his or her recommended callback invitations, is to extend such invitations only to those candidates who the on-campus interviewer would have been comfortable making an actual offer to at the conclusion of the screening interview if the on-campus interviewer had had the authority to do so. So if a candidate receives a callback invitation from our firm, at one level what that means is that the candidate has won over his or her on-campus interviewer and now has an important advocate within the firm for his or her candidacy. Having said that, at our firm, receiving a callback invitation does not give the candidate in question an assurance or a guarantee of receiving an offer. According to statistics published by NALP, somewhere between 70 and 80 percent of the applicants who come in for a callback interview at a large law firm like ours wind up receiving an offer from the firm. At our firm, however, the offer rate to callback interviewees is significantly lower than that. So at least at our firm, a candidate who receives a callback invitation is certainly off to a great start in our hiring process, but that process has quite a way to go, and the candidate has quite a lot still to do before an offer will be extended.

What are the most important success strategies for the callback interview in your opinion?

Mr. Meal: At the highest level of abstraction, I think the candidate's strategy should be to demonstrate as convincingly as possible a genuine interest in and excitement about the possibility of working at our firm. In an overall sense, our in-office interviewers, just like our on-campus interviewers, are evaluating each candidate as a potential colleague here at the firm. At our firm, the best colleagues are people who find their work to be engaging and energizing, who enjoy the challenge of taking on difficult projects and bringing all of their skills into play in order to complete such projects as well as they possibly can, and who enjoy and get excited about working collaboratively on matters. The callback interviewees who do the best job of exhibiting these characteristics during the callback interview are, invariably, the candidates who wind up getting offers from the firm. There are a number of tactics that a candidate can use in order to help himself or herself to succeed in this strategy. The more information about our firm that the candidate has obtained prior to coming in for the callback interview—whether through reading our print materials, looking at our hiring Web site, checking out third-party sources such as Vault.com, or talking to other students or to lawyers already in practice—the better armed the candidate is going to be to express his or her interest in the firm in a persuasive fashion and the greater interest the candidate is going to seem to have in becoming a part of the firm. Also, echoing what I said earlier about the screening interview, candidates who have really thought hard about why private practice interests them, and about which particular practice area they think would be a good match for their skills, can really distinguish themselves from the pack if they are able to articulate that thinking during the callback interview, because many, many second-year law students (and hence many, many callback interviewees) have made very little effort to think about this issue and as a result come across as being pretty much clueless on the topic when it comes up. Such cluelessness is not by any means a fatal mistake, but it is not particularly impressive either, and it is entirely avoidable if the candidate has spent some time genuinely thinking about why he or she is in law school and what he or she may want to accomplish coming out of law school.

Mr. McGrath: First of all, become well educated about the firm—where its offices are, and what its practice areas are. I don't think it is necessary to know the minutiae about cases that partners have been involved in or the practice areas that every partner specializes in, but it certainly helps to have good, generalized knowledge about the firm. It's always a good idea to pick up a newspaper in the city before your callback and at least skim it so you can be conversant about any major issue going on in town at the time. It doesn't make a convincing case for your interest in our firm if someone asks you about a significant issue going on in town and you have no idea what they're talking about.

Ultimately, you need to be yourself and you need to be comfortable, and as relaxed and as poised as possible. The people who receive callbacks at our firm are all extremely bright and have demonstrated accomplishment both at the undergraduate level and in law school. Despite a clear record of accomplishment, though, we're also looking for some measure of humility—which, to us, demonstrates a willingness to be taught, to learn from more experienced members of the firm, and to be willing to listen to other points of view. Finally, you need to show sincere enthusiasm. You may have fifteen callbacks during the hiring season, but with each one you do, you'll need to have thoughtful questions prepared, good answers to questions like "Why our firm, as opposed to some other firm?" and a sense of excitement about practicing with us.

How does the callback process work at your firm?

Mr. McGrath: Generally, the candidate will come in and meet with five or six people, including a mix of partners and associates, for about twenty to thirty minutes each. We'll then go to lunch with an additional group, usually four to six new people. If there is a particular partner or associate that a candidate wants to meet with because of an interest in a particular practice area or familiarity with a major case the partner handled, we try to accommodate those requests, either as part of the interviewing schedule or at lunch. These requests should be put to me in advance to give me some time to make the appropriate arrangements.

Mr. Meal: Our callback process is, I think, both somewhat more structured and somewhat longer than the callback processes of most firms our size. We think it is important to evaluate callback interviewees using a playing field that is as level as possible. What that means, in terms of our process, is that (1) every callback interview starts in the morning and concludes with a lunch; (2) every callback interviewee sees the same number of lawyers during the interview (six in one-on-one interviews and two more at lunch); (3) every callback interviewee meets me as one of his or her in-office interviewers; (4) the seniority mix is the same for every callback interviewee—three partners, including me, three midlevel associates, and two junior associates at lunch; and (5) every callback interviewee meets, if at all possible, with his or her on-campus interviewer at the start of the interview day in order to help get prepared for the interviews.

What are the most common mistakes made during callback interviews?

Mr. Meal: The biggest mistake, by far, is for a candidate not to take the callback interview seriously, either because he or she assumes (mistakenly, at least in the case of our firm) that he or she is pretty much guaranteed an offer by virtue of having received a callback invitation, or because he or she, for whatever reason, isn't particularly interested in our firm, notwithstanding the fact that he or she has taken the time to come in for the callback interview. Candidates who don't take the callback interview seriously typically don't do as much as they could to prepare for the callback and don't engage with the lawyers they meet during the callback in a way that leaves the lawyers excited about having the candidate as a colleague here at the firm. For example, a lack of preparation often results in the candidate either asking very few questions during the callback or trotting out generic questions that would work just as well at any other firm (such as "Tell me about your summer program" or "Tell me how your work assignment system works").

Candidates who have not really prepared for the callback interview and who have not done some good solid thinking about why they are even interviewing for a position at a large law firm like ours inevitably are going to suffer in comparison to candidates who have done those things. And since our hiring process really involves evaluating the callback interviewees against one another, those candidates who take the callback interview less seriously than most usually wind up not receiving offers no matter how high their law school GPA might be and no matter how sparkling their undergraduate record might have been. Indeed, at this stage of the process, the vast majority of the people we are looking at have both an eye-popping law school GPA and a brilliant record of achievement as an undergraduate, so those factors largely wash out of the equation when it comes to deciding which callback interviewees wind up getting offers.

Mr. McGrath: As I mentioned before, the callback interview at our firm is really a fit interview—to determine how well a candidate fits into the fabric of our firm's culture. Accordingly, this is not the time to come in stiff and nervous. The kiss of death in a callback interview is to be unable to carry on a responsive conversation with the person interviewing you. In my view, it doesn't matter how good your grades and scores are, if you can't carry on a twenty-minute conversation in an environment you're supposed to be familiar with on topics that you know better than anyone—your accomplishments and aspirations—it isn't going to work out. Also, some applicants fail to convince us that they really want to work at our firm. Come prepared to make the most of the opportunity.

What is the purpose of the recruiting lunch or dinner during callbacks?

Mr. McGrath: Sometimes, people will tell you that the recruiting lunch is an opportunity to let your guard down and have a relaxing time without having to worry that someone is evaluating you. I don't know how it works in other firms, but that's not how it works here. The entire time we are with a candidate, including, and sometimes especially, during the lunch, we are evaluating and assessing whether the person is somebody we would want to have as a summer associate, an associate, and perhaps someday as a partner. We'll frequently use the lunch to start a vigorous political debate or an argument over a legal issue, and while those of us who go to lunch together almost every day have these conversations as a matter of routine anyway, it is particularly interesting to see how candidates react to, and participate in, them. The worst thing you can do is just sit there and not participate. If you're not familiar with the issue, you can at least ask questions and show that you are interested in engaging on the subject. What we're looking at, though, is how you handle yourself. If you just sit there and don't add much to the dialogue, you're not helping your cause.

Mr. Meal: In our process, one of the purposes of the callback interview lunch is to help us evaluate the candidate. We ask both lunch interviewers to fill out evaluation forms on the candidate, which forms are identical to the forms completed by the other interviewers, and which evaluations are given every bit as much weight as the evaluations submitted by the other interviewers. Indeed, in some respects the interview lunch creates a better evaluative opportunity than the other interviews because it usually lasts for about an hour and a half, whereas a typical in-office interview is only thirty minutes long. But we also hope that, due to both its relative length and its relative informality, the interview lunch will be an opportunity for the callback interviewee to raise questions or concerns that he or she may have about our firm. As I mentioned earlier, in our process the interview lunch is always conducted by two junior associates—that is, two associates who joined the firm as entry-level associates the prior fall. Our thinking in doing that is that, because the lunch interviewers are much closer to being true "peers" of the candidate than any of the other lawyers the candidate met during the callback interview, such a structure for the interview lunch fosters our objective of having the lunch be an opportunity for the candidate to ask important questions of us.

What impresses you about a candidate at the recruiting lunch or dinner? What turns you off?

Mr. Meal: While I know I'm sounding like a broken record here, we train our lunch interviewers to evaluate the candidates using the same three criteria—intellect, interpersonal skills, and drive—that we look for in every other interview setting. So I guess the answer is that the same sorts of things impress us during the interview lunch that impress us in every other context. To some extent, the interview lunch is a bit more conducive than the formal interview to an evaluation of a candidate's interpersonal skills. But our lunch interviewers are trained to use the interview lunch as a way to evaluate the candidate in all three categories that we think are important, so I can't really say that the interview lunch has greater importance to us in terms of one particular category than it does in regard to the other two.

Mr. McGrath: It impresses me when a law student can sit at a table under somewhat stressful circumstances with senior partners and more junior partners and associates and hold their own in conversation and appear as if they've been coming to lunch with us for quite a long time. What turns me off is somebody who is either unwilling or unable to get engaged in the conversation at lunch. Somebody who is able to tell us about traveling in an interesting part of the world, or about some other interesting life experience that they had, can usually drive the lunchtime conversation. Lunch is a good time to get your hobbies and interests on the table and to get the conversation going about those things.

How does your firm typically handle the costs of the callback interview?

Mr. Meal: Our firm, like virtually every large law firm, reimburses each callback interviewee for his or her travel costs in connection with coming in for the callback interview.

Mr. McGrath: Our firm also pays all expenses related to the callback. If you are going to be meeting with more than one firm during the same trip, though, it is customary for travel-related expenses to be divided equally among the firms you visit.

Do people abuse the firm's expense account during callback interviews? Do people notice when that happens? Does it ever make a difference in whether someone gets an offer or not?

Mr. McGrath: Although I have heard stories from others about candidates throwing parties in their hotel rooms on a firm's expense account or charging expensive bottles of wine or massages to their rooms, I have never encountered any abuses of our expense account since I became the hiring partner here. If I ever did, I am certain that person would not receive an offer from the firm.

Mr. Meal: We do review the expense reimbursement requests that callback interviewees submit to us, although I am not aware of any situation where we felt an abuse had occurred. Certainly, if a situation ever arose where, after fully investigating the situation, we concluded that a callback interviewee had committed a serious abuse in his or her expense reimbursement request, that would have a significant—indeed, probably dispositive—negative impact on that candidate's chances of receiving an offer from the firm.

What percent of your callback candidates are typically extended offers?

Mr. Meal: The exact percentage varies somewhat year by year and is, in any event, confidential information that I am not in a position to disclose publicly. I can tell you, as I mentioned earlier, that our offer rate on callbacks is significantly below the national average for law firms of our size, which according to statistics published by NALP is between 70 and 80 percent.

Mr. McGrath: In a given year, we generally extend about six to eight callback invitations. We don't have any set quota, but on average, that is about how it works out. In a typical year, where we're looking to hire two candidates, we'll make rolling offers to our top callback candidates because historically our yield on offers has been relatively high.

The Summer Associateship Itself

What are the characteristics common to the most prized summer associates?

Mr. McGrath: Intelligence, excellent analytical ability, and diligence, not necessarily in that order. We want associates who, when given a problem, find a way to a solution—whether they find a way to that solution just by thorough legal research or by some combination of that and engaging other associates and partners at the firm about the issue. Legal issues are frequently thorny or fall into the interstitia of a doctrine, so we're looking for a willingness to doggedly pursue the issue to resolution—to drill deeper into advisory committee notes, legislative history, or to reason by analogy to the best answer—things that the best associates at our firm do as a matter of routine. Of course, the best summer associates also have strong interpersonal skills.

Mr. Meal: What we are looking for in our summer associates and what we tell them at the beginning of the summer that we would like to see is for them to demonstrate that they have the characteristics that we thought they had when we hired them: great intellect, great interpersonal skills, and great drive.

What are the most common problems you see in your summer associate programs?

Mr. Meal: It is very rare for us to encounter anything that I would call a serious problem. As I've said in response to your earlier questions, we have a very rigorous and unusually selective fall hiring process. Indeed, I think it is safe to say that we are sort of an outlier among large law firms in terms of how selective our hiring process is, not just in terms of the record of academic achievement we are looking for, but also in terms of the colleagueship skills that we insist on being demonstrated through the interview process before we are willing to make an offer to any given candidate. So our model is to weed out the "problems," not during the summer program itself, but during the previous fall, when we decide who we are going to include in the summer program. So for us, it is quite unusual for a serious problem to crop up among the group that actually joins us for the summer. In the rare case where such a problem does arise, the problem is almost never because the summer associate lacks the intellectual capacity to do our work. We seem to be pretty good at screening for that during the fall hiring process. Rather, what happens every once in a while is that a summer associate doesn't seem to have the interest in either our firm or in the work that we do at our firm that we thought we had observed during the interviewing process.

Mr. McGrath: Our hiring process has become so selective that I've been routinely impressed with our summer associates. If I had to point to one area of weakness that is most common, though, I would point to writing skills. We understand that skill in legal writing can take some time to develop, but I think it is a mistake for law schools to make legal writing courses ungraded or pass-fail, which often causes law students not to take the legal writing course as seriously as their other courses. The fact is, the legal writing course is one of the most important courses you'll take in law school because it is something you'll use every day in your practice, whether you are a litigator or a transactional lawyer. The ability to communicate clearly and concisely in writing is one of the most valued skills in the lawyer's arsenal.

What are the most common mistakes that summer associates make, and what is your advice on how to avoid those mistakes?

Mr. McGrath: I guess I could give you a list of potential pitfalls for summer associates. First of all, be sure to treat everyone at the firm well and with respect, and I mean everyone—from the person who answers the phone in the reception area to the person in the mail room to the most senior partner. Everyone deserves your respect, and you should be mindful of that. Similarly, avoid having any confrontation with anybody—secretaries, other summer associates, associates, or partners. If you feel you have been wronged somehow, handle it diplomatically through your adviser or other appropriate channels. Avoid being pretentious or obsequious—qualities that are clearly not genuine and not appreciated. Carelessness is another potential pitfall, and that usually shows up in documents that are sent to the partner with typographical errors or that are missing treatment of issues the partner has clearly asked that the summer associate address. When you are given an assignment, make sure you understand what is requested. Partners do not mind you asking follow-up questions either right away or as those questions arise in the course of research. What partners do mind is getting work product back that does not answer the question posed. Finally, be careful not to take on more work than you can reasonably handle within the deadlines imposed on you by the partners with whom you are working. It is better to decline a new assignment because of scheduling problems, or to get the partners to work out the deadlines with each other, than it is to try and take on too much and disappoint everybody.

Mr. Meal: One mistake that a summer associate will sometimes make is to communicate to an attorney who is supervising his or her work that the summer associate has little or no interest in the work that the supervising attorney is asking him or her to do. The attorneys at our firm feel, with ample justification, that the work they do for their clients is engaging and challenging and meaningful. They also feel that anyone who has been invited to join our summer program has been given an incredible opportunity that almost any law student would be grateful to receive. As a result, it really isn't very surprising that a supervising attorney will have a pretty negative reaction when a summer associate communicates his or her lack of interest in or respect for either the work that particular attorney is doing or the work that the firm is doing in general. So what I tell our summer associates at the beginning of the summer is that they should do everything they can to avoid giving any supervising attorney that impression, even if for some reason they genuinely feel that way.

How do you advise summer associates to solicit feedback from the partners they work for?

Mr. Meal: To some extent, we try to make that easier for the summer associates by soliciting the feedback ourselves through a formal process that we have put in place and then communicating that feedback directly to the summer associates. Our overall approach is to steer away from making the summer associates feel like it is their responsibility to solicit feedback from supervising attorneys because we think trying to get summer associates to solicit such feedback is a lot to ask. We supplement our formal process by going directly to the supervising attorneys and pushing them to provide such feedback to the summer associate in question, without waiting to be asked to do so by the summer associate.

Mr. McGrath: We have a mentoring system here, and as hiring partner, I monitor our summer associates closely. When I, or the associate's mentor, receive feedback about a particular summer associate, we deliver it directly to the summer associate. We also encourage and consider it entirely appropriate for summer associates, after completing a meaningful assignment, to casually ask the partner who gave them the assignment to assess the quality of the work product. The other thing a summer associate can do to get feedback on her work product is to look at the red-lined version of the document that she prepared or to look at the work product that was ultimately filed with the court or given to the client. You can learn a lot about your performance by evaluating the difference between what you delivered and what was ultimately filed.

How do you advise summer associates to get the kind of work they want during the summer?

Mr. McGrath: Ask for it! Ask your mentor or the associate adviser, either before you arrive at the firm for the summer or as soon as possible after you arrive, to get you the type of work you want. We want you to have a meaningful experience and, because we are a full-service law firm, can usually satisfy such requests.

Mr. Meal: This is something we work very hard at. To begin with, before the summer even starts we ask each summer associate to tell us, and then to confirm for us, which practice area or areas the summer associate is most interested in. We then assign each summer associate to two supervising attorneys—who we call coordinating lawyers—whose practice areas match up with the summer associate's preferred practice areas. In our model, the majority of each summer associate's work assignments come directly from those two supervising attorneys, so to us that creates sort of a fail-safe method of ensuring that there is a good match between the work each summer associate wants to do and the work he or she actually gets during the summer. We then supplement the coordinating-lawyer system with a central pool of assignments drawn from throughout the firm that we then spread out among the summer associates according to what they tell us during the summer about additional practice areas they may be interested in.

How do you advise summer associates to make best use of their summer adviser?

Mr. Meal: In addition to assigning each summer associate to the two coordinating lawyers mentioned in response to your last question, we also assign each summer associate to a more junior lawyer, whom we refer to as the summer associate's "adviser." Unlike the coordinating lawyers, the adviser does not assign work to the summer associate, nor does the adviser play a part in the summer associate's evaluation. Rather, the adviser's role is to be an informal resource for the summer associate by answering questions and addressing issues that may arise and also helping the summer associate to meet other summer associates and other lawyers in the firm.

Mr. McGrath: First, I'd make sure that you have enough work to do. Your mentor or adviser is typically the gatekeeper for your work, so you'll want to make sure that you're not only getting the diversity of work that you seek but also a sufficient volume of work. You want to have an opportunity to impress a number of different attorneys in the firm, and your adviser can help in that regard. Similarly, if you're getting overloaded with work, you'll want your adviser to serve as a gatekeeper to manage scheduling conflicts. In the past, summer associates have also used me as an adviser to act as a middleman in soliciting feedback from partners.

How important is participation in the summer social events? Is participation mandatory? How do you suggest striking a balance?

Mr. McGrath: I think they are very important. We don't go overboard, but we do have a few social events during the summer that various people at the firm have spent quite a bit of time organizing; and absent some extenuating circumstances, summer associates should attend those events. Similarly, if your firm has weekly departmental meetings, or firm lunches, you should attend those as well. Attendance at these events underscores your interest in and commitment to the firm.

Mr. Meal: Participation in the summer social events is irrelevant to our decision to make a summer associate an offer, but it is pretty important, we feel, in terms of recruiting our summer associates to accept our full-time offers, which in fact is the primary objective of our summer program. Participation is not mandatory, but we do encourage summer associates to attend the social events, provided a work commitment does not prevent them from doing so.

What are the most common mistakes you see summer associates make at summer social events?

Mr. Meal: I think the biggest mistake is that summer associates fail to take advantage of them, either by not attending them or by attending but not using them as an opportunity to meet either their fellow summer associates or the lawyers at our firm. We have a remarkably talented, and remarkably diverse, group of lawyers at Ropes & Gray, and that talent and diversity is replicated among our summer associate groups. Summer associates who get to know their peers invariably come away impressed and excited about having those peers as colleagues. Summer associates who don't make the effort to do that never realize what they missed by failing to do so.

Mr. McGrath: Stray a bit from your comfort zone. Don't just congregate with the other summer associates—mingle and interact with other members of the firm who are at the event. These events are a good time for you to get to know other members of the firm and to help them to get to know you.

How does your firm determine which summer associates to hire for full-time employment? Is there a vote of the partnership?

Mr. McGrath: Deference is given to the hiring committee to extend offers for summer employment after callbacks. That decision does not go before the full partnership. The decision about whether to offer an associate position to a summer associate is something that goes before our full partnership for a vote, usually in the middle or latter part of September. Although technically a majority of the partners' votes is needed for a candidate to be hired, in reality, it never comes down to this. If a candidate does not receive overwhelming support, the person does not receive an offer. If one or two of the twelve or fourteen partners that the summer associate worked with were mildly displeased with the summer associate's performance, that may not be enough reservation to cause that summer associate not to get an offer. Certainly, if one or two partners had severe reservations, though, that would likely be enough to derail an offer. Similarly, if there were several partners who had mild reservations, or if relatively few partners were enthused about a summer associate, that person might not receive an offer.

Mr. Meal: The partner in charge of the summer program solicits input from the other lawyers involved in administering the program, the supervising attorneys of the summer associate in question, the other lawyers for whom the summer associate has worked during the summer, and the summer associate's on-campus interviewer. Based on that input, the partner in charge of the summer program makes a recommendation to me as to whether or not an offer should be extended. In theory, I have authority to reject that recommendation. In practice, however, it is hard for me to imagine a circumstance where I would do so because I have tremendous confidence in the summer program head, and we work together very closely on the hiring program in general and the summer program in particular. Indeed, in my three years as hiring partner, I have never yet disapproved a summer program head's recommendation regarding an offer.

CHAPTER 21

The Future Is Now: Using the "Relevance Calculus" to Choose a Firm

All that glitters is not gold.
—CHAUCER

IF ALL GOES WELL, by the close of the recruiting season, you'll have secured a job offer for your 2L summer. Hopefully, you'll have several offers to choose from. But how do you decide which offer to take?

You'll mine the placement office, *The Insider's Guide to Law Firms,* and the *Law Weekly* citywide firm rankings. You'll talk to your friends to get their impressions. In the end, though, as so many other times in law school, it will be you, struggling, alone in the dark.

This chapter should help.

How to compare starting salaries

First of all, let's talk for a minute about starting salaries. If you are like most of us, actually having money in the bank at the end of the month is probably a foreign concept, so the very real possibility that you might be making well over $100,000 next year has probably blown your mind. Before you get smitten by dreams of vast wealth and sign on the dotted line, however, it's time for a reality check. Things, you see, are not always as they seem.

The following exercise will allow you to compare and chart out what is going to happen to the starting salaries at the various firms you're considering before you actually get to do much with "all that money" you'll be making. Flip to the Salary Comparison Chart on page 317. Start by filling in the names of the firms you're considering, and the starting salary at each firm, including any signing bonuses, and travel and bar exam preparation expenses. From there, figure out what tax bracket this salary and whatever other income you might be receiving from investments or other sources will put you in, and lop off the appropriate percent for federal income tax, state income tax, and any applicable city taxes. If you're not sure what percent state income or city tax you'll be subject to, call your firm's recruiting coordinator to inquire.

Now how much are you being paid? Those salaries don't look quite as impressive anymore, huh? Look across the board and compare them, however, because differences in state income tax percentages, and the presence or absence of a city tax can make a substantial difference in overall salary value. Circle these values, as these are your after-tax incomes before you spend a nickel on anything. Now enter the billable-hour goals for each of the firms, and divide your after-tax salaries by the number of billable hours you are expected to produce. The resulting figure is your after-tax salary per hour. Suddenly, that salary doesn't look so huge anymore, does it?

But now the fun really starts.

Determine the likely rental cost of an apartment for a year in the city where each firm is located. The difference in the cost of housing, alone, from one city to the next, can amount to over $10,000 per year, so take some time to get reasonably accurate numbers here. You may need to consult the real estate section of the city's newspapers or go online and consult a real estate Web site to determine average rental costs. When you have a number, subtract it from your after-tax salary (the values you circled) for each firm.

Now, are you planning to keep a car in the city? If you are, you're going to pay for it! Determine how much it is going to cost you to park the car for the year, and how much it will cost you to register and insure it. Subtract those costs from what's left.

If you're working in a big city, you're probably not crazy enough to drive to work every day, so you'll probably be taking some form of public transportation, right? Hopefully, your destination city provides commuters with some break on monthly commuter passes. How much are twelve of those babies going to set you back? Yup, you got it. Subtract that from your starting salary.

Now how much are you being paid?

But we're not done yet.

There's a not-so-little matter called a sales tax that you need to consider. Find out if the state where you're going has one, and what percent it is. The average American spends about 10 percent of his salary on taxable consumer goods, so take 10 percent of your starting salary, multiply that number by the percent sales tax your state features, and subtract that result from your starting salary.

Getting smaller, isn't it? But we're not done yet.

If you've done any traveling, you probably know that the cost of living can be wildly different from city to city. You have already noticed it in comparing the rents between the cities you are considering, but there are many other less obvious manifestations of this cost-of-living differential, such as food and entertainment costs, that can have a huge effect on your budget, and how much money you manage to squirrel away in any year. The following methods are not strictly scientific, but I have found that the calculations that follow can be surprisingly accurate in helping you to guesstimate the differences in the costs of living from one city to the next.

First, we'll deal with food. Whether you cook for yourself or are a sustaining member of the local sushi joint, the base cost of food in the city you choose will influence how much you end up paying for things. Accordingly, we're going to go shopping. Visit or call the largest chain grocery store in each city you're considering, and get prices on the following items: a gallon of milk, a half gallon of orange juice, a box of Cheerios, the per-pound cost of tomatoes and Granny Smith apples, the per-pound cost of bean coffee, the per-pound cost of boneless, skinless chicken breast, and the cost of a thirty-two-ounce jar of name-brand pasta sauce. Add up the cost of this "shopping list" to get a total cost in each city. Then add up the costs for all the cities, and divide by the number of cities to get an "average cost" of the shopping list among all the cities you are considering. Divide each city's cost by the average cost to get the "percent of the average" for each city. Multiply this percent of the average by $4,800, a mentor-estimated annual food budget, to get an estimated food budget for each city, adjusted for cost-of-living differences. Subtract this amount from your after-tax salary.

Now estimate the cost of an average night out with friends in each city. Take the cost of a movie ticket, and add it to the cost of three premium draft beers at the local bar to get a hypothetical "cost of a night out" total for each city. If you aren't sure of the exact costs of these items, make some phone calls to get them. Add up these totals for all the cities you are considering, and divide by the total number of different cities you're comparing to get an "average cost of a night out" among the cities. Then divide each city's actual cost by this average cost to get a value called the "percent of the average." This figure gives you some indication about how much more or less expensive one city is compared to another. Still with me? Now multiply this percent of the average that you derived for each city by $5,000, your mentors' consensus about how much you will spend on entertainment in a given year. The result is your estimated entertainment budget for the year, adjusted for cost of living in the various cities you are considering. It's not perfect, but it's a surprisingly good estimate. Subtract this from your salary.

After doing these calculations, you have a rough estimate of how much money you'll be looking at after you've paid your taxes and essential costs of living. Now take your after-taxes-and-expenses salary totals, and as we did before, divide them by the billable-hour goals for each firm you are considering.

Surprised?

I was. Doing these calculations revealed to me that I would actually be making a larger per-hour salary after taxes and expenses in New Hampshire than I would have made in Boston, even though the starting salary in Boston was about 90 percent higher, because the taxes, cost-of-living expenses, and the billable-hour goal in New Hampshire were much lower.

Fill out the chart below for yourself. You may need to spend a couple of hours and make a few phone calls, but the time you spend will be well worth the insights you can gain.

SALARY COMPARISON CHART

FACTOR	Firm: __ City: __	Firm: __ City: __	Firm: __ City: __
1. Starting salary at firm	______	______	______
2. Federal income tax percentage	______	______	______
3. Federal income tax (row 1 × row 2)	______	______	______
4. State income tax percentage	______	______	______
5. State income tax (row 1 × row 4)	______	______	______
6. City tax percentage	______	______	______
7. City tax (row 1 × row 6)	______	______	______
8. Total taxes (row 3 + 5 + 7)	______	______	______
9. After-tax income (row 1 – row 8)	______	______	______
10. Billable-hour requirement	______	______	______
11. Salary per hour after taxes (row 9 ÷ row 10)	______	______	______
12. After-tax income (same as row 9)	______	______	______
13. Annual rent	______	______	______
14. Subtotal (row 12 – row 13)	______	______	______

15. Parking/registration/insurance	______	______	______
16. Subtotal (row 14 – row 15)	______	______	______
17. Public transportation cost	______	______	______
18. Subtotal (row 16 – row 17)	______	______	______
19. Annual food budget*	______	______	______
20. Subtotal (row 18 – row 19)	______	______	______
21. Annual entertainment budget*	______	______	______
22. Subtotal (row 20 – row 21)	______	______	______
23. Billable-hour requirement (same as row 10)	______	______	______
24. Salary per hour after living expenses (row 22 ÷ row 23)	______	______	______

*See text above for suggested calculations

If you have taken the time to fill out the chart, consider the following thoughts. Are you working more hours for less money at one firm than you would be at another? Is there a compelling reason why you would want to do that? There might be—perhaps that firm offers more of the kind of work you want, has a better reputation, or is located in the city you most want to live in. Just make sure you know why you are choosing one firm over the other because, as the above exercise shows, a higher starting salary does not always translate to more money in your pocket. Remember a couple of other things. Minor differences should not be overemphasized since several of the calculations are rough estimations. Finally, keep in mind that the above exercise examines first-year starting salaries only. You might want to look into how much, and by what method, salaries typically increase from year to year at each of the firms you are considering. Are the annual raises merit based (based on your performance) or lockstep (based on the number of years you've spent at the firm)? Once you have this information, you can begin to eyeball how the comparisons between the firms you are considering might play out over time.

NALP comes at this issue from a slightly different angle, computing what it calls its annual Buying Power Index. Published in its annual monograph *Starting Salaries: What New Law Graduates Earn,* this index helps students compare the "buying power" of a salary in New York City with salaries in other major cities. Check out www.nalp.org/bookstore for more information about this resource, or inquire whether your law school placement office has a copy available for you to consult.

Choosing a firm using the "relevance calculus"

Below, you will find the list of the thirty-two defined factors that comprise the "relevance calculus"—a nonscientific system to help you decide in what firm, and perhaps even in what city, to practice. If you read the prior chapters on recruiting interviews, did your homework, and asked the right questions, you should already know where each firm you are considering stands with respect to each of these factors. After the list of these factors, you will find the relevance calculus chart, which will help you to really think about each of these factors and its importance to you and to your decision. You may want to photocopy this chart several times so you can fill one out for each firm you are considering.

Here's how it works.

First, read the descriptions of the various factors below, and assign each of these factors an "importance value" from zero to two in the space provided in the chart that follows. Give a factor a zero if it is of little or no importance to you, a one if it is somewhat important to you, and a two if it is very important to you. Be sure that once you assign a factor an importance value, you use the same importance value for that factor across all the firms you are considering. Note that a couple of blank spaces are intentionally provided in the chart in case you want to write in extra factors.

From there, assign each of the firms you are considering a score from one to five for each of the factors discussed. For example, on the factor "salary and bonuses," give a firm a score of one if the firm's salary and bonus structure is "lousy" compared to that of the other firms you are considering, a two if it is "below average," a three if it is "average," a four if it is "above average," and a five if it is "outstanding."

After you have assigned each factor an importance score (zero to two), and a factor score (one to five), multiply the two scores together to get the "total factor score" for each factor. For example, if you assigned the factor salary and bonuses an importance score of two (very important), and gave a particular firm a factor score of three (average) for salary and bonuses, the total factor score for salary and bonuses for that firm would be six (two times three).

Note that if you ruled a particular factor "not important," you will end up with a total factor score of zero for that factor because you are multiplying by zero.

Complete these calculations for each factor until you have filled the entire chart, then add up the total factor scores of all the factors. The number you end up with is the "final firm score." Compare the final firm scores of each of the firms you are considering to help you decide among them.

Description of factors in the relevance calculus

Salary and bonuses: Starting salary, including any bonuses (signing bonus, clerkship bonus), moving expenses, and the amount of bar expenses the firm will cover. Be sure to use the Salary Comparison Chart on page 317 to make a more accurate comparison among salaries.

Benefits/vacation package: The amount and quality of health, dental, and life insurance the firm will provide to you; whether your spouse and children are also eligible under the benefits package; number of weeks of paid vacation allowed per year; sabbatical program, if any.

Prestige of firm: Overall rank of firm in city and nationwide among lawyers and law students. By the time recruiting season is over, you should have a good idea about this already, but for more information, consult your law school placement office and the annual firm rankings provided in *The American Lawyer* or *Law Weekly*.

Length of partner track: The number of years you must work before you can be considered for partnership. Ask whether there are different levels of partnership (junior partner, nonequity partner), and determine the number of years required to reach each level.

Potential to become equity partner: Remember that only equity partners share in the firm's equity (and divide the lion's share of yearly profits), so if you're in it for money and control, find out what percent of first-year associates go on to become equity partners. If you receive an ambiguous answer, beware—the news is probably not favorable.

Billable-hour requirement: Eighteen hundred to two thousand hours is average, but don't just accept the firm's "party line" on what the billable-hour requirement is. Find out what the average associate billable hours were for the prior year, then ask several of the associates you met during your callback interview what their previous year's billable hours were. Remember that the most efficient associates can still only bill about 80 percent of the time they spend in the office. Assuming that you take your three weeks of vacation and don't work weekends, you will need to work ten-and-a-half- or eleven-hour workdays to meet a two-thousand-hour billable goal. Those are long workdays. If the requirement is higher than two thousand hours per year, well . . .

Ability to do type of work desired: First, does the firm have a thriving practice in the type of work you are interested in, or do they only do the occasional case or deal in that area? Will you be allowed to pick the department or the practice group you want to work with? Again, don't just accept the firm's party-line answer to this question. Check with the associates you meet to find out whether the person that came to the firm to do First Amendment work is actually getting that kind of work or has ended up getting stuck with routine contracts work instead.

Firm training/mentoring program: Will you be assigned a mentor in the area of law you are interested in practicing? What kind of training does the firm provide you, in terms of learning how to use the computer systems, and offering writing and trial workshops?

Distribution of assignments: Are assignments filtered to you through an adviser, mentor, or a central clearinghouse, or can partners and upper-level associates simply dump things on you willy-nilly? Will you be able to turn to anyone when your workload becomes unbearable, but the partners keep coming with more assignments? For incoming associates who have a difficult time refusing assignments from partners, this is a critical question to ask.

Firm hierarchy: Simply put, what is the partner-to-associate ratio? Top-heavy firms can be taxing on associates since there are only so many people around to field assignments from partners. You might also want to find out how projects are typically staffed. Will it be just you and a partner, or will there also be a midlevel associate on the project who can help you over the rough spots?

Associate satisfaction: How happy are the associates at the firm you are considering? Don't expect candid answers from the associates themselves. Instead, consult your law school placement office for the latest "Associate Satisfaction" poll anonymously collected from most of the country's largest law firms. If your firm ranks poorly, proceed with caution. There is no reason to expect that your experience will be any different.

Perception of the other attorneys at the firm: Largely a gut feeling here, since you probably only met these people for part of a day, but how did they look? Were they smiling and cordial, or were they generally scowling, walking around with their heads down, and looking exhausted? Did they greet each other in the hallways or just walk past each other like ships passing in the night? Did the people you meet seem to have interests outside the office, or was the office their life? Are these the kind of people that you'd want to hang out with socially?

Firm culture/environment: Is this a white-shoe firm from yesteryear where your kind might be welcomed at the front door, but not really welcomed in the back hallways? Is there an obvious old boys' network at play? Does the contingent of associates feel more like a college fraternity where boozing and partying after work is overemphasized? Is the place stiff and overly formal? Did it feel cold and austere, or warm and comfortable? More gut-feeling stuff here, but first perceptions can be accurate.

How do you think you would fit in here?: Still more gut-feeling stuff, but what do you think? Are the people at this firm enough like you that you'll have things to talk about? Would you be comfortable working in a place like this? Is this the kind of place you'd be excited to come to every morning, or do you already feel as if you'd have nothing in common with a lot of the people you met? How does your personal style mesh with the firm culture discussed above?

Maternity/paternity policy: Want to have kids someday but still keep your job? Better ask about this. While you're at it, inquire about whether the firm provides on-site day care for its lawyers. Some do.

Number of minority lawyers at firm: Want to work in a diverse or at least nonbigoted environment? Look around when you visit. What do you see? Does the place look ethnically diverse, or white as snow? Is there a mix of males and females in the partnership? If you have doubts, you'd better ask some questions. Better to find out now than after you start.

Firm's attitude toward alternative lifestyles: Are you gay, lesbian, bisexual, or transgendered? Better investigate what the firm's reaction will be when they find out. Are there any gays or lesbians in the partnership? Check the NALP directory for this information. Is there a nondiscrimination policy in place that includes a clause on sexual orientation? Ask to see the firm's policy. If there isn't one, you might want to look elsewhere.

Desirability of the firm's office space: Where is the building located? What does the office space look like? Will you have your own office? How big will it be? Will you have your own legal assistant? Completely a matter of personal taste here.

Perks: Does the firm have a luxury box at the arena or the ballpark? Does the firm provide discounted country club memberships or waived initiation fees? Health club memberships? Low-interest home loans?

Help getting a good mortgage? Meals if you are working late? A car to drive you home if you are working really late? Errand service? Ask!

Friends at or going to the firm: Don't underestimate the importance of having someone you can trust at the firm to commiserate with. Your job will have its moments, and having someone there to talk to who knows the personalities you are talking about and understands the firm culture can be helpful.

Potential to move laterally: If your job at this firm ends up being less than spectacular, how easy will it be to go somewhere else from this firm? The general rule is that it is easier to move from a large, big-city firm to another large, big-city firm, or to a smaller market, than it is to go from a smaller market to a large firm. Ask your law school placement office for more help here.

Desirability of city: Do you have a favorable or unfavorable overall impression of the city where the firm is located?

Housing options near the office: Are there affordable and attractive places to live near the office? Ask the younger associates at the firm where they live and for any recommendations. How do these options compare to the options in the other cities you are considering?

Length of commute to work: Pretty much speaks for itself, right? Also consider whether you will be traveling via public transportation or driving. Do you prefer one over the other? Are both options available and convenient?

Proximity to family: Can be good or bad, depending on your family. Whichever one it is, how do you feel about it? Are you close enough to them or far enough away from them to feel comfortable?

Proximity to close friends: Sure, you'll be meeting lots of new friends, but it helps to have an established network of friends in a new place to get you started, or at least to have a friend or two nearby to call on when times get tough. How far away are your best friends?

Proximity to significant other: Sure, some people try the long-distance-relationship thing, and a few of them even manage to make it work for a while. As a young associate at a law firm, you probably won't be one of them.

Potential to find a significant other in this city: Hoping to find a nice Jewish boy in Boise? Ever heard of a cowboy named Goldberg? Being single in rural anywhere probably isn't a good idea either.

Cultural activities: How are the museums? Is there a live-music scene? Good movie theaters? Exhibitions?

Nightlife: How is the local bar and club scene? Is it the kind of scene you'd enjoy? How close are the ballparks, stadiums, and arenas? Are there generally seats available to the games, or is every game sold out a year in advance?

Proximity to favorite outdoor activities: When the snow starts to fly, how far is the nearest good skiing? How far to the beach, the lake, the mountains?

Sports rooting interest: Can you stomach working in the same city as the Yankees? No, really. Can you?

After you've read through and considered these factors, make sure that you can give each firm an honest grade on each factor. If you need more information, it's time to make some phone calls. Once you have the information you need, fill out "The Relevance Calculus" below to get scores for each of the firms you are considering.

The Relevance Calculus

Firm: ______________________

Factor	Importance to you 0 = not important 1 = somewhat important 2 = very important	× Score 1 = worst 5 = best	= Total
Salary and bonuses*			
Benefits/vacation package			
Prestige of firm			
Length of partner track			
Potential to become equity partner			
Billable-hour requirement			
Ability to do type of work desired			

THE RELEVANCE CALCULUS (*continued*)

Firm training/mentoring program			
Distribution of assignments			
Firm hierarchy (# of partners to # of associates)			
Associate satisfaction			
Perception of other attorneys at firm			
Firm culture/environment			
How do you think you would fit in here?			
Maternity/paternity policy			
Number of minority lawyers at firm			
Firm's attitude toward alternative lifestyles			
Desirability of firm's office space			
Perks			
Friends at or going to the firm			
Potential to move laterally			
Desirability of city			
Housing options near the office			
Length of commute to work			
Proximity to family			
Proximity to close friends			
Proximity to significant other			
Potential to find a significant other in this city			
Cultural activities			
Nightlife			
Proximity to favorite outdoor activities			
Sports rooting interest			
Other:			

*See the Salary Comparison Chart above before scoring this factor

Surprised?

I was. I was having an extremely difficult time choosing between my favorite firm in Boston, and a great firm in the much smaller but rapidly growing city of Manchester, New Hampshire, where I grew up. After sketching out all the different factors that were relevant to my decision, I developed the relevance calculus to help determine which factors were more important to me, and to provide a way to objectively compare my options. After putting my two choices through the calculus, I determined that, given my interests, my career goals, and the factors that mattered most to me, my choice wasn't nearly as difficult as it first appeared.

Maybe the relevance calculus can do the same for you. At the least it should provide you with a way to think about and evaluate the factors that matter most to you in making this important decision. Remember, for most law students, a permanent offer of employment will come from the firm where you choose to spend your 2L summer, and accordingly it is also likely to be the firm you'll end up staying with for at least your first few years after law school. It is a big decision and should not be made cavalierly.

Here's what influenced your mentors in choosing their firms.

"I chose based on three factors: location, prestige, and variety of practice areas," Elizabeth explained. "I am close to my family, so I decided that I wanted to end up close to home. This turned out to be a good decision because the life of an associate is so busy there isn't much time to be traveling. I also wanted to make sure I ended up with a prestigious firm because in today's legal market no one knows how long they will be at their first job. My theory was that it's better to start off in a place that has a good reputation because from there you can go anywhere. Finally, I am interested in so many things that I wanted to get exposure to a bunch of different practice areas. I wanted to start my career with a wide variety of choices and then have the ability to specialize later."

"I paid particular attention to whether I liked the people I met, and whether I sensed that the attorneys were generally happy to be where they were," Carolyn adds.

"I ultimately chose the firm I did because when I went there for my callback, it just felt right," Megan agreed. "I genuinely liked all of the people that I interviewed with, and I felt like I fit right in. We went to lunch, and I had no problem relaxing and being myself. I was also convinced that working at this particular firm would allow me to maintain an acceptable work-life balance. While I might be making less money than I would be at a big national firm, I would not be forced to work so many hours that I would be unable to enjoy the other aspects of my life like my family and my hobbies. But in order to make the right choice, you have to know what you want in advance."

"Try to find a place where you can learn to practice law. You need to find a place where there are people you can learn from, a place where you'll feel comfortable, and a place that is going to allow you to practice in the areas you're interested in," Pat counsels.

"I also looked for positive experiences from the 3Ls who had worked at the firm the previous summer," Joel mentions.

Keith adds a final word for those being drawn to a particular city, firm, or firm size by peer pressure. "Avoid the lemming mentality. Don't go somewhere just because everyone else thinks it's the place to be. Decide what it is that you want, and then go after that. Forget what everyone else is doing. Most of them don't know what they're doing."

CHAPTER 22

Back on the Chain Gang: Advice About Journal Membership

We must, indeed, all hang together or, most assuredly,
we shall all hang separately.
—BENJAMIN FRANKLIN

MANY STUDENTS compete for membership on legal journals (in schools that offer writing competitions), or "walk on" to journals where membership is open to all, without ever considering what the experience entails or what benefits are to be derived from membership. For them, it is just another blind decision for students climbing the ladder of ambition. If you read chapter 15, however, you should already have given enough thought to the reasons why you want to be on a journal that the sometimes monotonous nature of 2L journal membership will be easier to take.

But what distinguishes the law review from the other "law journals" that you've heard about, and what does being on one of these journals entail?

Essentially, the law review or any other legal journal is an academic publication, kind of like a magazine for scholars, lawyers, and judges. As discussed in chapter 15, among its contents, a law review typically contains several articles on current, controversial issues in the law (typically written by professors, practitioners, or judges); reviews of the most current cases coming out of the Supreme Court or the circuit in which your law school is located, called "Notes" (typically written by law review members); "Comments" illuminating confusing areas of uncertain law or criticizing current doctrines (written by law review members); and perhaps a book review or an essay. A law journal, on the other hand, typically focuses on a particular subject or area of law (constitutional law, law and economics, mental health law, etc.) and restricts its articles, notes, and comments to that one subject area.

Generally, a school's law review is the most prestigious, because it has the widest circulation, receives the most funding, gets the best articles, and is the most selective in choosing its student membership. It is not uncommon, for example, for a professor who has written an article on a topic in constitutional law to bypass a school's constitutional law journal to get his article in the law review. In the publish-or-perish world of academia, reputation means everything.

So how exactly does this work, and what will your job be as a 2L working on one of these journals?

When you make one of these journals, you will probably be given a key to the office, a desk and a mailbox in that office, and a library card that will enable you to check books out to the journal. You will no doubt also go through an orientation where you will learn how the journal operates and what you can expect your schedule on the journal to be like. You will also be introduced to the journal's officers (read: 3Ls), the people who will really be running the show this year.

Who are they? you ask.

Every journal's board is slightly different, but generally it will look something like this. There will be an editor in chief, generally the intellectual and motivational leader of the board, who is ultimately responsible for overseeing the other teams of officers, and making all final decisions about the content and style of the journal. The managing editor is the money person, the individual who handles the budget, advertising, distribution, accounts receivable, accounts deliverable, and anything else financially related to running the journal. The executive editors, generally a team of three to six people, are responsible for typesetting, generating, dividing up, and distributing the copy to the 2Ls, entering the editorial changes made by the 2Ls into the computer system, redistributing second and then final edits of all articles, comments, and notes, and conducting a final check of all copy for errors. The articles editors, generally a team of three to six people, read every written submission and query made to the journal, check the author's background, and decide, usually with the editor in chief and the managing editor, which articles are selected for publication. They are also responsible for shepherding the author through the editorial process and acting as chief negotiators between the author and the journal when any controversies arise with respect to content or style. Comments editors or notes editors, generally a team of three to six people, are the people responsible for guiding the 2Ls and the 3Ls through writing their note or comment (or both), developing topic, outline, and draft schedules for each student, making editorial suggestions about each note and comment written, and selecting the best ones for publication in the journal. Each journal also typically has a resource editor, who is responsible for tracking down rare sources through interlibrary loan, making sure that the journal stays current on all its library accounts within the university system, and returning all sources back to their proper library at the end of editing. A symposium editor acts as the general overseer and manager of the journal's symposium issue (an issue devoted entirely to the treatment of one topic in the law).

As for you, well, you're just a plebeian this year, the worker bee that makes the hive run. Your journal likely publishes between four and eight editions a year, each of which must be filled with the articles, notes, and comments mentioned previously. After the articles editors select which articles to publish in an issue, and the executive editors divide up the manuscript into manageable segments, it's your turn to shine.

At the beginning of every "edit cycle," you will receive a piece of manuscript to edit. Your first job is to search through the citations and footnotes and retrieve all first-cited sources from the library system. Generally, these sources will be gathered on shelves and in binders devoted to the author in the journal office. Any sources you cannot find must be identified and handed off to the resource editor, who will then continue the search for you.

After you read the author's entire article to get a sense of what it is about, and how his argument develops, it's time to edit your piece of manuscript. Almost inevitably, you'll discover that your author has no idea what *The Bluebook* is and has never heard of proper citation form, particularly pinpoint citation. This will probably be your largest source of frustration, as you find yourself stuck in the library late at night skimming through a four-hundred-page tome looking for the two-line quote your author has cited to the source without pinpointing the page for you.

Frustrating. But all part of the game.

After you've finished your first edit and turned it in to the executive editors' office, you'll receive a "second edit," another section of the same article that has undergone its first edit in the hands of one of your fellow 2L editors. You are told to assume, however, that no one has seen the section before, and to check every source, quote, and citation again—and for good reason. Bluebooking is incredibly tedious and precise work, and even a momentary lapse of concentration can cause you to miss errors in a first edit. Of course, laziness, lack of effort, and the attitude that "someone else will catch it in a second edit" are more frequently the cause—which brings us to one of the most important pieces of advice about journal membership that you'll see in this chapter. It really should be obvious, but every year it seems that some people forget to heed this advice.

Do your share of the work, and do it well.

Nothing will destroy your reputation in law school faster than getting on the law review or another law journal, using the credential to secure a job and a clerkship, then being a slacker, turning in sloppy edits and dumping the burden to correct your work on your fellow editors. To police this problem, many journals post the names of the editors that worked on each section of a prior edit; but even if your journal doesn't do this, don't take advantage of the situation. In the law journal world, what goes around comes around, and generally the first thing to come around will be an angry fellow editor.

The cycle will continue with the circulation of "final edits," which are generally already in galleys and typeset and formatted as they will appear in the journal when it is published. At this stage, your job is mainly to check for typographical errors, numbers in headings, and cross-references in citations. Upon completion of your final edit, the article will go to the executive editors for a final read-through, and then off to press.

But your job is never done.

Usually even before you see a final edit for an article, you are working on the first edit of something for the next volume.

It is impossible to generalize a weekly time commitment for 2L law review or journal membership, as the commitment fluctuates significantly between schools. An initial barometer is to check how many credit hours the registrar has assigned to membership on your journal, but don't stop there, because this number usually significantly underestimates your actual time commitment. Twenty- or thirty-hour weeks (on top of your classwork) are not uncommon, particularly in the weeks when you are writing. Check with current members of the journal for an idea of what will be expected of you.

Writing your note or comment

The case note

Writing a case note usually entails dissecting a recent Supreme Court or circuit court opinion, reporting on its reasoning and conclusions, highlighting the controversial aspects of the opinion, discussing any dissents, and, depending on the style that your journal employs, perhaps editorializing a bit along the way. A case note is generally around ten pages in length.

Relax. You're basically writing a case brief on steroids. It's not as difficult as it sounds, and it can actually be an interesting and extremely educational exercise.

Unlike selecting a comment topic, choosing a note topic is fairly simple. The editorial board of your journal may select a case for you or provide a list of cases they want treated during the current year. If they don't, ask the professors in the subjects of your greatest interest about recent controversial cases that they feel would make good topics for a case note, or simply monitor the Westlaw and LEXIS legal news databases until you find something you like. Then follow your editors' instructions with respect to content and style.

The comment

Unlike the case note, the comment generally goes beyond the strict "reporting" of a recent case to a lengthier and more thorough evaluation of the controlling law in a particular area. Comments generally run between thirty and one hundred pages. The most fertile ground for comments is in areas of the law where splits among the circuit courts of appeals have left the status of the law in doubt or disarray. Poorly reasoned Supreme Court decisions, or decisions based on untenable or recently disproved scientific or social-science research are also common sources for comments.

Although each journal has its own guidelines for comment writing, there are two general rules to follow when selecting a comment topic. First, if you are writing on a topic that involves a split of authority in the circuit courts of appeals, the Supreme Court must not have already granted certiorari to a case (indicating that they will hear the case in the next tetra). The practical reason for this is that, by the time your comment is finished, edited, and published, the Supreme Court may already have issued its opinion resolving the controversy, which will render your comment moot and of little interest to readers. It is vital to monitor the appeals taken from circuit court cases in your area of interest, and the U.S. Supreme Court grants appeals, during the early stages of your comment writing. Nothing is worse than having already committed dozens of hours to a research outline, only to get preempted by a grant of certiorari.

Second, you must undertake a thorough review of all prior law review and journal articles written on your topic to assure yourself that you have not been preempted by another author. This does not mean that if someone else has written on the same topic, you can't write on it. You are only preempted if that other article makes the same arguments and reaches the same conclusions that you do. As long as you approach the subject in a different way, make different or additional arguments, provide a more thorough review of the subject, or reach a different conclusion, you should be fine. When in doubt, however, consult your comment editor. The last thing you want is to write a great comment and then to have it ruled preempted and barred from any chance at publication.

So how do you find a compelling comment topic?

The best way is to ask a professor in one of the subjects of your greatest interest about current controversies in the law. Inquire about circuit splits, vagaries in statutes, policy disagreements, or poorly reasoned U.S. Supreme Court opinions. Bring a pen and prepare to start writing. Professors usually have many of these areas on the tips of their tongues since they are also constantly searching for hot legal topics on which to write and publish. If the professor mentions anything that sounds interesting to you, always ask permission to use it as a topic for a journal comment and see if the professor has any books, case names, or other articles that might point you in the right direction. If the meeting goes well, you might consider asking the professor to mentor your work for you. Most professors are happy to assist students with journal articles.

Since every journal will have specific rules about the style and content of student comments, I won't go into further detail here. I will, however, offer a few pieces of advice that will be applicable to any comment written for any journal.

Choose a topic that fascinates you

Notice that I deliberately did not say *interests* you. I said *fascinates* you. Writing a comment, particularly a lengthy one, is a significant undertaking and may consume six months or more of your law school career. If you pick a topic that fails to hold your interest over time, that can be a miserable six months, and your final product will probably reflect your disinterest. Conversely, choosing a great topic can make working on your comment something you look forward to every day after class.

"Make sure your topic is not so general that you can't get it down to a clear thesis," Alison adds. "I picked what I thought was a sexy topic—

child-sex tourism and how to prevent it under international law. It turned out to be a mess because it was too general. I think the most specific topics work the best."

Whenever possible, choose a topic in the area of your greatest legal interest. If you can combine that topic with an area of expertise from your undergraduate major (such as history, political science, economics, or psychology), that's even better. The more layers of interest you have in your topic, the more likely that it will hold your interest, and the richer and more interesting it is likely to be. Take as much time as necessary to find a good topic, and be sure that you're not preempted before you begin.

"And make sure that if you're writing on an international or foreign topic, enough of your source materials are in English or some other language you can understand!" Keith counsels from experience.

Find a mentor on the faculty

Trying to write a comment without advice from a faculty member is inadvisable. In case you haven't figured it out yet, law is hard. Trying to keep intersecting doctrines straight and your argument on target in the midst of warring circuit court opinions discussing subjects you haven't yet studied can be difficult. Having a professor to guide you will help you to see the forest for the trees, keep you from veering off on unnecessary tangents, and help to pare down your topic to a sharp, solid thesis.

Stay organized, and stay on deadline

Writing a comment typically involves reading and citing at least fifty, and sometimes as many as several hundred, sources. If you're not careful, your apartment will quickly become littered with photocopies, and you'll end up spending more time looking for something that you previously read but now can't find, than you'll spend actually writing.

Stay organized!

Get yourself a couple of three-ring binders, some highlighters, some stick-on tabs, and a three-hole punch. When you begin reading source material, highlight any passages that you think are relevant, and when you finish reading a source, put it in a general section of your binder (cases, law review articles, legislative history, etc.) and tab it with an identifying moniker so you'll be able to find it again easily when you begin writing. Keep law review or scientific or news articles alphabetized by author's last name. Tab all passages in books, and keep a sticky note on the front of the book denoting what you plan to use it for.

Staying organized can shave many hours off writing the comment and will make the experience significantly less frustrating and more enjoyable. Finally, upon completion of your comment, you can also turn in your tabbed and organized source binders to your editor. If your comment was well researched and well documented with readily accessible sources, this could give you a leg up on your competition for publication.

Writing a comment for a law journal can be the most challenging and academically exhilarating experience of your law school career. Make the most of it!

CHAPTER 23

Restoring Balance: Moot Court, Public Service, and How to Reclaim the Life You've Lost

I am not now that which I have been.
—LORD BYRON

BY THE TIME you hit the halfway point of your law school career, you'll have weathered the worst that law school has to offer. With the dreaded first year, and all of its associated fears, behind you, with journal membership decided, and with recruiting season over, it is time to step back from the day-to-day grind and take an accounting of where you are in the big picture.

Take a look at your life.

Wow. Scary, huh?

How bad is it? Have you completely lost touch with your non-law-school friends? Have you put on fifteen pounds, fallen badly out of shape, or completely abandoned your hobbies and other interests?

When was the last time you took a whole weekend off without being worried or feeling guilty about it?

As much as I hate to admit it, I spent three years in Philadelphia without ever getting down to see the Liberty Bell, Independence Hall, or the Philadelphia Museum of Art or Museum of Natural History. I never got out to Pennsylvania Dutch country and only discovered the Reading Terminal Market, one of Philadelphia's most wonderful features, in the last months of my stay.

In short, I didn't do a great job achieving balance in my life until my third year.

And that's too late.

Your last three semesters of law school can provide a rich diversity of fulfilling experiences, and a much more relaxed pace, if you look up from your frenetic hustlings long enough to realize that the worst is over. It's time to restore some balance in your life.

Here's how.

First of all, you need to reclaim the life you've lost. In the first weekend after you get back from winter break (unless your school is on an odd schedule, in which case you should just shift all of this to after your third set of semester finals), take the weekend off. No books, no reading, nothing. Go out of town and visit the best friend you've virtually ignored for the past eighteen months or invite that friend to come visit you. Kick back and call friends and family. Reconnect with people. Give your spirit a lift.

Go out into the city (if there is one) and just wander around. See the sights. Go to a concert or an exhibit. Treat yourself to dinner at one of the city's renowned restaurants. Browse in the fiction section of the bookstore, or if the thought of reading anything makes you want to retch, spend some time on iTunes or Pandora. Bet there are a lot of new albums from your favorite musicians that you could catch up on.

Restore your gym membership if you've let it lapse, and recommit yourself to getting healthy again. Find a coffee shop somewhere with a waitstaff that isn't going to hustle you out as soon as you finish your coffee. Consider doing your class reading there as a change of pace.

When you're feeling relaxed and as if you've regained some perspective, look back over the last eighteen months of law school. Recognize how far you've come and credit yourself for having survived such a grueling experience. Now look forward to the time you have left. Are you still clearly focused on why you came to law school? Have your goals or feelings changed? Are you narrowing your interests on the kind of law you want to practice? Do you even want to practice at all? Prod yourself a little bit to come up with some answers to these questions, and recommit to or establish a direction to follow as you move into the second half of your law school career.

"I think a great way of maintaining your identity is to associate with people outside of the law school," John-Mark said. "If your law school is connected to a larger university, venture down there every once in a while. Join a main-campus student group. I made a regular practice of grabbing lunch and studying on the main campus, away from the law school. It was always stress-relieving, especially at exam times. My wife and I also had several groups of non-law-school friends whom we socialized with regularly. We also tried to take a hike once a week and go for a walk every day. It's amazing how minute the trials and tribulations of law school seem when you're on top of a hill overlooking the town or city you live in."

As you move into the second half of your law school career, you can start opening up to the myriad opportunities outside classroom study. In planning the spring semester of your second year, the first semester that you'll have the time and flexibility to pursue some different interests, look to areas other than just garden-variety classes to fill part of your schedule.

"I would just say do something," Joel notes. "Employers like to see extracurricular activities of all kinds, and participating in something can round you out as a person. If you made a good decision going to law school in the first place, then there is surely at least one opportunity that interests you."

"Definitely do something," Alison agrees. "The competitive activities like law review and moot court may seem the most appealing, but other activities can be equally rewarding. The important thing is to do something other than just studying and watching TV, for your sanity as well as your résumé."

Public-service opportunities

Almost every law school offers some form of course credit (or has a mandatory requirement) for public-service work. Commonly referred to as internships, externships, clinics, or practical, public-service opportunities come in all shapes, sizes, colors, and political affiliations. Depending to some extent upon where you are, there may be internships or externships with the attorney general's office, the U.S. attorney's office, or the public defender's office. You may have chances to earn credit in legal aid clinics or small business clinics working on real cases with real clients that may ultimately require you to make appearances and arguments in a real court before a real judge. There are opportunities to battle discrimination, bigotry, and anti-Semitism by doing research and writing legal briefs through the mail for organizations such as the Southern Poverty Law Center or the Anti-Defamation League. You can represent the poor in landlord-tenant battles against urban slumlords or work with judges and lawyers in mediation clinics.

"I think participating in a public-service activity is very worthwhile," Carolyn notes. "First, it gives you the opportunity to apply some of what you've learned in law school. Second, it gives you the opportunity to help someone who would otherwise have no one to turn to for help. Finally, participating in a public-service activity is a great way to get your perspective back. It is very easy to get wrapped up in your own stressful little world as a law student, but taking part in one of these activities is a way to avoid having this happen.

"I participated in a civil practice clinic and had an externship with the Philadelphia DA's office. The one thing I would strongly advise if you're going to do an externship is to research your placement thoroughly before you accept it. Don't bother going to work someplace where the program is unstructured, or where it is unclear both to them and to you what your duties will be, because you'll end up sitting around a lot and you won't learn anything."

The list of possibilities is so vast that you can almost certainly find something to satisfy even the most specific subject interest. Almost every law school has a public-service office or a public-service coordinator. Stop by, introduce yourself to that person, and get a sense for what the opportunities are. Public-service placements provide great opportunities to work with clients, hone your research and writing skills, anchor your legal education in the practical world, and do some real good. You'll be surprised at the life the law takes on when it is being applied to real situations involving real people, and the satisfaction you get from helping someone by using the law can help to cast law school in a whole different light.

Moot court

Whether run by your law school or an outside organization, moot court competitions provide an unparalleled opportunity to apply the research and writing skills you learned during your first-year legal writing class to a specific set of facts, then defend your work orally against an adversary and a panel of impartial judges. Generally, organizers of these competitions choose sexy topics that are the subject of widespread dispute in the legal community, especially issues that have produced a split of authority among the circuits or have just been granted certiorari by the U.S. Supreme Court.

"Moot court is a must for anyone thinking about litigation," Keith noted.

More than any other experience you will have in law school, moot court competitions prepare you for the realities of life as an appellate advocate and teach you to apply relevant law to the facts of different cases. In a well-constructed competition, you will be forced to analogize and extend existing law to the facts of your case and to defend your arguments against vigorous questioning from the judges. If you are a timid student who was rattled by the Socratic interlocutories of your first-year professors, you would be well served by forcing yourself through one of these experiences to build up your confidence and to help learn to think on your feet.

> My moot court experience is my fondest memory of law school. I would recommend it to everyone! There is just no substitute for free practice on how to think on your feet. The time to learn is now.
>
> —Elizabeth

Inns of Court

"The Mission of the American Inns of Court is to foster excellence in professionalism, ethics, civility, and legal skills for judges, lawyers, academicians, and students of the law in order to perfect the quality, availability, and efficiency of justice in the United States."* An American Inn of Court is an organization composed of judges, lawyers, law professors, and third-year law students that meets approximately once a month to discuss pertinent, cutting-edge issues facing the legal profession. Patterned after the traditional English model of legal apprenticeship, each Inn of Court is composed of Masters of the Bench (judges, experienced lawyers, and law professors), Barristers (lawyers who don't meet the minimum requirements to be masters), Associates (lawyers who don't meet the minimum requirements to be a barrister), and Pupils (third-year law students) and has a membership of around eighty people. Inns concentrate on issues raised in civil and criminal litigation practice, although some inns further specialize to address only specific areas of legal practice, such as intellectual property, federal courts, or white-collar crime.

The membership of a particular Inn of Court is divided into "pupilage teams," consisting of a few members from each membership category. Each team is responsible for conducting one program for the Inn each year and also assembles outside of monthly meetings to discuss general matters of legal practice, an arrangement that allows the less experienced lawyers in a pupilage team to learn from the more

*From the mission statement of the American Inns of Court on their Web site at www.innsofcourt.org.

experienced lawyers and judges. Finally, each less experienced member of the inn is assigned a more experienced member to act as a mentor and assist the member's development in the law.

A lot can be said for any opportunity to develop a mentoring relationship with more experienced people in the legal profession, since the law school atmosphere does not tend to foster these relationships between students and professors. There is no better way to learn the practical realities of legal practice. Investigate whether a chapter of the American Inns of Court is near you, and consider applying for membership if the concept interests you. You'll meet a lot of interesting people and learn a lot of things that are not taught in law school.

Law school committees

Finally, in your upper years of law school, you usually have chances to get involved in your law school's administration through memberships on various student-faculty committees. Although selection processes vary at different schools, membership is typically decided either by an election or by simply volunteering for the positions.

Among the more interesting of the committees usually seating one or more student members are the admissions committee (which decides admissions criteria and often reads files of aspiring applicants); the hiring committee (which seeks out, evaluates, interviews, and hires new faculty members); the curriculum committee (which proposes courses and designs the law school's curriculum); and the disciplinary committee (which enforces the law school honor code and conducts suspension or expulsion hearings for student offenders). Check with your law school's dean of student affairs to determine vacancies.

Membership on these committees can provide you with a great deal of influence in determining the philosophical direction of your law school. It also provides an excellent forum to cultivate close relationships with members of the faculty and to learn a lot.

CHAPTER 24

Keys to Ascension: Turning 2L Summer Employment into a Permanent Offer

To the victor belong the spoils.
—WILLIAM L. MARCY

WHEN YOU ARRIVE at the firm on the first day of your summer program, you will, no doubt, be somewhat nervous. All of a sudden, there you are in the big-city law firm, armed with two years of largely theoretical legal knowledge and some basic research skills that you're struggling to remember, thrown in with as many as sixty other 2Ls whom you've never met, with hundreds more nameless and faceless partners and associates going past you in a blur, and no idea what to make of it all.

Alternatively, you're at a smaller firm, or a public-service organization, and once greeted by the recruiting coordinator or the hiring partner, you are shown the library and your office, given some brief instructions about how to use the computer system and the phones, introduced to your secretary, and handed your first case file and a due date.

How are you supposed to deal with these situations?

Relax. That's what this chapter is here for.

Although the summer experience is radically different at large urban firms than it is at smaller firms or public-service organizations, basic performance concepts and rules of the road are common to all summer experiences. I'll address each of them below, making specific references to any relevant differences in strategy between large-firm and smaller-firm or public-interest practice. So let's get started!

> The summer associateship is basically just an extended interview. Use the time to really get a good sense what it is like to work at the firm. Ask a lot of questions about the partners, the lifestyle, the culture, the projects that associates are given, the expectations of associates, associate turnover rates, and take some time to figure out who the movers and shakers at the firm are, who the respected partners and associates are, and why that is. Finally, be yourself. You are going to want to be at a place where you are comfortable, and this requires that during the summer that you are there, you be yourself.
>
> —Pat

When you arrive

At large firms, your first week will likely be consumed by mixers to help you get to know the other summer associates in your summer "class," and by telephone and computer training. Carry a legal pad and a pen with you to take down anything important that you might not be able to remember, such as security codes, computer passwords, and the names of people you meet and want to remember. You'll either get your own office or share an office with another summer associate. If you're sharing, you must get along with your office mate, so spend some time early on cultivating that relationship. Whether you're on your own or have an office mate, strike up a friendship with your secretary. Chances are, your secretary has been around longer than you have and can teach you things and provide good advice. Don't overlook this obvious resource.

A number of social events will be scheduled for you during the first week. Make an appearance at all of them. As in the first days of law school, bonds are established during the first few days of a summer program—bonds that can enhance the experience. Having a good friend or a confidant in your summer program can go a long way to make the experience more enjoyable and less stressful.

Your first week at a large firm will be spent traveling from one orientation event to the next during the day, and one social event to the next in the evenings. Don't worry about it! You're being paid big money for doing nothing. Enjoy it while it lasts.

If you're at a smaller firm or a public-interest position, your experience will be much different. You may be the lone summer person, or one of only a handful. There may not be any organized orientation program, and you may be put directly to work upon your arrival. If so, you'll need to lean on the recruiting coordinator or the hiring partner to answer your questions and help you get settled. Don't hesitate to ask questions. They expect it, even if it doesn't seem that way.

In many ways the early days of a summer associate at a smaller firm or organization are often much more stressful, chaotic, and isolating than in a large firm. Because there are fewer clueless people like you, you'll feel somewhat self-conscious and unsure of how you fit in. At first, you may find yourself going to lunch by yourself and leaving at the end of the day with nowhere to go but home. It's not that nobody wants to spend time with you or to make the effort to get to know you; that's just the way things work in a small firm. Once people start seeing you around and working with you, you'll begin to assimilate. It just takes longer at these smaller places, and consequently your first days can feel pretty uncomfortable. That's normal, so don't worry about it.

Handling assignments

The way you handle assignments as a summer associate is almost as important as the work you ultimately produce. Organization, punctuality, clarity about what is being asked of you, and improvement in performance from assignment to assignment are all critical factors in determining whether you will be extended a permanent offer at the end of the summer. The advice that follows is applicable whether you work in a large firm, a small firm, or a service organization.

> Do what you are told, and do it well. It's really as simple as that.
>
> —Elizabeth

You may work on a dozen or more separate assignments during your 2L summer, and each one will likely start off the same way. You'll either choose a project from a central pool of available assignments, or, more likely, someone will wander into your office and hand you a piece of a project. This often happens in a hurry, and the person giving you the assignment is frequently unclear with her instructions and is often unclear herself on the precise question she is looking to answer. You must force the person assigning you a project to sit down with you for five minutes, take a deep breath, and express to you in the King's English what it is she wants you to do. She may claim to be in too much of a hurry, or she may try to weasel away from you by getting defensive and abruptly stating, "Just find out such and such, okay?"

and then walking away. If that happens, follow her. Ask for some context. Get clarification until you understand the issue and know exactly what you need to find out.

Yeah, it may feel awkward and uncomfortable to push someone on this, and, yes, you may get a hostile reaction initially. But you know what? If you don't get absolutely clear on what you're looking for, the chances are great that you'll go up to that great summer associate wasteland known as the firm's law library and end up flailing around for days on a project that should have taken you hours, and potentially coming back with an answer that is unresponsive to the question the assignor had in mind. And you know who ends up looking bad then? Not the person who gave you the ambiguous assignment. No doubt she'll insist that the assignment was crystal clear in her mind. So you know who ends up holding the bag?

Yup. You.

This is one of the toughest lessons of the 2L summer, and many people end up learning it the hard way. So it's your choice. A little discomfort now, or the potential for embarrassment and humiliation later. Trust me, this isn't much of a choice.

Managing your workload

The next monkey that many summer associates have on their back is how to manage their workload. Here's the typical scenario.

It's 4:00 p.m. You've been asked to research a difficult issue for a motion for summary judgment that a partner is filing. It was given to you yesterday afternoon and is due tomorrow morning. You've been working on it steadily, but you still have more research to do and you haven't even started writing yet. Then, out of nowhere, a partner comes into your office and without introducing himself or inquiring about your workload says, "I have an issue I need you to look into. The client wants an answer tomorrow morning, so read these cases, do some research, and have a memorandum explaining your position on my desk by eight a.m. tomorrow."

The partner then starts to walk out. Welcome to summer associate nightmare scenario number one.

What do you do?

Many summer associates would say that there is only one correct answer, and that is to pull an all-nighter and try to get both assignments done by the deadline. Of course, the likelihood of veering off course in one of the assignments at 3:00 a.m. is pretty high, putting you at risk of looking incompetent when you turn in average or below average work, and potentially leaving one or both partners without the answers they need. Option two is to tell the partner that you're sorry, but you can't take the assignment because you have another complicated, short-deadline project due tomorrow morning and that you won't have time to do a good job on both projects.

Believe it or not, most partners would prefer this answer to the former. Surely you're not so arrogant that you think that you're the only person in the office capable of handling this short-term research for the partner, are you? Remember that, at any one time, a number of other lawyers in the firm are *not* staring down a twenty-four-hour deadline on another project. While it might be uncomfortable to have to turn work away, particularly from a partner, it is certainly better to turn the work away than to take it on without saying anything and produce mediocre work for both people.

A third option, however, is the best response of all. The partner who just arrived told you that his client needs an answer tomorrow morning. But what about the guy writing the motion for summary judgment? He told you that your deadline is tomorrow, but is the actual filing deadline for the motion tomorrow or much later? You probably don't know the answer to that, but it is possible, if not probable, that the deadline he gave you is a "soft" deadline, meaning that it is a deadline for your part of the project to be completed, but is well in advance of the actual filing deadline. So here's what you do.

Explain to the partner with the client deadline that you'd be happy to help him, but that you've already been given another project that is due tomorrow morning. Give the partner the name of the attorney who assigned the other project to you, and let him know that if he talks to the other attorney and gets your first deadline pushed back by a couple of days, you could take on the partner's last-minute project.

This strategy does two things for you. First, it keeps you from having to say no to a partner, which many summer associates are (in most cases unnecessarily) afraid to do. Second, it puts the responsibility for restructuring your schedule in the hands of the person making the demands on you. If he needs you badly enough, he'll talk the other lawyer into pushing off his deadline. If not, he'll tell you not to worry about it, but he'll be left with the impression that you were proactive and willing to try to help him out. Of course, the partner may be unreasonable and tell you to work your scheduling out yourself. If that happens, you need to explain to the partner that you cannot take his project until you talk to the other lawyer. You should then immediately call the other lawyer, explain the situation, and let the two of them work it out.

"It took me a while to work up the confidence to actually do this, but I ultimately found that the best way to manage my workload was to be verbal about what I was capable of taking on," Megan explained. "If someone wanted to give me an assignment and I had too much backed up already, I would tell him or her all of the things that were already on my plate, explain when those things were due, and provide an estimate as to when I could feasibly complete the proposed assignment. Sometimes, the attorney had no problem with the offered date, and sometimes they chose to give the assignment to someone else. I never had anyone get upset with me for taking this approach, though. I think the attorneys appreciated my honesty and realistic assessment of when I could actually get their work done for them. I think they much prefer that to someone taking on an assignment and then later being unable to complete it on deadline.

"Of course, at times, I still misjudged how much time it would take to complete a particular assignment and ended up taking on more than I could handle," Megan added. "One time in particular, I ended up with two assignments that were due on the same day, and I knew that I was not going to be able to complete them both. I explained the situation to the two partners who had given me the two assignments, and rather than being frustrated with me, they discussed it between themselves and determined which assignment needed to be completed first. They were very understanding about this situation, and it all worked out fine."

Billing your time

There is one, and only one, thing to say on this subject. Bill all your time. That's it. No exceptions, no questions asked. Nothing to discuss. If you worked it, bill it. Period. End of story.

Yeah, but you got sidetracked on an issue that ended up being irrelevant, or you feel that it shouldn't have taken you twenty-five hours to write a memorandum, or you had no idea what you were doing because you never took Commercial Paper, or . . .

It doesn't matter. If you spent the time, bill the time.

In most cases the partner in charge of the client's account will look at your hours and bill the client according to what he thinks is a fair charge for the work you produced. Your billing rate as a summer associate already builds in a discount for inefficiency. Let the partner reduce your hours if those hours really need cutting. Your job is to write everything down so you get credit for the actual amount of time you spent working, and to give the partner a fair idea of how long something actually took you to do. If over the summer you actually worked five hundred hours, but only billed three hundred of those hours because you were afraid you were inefficient, since the presumption is that people bill all the time they spend working on client matters, the firm is going to think you only worked three hundred hours and conclude that you are lazy. The firm expects inefficiency from its summer associates and even from its young full-time associates. What the firm will not tolerate, however, is laziness. Thus, by reducing your own hours, you can end up shooting yourself in the foot.

So if you work the hours, bill the hours. 'Nuff said.

Using Westlaw and LEXIS at the firm

We've all heard the horror story of the hapless summer associate who, while working at a small law firm that had use-based online provider accounts, ran up a $25,000 bill doing online research for an internal memo to a partner. Doing this could be disastrous to your future employment prospects, but how do you find out the story about online research?

Simple. Just ask.

At the beginning of the summer, ask your adviser, the recruiting coordinator, or an associate about how the firm handles billing for its online services. Most large firms now have monthly or annual "unlimited service" arrangements with the firm paying a flat fee for unlimited access to all databases. Some firms, however, still pass these costs through to their clients proportionately, so if you spend two hundred hours doing online research on one project, and only one thousand user hours were logged by your firm that month, the client whose project you were working on is going to pay 20 percent of that month's bill. If you learn that the firm you are at uses proportional cost allocation for its online research services, you should ask every partner who assigns you a project whether you can use online research services, and if so, if he wants to cap their use at some level. This becomes even more important if you are working for a small firm or a service organization, where flat-fee payments are less common, and the cost of online services may be passed directly through to the client.

The one place you can still get into trouble on Westlaw and LEXIS is by doing research in online databases that are not part of your firm's flat-fee contract. When you try to enter one of these databases, a pop-up box will alert you that you are about to enter a database that is outside your firm's contract and for which you will be charged separately (read: obscenely). If you ever see one of these boxes, stop! Pick up the phone and call your firm's librarian or Westlaw or LEXIS administrator for guidance. Doing rogue research in these databases is how you can "accidentally" run up the mythical five-figure Westlaw bill and be the person that everyone talks about at the firm cocktail party. Trust me—I've seen it happen.

Getting the work you want

Nobody likes a complainer, but if after several weeks of work you have not been given a project in any of the areas you are most interested in, it's time to talk to someone about it. If you have a mentor, bring your concerns to him, express what your interests are, and go from there. If you don't have a mentor or your mentor is on vacation or unresponsive to your concerns, then go to the recruiting coordinator and ask for advice. If that doesn't work, go through the firm directory yourself, find a couple of partners who practice in those areas, and seek out the work yourself.

"I just went up and asked people who were working on issues I was interested in whether I could help them out," John-Mark stated. "Sometimes, those attorneys wouldn't have anything to give me right away; but inevitably, a few days later, something would come up, and they'd call me. If you want a particular type of work, advertise your interest to the people who do that kind of work!"

Again, there is a difference between brownnosing and expressing sincere interest in getting the work you want. Proactively soliciting work from partners, if the other channels fail you, constitutes the latter and should be done. While you want to be a team player and should not expect every assignment to be handpicked for you, the firm should make some efforts to find you projects in the practice areas you're interested in pursuing. If this isn't happening, you need to politely make it happen.

Getting feedback on your work

One of the most common complaints from both summer associates and full-time associates is that partners and upper-level associates don't provide any feedback to allow them to learn from their mistakes. As a summer associate, you will probably be scheduled for a "midsummer review" about halfway through your tour of duty, but you should certainly not wait until then to get feedback on your assignments. When you first talk to your adviser at the firm, explain that getting feedback on your performance is extremely important to you so you can learn from your mistakes and make adjustments. This should be music to your adviser's ears, and consequently you should ask him for advice on how to solicit feedback on a project if none is immediately forthcoming. My strategy was always to wait a few days after turning a project in, then to stop by the partner's office to follow up, ask if he needed anything else, and, at the same time, ask if he could provide any feedback.

Many times, the partner, impressed with my initiative, would sit me down right there and provide the feedback I asked for. Other times, if the partner was busy, he got back to me with feedback. Many summer associates feel that it is the firm's job to train them and to provide feedback on their performance. For the lawyers at the firm, however, life goes on, the work piles up, and deadlines come and go just as they did before you arrived. For them, giving you feedback is not a high-priority task, unless you make it one. In the two summers I spent in law firms, I got feedback on every single project I worked on by simply stopping by the partner's office to follow up and then asking for a suggestion or two for next time.

"My strategy was to wait for a few days after completing an assignment and then follow up with the attorney I did the work for," John-Mark noted. "Don't be afraid to ask directly what they thought of the research, presentation, at what you could do better. It can be tricky getting feedback because some lawyers just don't give it, and others are too busy to think about it . . . but people usually respond to direct requests."

There's really no magic to this. You just have to make it a priority, and the partners will come to appreciate your openness to constructive criticism and willingness to learn and improve.

Escaping the clutches of a possessive partner

Although it's uncommon, if you do good work for a partner early in your tenure as a summer associate, you may find your time monopolized by more and more work from this one partner. Although this can present a great opportunity to develop a mentor in the firm and a close working relationship that could lead to a permanent position, it can also work against you by limiting your exposure to other partners in the firm.

If you find that a partner is monopolizing most of your time, talk to your mentor or the recruiting coordinator about it. If you are happy with the arrangement and like the partner and the work he is giving you, explain this, but express your concern about not being exposed to the rest of the firm. Listen carefully to what you're told. If you hear that the partner is well respected in the firm and that you are lucky to have the opportunity to work so much with him, then count your blessings. If others agree with your concern, ask them for help in soliciting work from other partners at the firm to increase your exposure.

Confront problems immediately

Now and again, you might find yourself in a sticky situation at work. You may have a personality clash with another summer associate, your secretary may resent you, a partner may treat you unprofessionally, or you may discover a huge mistake in your work after you've handed it in. Personal problems between people are best handled directly after a discussion with your adviser or the recruiting coordinator, and after the situation has had a chance to cool down. Emotional responses are almost never productive, and drawing that kind of attention to yourself, justified or not, can jeopardize your chances of getting hired.

If you discover an error in your work, bring it to the attention of the person who assigned you the work immediately, apologize, and take responsibility for your mistake. While the partner may be upset that the mistake was made, it is hard to remain angry with someone who accepts responsibility for an error without making excuses or trying to cover it up. Fortunately, most legal errors, especially in the projects you'll be given as a summer associate, are easily remedied. Handling the situation poorly, however, by getting defensive, trying to cover up the mistake, or trying to pass the blame off on someone else only makes the situation much worse.

Getting along with the other summer associates

The most important aspect in this department is defusing any sense of "competition" for billable hours, attention of partners, or an offer at the end of the summer. The majority of firms and organizations do their screening while hiring 2Ls and do not bring on many more summer associates than they feel they have the need to hire permanently. Accordingly, if you do a good job on the assignments you are given and get along with people, assuming that the market remains steady, you should get an offer.

Overt arrogance, brownnosing, and gossiping or undermining others behind their backs is the way most summer associates get themselves into trouble. On the flip side, offering your assistance when another summer associate is in a crunch, asking questions, and being a good listener should put you in the good graces of your colleagues. Every once in a while, though, you'll meet someone who just seems to have it in for you. If one of those people is a summer associate with you, remember that you can never leave a battle with a skunk smelling like a rose. Steer clear, and involve your adviser if it gets really bad. Most of all, remember the bottom line—if you are productive, do good work, and get along with people, you will get an offer.

Proper etiquette at firm social events

In the two summers I spent as a summer associate in a law firm, I saw people make more clear blunders in this area than in any other area raised by this chapter. The first message, which you would think would be obvious, but apparently isn't, is to control your alcohol consumption. Yeah, there's an open bar featuring premium booze at most of the firm's social events, and, yeah, other summer associates and full-time associates get hammered and do really stupid things that people think are funny. Just make certain that you're one of the people laughing, not the one that they're laughing at. People get to meet you on a personal level and learn more about you at these events. If you are incapable of carrying on a conversation or, worse yet, end up embarrassing yourself, you may find yourself without an offer at the end of the summer.

> Don't be the person who is known to everyone merely as a big partyer. In the end, remember that you want to be remembered for the quality of the work you did; not for the quantity of alcohol you drank.
>
> —Allan

If you have a spouse or significant other and the firm makes it clear that such people are welcome at certain events, then by all means extend the invitation. Again, these events are organized to encourage people to socialize and get to know one another, and spouses and significant others are a part of that arrangement.

If the firm takes you out to expensive restaurants or to events where food and drink can be purchased and charged to the firm (such as golf outings, concerts, etc.), show some discretion. It is not appropriate to order the most expensive thing on the menu unless everyone around you, including the partners and the associates, are doing so. Similarly, it is not acceptable to be a glutton just because you're not paying for things. At a summer concert outing for a large Boston firm where a full, lavish dinner, drinks, and dessert had just been provided, I watched a summer associate order a large shrimp cocktail, two more alcoholic beverages, and two desserts when nearly everyone else was simply ordering a coffee or a beer. I was embarrassed merely to be sitting near her, and I later overheard several partners talking among themselves about this indiscretion. Remember that just because you're on a firm's expense account doesn't give you license to lose your sense of decency. If you act like a boor, people will notice.

"Also, don't feel compelled to maintain a frenetic summer associate social life, or that if you don't go to every impromptu social event you're invited to, that you won't get an offer," Joel adds. "There will be a few relatively formal events or dinners with partners that should not be missed. Otherwise, if an event sounds like fun to you, go; and if it doesn't, don't. No one has ever lost an offer or failed to make partner because he failed to go on the brewery tour as a summer associate—although someone probably has lost an offer because he threw up on a partner's shoes at the brewery tour."

Finally, as a summer associate, you need to be extremely careful about initiating romantic relationships within the firm. Dating secretaries, support staff, or other associates or summer associates can be risky—and should either be avoided entirely or entertained with extreme discretion. Such relationships, when they sour, can be divisive to the professional environment, and accordingly, many firms have policies to avoid the problem. Dating within the office is also frequently viewed as indiscreet by older partners and can work against you when hiring decisions are made. The summer is short. Use it to build a friendship, and if the relationship is still ready to bloom at the end of the summer, you can always entertain it then and look to move down the street for permanent employment.

> To use a golf analogy, during your 2L summer, two-putt. Smile, be polite, show up on time, and do good work on the projects you are given, but, at least if you're at a large firm, don't think

that you really have to distinguish yourself. Generally, the job is yours to lose.

—Keith

Some closing thoughts

Your 2L summer experience will probably be unlike anything you have ever experienced before in your lifetime. If you go to a large, urban firm, you will be wined and dined from start to finish. The firm's box at the ballpark will be at your disposal. They'll take you to concerts, museums, and on tours of the city. You'll dine at the city's finest restaurants, go yachting at partners' beach houses, and drown yourself at weekly open-bar happy hours. The excesses that you'll be exposed to can take your breath away.

That's the point.

You need to remember that once the summer is over, so is the fairy tale. With associate billable requirements of 2,000 to 2,250 hours per year (and many associates at these large firms routinely bill over 2,500 hours per year), most of the dining you'll be doing once you start as an associate will be at your desk. You'll be forced to work many late nights and weekends. Finally, because of the vast turnover at these firms, and their ability to routinely make students from the best law schools in the country swoon over them, if you aren't willing to produce at that level, you'll immediately be expendable. Forget about doing quality work for fifty-hour weeks and then taking a stand to reclaim the rest of your life. Most associates at these firms do great work, so it's not just quality that counts. It's quality and quantity both. The associates who do the most great work, and concomitantly bring in the most income for the partners, will survive the yearly bloodlettings.

A lot of my friends in law school went into these large firms naïvely and without seriously thinking about what the choice would mean. Now, after some of them billed 2,500 to 3,000 hours during their first year (do the math to figure out how much free time that leaves you for the "other things" in your life), bitterness, regret, and reconsideration abound.

"I laugh at people who go to these big firms," Steve notes. "They are fools. I guess some people just need to work hard all the time and have no social life to feel important. Some people get off on having a stressful life in an unpleasant work environment, and it's mostly those people that end up going to the sweatshops. I wish them the best of luck. The problem is that a lot of people go to law school right out of college and have never held a real job. They have no idea what it's like to work every day, with no spring break and no summer vacation. These people go to a big firm during their 1L or 2L summer because they think it's prestigious, and they get wined and dined and spoiled rotten in that artificial environment of excess. These people never look around long enough to see what kind of life the associates who actually work there lead because these summer associates are too busy going to theater nights and expensive lunches. Then they take a permanent offer there and get blindsided by the reality of what working at those places is really like, and they end up miserable! In choosing a firm, try to get a realistic view of what kind of lifestyle the lawyers lead there. Being a lawyer is hard enough if your job is 9:00 a.m. to 6:00 p.m. When you join one of these places and your work is 9:00 a.m. to 3:00 a.m. and there is a partner yelling at you and calling you a 'worthless sack of shit' every five minutes, and you are constantly being told that if you don't bill more hours, you'll be let go, that job gets even harder."

Wow.

It's not like that at every big firm, but I'm not making these quotes up, folks. I know several first- and second-year associates at some of the more notorious of these large firms who routinely pull at least one all-nighter a week, bill more than three thousand hours (figure *that* one out over fifty-two weeks), are routinely verbally abused, and in one case dodged a stapler hurled by an unhappy and stressed-out partner.

It's not my place to judge the choices you make. Just make them informed choices so you won't be surprised when the golden carriage you thought you were riding in turns into a pumpkin.

PART FOUR

. . . and the Third Year, They Bore You to Death . . .

CHAPTER 25

Demystifying Judicial Clerkships: Hie Thee to the Chambers

He that walketh with wise men shall be wise.
—PROVERBS 13:20

AT THE START of your fourth semester of law school, conversation will turn to the subject of judicial clerkships, and you will find yourself at the beginning of the newest law school feeding frenzy. But what exactly is a judicial clerkship, and why are all these people scrambling to get one?

A judicial clerkship is essentially a one- or two-year paid internship with a state or federal judge, which begins after your graduation from law school. A student accepting one of these clerkships must defer entering legal practice but, in exchange, will usually be given credit by her law firm for the number of years served. Thus, for example, a student deferring an offer with a firm in order to serve a two-year clerkship will typically enter the firm as a third-year associate. Although such policies vary from firm to firm (as do the bonuses offered by firms to students who clerk), they can be and should always be negotiated.

The exact job description of a judicial clerk varies depending on the kind of judge you clerk for and the judge's quirks; in most cases a judicial clerk functions as the judge's "research" person. The clerk's primary role is to read case files and the memoranda of law written by practicing attorneys and then write "bench memos" summarizing her findings, or "draft orders" of the actual opinions to be delivered by the court. In the past, a clerk would also serve as the judge's "runner" during hearings or trials—retrieving cases or statutes needed by the judge during the proceeding. With the growth of in-court technology, however, most judges now have access to Westlaw and LEXIS from the bench, absolving the law clerk of this duty. Unfortunately, this advance in technology has consequently reduced the amount of in-court time the clerk gets to log during his clerkship, since his presence is no longer required during every in-court proceeding. Most clerks, however, are still welcome and are often expected to join their judge in the courtroom for major proceedings in the cases they are assigned to. In such cases, the clerk's primary functions are to serve as an extra set of eyes and ears in observing the proceedings, to evaluate arguments and testimony, to feed the judge important questions raised by the briefs, and to alert the judge to any discrepancies between the written record and the live testimony.

Clerkships are available at all levels of the federal and state court systems. In the federal system, clerkships are offered by the U.S. Court of Federal Claims, the U.S. bankruptcy courts in each jurisdiction, the U.S. district courts in each jurisdiction, each of the twelve general federal circuit courts of appeals, the U.S. Court of Appeals for the Federal Circuit, and the U.S. Supreme Court. On the state level, clerkships are offered by every state's highest court (generally called the supreme court), and the majority of state appellate and trial courts. Competition for these clerkships ranges from competitive (state trial and appellate courts), to intensely competitive (state supreme courts, U.S. bankruptcy courts, the U.S. Court of Federal Claims, and the U.S. district courts), to extremely competitive (circuit courts of appeals), to damn near impossible (the U.S. Supreme Court). Experiences in these positions are widely disparate and are best summarized in turn.

State Court Clerkships

State trial and intermediate appellate courts

When considering a lower-state-court clerkship, it is important to remember that the state court systems vary widely. In some states, the courts may be divided according to subject matter (domestic issues, criminal issues, corporate issues, etc.), while in others, the subject matter may be lumped together but the courts' jurisdiction decided by the amount in controversy. In still others, the jurisdiction of state courts may be based on some combination of these factors.

Pay particular attention to whether the judges in a particular state court system are elected or appointed, as elected judges may have political agendas that you may be forced to adopt. Call the court and determine whether you will be in a central "pool" of clerks shared by all the judges in a particular court, or whether you will work one-on-one with a particular judge. As a member of a clerk pool, your opportunities to cultivate a mentor in the judiciary may be reduced. You should also keep in mind that many state trial courts carry exceptionally heavy caseloads, which may limit your opportunity to write extensive draft orders or bench memoranda, or to delve deeply into the theory behind the law.

When considering a lower-state-court clerkship, the best advice is usually found by consulting lawyers who practice in the state court system. They will typically have more insight into the particular courts and judges than you could ever gather on your own.

State supreme courts (highest court)

If you know for certain which state you intend to practice in, doing a clerkship in that state's highest court can be an extremely valuable experience both for the law you'll learn and the contacts you'll make in the judiciary and among the practitioners. Some states' highest courts, such as the Supreme Courts of California and New Jersey and the New York Court of Appeals, produce exceptional opinions. Others harbor judges esteemed on a level equal to their federal counterparts. U.S. Supreme Court associate justice David Souter, for example, spent many years on the New Hampshire Supreme Court before being tapped for the U.S. Court of Appeals for the First Circuit and then the U.S. Supreme Court.

Other state supreme courts seem to attempt to decide every case on its facts and show little interest in developing a body of well-reasoned, precedential case law. Other states still elect their supreme court justices, which, to put it kindly, opens the door for a more openly political experience.

Conventional wisdom says that the quality of legal scholarship is much higher in the federal courts than it is in the state courts, even at the highest level. There are, of course, numerous exceptions. To sum up, when pursuing a state court clerkship, you will want to do your due diligence and employ some quality-assurance tactics, as experiences vary widely.

Federal Court Clerkships

Federal district courts

Federal district courts are the "trial courts" of the federal system. Although they are courts of limited jurisdiction, the combination of federal question and diversity jurisdiction, coupled with state law issues bootstrapped into a case via supplemental jurisdiction, provides a vast array of subject matter likely to keep even the most curious law student happy.

If you have eyes on a career in litigation, a tour of duty in a federal district court will provide you with invaluable experience and insight. You will read and evaluate dozens of legal memoranda prepared by some of the best lawyers in the region, which will radically improve your understanding of how to construct, organize, and support legal arguments. You will argue close legal points and proper case outcomes with your judge, which will give you insight into how judges think, and an understanding of what is needed to convince them. Finally, you will have the chance to observe and participate in federal court trials, which will give you the opportunity to watch trial strategy in action—and to get immediate feedback from the judge about what is effective and what isn't. If you're lucky, the judge may even allow you to observe while he questions the jury about the case in the jury room after a verdict is reached, which will give you a rare glimpse into the confounding world of jury deliberations.

The heart of any clerkship is research and writing, and you'll do plenty of that as a district court clerk. Motion practice is the bread and butter of the federal clerk's responsibility, and consequently a large percentage of your time will be spent reading, researching, and writing draft orders deciding motions to dismiss, motions for summary judgment, and motions *in limine.* Although some district judges like to see their name in print, the majority of district court opinions are not published. Nevertheless, even in a quiet chambers, you'll still probably place two or three opinions per year in the *Federal Supplement* (the compendium of published federal district court opinions).

Finally, on occasion, a federal district judge will be asked to "ride the circuit" for a few cases to substitute for an ailing or otherwise indisposed circuit court judge. When this occurs, the judge's clerks go with him to oral argument and may even have an opportunity to draft a circuit court opinion.

A district court clerkship is perhaps best summed up as a one-year tutorial in federal courts litigation where you will learn from the practitioners, from the judge, and from your own performance. It is a once-in-a-lifetime opportunity and is viewed with the requisite prestige by even the largest firms in the country.

Specialty courts

Frequently overlooked, federal clerkships are also available in a number of the federal specialty courts, including the bankruptcy courts (which hear all cases arising under the Bankruptcy Code), the U.S. Tax Court (which hears income, estate, and gift-tax cases arising from decisions of the Commissioner of Internal Revenue), the U.S. Court of Federal Claims (which has jurisdiction over cases involving claims against the U.S. government), the Court of International Trade (which hears cases concerning the valuation and classification of imported goods), and the Court of Appeals for the Federal Circuit (which hears appeals from the U.S. Court of Federal Claims, the Court of International Trade, and the Patent and Trademark Office, among others).

Federal circuit courts of appeals

Appellate clerkships are viewed as the more scholarly of the two primary federal clerkships because there is a greater concentration on discrete issues and a frequent opportunity to make new law. Since circuit courts have the final word on the law in a particular circuit (save in the unlikely chance that a case is granted certiorari by the U.S. Supreme Court), as a circuit court clerk you won't spend as much time as a district court clerk worrying about the possibility of getting overruled. On the flip side, however, since most circuit court cases are decided by three-judge panels, your judge will not always be the primary author of an opinion.

As a circuit court clerk, your primary duties are to read the appellate briefs submitted by the lawyers in a particular case, research the applicable law, and prepare your judge for oral argument by highlighting in bench memos the uncertain areas of the applicable law. Since nearly all circuit court opinions are published in the *Federal Reporter* and are frequently complex and lengthy, a clerkship in these courts will help you to hone your writing skills and guarantee that much of your work will be memorialized in print for posterity.

Finally, a circuit court clerkship is virtually a prerequisite for a clerkship in the U.S. Supreme Court.

The U.S. Supreme Court

Referred to as the "mother of all clerkships," these positions are so intensely competitive that perfect grades, membership on law review at a top-ten school, a publication credit in your law review, and a distinguished circuit court clerkship may not even get you an interview. In a recent year, twenty-seven of thirty-eight Supreme Court clerks were drawn from Yale, Harvard, and the University of Chicago. Of course, that statistic also means that eleven clerks weren't drawn from those schools, and you never know what might draw the interest of a Supreme Court justice. However, no Supreme Court justice regularly draws clerks directly out of law school, so you'll need to secure another clerkship first and apply during your third year. If you think you have what it takes to get this most elusive of all brass rings, speak to a professor at your law school for more information.

Why People Clerk

Students give many reasons for pursuing judicial clerkships. Among them are the once-in-a-lifetime opportunity to observe and participate in the judicial process behind the scenes, to develop an understanding about how judges think and react to certain strategies, arguments, and approaches, and to gain a unique perspective on litigation by watching skilled practitioners in action and reading and evaluating their work. Students also note the opportunity to cultivate a mentor in the judiciary (someone outside your law firm who can render advice and guidance during your critical early years of practice), the opportunity to explore a new city or region of the country without making a long-term commitment to being there, the chance to further develop research and writing skills, and the obvious credential that one of these prestigious positions provides.

"I wanted to be at an appellate court, where I'd have a chance to see a diversity of legal issues," Patrick noted. "I wanted to improve my writing skills, and I wanted to gain the confidence to address partners and judges without an overwhelming amount of intimidation. I was happy to get all of these things out of my clerkship. It was a tremendous experience that I'd recommend to everyone."

> I applied only at the federal district court level because I was interested in litigation and felt that I'd learn more from the experi-

ence. I'd advise potential applicants to apply with judges and courts which would benefit them in a similar way. I also strongly suggest that you apply to judges who sit in the state you come from and to judges who went to your undergrad or law school since having these things in common may help put your application at the top.

—Bess

Whatever your thoughts, consider these reasons carefully before dismissing the chance to pursue a judicial clerkship. While the salary paid to judicial clerks does not begin to compare to that paid by larger firms, many firms provide handsome bonuses and/or credit for years served during a clerkship. Your loans will wait, and you'll have forty years to practice law.

How to Apply for a Judicial Clerkship

Choosing your judges

By now, you probably understand that securing a judicial clerkship is not going to be an easy task. Competition is fierce, and reminiscent of first-year recruiting, you'll probably need to send out dozens and dozens of letters. As was the case in looking for first-year employment, however, you only need to strike gold once to end up a clerk!

To get started, go to your law school placement office and ask them for a current list of members of the state and federal judiciary.

Chances are, your placement office keeps binders or computer programs with this information and may even have an event scheduled to explain the clerkship application process, or to teach you how to run mail merge software from their database. You should also explore oscar.symplicity.com, the online Web site for federal law clerk hiring.

I would caution you to ultimately apply only to places where you really want to go, and to judges that you really want to work for. I have several friends who were put in the awkward position of having to reject a clerkship offered by a federal judge, and several others who are instead clerking somewhere they wish they weren't because they haphazardly applied to forty or fifty judges without really thinking about whether these were all clerkships that they really wanted.

—Joel

In trying to narrow your focus, ask yourself a couple of questions. Are you more interested in a federal clerkship or a state clerkship? Trial court or appellate court? It is okay to be interested in, and to apply for, both trial and appellate court clerkships, but it helps to have one as your primary focus. Here's how I did it.

When I began my clerkship search, I decided that, given my interest in litigation, I would be best served by pursuing a federal district court clerkship. I also knew that I wanted to settle in New England, and most likely in New Hampshire, the state where I grew up. Accordingly, I decided that my optimal clerkship would be in the U.S. District Court for the District of New Hampshire. The problem is, that court had only four judges, two of whom were not hiring for the term I was interested in (directly after law school). Accordingly, I expanded my horizons to include the districts of Maine, Vermont, Massachusetts, and Rhode Island, which brought me up to about twenty-five district judges. Since that number was still far too low to provide a good chance at success, I expanded my horizons further to include the U.S. District Court for the District of Connecticut, located in New Haven, where I did my undergraduate degree, and the U.S. District Court for the Eastern District of Pennsylvania, located in Philadelphia, which was familiar with and tended to hire Penn students. That brought my number up to about forty district court judges. I then did a search for all district court judges who were alumni of either my undergraduate university or my law school and applied to all of them, irrespective of their geographical location. This gave me about twenty more judges, bringing my total up to about sixty. I then consulted the list of newly appointed district court judges and added all of them to the list, figuring that they might not be on everyone's radar screen yet, which could increase my odds at getting an interview in those chambers.

I then decided that since I had a strong interest in research and writing, I should also pursue clerkships on the appellate level. Given the degree of competition for these clerkships, however, I thought it best to target certain judges with whom I had at least some connection. I chose the judges of the First Circuit Court of Appeals, the judges in the Second Circuit Court of Appeals, who sat in New Haven, a judge in Little Rock whom I knew lectured and wrote extensively on my law review comment topic, and all alumni of my undergraduate university and my law school, irrespective of their circuit. This brought my list to about eighty judges.

I then talked to the professors I was planning to use as recommenders and asked them if they had any friends or colleagues in the judiciary. Most of them were able to give me at least a name or two, and I added these names to the list, figuring that my odds would increase with those judges because I had a recommendation from someone they knew. To top it off, I added the justices of the New Hampshire Supreme Court, figuring that since I knew I wanted to practice in New Hampshire, getting a clerkship in that appellate court would be a particularly relevant and worthwhile experience.

When I had my list, I went through each judge's biography looking for interests in common that I could highlight in a cover letter or on my résumé. Whenever I found such commonalities, I noted them on the list next to the judge's name to assure myself that I would personalize his or her cover letter accordingly.

What to send

Whether you are seeking a state or federal clerkship, your application materials must contain (1) a brief, well-written cover letter; (2) a current copy of your résumé, updated to contain membership on journals, forthcoming publications, and any other relevant law school honors or activities; (3) a copy of your law school transcript; (4) a copy of your undergraduate transcript (if it helps you); (5) a carefully edited, concise writing sample; and (6) two or three letters of recommendation from law school faculty members.

The cover letter

Your cover letter should be brief, certainly not more than one page, and laser-printed on conservative, white bond paper. As before, avoid ostentatious monogrammed paper, and don't do anything funny with fonts.

In two or three paragraphs, describe your interest, as specifically as possible, in the type of clerkship that judge is offering. See my descriptions of the various clerkships above to help you highlight specific reasons for your interest. A cover letter expressing a well-reasoned and relevant desire to clerk for a particular court can go a long way in separating your application from the rest. It is also critical to highlight any geographic connection you have to the city, state, or region that houses the court you're applying to, and to put the name of your undergraduate school and/or your law school front and center if the judge is an alumnus. Although there is no official policy, many judges show a trend toward hiring former, present, or future residents of the city or state where their court is located, and graduates of their undergraduate and law schools.

Close by (1) mentioning what you've enclosed; (2) stating that, if invited, you'd be willing to travel to the judge's chambers for an interview at your expense (since judges don't have interview budgets, there are no judicial flybacks, and a judge might be disinclined to interview you if you will have to travel a long distance); and (3) providing a contact number and e-mail address.

Since you are personalizing these letters whenever possible, go over each one carefully to make sure that it is free of typos and other errors, as such mistakes show carelessness and are likely to be fatal to your chances.

Your résumé

We've already discussed résumés a couple of times in this book, so I won't belabor the point here. Just make sure that the résumé you send to judges is updated with your most current achievements, including journal membership and position, forthcoming publications (if any), moot court participation, externships, teaching assistantships, and first- and second-summer (forthcoming) employment. In addition, you should include a "personal interests" section on the résumé you send to judges if you don't already have one. You will be spending a great deal of time in close quarters with your judge during your clerkship, and mutual interests can be influential in hiring decisions. Hobbies, recreational interests, and sports-rooting interests can all be placed in this section.

Your writing sample

Whatever it is, make sure it is the tightest, best organized, and smoothest piece of legal writing that you've done to date. No matter how wonderful your grades are, to function successfully as a judicial clerk you have to be able to research thoroughly and accurately and write in a fluid, clear, and well-organized fashion. Unlike law firms, which may not closely evaluate your writing sample, a judge considering whether to invite you to chambers for an interview will read your writing sample closely to determine whether it meets those qualifications. In many chambers, evaluation of the writing sample is the final cut before the interviews are granted.

Most judges will not want to read anything longer than ten pages, so unless you have a good reason to submit something longer (such as a strong draft of a journal article you are authoring), keep your sample to ten pages or less.

In selecting your writing sample, be wary of submitting something you produced either for a judge or for a law firm during your 1L summer. Remember that strict confidentiality rules apply to the use of these works, and that you will need to obtain specific permission prior to submitting either to a judge. If you plan to submit work produced for a law firm, replace any identifying names or products with generic terms to maintain the flow of the written prose (in other words, do not simply black out identifying terms), then obtain written permission from your employer to use the work. When submitting the writing sample, be sure to include a cover sheet explaining to the judge that you obtained written permission for the use of the work. This rule applies with even more force to draft orders prepared during a judicial internship. Don't even think of sending a photocopy of a judge's signed opinion as your writing sample without obtaining explicit permission from the authoring judge. If you plan to use a draft order as your writing sample, send a copy of the sample you intend to use to the authoring judge and request permission, in writing, to use the draft as a writing sample. Ask that, in granting you written permission, the judge affirm, in writing, that the sample you are submitting is indeed your work. If permission is granted to you, send a copy of your draft (not the signed, final order) with a copy of the authoring judge's permission letter to every judge you apply to. Note that failure to follow these instructions explicitly can be fatal to your candidacy for a clerkship.

How to choose your recommenders

Yeah, yeah . . . you don't know any professors well enough to ask them for a recommendation. Few law students do. But you gotta ask anyway, so here's how to determine whom you should ask.

Look at your transcript. Find the classes you did best in. If you have the luxury of choosing from among these classes, pick the professors who taught the classes most relevant to your clerkship. For example, if you are applying to a federal district court and you got A's in Constitutional Law, Federal Courts, and Real Estate, choose the Con Law and Fed Courts professors.

Make a photocopy of the most recent version of your résumé, then, in three or four double-spaced pages, type up a brief, autobiographical sketch of yourself, highlighting your major accomplishments in detail. Note that I said major accomplishments. You don't need to include the story of how you rescued your neighbor's cat from a tree in third grade and got your name in the town paper. We're talking major things here. Two or three major things you did in college, what your thesis was about, what you did if you took a year off between college and law school, how you chose to go to law school, what you did last summer. What you're trying to do is make your résumé come to life by putting some meat on the bones. Then write a brief note to the professor (one paragraph will suffice) alerting him that you'd like to solicit his recommendation and that you are enclosing your résumé and a brief autobiography for his evaluation.

When you've finished your autobiographical sketch, go to each professor's secretary and set up an appointment. Leave your note, résumé, and the autobiographical sketch with the secretary and ask that the professor review them in advance of your meeting. You should expect that it will take your professor six to eight weeks to prepare your letters of recommendation, so don't ask too late!

When the day of your meeting arrives, be on time for your appointment, and thank the professor for his time. Ask him if he has had the opportunity to review your materials, and if he has, whether he thinks he could forcefully recommend you as a clerkship candidate. In almost all cases, this method will produce the affirmative result you seek. Using this method will also provide the professor with a base of knowledge from which to ask you further questions. He can then use these materials to highlight the things in his recommendation that he feels will be most influential in the eyes of a judge. Take advantage of this opportunity to ask the professor whether he knows or thinks any particular federal judges would provide an excellent experience. This is your opportunity to add three or four names to your list where your chances for success may be highest.

Navigating the new law clerk hiring plan

Until 2002, most federal judges and many state judges accepted applications for judicial clerkships from law students in the fall of their second year. Judges would typically pore over applications in midwinter and begin scheduling interviews with selected candidates in February of the students' second year. Accepted candidates would then be offered one-year or two-year clerkships beginning in the fall after graduation—nearly two years after the application process first began.

One of the many problems with this hiring scheme was that because candidates applied in the fall of their second year, only first-year grades were available to the judges for consideration, which many judges thought was an insufficient sample by which to judge a candidate's intellectual capacity. Further, in the fall of the second year, many students still haven't decided on a direction or concentration in law school, which makes it difficult to determine whether a judicial clerkship would be beneficial to one's career or even of interest. Finally, in the fall of the second year, students accepted on their school's law review (virtually a prerequisite for federal clerkships) had not yet had the opportunity to even select a note or comment topic, much less begin drafting one . . . and many judges look with interest on these significant writing projects to gauge an applicant's writing ability and the applicant's capacity to reason out a convincing thesis and argue persuasively for it.

As a result, in the spring of 2002, an ad hoc committee of federal appellate judges cochaired by Chief Judge Edward Becker of the Third Circuit Court of Appeals and Judge Harry Edwards of the D.C. Circuit Court of Appeals and composed of at least one judge from every federal circuit court approved a new plan for law clerk hiring. Under this new plan, applications for law clerk positions should not be accepted from any candidate prior to Labor Day of the candidate's third year of law school. This plan is now being followed by all of the appellate judges in the federal circuits, the vast majority of the federal district court judges, and by many, but not all, judges and justices in the state systems.

Your law school's career services office is the clearinghouse for judicial clerkship applications, so at some point during the second semester of your second year of law school, pay them a visit. Ask one of the career services officers for the latest updates on the implementation of this new hiring plan, for a list of courts (state and federal) that are abiding by the new deadlines, and for clarification on your law school's rules about how to obtain the necessary supporting materials (recommendations and certified transcripts) to apply to state judges and others who are not following the new federal plan. You can monitor the implementation progress of this new plan, and any changes made to it between editions of this book, by visiting the committee's law clerk hiring plan Web site at www.cadc.uscourts.gov/lawclerk. You can also search an online database of law clerk hiring schedules and application criteria supplied by federal judges at oscar.uscourts.gov.

Schools that participate in the new law clerk hiring plan will not send out letters of reference and official transcripts until the threshold day designated each year by the federal courts—and will then send out letters of reference and official transcripts only from third-year students. Under the prior system, when judges generally adhered to a March 1 date (of 2L year) for the commencement of candidate interviewing, many judges began their interviews at 8:00 a.m. on March 1, even if that date fell on a weekend, in order to see the best candidates as early in the process as possible. You should assume that the same scenario will prevail under the new plan—namely that judges will begin to schedule interviews and make offers as soon as possible after the threshold date has passed.

This means you'll need to have your applications ready for mailing by late summer of your 3L year. And that is going to take some serious planning.

Preparing your applications

Pursuant to the requirements of the new plan for law clerk hiring, applications, letters of recommendation, and certified transcripts from third-year students cannot be sent out by law schools until the day after Labor Day. A deluge of application materials thus hits the U.S. Postal Service on the day after Labor Day, and to maximize your chances of success in this incredibly competitive process, you need to make certain that yours are among them.

The date-limiting step for your applications will be your requests for faculty recommendations. Remember that earlier in this chapter we advised you to prepare an autobiographical outline for your recommenders, drop it off with them in advance, ask for a subsequent meeting to talk them through it, and then allow six to eight weeks of lead time for your recommenders to complete the recommendations. This means that you need to do all of these things before you leave for the summer after your second year.

Let's repeat that for emphasis.

That means that you need to do all of these things before you leave for the summer after your second year.

Got that?

The end of your second year is already a hectic time. You'll be studying for and taking finals, and then, in all likelihood, jetting off to a different city for your all-important summer associateship. That means packing up clothes, arranging for a sublet of your law school living space, finding housing in the city of your destination, and a host of other disruptions. Don't leave your clerkship planning for the last minute, or you won't get it done.

Ideally, you should research and select your judges during the early part of the second semester of your 2L year, when there are fewer demands on your time. As you saw from our discussion of this process in the early part of this chapter, it is relatively involved and time-consuming. You can't do it well in a rushed afternoon, so don't do it that way. Take your time, and pick your judges thoughtfully. Doing so will greatly increase your chances for success.

Once you have your list of names finalized, draft your cover letters, postdating them to the deadline day, and run your mail merge. Sign the letters and put them into a file where you can quickly assemble them into application packages upon your return to school in the fall.

When you return from spring break in your 2L year, contact the professors you intend to use as recommenders. Once you've decided on who those recommenders will be, complete and distribute your autobiographical outline, and set up appointments for your follow-up meetings. Do all of this right away—before the crush of finals begins.

Once finals are over, contact your faculty recommenders and make sure they have all the information they need, including the list of the judges to whom you intend to apply. Before you leave campus, order your certified transcripts so they'll be ready for you when you get back to campus. Remember, the goal is to get everything in the mail the day after Labor Day. Chances are, you won't be returning to campus much more than a week before that date, so you want to make sure you have your house in order before you leave.

When you return to campus

As soon as you return to campus in the fall, touch base with your faculty recommenders and be certain that your letters are done and ready to go. Pick up your certified transcripts and check in with the career planning office to find out whether they plan to schedule a day for the assembly of your clerkship applications or whether you are on your own.

In many cases, your law school will insist that certified transcripts and faculty recommendations be sent to your judges directly by the school. If this is the case, it is your responsibility to check that everything was actually sent out. We've heard horror stories about professors who have forgotten about deadlines, stacks of letters and transcripts being mislaid in the placement office, and even stories about the wrong recommendations being included with the wrong application materials.

Take whatever affirmative steps you can to make sure that these disasters don't happen to you.

Scheduling interviews

Anytime after deadline day, your phone may start ringing with offers to schedule interviews. Before you schedule anything, however, you need an important piece of information.

You may get an offer at the end of an interview, and you may be asked for your answer right then and there. These are called exploding offers, meaning that the offer is rescinded if not immediately accepted.

Yeah, you read that right. You might have to make an on-the-spot decision whether to accept the offer. Right there, with the judge looking at you! No time to make phone calls, no time to mull it over, no time to wait for some other judge to make a decision. Yes or no. Simple as that.

Needless to say, this possibility puts you in a precarious position because you may be faced with the choice to (1) decline with the hope that your first-choice judge will accept you, thus running the risk that you will end up without a clerkship altogether if he rejects you; or (2) accept the offer and be happy that you have a clerkship, but have no chance to end up in the court or with the judge that you wanted most.

While this scenario may play out despite your best efforts, you can attempt a couple of things to control this mayhem.

First, prioritize your list of judges. As multiple interview offers begin to arrive (and may you be so lucky), try to schedule your most favored judges as early in the process as possible. That way, one of your top-choice judges might make you an immediate offer, and even if that doesn't happen, the possibility of getting an exploding offer before you interview with your preferred judges is reduced.

Although this seems simple enough, it may not always work because some judges may call and require that you interview on the first day of interviews. You see, at the same time that you are angling for the most prestigious clerkship, the judges are also angling for the best candidates. They know that a delay of even a day or two can cost them their top-choice applicants, so some judges rigorously pursue their top candidates by requiring them to interview on the first day. If you are invited to interview with a judge and you are given an early interview slot, ask yourself a single question before you accept the interview: Independent of my other options and considered in a vacuum, would I be happy clerking for this judge? If the answer is yes, take the interview. If not, decline.

One final thing about scheduling interviews. As soon as you are granted an interview with a judge in a particular court, it is appropriate to call the other judges in the area to let them know you will be there on a particular day. This may trigger one or more of these other judges to grant you an interview as well, significantly increasing your chances for success. Oh—and feel free to define the term *area* loosely!

The interview itself

You've been through many of these by now, so the standard rules for a legal interview apply. Arrive fifteen minutes early, dress conservatively, be prepared to be thoroughly searched by court security personnel, and try to relax.

When you arrive in the chambers, you will likely be greeted by the judge's secretary. Remember to treat this person respectfully as, even more so than secretaries in law firms, a judge's secretary is likely to be tight with the judge. Try to make some idle chatter while you wait.

When the judge arrives, it is proper to greet him either as "Your Honor" or as "Judge So-and-So." He will likely then take you into his chambers and close the door. Don't let this rattle you.

From there, things can vary widely. The judge may chitchat or jump right into things. Sit up straight, make good eye contact, and watch your body language. Remember that most judges are former prosecutors or trial lawyers and have been trained to read people. Crossed arms, leaning away, and downward glances show intimidation, which is not what most judges want in a law clerk. As a clerk, you'll need to have the confidence to argue legal points with the judge, and you can't do that effectively if you are intimidated. But don't adopt a cocky attitude either. Deferential confidence is what you're aiming for.

Know your résumé cold, be sure you can talk specifically about why you want a clerkship in the particular kind of court you're in (see above for help on this), and be ready to discuss your connection to, or interest in, the geographical area. If you submitted a draft of a journal article you are writing as your writing sample or listed one on your résumé, be prepared to discuss it in depth. The judge I ultimately clerked for grilled me for almost forty-five minutes on my comment topic based only on the title I listed on my résumé (the subject interested him a great deal, and he knew a lot about it).

Know the judge's biography, and remembering that people like to talk about their families and their own accomplishments, try to get in a question or two about the judge's background at an appropriate time. Many times, these biographies also provide hints about the judge's hobbies and interests, and if you have anything in common in this area, find a way to get those common interests in play. Be sure to glance around the chambers and see if anything strikes your eye. For example, my judge had several pictures in the chambers showing him hiking with his family. Because I shared his passion for hiking, I acknowledged his interest, and we spent several minutes discussing the various mountains that we had climbed. Remember, a judge has to work in proximity with his law clerks for a minimum of a year, so in addition to your academic qualifications, he's going to be looking for someone he likes and can comfortably work with. Common interests help.

Some people may tell you that you should brush up on the judge's recent written opinions, but none of the judges I interviewed with asked me about them or expected me to know about them. Nevertheless, to cover your bases, check the judge's five most recent opinions on Westlaw, find one that interests you, and read it for a basic understanding. That way, if you need to talk about an opinion for some reason, you'll have one. Anything more than that is probably overkill.

When the interview is over, shake hands and thank the judge for the opportunity to interview with him. Listen carefully to anything the judge might say. He might give you a timetable as to when you might expect an offer. He might ask you to call him before you accept an offer from another judge. He might say nothing, in which case it is appropriate to ask him when you might expect a response. Finally, he might make you an exploding offer.

If the judge making an exploding offer is one of your top choices, you can happily accept on the spot and begin celebrating. If you are confronted with an exploding offer from a judge who is not one of your top choices, you may be able to use one tactic to buy yourself some time. Whenever a judge makes an offer to you, react enthusiastically and humbly. Thank him sincerely for his faith in you, and express how fortunate you feel to have been granted such a rare and exciting opportunity. Then, when the judge asks you for an immediate decision, explain that you were not expecting this outcome, and that you'd like to have a few hours to discuss the ramifications of taking the position (e.g., the location of the position) with your spouse/fiancé/significant other, and ask when the judge would like to have an answer. If you're lucky, your judge will give you twenty-four hours, though some will insist that you get back to them by the end of the day.

In either case, if you have an exploding offer and a brief window of time in which to accept it, as soon as you leave the chambers, call every other judge ranked higher on your list with whom you have already interviewed and explain your predicament. Make it clear on the phone that you will accept an offer if one is tendered, but that you'll need an immediate answer. These situations will generally work themselves out. Either the judges you've already interviewed with will make you an offer on the telephone, or they'll tell you that they cannot make a decision yet, which, in essence, is their way of telling you that you're not tops on their list and that you should probably accept the offer. No matter what the result, at least you'll have had one last chance to canvas your top-choice judges. Whether you reach every judge or not, however, be sure to respond to the judge who made you the offer well within the time frame he gave you. A delay of even an hour beyond what he allowed could cost you your clerkship.

Finally, either before or after you meet the judge, you will likely spend some time talking to the judge's current law clerks. Use this time to ask the clerks questions about their experiences. Unless the judge has already made you an offer when you meet the clerks, do not let down your guard during this discussion. Many interviewees are under the false impression that their time with the law clerks is not part of the interview. Nothing could be further from the truth. Law clerks have the ear of their judge regularly, and in most chambers law clerks play a vital role in the clerk selections. No matter how comfortable it might feel, the time you spend with the law clerks is a crucial part of the interview. Treat it accordingly.

Accepting an offer

Absent an exploding offer from one of the judges you interview with, you'll be playing a waiting game. Any offer you're going to get will come by telephone, so check your messages at least twice daily, especially if you are away on spring break, as you will need to make an immediate response to any offer you get. If you receive an offer from a judge other than your top-choice judge, use the same stalling tactic I provided you in the section on exploding offers above. If you are granted a reprieve of any length, use the time to call your top-choice judges and explain your situation. As before, the situation will likely resolve itself. Even if you don't get an offer on the phone from one of your top-choice judges, you'll at least have given yourself one more chance.

> I wanted my clerkship to approximate an apprenticeship. In other words, I hoped to learn the essentials of lawyering by one-on-one instruction from my judge. What I neglected to consider before the clerkship was the extent to which the clerks learn from each other. Some of my most memorable experiences as a clerk are of the judge and the clerks gathered around a table discussing cases. It was a truly collaborative project, and it made me realize that the best way to develop as a lawyer was to work with and under other good lawyers. I think my clerkship has given me the ability to home in on the more important issues in a case. The first step in legal problem solving is identifying the problem or issue. Law school exams will primarily test you on your ability to spot issues, and law school generally gives you the ability to identify issues. Being a clerk and reading brief after brief taught me an additional skill: being able to quickly identify the most important issue of all those I have identified. Cases generally raise multiple issues, but they usually turn on one or two. As an advocate, it is worth your while to focus on the most important ones.
>
> —A mentor

When you do accept an offer, ask the judge whether he requires some form of formal acknowledgment. He may require a written acceptance letter from you, or he may send you a letter confirming your arrangement. If no formal acknowledgment is offered, call the judge's secretary and request a letter confirming the arrangement.

Once you have accepted a clerkship, you are expected to call the other chambers where your candidacy is still active and withdraw. Don't even think about waiting to see if your first-choice judge accepts you, then calling the other judge back and rescinding your acceptance. The judiciary is a brotherhood, and exhibiting such unethical conduct will likely cost you both offers.

Finally, remember that getting a judicial clerkship is a crapshoot, and every year many qualified candidates fail to land one. If you are unsuccessful, it is not necessarily a reflection on you or your abilities. Connections, alumni preferences, personalities, and timing all play roles that you cannot control.

CHAPTER 26

Opportunity Knocks Again . . . a Second Chance at Recruiting

The foolish and the dead
alone never change their opinion.
—ROBERT LOWELL

IN THE FALL of your third year, after you know whether you received an offer from the firm where you spent your 2L summer, recruiting season arrives anew. Although the primary focus will be on the 2Ls in the class behind you, almost every firm will be willing to talk to and hire 3Ls for permanent employment beginning in the fall after graduation without the need to summer at the firm.

Some 3Ls feel that a stigma attaches to reentering the employment pool as a 3L and, thus, refuse to do so even though the firm they worked at during their 2L summer failed to live up to expectations. Nothing, however, could be further from the truth. Once you've been through a full summer of employment at a firm or a public-interest placement, you will inevitably have a much better idea about what the real-life lawyering experience will entail. Did you like what you saw?

> I would suggest participating in 3L recruiting to anybody who is not 100 percent certain about the place they have an offer from.
>
> —Pat

Think about the experience you had at the firm last summer. Did the people there treat each other with respect? Did they treat you fairly? Does the firm specialize in the kind of work that you are most interested in doing? Did you get to do any of it while you were there?

Did you get good feedback from the partners you worked with? Can you see yourself working closely, on a longer-term basis, with the people you met?

> I recruited third year because I wanted to do trusts and estates and I hadn't yet heard whether I would get a specific offer from the trusts and estates department at my firm. I went through five or six on-campus interviews with firms that had trusts and estates departments, got three or four callbacks, and then got an offer from the trusts and estates department at the firm I had worked at, which I immediately accepted.
>
> —Alison

Now step back and get a panoramic view of things. Did you like the city or geographic region that the firm was in? Have any factors in your academic or personal life changed since last fall that are prodding you to look in a different direction?

While few 3Ls are ever really secure about the employment choices they make, if any of the aforementioned concerns are nagging at you, there is no harm taking another lap or two in the recruiting pool before you make a final decision about the firm where you worked last summer. With an offer in hand, you are likely to be even more attractive to firms than you were last time around, since another firm has already staked its claim to you. This time, with a summer's worth of experience to draw upon, you can ask the tough, insightful questions that you may not have known to ask, or dared to ask, last time, you can pursue the really selective firms, or you can barter for department-specific placements in a particular firm with more force and more credibility. With a much more clearly defined idea of what it is that you are looking for, it can't hurt to take another look around.

You'll typically have until November 1 to make a final decision about whether to accept the offer from your 2L summer firm, but you'll want to confirm this arrangement with your specific employer. There is nothing disingenuous or disloyal in exploring your options and seeking other offers until that date, nor is it improper to tell other employers, if you are asked, that you have an offer from the firm that you worked at last summer. People understand that interests change and that the choice of a first job is a large and important decision. Take your time, and make your decision the right one.

How to handle phone calls from people at your old firm

By the way, while you're shopping yourself around, don't think that the firm you got an offer from is going to sit idly by and let you get away. Although firms understand why you might want to take a second look around, they don't like it when people they wined, dined, and trained end up going elsewhere. There's nothing they can do to stop you, except one thing.

They'll start calling you.

It will start out as a casual call from the recruiting coordinator asking if you received the firm's offer letter. When you respond affirmatively, the coordinator might inquire if the firm can provide anything to help you in making your decision, or outright ask you if you've made a decision yet. It is perfectly fine to respond by saying that you are weighing your options and will give the firm an answer well ahead of the November 1 deadline.

That won't be the end of it, though.

By delaying your decision, you're opening the floodgates. You'll get more calls from people at the firm than you get from telemarketers. You'll hear from associates you socialized with, and partners you worked for. If the firm really wants you, you might even get a call from the hiring partner asking if your decision hinges on financial concerns.

How do you respond to all of these people?

I used my answering machine a lot during those days and screened my calls to avoid having to tell the people at my firm for the third or fourth time that I was weighing my options and trying to come to a difficult decision. If a firm subscribes to the NALP guidelines, they cannot force your decision before November 1. If you're dealing with a smaller firm that is only going to hire one or two people and is waiting on your decision, you should certainly understand their desire to fill their slots as quickly as possible with the most qualified candidates and get them a decision as soon as you can.

Until you've made a decision, however, there's not a lot you can say. If you have any questions or concerns, call the firm and get them cleared up. If you need advice, get it from people you trust. At the end of the day, though, as with so many other things about law school, you alone must step up and make the call. Make the decision, then don't look back.

If you didn't get an offer from your 2L firm

You can get two different species of "nonoffers" from a law firm. A "soft offer" is an understanding that, although you are not welcome to return to the firm, you may, to avoid being stigmatized, tell other employers that you were, in fact, extended an offer. These nonoffers are typically extended by firms that would have hired you but for a downturn in their business or a strategic restructuring that has reduced their need for young associates. These offers can also be given to people with strong constituencies within the partnership favoring their being offered permanent employment, with a couple of strong detractors blocking the offer. A soft offer is an effective tool because it permits you to spin your nonoffer any way you like.

The second, and much more difficult, nonoffer is the simple thanks-but-no-thanks. Fortunately it is rarely a surprise to its recipient, since most firms provide adequate warnings to summer associates at risk of failing to secure an offer. Typically, some people who get nonoffers have done something egregious during their summer associateship, such as making a pass at a partner's spouse (don't laugh, it has happened) or betraying client confidences. Others have shown no effort during the summer associateship, displayed intolerable arrogance, or repeatedly been unable to handle the rigors of law practice. The first two of these examples would get you fired from your summer position; the last three would probably get you a warning at your midsummer review first.

Occasionally, however, a nonoffer will come pretty much out of the blue from a particularly compassionless firm that has simply determined it doesn't need you. This situation, although rare, can leave you in the lurch. So what do you do if this happens to you?

If you get an unexpected nonoffer from a firm, the first thing you need to do is swallow your pride and call the recruiting coordinator at the firm to make sure that your nonoffer was not the result of an administrative error (which has happened). If your fears are confirmed and you had no idea that your performance was lacking, it is appropriate to explain your surprise and ask the recruiting coordinator for an explanation. If you get some kind of equivocation that falls short of "you didn't get an offer because your work product was pathetically inept and so were you," you might ask the recruiting coordinator if the firm would consider making you a soft offer, or providing you with a blanket letter of recommendation to use in 3L recruiting. If you didn't get an offer because of a downturn in the firm's hiring needs, you are on solid ground making this request. If you don't get satisfaction from the recruiting coordinator, call your adviser at the firm and put the request to him. Do not simply roll over and play dead because an unexplained nonoffer from your 2L firm can be the kiss of death in 3L recruiting.

Almost every interviewer you'll see during 3L recruiting will ask if you received an offer from your 2L firm, and just in case you were wondering, your unfortunate circumstances do not justify a lie. Most employers will call your 2L firm to verify that you got an offer, and if you are discovered to be lying, you'll be finished anyway and potentially subject to disciplinary sanctions by your law school. Accordingly, if at all possible, try to get a soft offer or, at the least, a letter of explanation from your firm explaining the circumstances that led to your not getting an offer. Without such a letter, you're in for some tough sledding.

So, what if you didn't get an offer because you really were arrogant or lazy or you rubbed somebody the wrong way? How do you spin that reality in 3L recruiting to make some other firm take a flier on you? That's not easy, even in a good economy, but here's my advice.

First, be completely candid. Come clean about the mistakes you made, and what you learned from them. Don't try to explain why you behaved the way you did, just make it clear that you understand what you did wrong, why it was wrong, and most important, that you are now clear about what the expectations are. Contrition goes a long way in a situation like this, and you're now a gamble, so you need to convince the firms you interview with that you're a normal person who made a mistake but you are now ready to take your place in the adult world.

A lot of firms will pass on you despite these efforts because when another firm decides that you're not employable and not even worthy of a soft offer or a letter, that's pretty stigmatizing. You may need to call in reinforcements from your law school's placement office or get letters from faculty members to help you overcome the stigma—that is, if those people don't share the firm's opinion of you. If they do, and you don't have any family connections you can count on to bail you out, your last hope is volunteering to work at a firm for free to prove your worth.

CHAPTER 27

Last Semester Cross-Checks

Caution is the eldest child of wisdom.
—VICTOR HUGO

LIFE IN THE REAL WORLD is fast approaching. As you make the turn into your last semester, you need to make a number of cross-checks with various members of your law school administration—and with yourself—to ensure that no important details slip through the cracks as graduation nears.

Ensure that you have enough credits to graduate

Don't laugh—I've seen more than a few frantic "independent study" papers spring up after a call from the registrar around spring break. Your law school has a minimum number of credits or credit hours required for you to graduate. Do you know what that number is? Do you know how many credits or credit hours you've earned to date? Have you scheduled enough credits in your last semester to graduate?

Before the close of the registration period for your last semester, be sure you have a comfort zone here. Count the credits for the classes you've taken, making sure that you've assigned the proper number of credits for moot court, journals, and any externships you've completed. When registering for your final semester, don't put yourself in the position where failing a class would mean not having enough credits to graduate—motivation can be a significant problem in the final semester.

When you think you have an accurate count of your credits earned, stop by the registrar's office and check your count against the registrar's count—because it's the registrar's count that matters. Although this may all seem a bit paranoid, these cross-checks are for your own peace of mind. Clerical errors can, and do, happen.

Ensure that you've taken and passed all required courses

Most law schools have a number of courses that you must take to graduate. Many schools require you to take the majority of these courses during the first year, but a few other required courses, often Corporations, Federal Income Tax, or Professional Responsibility, may be reserved for the upper years. Do you know what courses your school requires? Before the registration period closes in your last semester, ensure that you've met each of your school's curricular requirements or have registered for any that you've missed. Schools tend to be pretty unforgiving of mishaps and oversights in this area. A forgotten course could easily derail your graduation.

Cocurricular or extracurricular requirements

Many schools impose an upper-level writing requirement, an oral advocacy requirement, and a pro bono requirement. Does yours?

If your school allows a note or comment written for a legal journal to satisfy the upper-level writing requirement, have you checked to see if there is a length requirement or if your journal piece needs to be advised and approved by a faculty member? Check now so you won't be disappointed later.

What about public service? Some schools require you to have completed—and have the documentation to verify—a certain number of hours of public-service work during your three years of law school. Have you met the requirement and verified that your paperwork is in order? Don't make any assumptions here because clerical errors can happen and paperwork can be lost or forgotten, especially if you're assuming that your externship sent the required documentation to your law school. Remember that in cases like this, the paperwork is important only to you—to someone else, it's just a nuisance that can easily be overlooked or pushed to the back burner. If your school requires public service to graduate, verify that you've made your hours, and be sure that the public service office concurs.

Verify that your tuition has been paid

Nothing can stop your graduation faster than an unpaid tuition bill, and remember that without a copy of your diploma, you will not be able to register for the bar exam in most states. When you visit the registrar to cross-check your credits and required courses, verify that you've satisfied all financial obligations to your school. Don't wait until the last minute to do this, because if you discover any shortfalls, you might need time to secure additional funds to clear the lien against your diploma.

Once you're satisfied that your academic house is in order, it's time to start looking to the future. You'll need to take care of a number of housekeeping items early in the semester before the approach of exams and the imminence of your graduation start to compete for your attention.

Register for the bar exam and get your firm to pay for it

I took the six-week BARBRI preparatory course for the New Hampshire Bar Exam and found it to be excellent preparation for both the MBE (the Multistate Bar Examination, the two-hundred-question multiple-choice part common to all bar exams in all states) and the state essay section. Many students wonder whether these courses are worth their hefty fees (the average bar review course costs $2,000 to $3,000) or are just business ventures designed to prey on students' fears. The mentors and I can't imagine trying to study for a bar exam without taking one of these courses.

In addition to keeping you on a strict study schedule, showing you the common tricks used by the exam writers, and providing you with an endless supply of sample questions to work on, you will probably learn more black-letter law during the six-week bar review class than you learned during your entire three years of law school. That's valuable! I kept my bar review books and notes handy and used them frequently as a quick reference and a starting point while researching issues during my clerkship. They're a great source of legal outlines for most of the common legal subjects you'll encounter in practice.

Once you've decided that you need to take one of these courses, how do you choose which course is right for you? You'll want to, and should, do your own research, but I wanted the best-known and most reputable company in my corner—and that came down to a choice between BARBRI and PMBR. I, and many of your mentors, chose to take both.

Now wait . . . before you throw the book across the room in disgust, hear me out. BARBRI offers the most widely reputed full-bar preparation, a six-week class that provides you with two- or three-day lectures on all of the MBE subjects, one-day, state-specific lectures on all topics covered on your state essay section, and comprehensive outlines for all of these subjects. PMBR offers (among its options) a fantastic three-day MBE-only review course designed to be taken in conjunction with BARBRI, after you have completed your study of the multistate subjects. This course assumes that you've already studied the substantive law and simply want to practice applying your knowledge.

On the first day, you take an entire MBE in real-time test conditions—a harder-than-the-real-thing exam that provides a great exposure to what the real thing will be like. On days two and three, an instructor (live or on videotape) will walk you through the entire exam question by question, discussing all the tricks used in each subject, and going over each wrong-answer choice and explaining why it is wrong, and how you are tricked into picking it. I found this dry run and review extremely helpful and highly recommend it as a supplement to BARBRI.

Way back in the beginning of the book, I told you not to sign up for a bar review class during your first year of law school despite the discounts that the various companies might offer. The two reasons for this were, first, you probably didn't have as clear an idea then about which courses you'd want to take, and second, now if you have a job offer from a firm, the firm should be willing to cover some, if not all, of your bar-related expenses—including the review course.

How do you ask them to pay?

If you have signed on with a large film, they may already have offered to pay your expenses or to cover up to a certain amount. If so, simply call the recruiting coordinator to request the necessary paperwork, then send it in. If your firm has not broached the subject with you, contact BARBRI and PMBR, or whichever company you choose to use, and obtain the course registration paperwork from them. Among the materials you receive will be a sign-up form that includes a space for your firm's billing address and contact person. Once you have this form, call the recruiting coordinator at your firm and ask him what the firm's policy is on bar fees and expenses. Explain that you have the necessary paperwork and ask if you may send it directly to the firm for payment. Most firms (even small ones) will either cover some or all of your bar expenses or will, at a minimum, advance you the money to cover these expenses. You should certainly negotiate with any firm that does not immediately offer to do so, as covering these expenses is virtually standard practice these days.

Register for and take the MPRE

Officially, the MPRE, or Multistate Professional Responsibility Examination, is the first part of your bar exam and is required by almost every state's board of bar examiners. Requirements change from year to year, so check with the state where you intend to practice to confirm that you must take it. The MPRE is a somewhat tricky, fifty-question, 120-minute, multiple-choice exam administered three times each year (in March, August, and November), with a curve so generous that the exam is more of a nuisance than a threat for those students that take it seriously. Note that I did not say that you can blow off the exam and still pass it. I said it is relatively easy to pass if you study for it.

The exam measures your knowledge and understanding of the rules of professional conduct as established by the American Bar Association's (ABA) Model Rules of Professional Conduct, the ABA Model Code of Judicial Conduct, controlling court decisions, and generally accepted principles established in federal procedural and evidentiary rules. Note these three major points about the MPRE. First, when do you take the exam? Many law schools offer the required course in Professional Responsibility as an elective during the first or second year, and consequently students wonder whether they should take the exam during or shortly after completing this course. Take the exam early if you can, but check with the jurisdiction in which you intend to practice because some states require you to pass the MPRE before you take the bar exam, while others will not allow you to take the MPRE until you've graduated from law school.

Point number two is, what do you study to prepare for the MPRE? When you register for the exam, the National Conference of Bar Examiners (NCBE) will send you a nifty little package of preparatory materials, including a study guide and a series of sample questions. You can order more sample questions from the NCBE Web site (and you should if you're having trouble with the questions provided). I, and most students I know, carefully read through the materials provided by the NCBE, worked all of the sample questions provided, and never consulted the materials from our law school ethics classes. If you have signed up for BARBRI already and made at least a $250 payment toward your bar review course, you can attend a four-hour MPRE video review lecture complete with a comprehensive outline, practice tests, and a review book.

For the average student, a few hours a night for a solid week or ten days should be sufficient preparation to pass the exam, but leave enough time to work additional practice problems and to conduct additional review if you're not getting 75 percent of the practice problems correct. In an informal canvas of my classmates, 70–80 percent correct on the practice problems was about average, and assuming that the NCBE's grading scale doesn't change, getting 70–80 percent of the real MPRE questions correct should get you a passing score in every jurisdiction.

The third thing about the MPRE is, don't worry if you feel as if you failed it after taking the real exam. Most of us felt that way. Remember that the scale is friendly. The consensus is that if you take the exam seriously and study diligently for it, you'll have little trouble passing it. Those who fail the MPRE typically (1) didn't study seriously for it and tried to take the exam cold, (2) misbubbled on their answer sheet, or (3) had problems with time by getting hung up on a question. These things are all preventable and should not happen to you. If you have further questions about the MPRE, consult the NCBE's comprehensive Web site at www.ncbex.org.

Arrange a start date with your firm, judge, or placement

The bar exam is typically given in the last week of July. Judicial clerkships usually begin right after Labor Day. Everything else can be negotiated.

Smaller firms may be counting on your presence in the office soon after the bar exam, while big-city firms may grant you a start date as late as November. Whatever your individual situation is, make your arrangements early so you know what the expectations are and can plan accordingly.

Two bits of advice here. First, if you have any other option, don't work while you are studying for the bar exam. The schedule you'll get from your bar review course will be demanding enough, and any free time you have should be spent doing sample problems or relaxing. If money is tight, ask your firm for an advance on your salary to cover summer living expenses, and if they won't give you that, then ask them for a low-interest loan. Most firms have an interest in your passing the bar the first time around and will do whatever they can to help make sure that happens. If all else fails, get a loan from a relative or a bank.

It's only two months we're talking about here, and during those two months your time is best spent studying and resting. There will be plenty of time to pay back your loans later. First things first.

Once the bar is over, plan to take a vacation if you can afford it. You'll be wiped out, and many students report feeling a kind of post-partum depression when all of a sudden, every moment of your day isn't scheduled. Remember that the days between the bar exam and the beginning of your employment may represent the largest chunk of free time you'll experience between now and, well . . . retirement.

Make the most of it.

Make advance accommodations in your new place of employment

Most bar review courses begin around June 1, which may not leave you a lot of time between graduation and the beginning of the course to find living arrangements in your new city and to get settled there. Remember the importance of this choice—you're choosing the place where you'll be studying for the bar and probably living for the foreseeable future, and if you're going to work for a large firm, they may pay your relocation expenses, including moving costs. They'll only pay this once, however, so you'll need to get it right the first time. For this and many other reasons, many students like to stay in their law school accommodations through the bar exam because the surroundings are familiar and their living arrangements are already established.

Whatever your choice, let it be guided by two primary considerations. First, choose a place with minimal distractions, where you'll be comfortable and able to concentrate. This is not the time to risk failure for the fleeting pleasures of studying on a crowded beach. An isolated carrel in an air-conditioned, quiet library, away from phone calls, e-mail, and the Internet, is a good choice. As unappetizing as this seems, the sacrifice must be made, as the alternative—possibly failing the exam—is definitely worse. The goal is to take the bar exam once and to never have to think about it again. For most law students, this means giving up most of June and July to study, and taking (at least) the month of August off to play and recover. Second, try to find accommodations reasonably close to the location of your bar review course. Typically, the daily classes begin at 9:00 a.m. sharp, and these are not classes you'll want to miss or walk into late. Every missed class or late start translates directly into lost opportunities to score points on the bar, and if you're like most people, you can't afford to give any points away. Tacking a long commute onto your day won't make things any more pleasant.

Make arrangements for your move well in advance

If you live in a high-rise or a large apartment complex, don't assume that you can just move out whenever it suits your schedule. I had already rented a U-Haul and signed a lease to move into my new apartment before I discovered that my apartment building in Philadelphia had strictly enforced moving times—and the date I needed was completely booked weeks in advance. Only a fortunate "arrangement" struck with the keeper of the freight elevator key and loading-dock schedule saved me from disaster.

Don't get yourself into this situation. To be safe, make your moving arrangements at least sixty days in advance, and remember that you'll need to make compatible arrangements on both ends of your move. Oh, and you might as well assume that the day of your move will be the hottest and most humid day of the year to date. Somehow, it always seems to work out that way.

"And don't miss the deadline for picking up your family's commencement tickets!" Joel urges. "This is the voice of experience speaking."

CHAPTER 28

The Final Hurdle—Strategies for the Bar Examination

But you're not a Jedi yet.
—DARTH VADER TO LUKE SKYWALKER

SO YOU'RE A LAWYER.

Congratulations! You now have an impressive-looking piece of parchment that you can hang on your wall to commemorate the struggle you've just endured. There's just one problem. If your intention is to practice law, that diploma isn't worth the paper it's written on until you slay the dragon.

Your law school diploma is merely your ticket into the final and grandest battle of them all—the bar exam.

It's time for a reality check here. Although this is the penultimate chapter of the book, and the bar exam is your final antagonist, this is not Hollywood, and you are not guaranteed a happy ending.

Do not underestimate the difficulty of the bar exam. It is a worthy adversary.

In many states, the failure rate for the bar exam lies around 50 percent, and no one stands invincible against it. Every year, the bar exam claims unsuspecting victims from top law schools around the country, primarily individuals who failed to give the exam the respect it deserves.

Don't be one of them.

Around June 1, bar review classes begin in cities and towns around the country. If you read the last chapter, you should have registered for one of the six-week preparatory classes, and if you took our advice, you'll be supplementing that with the three-day PMBR mock exam and review.

Yes, I've known a couple of people who wrote away for a couple of sample bar exams, never took a review class, and passed the bar exam. I also know someone who won the lottery. You bought this book because it provides the best advice available to you as a current law student—in this case, advice from sixteen people who took bar exams in ten different jurisdictions without a single failure—and we're telling you that it's worth every penny for you to take these bar review courses. Disregard this advice at your own peril.

"Take a bar review course, despite the expense. How much is failing worth? Plus, the course will give you a modicum of comfort, and every ounce of comfort is priceless. When in doubt, study. I studied at least forty hours a week. Treat it like a job," Yvette suggested.

On the morning of your first bar review class, bring a duffel bag to class as you'll be on the receiving end of about sixty pounds of books and binders, and you'll need a way to transport these items home with you. You'll also be given a class schedule, and a lot of advice about how to pace yourself through the summer as you prepare for the exam.

Every student that takes the bar exam has a slightly different war story and a slightly different idea about what is the best way to prepare. This includes all of us as well, and several of your mentors' bar exam study suggestions are abstracted for you throughout this chapter. However, the consensus is that, if you're taking the July exam, you should follow the class schedule given to you as closely as possible during the month of June. Treat each day as if it were a day at the office. Clock in at 8:45 a.m. to prepare for your 9:00 a.m. lecture. Drink as much coffee as it takes to remain rigidly attentive, because unlike your lectures in law school, these lectures are crammed full of black-letter law and explanation, and you can't afford to miss a minute. In BARBRI, the lectures closely track the course outline, so highlight the material covered in the lecture in that outline. Take written notes only where necessary to supplement or clarify the outline. Listen carefully and actively and try to process the information.

When the lecture ends, take a quick break for lunch, and follow that with whatever preparation the course schedule recommends. Generally, among the tasks assigned to you that day will be to go over your outline and notes. Take that time to consolidate your lecture highlights and anything additional you wrote onto the large outline onto the small, concise outline also provided to you. After this consolidation, study only the concise outline, and do not refer to the large outline for that subject again. You can retain only so much information for each subject. Concentrate on what's most important, and in BARBRI, that's what's covered in the lectures.

"I think I had an effective strategy in preparing for the bar exam," Carolyn recalls, "which was passed down to me by my brother Keith, who took the exam the year before. I took BARBRI and the three-day PMBR strategy course and never missed a moment of the classes. During the first month, I treated studying for the bar exam like a job: I went to class at 9:00 a.m., did my assignments, quit by 6:00 p.m., and didn't do a whole lot on the weekends. Starting July 1, though, I pretty much worked from 9:00 a.m. to 11:00 p.m. with breaks for meals and exercise, and spent lots of time doing and going over problems."

"Slow and steady wins the race," Keith insists. "It's a marathon, not a sprint, and you want to peak at the right time. Start preparing early so you can leave a little bit of time each day for some fun."

"Go to the bar classes, do the work they assign you, but don't overdo it too early or you'll burn out before the critical days," Bess agrees. "Heavy-duty studying should begin around July 1. Eat well, exercise, and try to stay healthy."

"I studied like hell for two months," Pat notes. "I took BARBRI and studied with a friend. Studying with someone else helped me because it provided me with an additional source of motivation. Knowing that another person was relying on me helped me to stay committed to my study schedule."

"I'd rather study ten times harder than I need to and pass, than underestimate the exam and fail," Allan noted. "Having said that, try to remember that the bar exam is designed to be a minimum proficiency exam. If you do the recommended studying, you should pass."

"Try to relax. Lots of people who are not that smart pass this exam," another mentor adds. "Don't be too rattled by the low pass rates. You have an advantage simply by being a native speaker of English because a number of people who take the bar, particularly in New York, are international students."

Steve agrees. "Think about this: For every person sitting in your bar review class, there is a hapless person who decided that he could review old outlines from classes to prepare for the bar exam; or an even more hapless person who decided that the summer after third year of law school was the last bit of free time he would have and chose to spend that time traveling around and cramming for the bar exam in the last week instead of studying for two months like you will. Then there are the people who speak English as a second or third language, who will be at an immediate disadvantage to those of you who will be taking the exam in your native tongue. Essentially, it comes down to this: The people who work diligently and put forward a legitimate effort usually pass."

The key to your success on the bar exam lies in those practice problems. Don't forget to take advantage of all of the online tools available to you. For example, BARBRI offers practice tests online that calculate how many questions you got wrong in each MBE area, then further breaks down those errors by the particular topic in each area. Drilling this way will enable you to focus on your areas of weakness. Remember that simply doing the problems and correcting them is not enough. You must not leave a problem you got wrong until you understand why you got it wrong and how the problem tripped you up. If the problem contained a legal point not in your concise outline, go back and write it in so you won't forget it. The little distinctions that you'll make by getting hundreds of practice problems wrong in each subject, and learning from your mistakes, over the next six to eight weeks, will earn you points when it counts. Keep a cheat sheet for each subject, noting the things you got wrong and the tricks that kept tripping you up, and consult it and add to it every time you work problems. Avoid the temptation to be lazy. Repetition is the mother of skill.

Many students wonder how to strike a proper balance between the MBE and the state essay topics. In BARBRI, sometime near the end of June there will be a transition from the six multistate topics (constitutional law, torts, property, contracts, criminal law and procedure, and evidence) into the essay subjects listed as "in play" by your state's board of bar examiners. Again, the best advice we can give is to follow the schedule provided to you. Prepare for each state subject on the day it is to be introduced, particularly if it is a subject that you did not study in law school, but do not go overboard trying to master the intricacies of these subjects. Read the subject outline provided by BARBRI and try to master the material it provides. Do not even consider going to outside sources to supplement your understanding. Your degree of understanding will be stronger in some subjects than in others. Accept that and move on.

Once you have a working knowledge of a state essay topic, take the outline provided to you by your bar review course and boil it down to a one- or two-page bullet-point outline. Going through this process accomplishes two things. First, it forces you to engage the material, select what is most important, and organize it in a way that makes sense to you—all of which will help you to understand the material and commit much of it to memory; and second, with every bullet outline you complete, you progressively reduce the amount of material you need to cover. Remember, you can't possibly memorize everything the bar review course will give you. You need to make choices.

Every state's essay day is different. Some states put ten subjects in play and put six one-hour essays on the state portion of the bar exam. Other states put as many as sixteen subjects in play and ask twelve thirty-minute essay questions. Still other states fall somewhere in the middle. Your strategies for these state essay sections would thus be quite different. On the former, there are fewer subjects to master, but the level of mastery required to write a one-hour response can be fairly sophisticated. On the latter, you have more subjects to master, but with only thirty minutes to craft a response, a rudimentary, working knowledge of each subject will probably suffice. Listen carefully to the advice of your bar review instructor, and don't be afraid to ask questions about allocation of study time if it is not clear to you from the outset.

For the state essays, the consensus is that you might attain three possible levels of knowledge. The first level is superficial competence—an understanding of what's in the outline, and no knowledge of the subject outside of that. The second level is angry confusion—understanding what is in the outline, thinking that things in the outline contradict what you learned in your law school classes, and spending lots of time needlessly and frustratingly attempting to reconcile the two. Finally, the third level is mastery—which can only be the product of long hours working on the intricacies of a subject in law school.

It should be obvious what level of knowledge you're looking for on the state essay section of the bar exam. Sure, some subjects that you have mastered will be fair game for the state bar exam, and be thrilled for each of those you can count. For the rest, you're looking for superficial competence, enough to comprehend the rudiments of the subject, but nothing beyond what's in the bar review outline. Forcing yourself to settle for superficial competence is one of the keys to staying on pace in your preparation, and however uncomfortable it might feel, you must do it.

Once you have a working knowledge of the state essay subjects and determine the depth of knowledge required, work up a bullet-point outline for each subject, work at least one sample essay in each topic in play, and figure out the timing for your particular state's exam. Most students feel that the majority of their time is best spent drilling on MBE questions. This strategy actually serves a dual purpose, as nearly every state essay exam will feature at least one torts question and at least one contracts question, so the time you spend working with those subjects on the MBE section actually helps you with the essay section as well. Don't obsess about the essays. By the time you graduate from law school, you've probably written dozens of them. Conventional wisdom has it that few people who do well on the multistate day fail the bar exam because of their performance on the state essay day. As long as you have a rudimentary understanding of the subjects in play, you'll survive the second day. Spend your time on the MBE.

The magic number is 75 percent. If you can routinely get 75 percent of the questions in an MBE subject correct, you're ready for the big day.

When exam day nears

The two or three days that you spend taking the bar exam will be among the most stressful and grueling days of your life. The worst thing you can possibly do after six to eight weeks of intense preparation is deprive yourself of sleep or relaxation on the eve of the exam. Your bar review course will work hard to drum this into you, and for good reason. You should approach the bar exam the way an athlete approaches the most important athletic event of his training year. A day or two before the exam, you should begin to taper your studying to a few hours a day, coupled with lots of rest and relaxation. If you've stayed on schedule and worked hard for the entire six-to-eight-week preparatory period, this should pose no problem for you.

The day before the exam, shut down no later than midafternoon, and make peace with yourself. You've done everything you possibly could to prepare, and you must now try to relax and get ready to show the examiners how much you know. Nothing is to be gained by studying up to the closing bell. Go to a movie, go out to dinner, and do whatever you do to regain your center and your perspective. Remember that, in spite of the stress and anxiety you feel, you are not suffering from a fatal disease, and your life will go on no matter what happens. Think of the thousands of people who have gone before you and passed this exam.

Rest easy—you can do it.

Final thoughts

You'll get all the strategy you need from your bar review course, but given that we've been looking over your shoulder since you started law school three long years ago, permit us to make three final suggestions. First, on the MBE, watch your time and stay on pace. Break the morning section up into workable segments with time checkpoints, and make sure that you hit every one. The only sure way to fail the bar exam is to fail to finish the exam. Be disciplined! Remember, you don't need to get every question correct!

Second, no matter how you feel about the morning session of the

MBE, go back for the afternoon. Almost every year, either the morning or the afternoon session of the MBE is noticeably harder than the other. Don't get rattled.

Finally, on the state essay section, watch your time and stay on pace. Take the time to read the question carefully and sketch out a response before you start writing. Don't worry if you don't have time to cover everything. Write a well-crafted response that hits the major points and you'll be fine. Never spend more than the allotted time on an essay response. Better to get three eights in the morning session and complete every essay than to get two tens and a three because you took too much time on the first two essays. Rudimentary understanding wins the day.

CHAPTER 29

Parting Thoughts

There is a certain relief in change even though it be from bad to worse; as I have found in traveling in a stagecoach that it is often a comfort to shift one's position and be bruised in a new place.
—WASHINGTON IRVING

SO THERE YOU HAVE IT. The secrets to law school success neatly packaged between the covers of a book. Suggestions gathered from students of different backgrounds and interests from law schools across the country, and advice gleaned from more mistakes, gaffes, and errors than any of us thought we would ever publicly admit to.

But you know what? We survived and we've gone on to chase a hundred different dreams all over this great country, and so will you.

In the end, I think law school is less about the degree you get, or the first job you take, than it is about the things you'll learn along the way. Yes, to some degree, especially in the first year, law school is about survival. It's about reading more than you ever have before, forcing yourself to be more disciplined than you ever thought you could be, and replacing confusion and fear with confidence and mental acuity. It's about learning to write clearly and concisely, to question the way you think about things, and to look at everything in the world through a more critical, analytical prism.

"The main lesson I learned in law school was to be myself and make my own decisions," Joel counsels. "I think the peer pressure in law school, especially during the first year, is greater than it is at any time since junior high. It is crucial that you not blindly do whatever it is that the majority of your peers are doing. Make informed decisions. I truly believe that most unhappy law students and most unhappy lawyers are the people who did not know what they were getting themselves into. Reading this book is a good start."

"It's really all about being committed to law school before you start," Carolyn concluded.

"Once law school begins, every choice you make opens some doors and closes others," Megan cautioned. "It's important to carefully consider all of the options before you, as well as the implications of choosing one option over another. My parting advice is to just be intentional about everything you do and every decision you make."

"A lot of people end up unhappy as lawyers," Steve concludes. "Maybe they just weren't cut out to be lawyers. More likely, though, is that they didn't think about the choice they were making before they made it. The people I graduated with who enjoy being lawyers each put a lot of thought into the kind of lawyer they wanted to be, and the kind of lifestyle they wanted to live, and made their choices accordingly. You do the same."

"The one thing that good lawyers know is that an issue is almost never completely black-and-white," Chief Justice Dalianis said. "Therefore, a good lawyer recognizes and admits the weaknesses in a position. In other words, 'We think the answer should be this, we recognize that there is some authority to the contrary, and this is our response to that.' Don't puff your position, allow for the fact that it might not be absolutely correct, and work with that. That's rare, but it immediately sets a good lawyer apart."

"And understand that you only get one crack at a reputation," Professor Garvey added. "Make deciding which one you want your first decision as a lawyer, and then make all subsequent decisions for the rest of your career with that first decision in mind."

Law school is exhausting and exciting, annoying and awe-inspiring, frustrating, all-consuming, and exhilarating. It will, at times, drive you to tears, drive you to drink, and drive you to the edge. It will tear you apart as you've never dreamed, but, just when you feel that you've irreparably been reduced to an emotionally wrecked, mentally ravaged, vacant bundle of exposed nerves, it will rebuild you into a more thoughtful, more intellectually critical, and more mentally astute human being. At its core, law school is really about teaching you a different way to think, and once you've experienced it, it's impossible to ever go back to the way you were before.

Like most people, I had a love-hate relationship with law school. In the end, however, the experience, as miserable as it sometimes was, was definitely worth its benefits. You can do an awful lot with a law degree, and despite the rather sorry state of the profession in the minds of the public these days, people still have a lot of respect for the degree and the set of skills it stands for. For all the jokes and punch lines, people still look at you with a certain respect when you tell them you're a lawyer.

So get clear on whether you want any of the things a law degree can provide. If you decide you do, you've thought carefully about it, and you've committed completely to the experience, then there's only one thing left to do.

Go for it.

ABOUT THE AUTHOR

ROBERT H. MILLER, thirty-nine, is now an equity partner and a member of the Management Committee at the New England law firm of Sheehan, Phinney, Bass & Green (www.sheehan.com), where he specializes in business litigation in the federal courts. He is the immediate past chair of the firm's Hiring Committee, which he led for five years, and is also currently serving on the firm's Strategic Planning Committee. Prior to joining the firm, he served as law clerk to the Honorable Paul J. Barbadoro, Chief Judge in the U.S. District Court for the District of New Hampshire.

Mr. Miller graduated from the University of Pennsylvania Law School in May 1998, where he was a senior editor of the *University of Pennsylvania Law Review,* an H. Clayton Louderback legal writing instructor, and the chairman of the Executive Committee on Student Ethics and Academic Standing. His article "Six of One Is Not a Dozen of the Other: A Reexamination of *Williams v. Florida* and the Size of State Criminal Juries" was published in the January 1998 issue of the *University of Pennsylvania Law Review.*

Mr. Miller graduated with distinction from Yale University in 1993. He lives in New Hampshire with his wife, Carolyn, and their two boys.